*f*P

Why Our Children Can't Read

and What We Can Do About It

A SCIENTIFIC REVOLUTION
IN READING

DIANE McGUINNESS

THE FREE PRESS
New York   London   Toronto   Sydney   Singapore

THE FREE PRESS
A Division of Simon & Schuster Inc.
1230 Avenue of the Americas
New York, NY 10020

THE FREE PRESS and colophon are trademarks
of Simon & Schuster Inc.

Manufactured in the United States of America

10   9   8   7   6   5   4   3   2   1

Library of Congress Cataloging-in-Publication Data
McGuinness, Diane.
    Why our children can't read—and what we can do about it: a scientific revolution in reading /
Diane McGuinness.
        p.   cm.
    Includes bibliographical references and indexes.
    ISBN 0-684-83161-9
    1. Reading.   2. Literacy.   3. Remedial reading.   4. English
language—Study and teaching.   I. Title.
LB1050.M314   1997
372.41—dc21   96-24112
                                                                              CIP

ISBN 0-684-83161-9

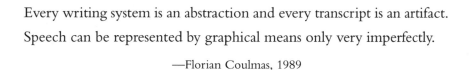

Every writing system is an abstraction and every transcript is an artifact. Speech can be represented by graphical means only very imperfectly.

—Florian Coulmas, 1989

CONTENTS

FOREWORD

Man has an instinctive tendency to speak, as we see in the babble of our young children; while no child has an instinctive tendency to bake, brew, or write. More than a century ago, Charles Darwin got it right: Language is a human instinct, but written language is not. Language is found in all societies, present and past. All languages are intricately complicated. Although languages change, they do not improve: English is no more complex than the languages of stone age tribes; Modern English is not an advance over Old English. All healthy children master their language without lessons or corrections. When children are thrown together without a usable language, they invent one of their own.

Compare all this with writing. Writing systems have been invented a small number of times in history. They originated only in a few complex civilizations, and they started off crude and slowly improved over the millennia. Until recently, most children never learned to read or write; even with today's universal education, many children struggle and fail. A group of children is no more likely to invent an alphabet than it is to invent the internal combustion engine.

Children are wired for sound, but print is an optional accessory that must be painstakingly bolted on. This basic fact about human nature should be the starting point for any discussion of how to teach our children to read and write. We need to understand how the contraption called writing works, how the mind of the child works, how to get the two to mesh.

It is a national tragedy that this commonsense understanding has been so uncommon. We are turning into a nation of illiterates, the victims of misguided ideas about the nature of reading and how to teach it. All the familiar techniques were devised before we had a scientific understanding of reading, and they are based on theories that we know are wrong. Parents and policymakers are bewildered by contradictory advice from a slew of well-meaning but uninformed romantics, over-simplifiers, entrepreneurs, and quacks.

The book you are now holding is a profound and wonderfully readable essay on reading and writing and how they should be taught. Diane McGuinness is an applied scientist in the best sense of the word—not a self-appointed "expert" spouting mumbo jumbo, but someone who works by the guidelines: know what you're talking about, think clearly and logically, and try to let the world tell you whether what you are saying is true. She combines these virtues with style, vigor, insight, and compassion, Anyone who has tried to teach children will recognize the vignettes in this book.

Modern illiteracy is a story of needless misery and waste. *Why Our Children Can't Read* is part of the solution and one of the most important books of the decade. Read it for your own pleasure and enlightenment, and buy copies for the people in control of your children's education.

—STEVEN PINKER
Professor and Director of the Center
for Cognitive Neuroscience, MIT
Author of *The Language Instinct*
and *How the Mind Works*

PREFACE

When you think back on your schooldays, funny things stick in your mind. These memories stick because of experiences that jolt you into vivid consciousness. My earliest memories were of first grade, probably because I spent a lot of time in the cloakroom that year. I have forgotten the crimes. My main misfortune was to finish my work too quickly and get into trouble. It seemed nothing could be done about this. The whole class worked on the same assignment at the same time. My mother was called in for a conference with Miss Chenette, my teacher at James Madison elementary in Pasadena, California. They had a discussion about skipping me a grade, but Miss Chenette said I was too immature.

I learned to read in Miss Chenette's class, although I don't remember how. I would never have remembered even this fact except for an experience with a neighborhood boy of twelve who couldn't read. Early most Sunday mornings, I used to read him the comics section from the Sunday paper. "But everyone can read," I remember saying. I decided that there must be something wrong with him. If I'd had a larger vocabulary I would have thought he was "retarded."

How was it that I could read and he couldn't? These are the twin mysteries of reading research. Fortunately, we have solved the most important one—why children fail. So far, scientists have not studied the reasons why children *don't* fail.

This early experience plus the contrast between my education in the California school system and my children's superb education in Hertfordshire, England, fostered my interest in education. I was witness to what *could be* versus what *is*. However, I didn't realize at that time that 80 percent of English children were shut out of this experience.

A specific interest in reading and literacy came about through serendipity in the form of being in particular places at the same time as particular people. Phyllis Lindamood was one of my students at the University of California at Santa Cruz. She did her senior thesis project on blind readers learning Braille and introduced me to her parents' work with poor readers. Based on their work, Phyllis predicted that blind people would fail to learn to read Braille to the extent that they are unable to *hear* individual sounds in words. This hypothesis was overwhelmingly supported. The Lindamoods' work on the importance of auditory analysis to reading was virtually unknown by the scientific community at that time. Today, this work has been recognized as one of the major breakthroughs in reading research of this century.

Soon after this, I got an invitation from the Orton Dyslexia Society to present a paper at a conference on sex differences in reading. This prompted me to make connections between the research on poor readers and my own research on the development of perceptual and cognitive skills of boys and girls. This meeting was a major turning point. I met Isabelle Liberman, one of the great pioneers in reading research, who strongly influenced my thinking. I also benefitted enormously from future conferences and a close association with the Orton Dyslexia Society, which has consistently supported good scientific research on reading.

Later, I joined the faculty at the University of South Florida. One day, in a class on cognitive psychology, I outlined in detail what the next major step in reading research should be. The following week, some students met me in the hallway, and said: "We want to do it"— meaning the "next step."

Two of these students were Carmen Adams (later to become Carmen McGuinness when she married my son Geoff) and John Donohue. Carmen, Geoff, and John are still intensely involved in reading research, and Carmen, in particular, in program and curriculum development for reading instruction. No one realized at the time where this initial project would take us, nor how many hours (years) of testing, data entry, data analysis, and the endless revisions of research reports that would follow. The outcome of this collaboration has been beyond our wildest dreams.

This book is the culmination of that work, which has continued for nearly a decade, as well as a synthesis of modern research on reading. It describes a revolution in teaching methods that so far has escaped the notice of most educators. This revolution is the result of four major discoveries or principles:

1. From paleography and structural linguistics, we have learned that all writing systems are based on the syllable structure of the language for which they were written. The way a writing system is designed determines how it should be taught.

2. From cognitive and educational psychology, we have learned that children must be trained to hear the individual sounds (phonemes) of their language. They must be able to disconnect or "unglue" sounds in words in order to use an alphabetic writing system.

3. From an analysis of the structure of the English alphabet code, we have discovered that it encompasses four systems of mapping logic: simple reversibility (1-to-1 mapping), and various forms of propositional logic (1-to-1(2), 1-to-many, and many-to-1 mapping).

4. From research in the classroom and the clinic, we have discovered that when the sequence of reading and spelling instruction is compatible with the logic of the alphabet code *and* with the child's linguistic and logical development, learning to read and spell proceeds rapidly and smoothly *for all children* and is equally effective for poor readers of all ages.

Only a handful of reading programs are based on one or more of these principles. These programs are unlike anything that is seen in the classroom or taught in teacher training colleges. This revolution is outside the current debate between "whole language" and "phonics." Neither of these methods, *no matter what form they take,* is based on even one of these principles.

True scientific research on literacy only began about twenty-five years ago. What this means is that every "theory" or "model" or "method" of teaching reading, past or present, has been based either on human reason alone, or on empty theorizing or "fads," rather than on solid scientific research. Because of this, success in learning to read is largely accidental, due to parental input, or the intelligence, talent, and integrity of the classroom teacher, plus the chance connection between the parent's or teacher's ability and the aptitudes of particular children. Learning to read in every English-speaking country is like a lottery. It doesn't have to be. New programs described in this book allow us to teach anyone to read at any age.

This book examines new data on the analysis of writing systems which reveal how they are constructed, and, therefore, how they must be taught. It reviews the scientific evidence on the subskills important to mastering an alphabetic writing system, along with exciting new research on reading programs that work for *everyone,* including children and adults who can't read a word.

To help you with technical terms, there is a Glossary at the end of the book. A standard format for pronouncing the sounds of the English language follows this Preface.

Please note that all names of persons in examples are pseudonyms.

This book would not have been possible without the support of some very special people. In addition to those mentioned earlier, I also want to express my appreciation to my agents, Felicity Bryan, who believed in this book, and Peter Ginsberg, who, with great kindness and tact, guided me through revisions to make the book more salable. Susan Arellano at The Free Press has been a superb editor, asking just the right questions to force me to have a better perspective of the nonspecialist reader. Her ability to remain focused over hours of discussion is amazing and incredibly gratifying to an author. Without her input and enthusiasm this book would have been much more dull and academic than it is.

I owe a special debt of gratitude to Carol Tavris and Steven Pinker, who liked and understood earlier drafts when nobody else did. Thanks a million. Writers write in a vacuum, and without this encouragement, I probably would have given up.

I am especially grateful to Peter Bryant and the Department of Psychology at Oxford University, who gave me a home for five months while I did research for this book. Thanks also to the staff of the Bodleian Library, who responded graciously to my many questions and requests. Thanks to my daughter Julie, who gave me home and hearth at Oxford, and who listened so patiently while I struggled to put new insights and discoveries into words.

Last, but not least, special thanks to the teachers, the parents, and the children with whom I have had the privilege to work over the years. It's their voices that make this book and its message come alive.

Pronunciation Key for English Phonemes

Consonants		Vowels	
Sound	*Key Word*	*Sound*	*Key Word*
/b/	boy	/a/	hat
/d/	dog	/e/	bet
/f/	fan	/i/	sit
/g/	get	/o/	hot
/h/	hot	/u/	cut
/j/	jog	/ae/	cake
/k/	key	/ee/	seem
/l/	log	/ie/	time
/m/	man	/oe/	home
/n/	not	/ue/	cute
/p/	pan	/aw/	law
/qu/ (kw)	quit	/ou/	out
/r/	red	/oi/	oil
/s/	sit	/oo/	book
/t/	top	/o͞o/	soon
/v/	vet	/ar/	car
/w/	win	/er/	her
/x/ (ks)	fox	/or/	for
/z/	zip		
/ch/	chin		
/ng/	ring		
/sh/	ship		
/th/	thin		
/<u>th</u>/	them		
/zh/	vision		

In this book English phonemes are represented by the most probable spelling rather than the International Phonetic Alphabet, which is unfamiliar to most readers. Sounds are enclosed in slash marks. Letters are underlined. The sound /b/ is spelled <u>b</u>.

VOWEL+R

The phoneme /r/ is both a consonant and a vowel. The vowel /r/ is spelled <u>er</u>, <u>ir</u>, or <u>ur</u>. Eight other vowels can combine with /r/. Two need to be taught specifically because the /r/ alters the pronunciation of the preceding vowel: cap/car   fog/for.

The other six Vowel+r combinations tend to keep the same sound and spelling pattern with or without the /r/.

/ae/–/er/	(date/dare)	/ee/–/er/	(see/seer)
/ie/–/er/	(time/tire)	/ue/–/er/	(cute/cure)
/ou/–/er/	(out/our)	/o͞o/–/er/	(too/poor).

SECTION I

WHY IT'S HARD TO LEARN TO READ

Chapter 1

READING REPORT CARD

The Jamesons were a model middle-class family. Jim and Pat had college degrees. Jim earned good money as an engineer, and Pat had a part-time consulting job setting up computer systems for small businesses. They were devoted parents to their three children, umpiring for little league, running car pools to diving lessons, dancing lessons, and soccer practice. They valued learning and read bedtime stories every night. They often consulted dictionaries and encyclopedias whenever one of the children introduced an unfamiliar topic. Dinner conversations were lively, and filled with accounts of the children's daily activities.

Their youngest son, Donny, started kindergarten after two years at a well-run preschool. Donny could recite the alphabet, write most of his letters, his first and last names, and could count to 2,000 if anyone would let him. In kindergarten, Donny got more practice reciting the alphabet, copying out letters, and memorizing "sight words." He could read several short words. During first grade he taught himself to read simple books and enjoyed writing stories about airplanes, guns, and robots. He got an A on his report card for Language Arts. His teacher said he was the "best reader in the class." Mom and Dad were pleased, the teacher was pleased, and Donny was pleased. As he told his Grandma: "I can read faster than anyone in the school."

In second grade the words got longer. Donny had trouble remembering all of them. He began to ask his friend, "What does this word say?" He would try to memorize it for the next time he saw it in a story. As the year went by, he had to ask his friend more and more often. Meanwhile, his stories got more interesting, and his handwriting a little neater. This year he wrote a lot about submarines. He could spell "submarine" correctly. The word was on the cover of five books he had at home and he practiced copying it over and over again. Here is one of his stories:

The Submarine Rtet

Kpn John tol hz cru fl sdm a ked. Takr dun. The submarine sek to the osn flor. It was qit. Tha cud ker the df crjz fling ner bi. But tha yr saf.

[The Submarine Retreat. Captain John told his crew full steam ahead. Take her down. The submarine sank to the ocean floor. It was quiet. They could hear the depth charges falling near by. But they were safe.]

This particular story, replete with spelling mistakes, was up on the wall on parents' night. Jim and Pat were alarmed. In fact, they had already discussed asking the teacher about Donny's written work. The teacher told them not to worry. She pointed out that Donny was a model student. He worked very hard. She asked them to notice the excellent vocabulary in the story (she was adept at reading her students' spelling). She asked them to notice that Donny was the only child who put a capital letter at the beginning of every sentence. She said that this was "transitional spelling." The children would be taught to spell with "conventional spelling" in third grade.

In the middle of second grade the children were given a nationally normed reading test. Donny scored just below "grade level," about average for his age. His teacher was pleased, because most of the children in her class were "at grade level," just where they should be. She was proud of her record in getting most children "at grade level" over the six years she had taught second grade.

In third grade the words got longer still. The books had more pages. Donny couldn't remember lots of these words, even when he asked several times. He had to guess so many of the words when he was reading that he couldn't make sense of the story. It helped a lot if there were pictures. Pat spent more time listening to Donny read and correcting his mistakes as they went along. Despite this extra tutoring,

Donny's reading did not improve. When he wrote stories, they looked pretty much the same as "The Submarine Retreat." Paradoxically, Donny was the best speller in the class. His teacher told the Jamesons that his spelling was perfect. He got 100 percent week after week on the class spelling words. She said not to worry, because the "conventional spelling" he was learning would eventually transfer to his creative writing. "It just takes time." The teacher saw nothing odd about the fact that Donny's spelling was "perfect," yet he could scarcely spell a word in his creative writing.

At the end of third grade, Pat went to see the school counselor about Donny's poor skills. By now, she had discovered that Donny could memorize the week's spelling words long enough to pass the test, but forgot them completely only days later. The counselor said that Donny was "not severe," that there were scores of children worse than him, and there was a ten-month waiting list for testing. Instead, Pat and Jim got Donny tested by a school psychologist in private practice. It cost them $600.00. Donny was a year and a half behind in reading, two years behind in spelling, and had an IQ of 124. The school psychologist said he needed private tutoring. She said it could take up to two years, but that she didn't do private tutoring herself and couldn't recommend anyone.

They found a tutor in the Yellow Pages. The cost was $40.00 an hour, and Pat took on more consulting work to pay for the extra expense. Meanwhile, Pat and Jim didn't tell anyone about Donny's problem except the immediate family. They were embarrassed and upset. How had they failed their child? Why was it that Donny had these problems when the other two children were fine? Did he have some kind of brain damage? What would happen if the reading specialist couldn't teach Donny to read and spell? Mealtimes changed from joyful, happy occasions, to a tension-filled experience, as Donny was asked to tell everyone *exactly* what he had done in school, *exactly* how many pages he had read, and *exactly* what his spelling words were for that week. Pat accused Jim of not taking enough time with Donny, so Jim spent every evening listening to Donny read. Jim wasn't always patient ("I've told you that word a hundred times"), and the session often ended in tears. Pat and Jim read books on the subjects of "dyslexia" and "learning disabilities." Nothing they read held out much hope. While all this was going on, the other children were pushed into the background and became silently angry and resentful.

What is the ending to this story? It depends on whether Pat and Jim found the right reading clinic. If they did, they would be given an accurate diagnosis of Donny's problem. The clues are all contained in the story. Donny's problem was quite simple. He didn't understand the alphabet code *because he had never been taught it*. Instead, he was using letter names instead of "letter sounds" to create his own code ('captain' = "kay-pee-en" kpn), or trying to memorize whole words by sight. This made it impossible for him to decode text (read) and encode text (write and spell). There was nothing wrong with him. He had excellent auditory skills as shown by his use of letter names to spell sounds in words. He had a superb visual memory. Not many children can memorize a list of spelling words they can't read entirely by *sight*. He had a terrific vocabulary. These are the ingredients that should have produced an expert reader. A good reading specialist could teach Donny to read and spell in about twelve hours or less, and family life would quickly return to normal. Donny would shoot ahead to near the top of the class, which is where he should be with an IQ of 124.

Unfortunately, an unhappy ending is considerably more likely. Instead of an expert reading specialist, Pat and Jim found a reading "tutor." This person was kind and patient, but knew as much abut how to remediate reading problems as Pat and Jim, especially after all the books they had read on the subject. The tutor merely listened to Donny read and corrected his mistakes, just as Pat and Jim had done. The unhappy ending can continue for a lifetime unless proper help is found. The unhappy ending includes expensive schools for "dyslexics," more private tutoring, more family worry and discord. Donny would eventually get a high school diploma from his special school, go to college and flunk out, and end up in a job where he didn't have to read anything. If parents aren't as lucky as Pat and Jim and can't afford to pay for outside help or private schools, the situation is even more hopeless. Ultimately, a child with an unremediated reading problem can never function at his full potential and suffers incredible emotional damage and loss of self-esteem.

The Jamesons are fictional, but Donny is not. He is the prototype of many real children we have seen in our research and in our clinic. Donny is the product of the "whole language" classroom, the dominant reading method in most English-speaking countries today, sometimes called "literature based" reading or "real-books." According to the tenets of whole language, children can "discover" how to read and spell on their own. They can do this because whole language advocates believe that spoken and written language are essentially alike, and should be learned the same way, "naturally." Whole language is not the only reading method that fails many children.

THINGS ARE WORSE THAN YOU THINK

How many children are like Donny? Outside the United States there is no answer to this question. There is no literacy testing using accurate demographic sampling and controlled testing procedures. Instead, there is either no testing at all, testing by the classroom teacher, or the use of standardized tests normed on large samples of children. These are tests like the California Test of Basic Skills (CTBS) or the Schonell Reading Test used in England and Australia. Standardized tests provide information on how a particular child is reading compared to all other children in the sample population. If the population as a whole has poor reading skills, then a score of "average" means you are a poor reader. If the population as a whole has good reading skills, then a score of "average" means you are a good reader.

To assess literacy properly, you need an objective definition of literacy for each age. This means setting an absolute standard of literacy which is *independent* of the population's reading level. To date, only the United States and Canada have carried out this type of testing on very large population samples, and only the United States has tested children.[1] This puts the United States in the unenviable position of being the first nation in the English-speaking world to discover the shocking truth about actual literacy rates, truth which has revealed a "literacy crisis" in America.

The National Assessment Governing Board, in conjunction with the National Center for Education Statistics, carried out two studies in 1992. One tested nearly 140,000 American children in grades 4, 8, and 12. The second tested 26,000 adults in the age range sixteen to sixty-five years. ETS used careful demographic sampling with accurate proportions of males and females, all ethnic and racial groups, and balanced for geographic location (urban, inner city, rural, etc.).

An important innovation was the development of an *objective* way to measure reading by setting absolute standards or "achievement levels." A panel of experts determined ahead of time what literate adults and children in various grades *should be* able to do. They emphasized "functional literacy," the ability to read text, find information, and perform operations ("functions") on that information. All test items were

drawn from published materials and included stories, poems, nonfic-
tion, newspaper articles, and common "documents" such as bus
timetables and simple graphs.

Equally important was the methodological rigor in which the testing and scoring was carried out. Up to this time, school-district testing
had become a national disgrace. Some schools blatantly teach to the
test, using the same test year after year. Parents have told me that teachers asked their child to stay home on the day of testing because he or
she was a poor reader. To circumvent this, ETS ensured that all partic-
ipants were monitored during testing by an outside tester. Strict guidelines were set up for scoring responses, and data analysis was done by
trained specialists at a central location. All test items were secured, and
no school had access to any of them or even examples of them.

Using a complex scoring procedure and statistical model, NCES established "levels" of competence based on achievement criteria and
test item difficulty scores. For the student population there were four
levels: advanced, proficient, basic, and below basic. Students who were
"below basic" could not understand the overall meaning of what they
read and were considered to be functionally illiterate according to expectations for that particular grade. I want to spend some time addressing these findings because they provide a number of clues about what
is wrong with the way schools in America teach reading, and no doubt
in other English-speaking countries as well.

The report on the student population provides a detailed breakdown
of the fourth-grade data. Buried at the back of the report, on page
250, is an astonishing table. It reveals that, on average, the states
claimed that 12 percent of the students were untestable! Think what
this figure means for the validity of typical district-wide testing. ETS
personnel disallowed 4 percent of these exclusions. This left 3 percent,
who were excused because of limited English proficiency (LEP) and 5
percent who were in special education programs and had an individual
education plan, or "IEP." These children spent less than 50 percent of
their time in the classroom. Typically, the majority of students with an
IEP have been diagnosed with a learning disability (LD), meaning they
"can't read."

National statistics show that about 2 to 3 percent of school children
are mentally retarded, blind, or deaf. The remaining 2 to 3 percent,
who were excused from testing, could have been tested.[2] This means
the results are biased toward higher reading achievement than is actually the case.

States were ranked according to statewide proficiency scores. The literacy rates for states in the top and bottom five ranks in the continental United States are shown in Table 1–1. Bear in mind that this table underestimates the number of otherwise normal children who are below basic levels in reading.

The top five states averaged 29 percent of all students below basic-level reading skills. The bottom five states had double this rate. The national average for fourth grade was 43 percent of children reading "below basic level."

These dismal results continue to dominate the adult survey. Remember, all test materials were drawn from printed text that a normal adult would be *likely to encounter in everyday life*. For adults, there were five levels of competence. Level 1 required only the most minimal level of competence. For example, from an eight-sentence newspaper article, the reader had to find this information about a cross-channel swimmer:

What did Ms. Chanin eat during her swim?

TABLE 1–1

Percentage of Fourth-Grade Children Scoring Below Basic-Level Reading Skill

	States Identified % IEP	ETS Allowed % IEP	% Below Basic
TOP-RANKED			
1 New Hampshire	12	4	27
2 Maine	12	5	28
3 Massachusetts	14	5	29
4 North Dakota	10	2	29
5 Iowa	9	4	32
BOTTOM-RANKED			
38 Louisiana	7	4	60
39 Hawaii	9	4	58
40 California	7	4	57
41 Mississippi	7	5	64
42 Wash. D.C.	9	7	75

IEP = "individual education plan" applied to students who spend less than 50 percent in the normal classroom.

State ranks are for forty-two states, based on average scores for all reading levels.

Source: Data from NAEP 1992 Reading Report Card for the United States.

Altogether, 22 percent of the adult population were only able to perform at a Level 1 proficiency or *lower.* This translates to forty-two million functionally illiterate American adults. Forty-eight percent of all adults scored at Level 2 or worse, barely literate. Hardly anyone (3 percent of all adults) performed at Level 5, the "advanced level." One Level 5 test item was a fact sheet sent to potential jurors outlining jury selection procedures. It is sobering that only 3 percent of potential jurors can read and fully comprehend how the jury selection process works. Statistics Canada, which carried out the same kind of testing in the United States, Canada, and five non-English speaking European countries, replicated these findings for the United States. The study also showed that U.S. high school students and young adults (16 to 25 years old) were six times more likely to be functionally illiterate (Level 1) than those in Sweden, and twice as likely as those in Canada.[1] Both surveys show that the "golden age" of literacy in the United States is the 35- to 45-year-old age group, with 30 percent scoring at Levels 4 and 5. This group learned to read during 1955–1965. Only 13 percent of today's 16- to 25-year-olds scored at Levels 4 and 5.

There is little evidence that the number of years of schooling plays any major *causal* role in improving literacy. Only ten percent of college graduates and 16 percent of graduate school students scored at Level 5 proficiency when the majority should score at this level. Four percent of college graduates were functionally illiterate (Level 1). Fifteen percent of college graduates scored at Level 2 or worse, showing they could not function in a sophisticated work environment. National statistics show that about 80 percent of the American population graduates from high school. Half of these students enter college (40 percent of the population), and only half of this group (20 percent) gets a four-year college degree. Fifteen percent of these students have marginal literacy skills. This means that about 17 percent of working adults, thirty-three million people, are both well educated *and* sufficiently literate to work effectively in a complex technological world. We are dooming the vast majority of Americans to be second-class citizens.

The authors of these reports do not speculate on causes for these extraordinary illiteracy rates, but causes can be inferred from the statistics. There was an extreme range of literacy levels between the states as shown in Table 1–1. With such a large population of children, this cannot be attributed to chance or random variation. We can conclude, with some confidence, that some states train their teachers better and use more effective methods in the classroom.

There was also a large discrepancy between the states in the number of students identified as "IEP" and in need of special remedial classrooms. IEP rates varied from 14 percent in Florida and Massachusetts to 7 percent in six states. As no one state could possibly have a monopoly on students who *inherently* require remedial education, this discrepancy also must be due to pedagogic factors and to different methods of identifying "LD" children.

The student survey included data on Catholic and other private schools. Students from these schools were far and away superior to those in public schools. Catholic schools draw from a similar population to public schools, including a high percentage of Spanish-speaking children. Based solely on demographics, their results should be identical to those of the public schools. But Catholic schools had 17 percent more students at or above basic level skills at all grades tested (grades 4, 8, and 12). This shows that some *schools* have better programs for teaching reading, and/or are run more effectively, due to greater academic rigor, higher student expectations, more homework, and better discipline. Catholic schools, for example, tend to use a phonics-based reading method.

Comparisons of teacher salaries and per pupil expenditure across states show, yet again, that throwing money at the problem doesn't make a difference to literacy rates. The Catholic school results are a powerful illustration of this fact, as these schools spend less money per student than the public schools.

Fourth-grade teachers were asked to provide information about which method they used most or least for reading and spelling instruction. In general, these reports are too idiosyncratic to be of much value, especially as fourth-grade teachers are not responsible for teaching children to read. However, there is one state where a single reading method was mandated statewide in 1987. This state is California, and California teachers were overwhelmingly more likely to report "heavy use" of whole language/literature-based reading methods (87 percent of teachers) than teachers in any other state. Table 1–1 shows that California ranked near the bottom in the nation, and results from the 1994 testing, published in 1996, place California in a tie for dead last with Louisiana. In 1996, California passed legislation to reintroduce "phonics" back into the classroom along with 1 billion dollars of funding for teacher workshops, new guidelines for teacher training, and new textbooks and curriculum.

When nearly all teachers in a state report a "heavy use" of a particular method, and the state in which they teach has nearly 60 percent of its children below basic levels in literacy, this means the method isn't working! There is simply no other argument for these kinds of numbers. Nor, I might add, is 27 percent of children below basic level acceptable either, which is the *best* any state could do.

The truth provided by these statistics is that children's reading problems, and ultimately adults' reading problems, are *caused by the school system,* and not because there is something wrong with poor readers. It is impossible that 30 percent to 60 percent of all school children have an inherent or "brain-based" deficit leading to reading failure. In any case, reading and spelling are not biological properties of the human brain. People are illiterate because none of the current methods of reading instruction work for everyone. Later, I will review evidence which shows that *any child or adult* who isn't mentally retarded or deaf can be taught to read if given proper instruction.

Over the last quarter century, there has been a revolution in our understanding of how to teach reading, the outcome of an explosion of scientific research. So far, this revolution has escaped the notice of most educators. These studies show conclusively that to learn an alphabetic writing system, a child must be taught the sounds of his language and be trained to *hear* the order of these sounds in words, because it is these sounds that the letters represent. Furthermore, while this ability is highly trainable, it doesn't appear spontaneously in all children simply because they are exposed to print or taught "the sounds of letters." The next step is to teach children how each of these sounds can be spelled in a carefully sequenced way. We now have the knowledge to teach these skills correctly, leaving nothing out. When programs based on this knowledge are tested in the classroom and the clinic, all children learn to read rapidly and accurately.

THE PLAN OF THE BOOK

This book is divided into three sections. The first section looks in depth at writing systems and reveals firsthand why children can easily become confused about our writing system and fail to learn to read and spell. The section begins with typical examples of the incorrect strategies that children routinely adopt to decode text. These strategies harden into habits that are difficult to overcome without remedial help. The next two chapters show that *all* current teaching methods (yes, even phonics) will fail at least 30 percent of children, because they are based on ignorance about how writing systems work. The last chapter in this section provides an analysis of the sounds of the English language, how the English spelling code evolved over 700 years, and what the structure of this code looks like. The complex syllable patterns in our language, plus the complexities of our spelling system, make the English alphabet code one of the most complex writing systems in the world. Unless we understand how it works, we cannot teach it.

The middle section focuses on the scientific evidence. This has shown that certain subskills must be in place in order for a child or adult to master an alphabetic writing system. The good news is that these subskills are highly trainable. Additional research has shown that children's linguistic and logical development are of critical importance in setting up the proper sequence of instruction. The last chapter in this section reviews training studies based on this research, studies which prove that auditory-linguistic skills are a major missing link to reading success. These skills are so trainable, *at any age,* that the terms "dyslexia" or "learning disabilities" cease to have any meaning.

The final section of the book is devoted to method. Given what we know about the skills involved in learning to read, about how the English alphabet code actually works, and our new understanding of the young child's linguistic and logical development, what does a reading program look like which takes advantage of all of this information? Chapters 9 and 10 set out the details of such a program for the classroom or for home instruction.

Millions of youngsters and adults have serious reading problems through no fault of their own. Reading and spelling problems are completely remediable with proper training. People who cannot read a word can be taught to read, write, and spell, fluently and efficiently, if they are taught by the right methods. Chapters 11 and 12 are devoted to the topic of remedial instruction, reviewing programs with solid research support. These chapters provide a detailed explanation of how a good clinical method works. As well, there are diagnostic tests and techniques to pinpoint individual learning deficiencies and guidance on how to deal with the emotional problems of children or adults with severe reading delays.

The final chapter offers suggestions about what parents can do to help rather than hinder their children before they go to school, along with some practical ways to help develop skills that are important in learning to read. For families with a child or other family member who has reading or spelling problems, there is advice about how to work with the school system, and how to evaluate a remedial reading program in your school or private clinic.

We have the answers to the problem of illiteracy. We have had many of the answers for over 25 years. So far, members of the educational community either do not know about these research findings or are threatened by them, because it will mean an overthrow and a restructuring of everything that is familiar. These new ideas belong in the classroom, because we are harming our children and ourselves by creating a nation of illiterate citizens.

This book is for the millions of concerned parents, the millions of intelligent people with poor or absent reading skills, the thousands of teachers who have been falsely blamed for the literacy crisis, for the dedicated scientists and reading specialists who persist and persist, as well as for the enlightened members of the educational community who care enough to make a difference.

Chapter 2

READERS READING

How Do We Do It?

Everyone who bought or borrowed this book is a reader. Readers don't understand why someone can't learn to read. Many are dumbfounded and troubled by the very high illiteracy rates in America. They are justifiably upset that no solutions have been forthcoming for over 100 years. In fact, things appear to have gotten worse. Some people will have more specific concerns, because they have a child or family member who can't read. Teachers of young children worry that many of their charges will fail to learn to read, and they don't know why. Teachers in higher grades are angry with first- and second-grade teachers because children are coming into their classes unable to read, write, or spell. This means that they can't move ahead with their lessons like they're supposed to. These teachers are not trained in how to teach reading, nor do their curriculum guidelines include reading instruction, so the problem never gets solved. Instead, children are either held back, passed up the system, or put into remedial classrooms from which they rarely escape. At the end of the line, these young people will either seek employment where reading isn't necessary, or enroll in community college literacy programs.

As a fourth-grade teacher told a friend: "Your child can't read, because no one taught him to read. Get him a good reading tutor now, or he will never learn to read."

What is reading, and why is there such a problem in figuring out how to teach it? This is the topic of the first part of the book. To illustrate the problem directly, let's begin with a simple exercise. Read this passage and think about how you did it.

Bad Fruit

The fructificative goosefoot was foveolariously assembled. The frugivorous and frowsy fricatrice, whose epidermis was of a variegated fuchsinophillic consistency, masticated her chenopodiaceous repast morosely.

Reprinted courtesy of Read America

[The fruit-bearing goosefoot was full of pit-like indentations. The fruit-loving and frowsy chewer, whose skin was of a mottled and purplish-red consistency, chewed her goosefoot (species) meal morosely.]

Good readers can read this with relative ease, even though they don't understand many of the words. People who can read this passage know how the English alphabet code works. They know that individual letters, letter-pairs, and sometimes three or four letters in a row ("igh," "ough") stand for only one sound in a word. These people decoded this passage from left to right, one sound unit at a time. They know this implicitly, and only noticed what they were doing because the words were so unfamiliar, forcing them to slow down and analyze each word sound by sound.

Some people who are reading this book will not be able to read this passage. Most of them are using a "part-word" decoding strategy in which parts of words are assembled into a longer word. Part-word "assemblers" search for familiar little words or word fragments *inside* a longer word. These letter fragments stand for *more than one sound.* Often they reuse letters in different combinations. When familiar patterns can't be located, or aren't helpful in constructing a word, as in the words "fructificative" (/fru/ /tif/ /cat/ /tive/) or "chenopodiaceous" (/chin/ /no/ /pod/ /dice/ /ace/ /ous/), the word cannot be read. Instead, they have to ask someone else to read it for them. When I play this game with my college students, it turns out that a surprisingly large number of them are part-word assemblers. They never knew there was any other way to read. These are the students with poor spelling, who misread words, and who have to reread passages over and over to understand what they are reading.

The example is here for another reason. Many educators claim that efficient readers read so quickly that they ignore individual letters, re-grouping them into patterns of letter strings or "chunks" and whole words. Therefore, they argue that children should be taught whole words from the beginning. It's true that good readers read quickly, skimming along, unconscious of how they are reading, but they didn't start out like this. Furthermore, careful research has shown that adult good readers look at nearly every letter, and can see only about three letters beyond the focal point as they read. When reading complex text, fixation duration is increased, as is the number of repeat fixations, and the number of words read per minute decreases.

Reading is a skilled behavior and, like all skills, it has be taught from the bottom up, from the simple parts to the complex whole. No one would dream of asking a novice diver to attempt a complex dive, like a reverse jackknife. Nor would one teach a beginning piano student to use all ten fingers at once at the first piano lesson. All skilled learning builds piece by piece, through practice, until the skills are integrated.

Writing systems are codes for spoken language. Someone has to teach the code, because most people can't figure it out alone. We have learned this lesson from the reports of scholars trying to decipher ancient writing systems. Later, I will be discussing the exact nature of the code for written English in more depth, because the complexity of our alphabet code is a major cause of reading failure. In fact, *nobody* can unravel a written code without knowing something about how the code works, even when they are told that symbols on a page stand for sounds in their native language. Look at this recoded version of the first line of a famous nursery rhyme.

ytoxto hrusxz ub ldyyuos xtmo

The letter-sound relationships are based on English spelling patterns and recoded by simple substitution. There are even helpful clues here. When more than one letter stands for a single sound (as it does in the original spelling), those letters are underlined. The answer is at the end of the chapter.

This example provides the adult reader with some idea of the child's first experience with print. But in most classrooms today, the child doesn't have the advantage of knowing which letters work together to stand for one sound. Nor do most children know that letters stand for sounds, or even that there *are* sounds in words. The point is this: if you stared at this passage for *years,* you wouldn't have the slightest idea how to decode it. Why, then, should we expect a child to teach himself to decipher the English alphabet code, one of the most complex ever designed, without any instruction? Yet, this is precisely what is going on in classrooms throughout the English-speaking world. When Rudolph Flesch wrote *Why Johnny Can't Read* in 1955, he complained about the illogical teaching method called "look-say," where children were taught to memorize whole words by sight. Today, our children learn that if they look at the pictures, hear the story read while they look at the words on the page, they can teach themselves to read. They are encouraged to do this through getting the maximum information from the minimum cues as a "psycholinguistic guessing game."

Let's see how they do this.

First of all, children are taught something. They learn the names of the letters of the alphabet from Mom, Dad, Sesame Street, and the kindergarten teacher. As the names for letters of the alphabet have no relationship whatsoever to the sounds in speech those letters represent, this sets up the first roadblock for the young reader. To get past this roadblock, the child has to figure out that letters have "names" *and* "sounds." In most classrooms he is supposed to do this by himself. Many never figure this out. This leaves open several possibilities for decoding text.

To illustrate this, I am going to transcribe some lines of *How the Grinch Stole Christmas* by Dr. Seuss. We will look in on several children reading this passage. If your child has a reading problem, you might recognize him or her in these examples.

First is Sally, who is 7½ and is in second grade. Miss Jones has told Sally, who has just finished reading, or I should say, memorizing, *The Three Little Pigs* (with considerable help from her Mom and her best friend Jane), to find another book. The teacher is busy and Sally gets no help from her about this book. This means that Sally doesn't know the title and therefore has no "context clues" to help her read the story. There are pictures. Branches of a Christmas tree are in the first illustration, and a wreath is on the second page, but these pages got stuck together with chewing gum. Sally opens the book at the page where the following quote appears. On the facing page, the Grinch stands in the opening to his cave, looking mean and disagreeable. The landscape is bleak. There are snow and icicles clinging to the rocky entrance to his cave.

Here's the quote:

The Grinch hated Christmas!
The whole Christmas season.
Now please don't ask why.
No one quite knows the reason.

Here are examples of how this passage would have been read by Sally about a year ago when she was using letter names to decode, just like Donny used letter names to spell:

The jeerienseetch aitchaiteedee seeaitchericeteemace——
(The)   (grinch)   (hated)   (Christmas)

It's too painful to continue this transcription. It was also too painful for Sally, who gave up completely until her mother intervened. Sally had been drilled on the letters of the alphabet from the age of four. She could recite them at lightening speed: "aybeeceedee-ee-ef-gee/aitch-ie-jaykayelemenopee/kewaresteeyouvee/doubleyouekswhyzee." When Sally didn't learn to read, her Mom decided to teach her the sounds of the letters as well. Sally's Mom taught these sounds incorrectly, attaching vowels to each consonant that shouldn't be there (buh, duh, kuh). Now Sally has a mixed strategy. She starts with the letter name out of habit, knows this is wrong, cancels this in her mind, translates or substitutes a possible sound the letter might stand for, and proceeds along like this (bear in mind, much of this will be subvocal and inaudible):

"The gee/guh, are/rrruh, ie/i, en/nuh, see/kuh, aitch/huh," (pause: "umm, umm, umm") "guhrink." Not a bad guess. She did this *very* slowly and it has taken about thirty seconds to decode "Grinch" incorrectly. And so it goes on, and about ten minutes later, Sally may have decoded four lines, most of which will be meaningless because she is so inaccurate and so slow. Personality comes into play here. Sally has always wanted to please her parents and her teacher. She is determined to succeed and just keeps trying. She never gets any better. Most kids are not like Sally and would have given up long before this. Sally will give up in third grade. Sally will think she's dumb.

Let's talk about Nigel. He's in Sally's class. Nigel is reading the same story. Nigel hasn't been taught anything. He figured out that random letter sequences stand for whole words: sjboidntl = "baseball." In fact, he is encouraged to think this way. "What is the story about, Nigel? Look at the picture. Say the whole word. Don't sound it out. Say it fast," says Miss Jones over and over again. Nigel has memorized some words, so he can read some of the story about the Grinch. Words he's never seen cannot be read, and his memory is faulty, because some letter strings look so much alike.

The————hat————the————while————Now please
        (hated)   **(whole)**
don't———— ————. No one quick——— the ———.
                            (quite)

Nigel has no way to read words that don't look like words he has already memorized. Nothing he reads ever makes much sense. Nigel has just decided to give up reading the Grinch. He is frustrated. He makes a paper glider and fires it at a classmate's head. He loses the star he got yesterday for good behavior, and has to move his chair to face the wall.

On the other hand, there is Albert. He has figured out something pretty nifty. He has discovered that letters stand for sounds at the beginning of words and sometimes at the end as well. So if he can work out the beginning sounds, he can guess the rest of the word because words have different shapes. He looks at the word's overall shape and how long it is. He knows that each string of letters stands for a word, a real word. So here is Albert's rendition of the Grinch. The individual letters he actually looks at are underlined. The rest of the word is a blur.

"The **Gr**anny **ha**d **ch**ocolate. The **wh**ile——**wh**ite **ch**ocolate **se**es.
No **pl**enty **d**on't **a**nd **w**ont. **N**o one **qu**ick **n**ow, the **rea**lly.

Albert is trying to rely on picture cues to help him guess words. He thinks this story is about Granny and how she has plenty of white chocolate which she got from Sees Candies. The snow and icicles around the Grinch's cave he thinks is white chocolate. Judging by her sour expression in the drawing, she is guarding this chocolate so no one else will get it, even if they're "quick." "Really!" the author says. This is too bad!

Oh, dear! If only Miss Jones had given Albert some context clues, like the title of the story, he would have been in better shape. If he takes the book home, his Mom will tell him the title, read the words he can't read, and Albert will store away some more beginning letter-sound combinations and more word shapes in his brain than he has stored at the moment. After awhile, his brain will overload and he will quit reading. This will happen around third grade if Albert is very smart and has a good visual memory. If he is not, he will have stopped by now, and he will just be looking at the pictures.

So far, we have been talking about what children do when they have been taught essentially nothing, or have been misinformed about how our alphabet code works by being encouraged to memorize letter names and guess whole words from context cues. This means that teaching the alphabet code becomes the parents' problem. These children may have parents who are both working and can't spend time with them, or parents who have tried and failed to teach them to read. Maybe the parents also have a reading problem themselves, or they're doing what the Jamesons did in the story about Donny, supplying the correct word as the child goes along, but not teaching a system their child can use without their help.

The next examples come from schools in a different state, probably somewhere in New England. Children have actually been taught something about the alphabet code. They are taught various types of "phonics." I am going to stick to the more generic forms to illustrate the typical patterns of errors children make with phonics instruction. The first type of phonics comes mainly from major publishing houses and teaches what are called "word families" or "analogies." Word families are parts of a word, usually a group of ending sounds combining a vowel and final consonants. These are often taught in rhyme: "the cat sat on the mat," and are known technically as "rimes," which are vowel+consonant(s) endings to words. Dr. Seuss is a favorite author. The letter strings: ing, ent, unch are examples of word families or rimes. In these examples, the letter strings stand for the following number of sounds in English: 2 (/i/ /ng/), 3 (/e/ /n/ /t/), 3 (/u/ /n/ /ch/). However, children are taught, or led to believe, that these letter sequences *are only one sound*. This means that if they are taught unch, as in "bunch," "hunch," "lunch," "punch," they will not be able to transfer this knowledge to other similar sounding endings: "bench," "ranch," "launch," because they learned 'unch' as one unit or one 'sound.' They don't know that n stands for the sound /n/ wherever it appears in a word, or that ch stands for the sound /ch/ most of the time (except when it stands for /k/ in words like Christmas, character, chaos, choir, anchor, mechanic, etc.). This means each word family or "rime" has to be taught one at a time, but there are 1,260 possible rhyming endings in English. Even if teaching rimes was an efficient way to teach spelling patterns (which it isn't), phonics programs never teach more than a fraction of them.

Many children discover that longer words can be broken up into smaller words or word fragments, such as the letter pattern: <u>an</u> (two sounds). The child scours text for <u>an</u> in words: "and" "ant," "Martian," "pleasant," "branch," "answer." Here is Sam, in Mrs. Finch's second-grade class. The whole school is working in an off-the-shelf phonics-based program.

Sam reads:

The Ger-inch hat-ate-ted cris-tams. The who-ell crit-muss see-son. Now pless-as do-ont as whee. No one quit kuh-na-now the re-are-son.

Notice that Sam is continually reusing letters in different combinations. He knows he has to break the word apart, but he doesn't know how to do this. When he reads 'hated,' he sees 'hat,' 'ate' and 'ted,' and so he reads "hat-ate-ted." He also knows he isn't reading real words. He is hoping that what he reads will sound similar to a real word so that he can figure it out. He tries different options. That is why he reads "Christmas" differently the second time, but it still doesn't make sense. Sam is scanning the words from left to right and from right to left to locate these letter strings standing for word parts. He has done a pretty good job of putting these word parts in the right sequence, from left to right. Some part-word assemblers don't do this. They get the sequence scrambled.

At the beginning of this chapter, I pointed out that college students use this strategy. If Sam keeps on like this, which he probably will, he will improve to some extent as his vocabulary grows. But this strategy is very prone to error and Sam is seriously at risk for giving up. Even if he persisted and became more accurate, he would always misread a large number of words on every page and have to reread many sentences.

Across town, there is an experienced teacher named Mrs. Earnest. Mrs. Earnest is about five years from retirement. She thinks that what is going on in most schools today is nonsense. She particularly hates "whole language" and thinks it's ridiculous that children are supposed to teach themselves to read and spell. Mrs. Earnest strongly believes that "phonics" is important. She was taught some phonics in her training, and her students do well on standardized tests. However, Mrs. Earnest never learned the entire alphabet code. She knows the sounds for the twenty-six letters of the alphabet, but she is uncertain about how many other sounds are in the English language (twenty-one more). She knows that there are consonant clusters or "blends," that is, two consonants side-by-side, as in the letters b̲l̲ in the word "black." She knows that each of these letters stands for a different sound /b/ and /l/, but she *thinks* it's easier for the children to learn clusters as "one sound" /bl/. She is supported in this incorrect viewpoint by several well-known phonics programs. But neither Mrs. Earnest nor the authors of these phonics programs know how many clusters there are in the English language (there are seventy-six), so most clusters are never taught.

She also knows that certain letter pairs can stand for *only one sound* (e̲a̲ c̲h̲ has two sounds). She even knows the technical name for this: "digraphs." It never occurs to her that these two pieces of information are contradictory: two letters stand for "one sound" which is *really two sounds* (b̲l̲), but two letters also stand for "one sound" which is *really one sound* (c̲h̲). Apart from these problems, as Mrs. Earnest never learned the entire spelling code, she can only teach as much as she knows. The kids have to figure out the rest. Here is Andrew, a seven-year-old, reading the Grinch.

The Grin hatted chuh-ristmas. The wall Christmas seesson. Now pleece don't ask wee. No one quit k-noass the reeson.

Andrew has a strategy that is partially working. Notice how he corrects "Christmas" the second time he sees it. First he tries the sound /ch/ and then the sound /k/, which is right and makes sense. He does this because Mrs. Earnest told the children to try out both ways to read c̲h̲. But Andrew was never taught the final consonant cluster n̲c̲h̲. He wasn't taught about "e-controlled" vowel spellings either. This is where the letter e̲ "controls" the pronunciation of the vowel letter coming in front of it. It controls this pronunciation backwards across one consonant but not two: hat, hate, hated, hatted. So he misreads 'hated,' 'whole,' and 'quite' as "hatted," "wall" and "quit." Mrs. Earnest never taught the children that the sound /z/ is often spelled s̲ or s̲e̲ (please, season, reason). Mrs. Earnest taught the children that final y̲ stands for the sound /ee/ at the ends of a lot of words (baby, lady, crazy), but *not* that the letter y̲ stands for the sound /ie/ at the ends of one-syllable words (why, by, cry). Andrew will learn to read eventually, because he has a strategy that is partially working, and this will allow him to work out more of the code. Right now he is not independent of adult help, but he probably will be in a year or two.

Now let's look in at Mrs. Able. She is teaching in a different school than Mrs. Earnest. The principal is a strong proponent of a "phonics"-based approach to early reading. No child is taught sight words first (memorizing whole words by sight) and phonics last, so that they are misled about how the code works. Within this general framework, the principal encourages her teachers to be innovative. Mrs. Able had some excellent training at Columbia Teacher's College about twenty years ago where she learned the sounds of the English language and the logic of the alphabet code: that letters are arbitrary symbols for sounds in speech. She then went on to make a thorough study of the issue. She tried out various approaches in her classroom and actually noted down the results she got year after year. Her children got better as a result of her efforts. By the time we look in on Mrs. Able, she had worked out how to teach children the entire alphabet code in a carefully sequenced way, so that no child was ever confused or lost. Mrs. Able had to write most of her own curriculum materials, because she couldn't find anything that was complete, accurate, *and* interesting to the children. Here is Luz, a little Hispanic girl who is bilingual, reading the Grinch.

The Grinch hated cheristmas—Christmas. The whole Christmas season. Now pleass—please don't ask why. No one quite knows the reason.

And by the way, I forgot to mention that Mrs. Able teaches first grade, and Luz is only six years old.

I hope this exercise has been enlightening for many parents and teachers. Many of you will recognize your child or family member, or one of your students here. It was intended to show that people can decode text in many different ways. When the beginning reader has to try to decipher the alphabet code unaided, he will come up with at least one of the strategies I have outlined here. Most children will use more than one. If a child sticks with any of the first four strategies: letter-name-decoding, name-to-sound-translating, sight-word-reading, real-word guessing, this will *inevitably* lead to reading failure (no exceptions). Failure could come as early as first grade or as late as third grade, when the real-word guesser with the fabulous visual memory and terrific vocabulary finally breaks down. A child's poor reading strategy will not self-correct without appropriate remedial help.

Most of the time, a child's decoding strategy is invisible to the teacher and the parent. In order to discover a child's strategy you need to listen to him read individual words and record each misread word phonetically. You need a good ear and knowledge of the spelling code to make these transcriptions. I can share these examples with you only because I have spent hundreds of hours testing children, and transcribing and analyzing errors, as have other scientists. I can confirm this in a different way, because we see these strategies every day in our reading clinic and some even more bizarre than these. One adult client decoded each unfamiliar word after she chanted letter names out loud: "Let's see—double-you aitch ay el ee—that's 'while' isn't it?" (No. It's 'whale.')

It probably wouldn't surprise anyone that the strategy the child or adult is using is highly correlated to reading test scores on standardized tests. The strategies were introduced in the stories in order from the worst to the best. In our research, children's reading test scores could be predicted from the proportions of each type of strategy error they made at around 65 percent accuracy. More important, this prediction holds up over time. The types of strategy errors a child makes in first grade predict his reading ability *in third grade* with about 38 percent accuracy (38 percent of the variance). Examples of student errors from our research are shown in Table 2–1.

The table illustrates some of the 1,780 errors made by 137 first and third graders. The words the child was asked to read are on the left. The errors the children made were phonetically transcribed. Examples are from an easy and a more difficult part of the test. Notice that there is a huge margin of error for strategies where the child guesses a whole real word or assembles word fragments into something like a word. The test ends when the child makes six errors on the same page, which explains why there are so few whole word errors in the harder part of the test. Most "whole word guessers" drop out before they get this far.

The errors in the two columns on the right are made by children who attempt to decode phonetically from left to right, getting the correct number of sounds in the word. "Orthographic errors" occur when there is an incomplete knowledge of the spelling code. For example, one child read 'without' as "withut," because he couldn't decode ou with the correct vowel sound. "Phonetic errors" are accurate phonetic decodings of irregularly spelled words. For example, the word 'money' uses the spelling o-e (bone, cone, alone) for the sound /u/ (fun). An accurate phonetic decoding of this spelling is mone-y, an error. Note, however, that the margin of error for orthographic and phonetic decoding is minimal, despite the fact that this particular test contains a high proportion of irregularly spelled words. (A strategy test is provided in chapter 11.)

Are the teachers in the stories unusual? Not really, except, perhaps, for Mrs. Able. Mrs. Able is fictional. I have never actually met anyone

TABLE 2–1

	Whole Word	Part Word	Orthographic	Phonetic
money	mommy	mo-ness		moany
	mom			
	many			
	morning			
lemon	lawn	lee-mo	leemon	
	woman	lemola		
	none	lev-on		
	loan	el-mon		
without	shouted	witch-shot	withut	
	what	what-out		
	whole	went-about		
	washout	wi-hut		
		withit		
		went-hunt		
		with-ert		
exit	next	ex-is		
	eat	ox-it		
	axe	ex-ch		
	except	ext		
	picket	ex-out		
chew	cherry	ch-wah	shoo	
	cheer	chelm	chow	
	cow	chale		
	show			
	chill			
question	position	quest-unt	questun	
	present	quock		
	construction	quiss		
		plush-on		
		quest		
		quist-on		
		clitton		
		bus-tom		
piece	press	pie-eck	peek	pice
	people	pie	pike	
	picnic		pies	
	picture			
	price			
	picket			
	place			
	pipe			
	person			
	pick			
strange	starting	star-nag	strang	
	stand	stamp-gate		
	string			
	strong			
	straight			
	starch			
	strain			
	scared			

TABLE 2–1 (CONT.)

	Whole Word	Part Word	Orthographic	Phonetic
prudent	parent	pun-dent	proddent	
	pretend	per-dent	pruddent	
	predict	per-dint		
	rodent	por-dunt		
	president	pron-dent		
		prun-tent		
		pre-dent		
		proud-ent		
		per-du-tent		
circumstance	circus	kirkum-ston	kirkumstance	
	Christmas	kircum	kirkumstens	
	cricket	criss-ums		
	customers	circus-tant		
	Christmas/	circus-stance		
	dance	kirkus-men-stem		
		cirma-tense		
		cree-cum-stance		
		cir-quum-stan		
		circum-stess		
		circum-steak		
		cru-cumst		
		curse-coms		
occasionally	association	occasion	occa-sinally	occashunally
	o-consequently	os-conally	ockushenally	
	socially	oki-den	occasonally	
		oko-lus		
		ock-us-shun-ality		
		ock-sit-on-ally		
		ocka-sallony		
		ock-ish-inly		
		ock-sin-sin-ly		
		ock-us-on-allay		
		on-son-ally		
		on-cass-on-ally		
		us-colly		
		o-can-selly		
		o-can-sarly		
		ass-ocean		
		o-cash-in-alley		
		ack-sit-olly		
flamboyant		fam-boyantly		
		flam-bio-ant		
		flam-bonnet		
		flam-bout		
		flab-bay-ent		
		fail-boy-ant		
		fan-boy-ant		
		flame-boy		
		flame-bone-yant		
		fame-boy-ant		
		flame-boy-ant		

like this, though I have met teachers who come close. But Mrs. Able is very, very lucky. She had excellent training, an enlightened principal, and she took advantage of her freedom to be innovative and carry out her own research. This combination of factors is rare.

Are the children in the stories unusual? This is a harder question to answer. Although we see children use these strategies daily in our clinic and in our research on normal children, there is not sufficient evidence on what percentage of children fit these profiles. You may have noticed that I never mentioned anything about their abilities, other than the fact that some children with superb visual memories can end up reading poorly because they rely so exclusively on this skill. Of course not all children read like the children I have just described. The majority learn to read and score normally on standardized tests. Fifty-seven percent of fourth graders are reading at "basic level" or higher as shown by the national literacy survey. But is this due to something going on in the classroom or something going on outside it?

Reading researchers in England routinely include parents' educational level as one of their measures. Peter Bryant and his colleagues at Oxford University studied factors that predict children's reading ability across the age range four to seven years. The strongest predictor at age seven, on three different reading tests, was *mother's education,* which predicted overall reading skill with 40 percent accuracy. Mother's education contributed above and beyond the child's intelligence, and IQ added another 15 percent to the accuracy of the prediction. Reading researchers in the United States don't usually include parents' educational level in their data. The Educational Testing Service did collect information about parents' education as part of their survey material, but this was based on student reports and is inaccurate. Thirty-six percent of fourth graders responded "don't know" to the question about their parents' education.

What can English mothers be doing that English classroom teachers aren't doing? We can only guess, as this hasn't been studied. More education equates to more money, and a greater likelihood of finding remedial help or paying for a good private school. There is evidence that the amount of one-on-one instruction is directly related to how fast you learn to read, and how fast you learn to read determines your placement in the classroom. This placement has been found to stay relatively constant over time. Educated moms are likely to spend more time teaching their children to read, and from our clinical experience, most parents we meet believe that training children to sound out words is the best way to teach reading.

Another problem in trying to determine whether these children are unusual is what is meant by "being able to read." Young children can read "at grade level" or "age level" using quite inefficient reading strategies. Does this mean that norms on standardized tests are essentially meaningless? Certainly, this was the rationale behind the development of "achievement levels" by the National Assessment Governing Board and completely borne out by their results.

In our research, we found some "real-word guessers" who were among the best readers in the class in first grade, when there aren't many words, but who fell apart completely at second or third grade, just like Donny in the opening story. So, it matters a lot *when* children are tested. We found that by far the most common type of reading strategy in third grade was "part-word assembling." Children who used this strategy were all reading at or above grade level, showing that this must be common. The next most common was the phonetic decoder who makes "orthographic" decoding errors due to an incomplete and inaccurate knowledge of the alphabet code. Only two children in our entire sample of 137 children had accurate phonetic decoding skills. One was a first grader, whose parents were both teachers, and one a third grader. Needless to say, they scored the highest of anyone on the reading test. The first grader whizzed through the test and scored at a comparable level to a thirty-three-year-old adult. He was known affectionately as "the little professor." He would need a good vocabulary to do this, but he didn't understand all the words he could read; he just knew how the code worked. *Shouldn't every child know how the code works?*

The children in our study attended an excellent private school which boasted a 90 percent success rate for university placement. Yet after 3½ years of schooling, totaling over 3,600 hours in the classroom, in this best of all possible schools, with dedicated teachers, small classes, and highly involved parents, only 2 percent of the children really knew the alphabet code. That things are much worse in the average public school is illustrated by the results from the national literacy survey comparing public and private schools.

HOW DO GOOD READERS LEARN TO READ?

About now, you may be wondering how does anybody ever learn to read? How did Donny's brother and sister learn to read? How did you learn to read? In the Preface, I described my recollection of being able to read anything in print in first grade. But I only remember this because of an unusual event, having to read the newspaper to a boy twice my age who couldn't read a word. Beyond this, I remember nothing at all. Many people are familiar with this experience, and many parents report that their child suddenly "took off" and could read.

How does this happen with the same teaching that fails so many other children? This is a fascinating question that, so far, nobody has attempted to answer. One can only suppose, on the basis of extensive research on poor readers, that good readers have a "talent" for hearing individual sounds in words, which are the basis for our alphabet code, *and* that they somehow understood that these sounds, and no other combinations of sounds, are represented by a specific letter or letters. These children will also have a "talent" for remembering visual detail and need less time to memorize letter-sound correspondences. In addition, they will have been given instruction which was sufficiently accurate so as not to be misleading.

How common are people like this?

The truth is that good readers are relatively rare. Only 13 percent of fourth graders in the bottom-ranked states were in the combined reading levels: "proficient" + "advanced" in the national reading study. This value was 31 percent for the top ranked states and 24 percent nationwide, about the same proportion of the population who succeed in getting a college degree.

In every skilled behavior, there are degrees of competence. Reading is no exception. As an analogy, think about swimming. Everyone should know how to swim and have swimming lessons sometime in childhood. Whether a child becomes an expert swimmer depends upon the teaching method, the teacher's skill in teaching it, parental support, the child's motivation and talent, and the number of lessons and hours of practice. Few of us are expert swimmers, but *most of us could be* with appropriate training. We certainly *should be* if we had spent over 3,600 hours in swimming classes, which is the number of hours our third graders had spent in the classroom trying to learn to read.

It's nice to be able to swim, but swimming only matters because you might fall into a swimming pool or pond. If this should happen, all you need is sufficient skill to stay afloat until you are rescued. You don't need Olympic-quality style or speed. Learning to read is similar to learning to swim in one sense (both are skills that must be taught), but completely different in another. To be effective in a modern world, it matters whether or not you are an expert reader. Keeping afloat isn't good enough. Keeping afloat is tantamount to drowning.

So what is reading all about? Is there a better way to teach reading so everyone can become an "expert"? In the next chapter, we look at exciting new discoveries about how writing systems work. It turns out that every writing system is determined by the sound-based structure of the language for which it was written. This startling new information has important implications for how a particular writing system can and *cannot* be taught. These findings are compared to current teaching methods and to the philosophies behind them.

Answer to nursery rhyme on page 17: "London bridge is falling down."

y=l   t=o   o=n   x=d   etc.

Chapter 3

TRANSCRIBING TALK

In the last chapter we saw that when children are given no instruction, or misleading instruction, they develop different strategies or hypotheses about which unit of talk the letters stand for. Some psychologists and educators believe that these strategies reflect "stages" of reading development. Some go further and argue that these stages mirror the progression of the development of writing itself, an idea which begins to resemble biological determinism. In this view, children are not really making errors, they are behaving "naturally" as they progress along a developmental path.

There are various forms of quasi-biological models in reading instruction, whole language being a primary example. The "stage" theorists advocate teaching reading in as many as four separate steps. The child is first taught whole words, then whole syllables, then initial consonant plus rhyming endings ("onset-rime"), and finally individual sounds (phonemes). One extreme view advocates using different symbols for each of these steps. These ideas have impacted teacher training and curriculum design in countries around the world. One major education publisher has implemented a whole-to-part/whole language curriculum for kindergarten through third grade. Children begin learning "sight words" (memorizing whole words), followed by "onset-rime" (alliteration plus rhyming endings or "word families"), then whole language for a year or two, and finally, traditional "phonics" at third grade. This is the ultimate in hedging your bets, a trend in curriculum design known as "eclecticism," which wastes three years and can derail many children.

The idea that writing systems, or children learning them, go through developmental stages is incorrect. It is based on ignorance about how writing systems actually work, and also upon a type of reverse logic. Children's confusion and misunderstanding about our alphabetic writing system, instead of being seen as correctable, *becomes the platform* for designing a program of instruction.

In the next two chapters we will be looking at writing systems in the light of modern teaching methods, to see if there is any fit between the way writing systems are designed and the methods which should be used to teach them.

For over 200 years scholars have grappled with the mystery of deciphering ancient writing systems. Eleven writing systems still defy a solution. This extended effort has revealed that writing systems aren't arbitrary; that is, you couldn't use the Chinese writing system for English, and it wouldn't make sense to use the English writing system for Chinese. The evidence shows conclusively that the design of every writing system is constrained by two main factors:

1. the limits of human memory for abstract visual symbols
2. the syllable structure of the language

This information is critically important in knowing how a writing system should be taught, and in knowing how it *cannot* be taught.

We're going to start by comparing the development of writing to "whole language" and the "progressive stages" approach. Whole language advocates make specific predictions about how all writing systems should be taught, predictions which can easily be checked against the evidence.

The whole language or literature-based ("real books") method has been the dominant teaching approach in most English-speaking countries for over a decade, but there is considerable confusion about what whole language actually means. The central idea behind whole language is that "reading is natural" in the same way that learning to speak is natural. According to Kenneth Goodman, the leading expert on whole language, children come to the classroom with a wealth of knowledge about the meaning of words and the grammatical structure of their language. They have acquired this knowledge without any direct instruction. He also assumes that as children speak fluently, they have an awareness of the sounds in their own speech. From this knowledge, which Goodman describes as three "cueing systems," children can easily acquire an understanding of the written code for their language by maximal use of all three cues: context cues to determine meaning, grammatical structure to anticipate which word is most likely in a sequence, and knowledge of patterns of sounds in speech. Goodman predicts that this approach would work for all written languages, commenting that "theoretically, any type of writing system would work for any language."

As reading is supposed to be just like learning to speak, the child needs to be exposed to good children's literature, using books and stories which use *natural* or "normal" language, and not unnatural language like the old Dick and Jane readers, where words were repeated over and over again.

See Jane, see. Look, look, look.

The idea is, that if children hear natural language from children's books, while they are looking at the print as it is being read, and at the same time "invent" their own spelling system as they're learning to write, children will naturally teach themselves to read and write by trial and error. Goodman states that the reader should "use the least amount of information possible to make the best guess possible." By "information," he means pictures, context, and print. In other words, readers should guess whole words in context and work at what makes sense, rather than sounding out words letter by letter, and participate in what Goodman has called "a psycholinguistic guessing game."

It was this approach that Miss Jones was using in her second grade classroom. This is why she said to Nigel, "don't try to sound out the word, just look at the pictures." What she meant was, that if Nigel could understand the *context* of the story, he could figure out which words made sense in that context. As he figured this out, he was supposed to automatically learn the relationship between the sounds in words and the patterns of letters on the page by a process of osmosis.

This certainly makes life a lot simpler for Miss Jones and for the children, and a lot more fun. But is reading and writing "natural" or not? Can children learn to read by context clues, guessing whole words as they work through text? To find out, we're going to look at how writing was invented in the first place.

Here is the problem in a nutshell. Writing is a coded transcription of talk. Talk isn't like words on a page, neat little bundles of sounds separated by spaces. Words are glued together in phrases. Talk sounds like this hypothetical conversation between two people we'll call Ethel and Howard. Howard has just arrived home from the office.

Howard: Hi. Wujjadoodaday?
Ethel: Wentoothemall. Haddasale.
Howard: Bynything?
Ethel: Botchuaparrapanz.
Howard: Howmuchaycos?
Ethel: Nahmuch. Wanmeedagiddumenshowya?
Howard: Inawhile. Wuzferdinner?

Conversations sound like this in every language. Howard and Ethel speak pretty much the same as other folks, connecting badly enunciated speech sounds across an entire phrase. Certainly, no one would ever want to create a written record of conversations like this one. Something very important has to be going on to make the invention of writing absolutely necessary.

We are fortunate to have a treasure trove of documents providing a blow-by-blow description of what it was like to design a writing system from scratch. This detailed history comes from ancient Sumer in the Tigris-Euphrates delta. Our alphabet is a distant descendant of the writing systems of Sumer and Egypt. Beginning around 3500 B.C., the Sumerians had a problem with storing grain, dates, oil, and wine in a communal warehouse. It was the warehouseman's job to remember which farmer was storing which commodity, what kind of grain (emmer, wheat, barley, millet), how much of each type, and what was owed to whom in either exchange or money. He had to keep all this in his head, and no doubt he and the farmers had arguments almost daily. To solve these problems, the farmers and city administrators got together and devised a code using pictures for the types of grain, for oil, wine, and dates, along with little slashes and dots for numbers. These were carved onto clay tablets or tokens. Now they had a method for keeping ledgers and inventory control, a method that got more sophisticated over the next thousand years. An accounting tablet is shown in Figure 3–1. Translations of lower figures are unclear.

This solution worked fine until the crime rate started to go up as the harvests increased, artisans flourished and became famous for their wares, and the towns generally grew more prosperous. There were disputes over ownership to the land, positions of boundary markers, irri-

FIGURE 3–1

Photo reproduced with permission of Christie's
Images

quantity of the product:

c. 135,000 liters

type of the product:

barley

accounting period:

37 months

gation rights, and disposable property. This is the awful consequence of owning land and goods. Somebody always gets more than somebody else, and the "somebody else" hits back.

The Sumerians needed laws, courthouses, and judges, and some way to remember the laws and record the judges' case decisions, because the judges couldn't remember them all. But how? Laws aren't commodities, things, or numbers. You can't draw pictures of laws. Laws are just talk, and talk sounds like Ethel and Howard's conversation about the pants. It's not easy to try and represent talk in symbols. What part of the talk do you choose? The most obvious units are words. You could symbolize words with the pictures you already have from the warehouse inventory control system, but this doesn't get you very far with statements like this from a hypothetical plaintiff:

Hewuzpickinmygrapesoudamyfield. Iknowidwuzim. Isawim.

It needs a sharp ear and a keen understanding of the language just to find out where the words start and stop. And anyone smart enough to do this and to begin to develop a writing system will know in a hurry that pictures won't work:

He   was   picking   my   grapes   out of my   field.

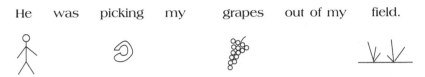

The pictures could mean: "He was picking grapes in his field," or "We're hiring men to pick grapes in the field," or "The man planted seeds in Fred's grape field."

The Sumerians hit upon the idea of using abstract symbols for words that couldn't be drawn as a picture. These symbols could look like anything at all.

Here's where the trouble began and the story gets really interesting, except no one thought so at the time.

These difficulties were not unique to Sumer. They caused problems everywhere during the agricultural revolution, in all the places where it was easy to grow wheat and rice. The same ideas and the same types of solutions cropped up whenever people had to keep inventories, write out wills, contracts, bills of sale, rules, laws, and case decisions. This happened in the Nile delta in Egypt around 3000 B.C., in the Indus valley around 2500 B.C., along the Yangtze river in China sometime around 2000 B.C., and in places as remote as the Yucatan jungle, where exactly the same kind of writing was invented by the Mayans.

All early writing systems begin by focusing on meaning. First, words are isolated from phrases. Words that can be drawn, (ship, ox) are represented by pictures (pictograms), and words that can't are represented by abstract symbols, called "logographs," which is Greek for "word-writing" or "word-carving." After a while the Sumerians had hundreds of these logographs.

Unfortunately, this doesn't work. People may have a natural talent for learning language and rapidly acquire huge vocabularies without much effort, but they have almost no talent for remembering *either* thousands of abstract visual patterns *or* the connection between each abstract visual pattern and a particular word. This meant that the Sumerians couldn't represent most of the words in their language. The average number of words in daily conversations on the streets of any town in the world today is about 50,000. The *Oxford Companion to the English Language* estimates that the total number of all possible English words, including abbreviations and specialist vocabularies, exceeds one billion! But when people are asked to memorize what word goes with which abstract visual symbol scribbled on clay, or papyrus, or paper, the upper limit is around 1,500 to 2,000, not enough for any language. Not even close.

Instead, the Sumerians were faced with a totally different problem, how to limit the number of symbols so that people could remember them, and at the same time transcribe all possible words they needed. They tried to use the symbols more efficiently. For instance, the same symbol was adopted for two words related in meaning. The symbol for "mouth" was used for the verb "to speak," and the symbols for "mouth" and "food" were combined to stand for "eat."

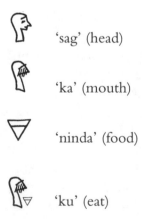

'sag' (head)

'ka' (mouth)

'ninda' (food)

'ku' (eat)

All languages have words that sound alike with different meanings. In English, we bury our dead and pick a berry off a bush. We see a bear in the woods, bare our chest, and bear our burdens. We trip on a stair and people stare at us. We pare a pair of pears and reel in a real fish. These kinds of words are called "homophones" (Greek for "same sounds"). The Sumerians used one symbol for homophones, instead of inventing different symbols for words like "berry" and "bury." The reader was supposed to figure out which meaning was correct by using context clues.

There were lots of homophones in Sumerian and this made the writing ambiguous. This could have important implications down at the courthouse. Arguments might break out in court over whether a man had been blinded by his son, or was blinded by the sun, and this would never do. The Sumerians had another idea. They divided the words in their language into categories, and then invented symbols for each of the categories. In the hypothetical example, if you wrote the symbol for the word "sun," you could add the category symbol for "heavenly body," and "son" could be written beside the category symbol for "man." These category signs are called "determiners" because they *determine* the meaning of a word. How many of these determiners you need in the writing system depends upon how many symbols have multiple meanings. Sumerians used determiners only for nouns.

It's difficult to duplicate these effects in English, because the symbols in our writing system stand for sounds, not words. English homophones usually have different spellings. But it might look something like this:

Aunt Eloise picked four ripe pears (⏖) and took them into the house to pear (⏚) and served them in pears (⏛) to the guests.

The determiners to help interpret "pear" are:

⏖ = fruit

⏚ = utensil

⏛ = quantity

Alas, this solution was only marginally useful. Most Sumerian words were not homophones. There were still thousands of words without symbols and new words coming into the language almost daily. There was no way to write people's names, and no way to mark grammatical tenses, like past, present, and future. To add to the confusion, the pictographs began to disappear after the stylus was invented. It made wedge-shaped marks, known as "cuneiform" (wedge-shape) writing. It's difficult to draw with a wedge-shaped tool, so the pictograms were turned on their side and ultimately became as abstract as the logographs. The pictograph for "eat" went through these transformations:

3000 B.C.——————————————————————————————600 B.C.

So far, the Sumerians had focused exclusively on meaning, developing the writing system entirely at the level of the word. They had pictographs standing for words, logographs standing for words, logographs that stood for several words with the same sound, logographs that stood for words related in meaning, and symbols called determiners that stood for categories of meaning. From a whole language perspective, a writing system that focuses entirely on meaning should have been nearly perfect. The only problem was, *it didn't work.* No matter how efficiently the symbols were used, they still kept creeping above the limits of human memory.

Eventually, scholars had a better idea. Suppose you invented symbols to stand for fragments of a word, the meaningless *sounds* in the word, instead of the whole word? This would give you two kinds of clues, category clues (determiners) for words that sounded alike (son/sun), and sound-based codes for words that were ambiguous or had no symbols, like parts of speech. Once they made this decision, they discovered something amazing. There were only three main types of syllables in Sumerian: consonant+vowel (CV), vowel+consonant (VC), and consonant-vowel-consonant (CVC). Furthermore, the total number of possible syllables was incredibly smaller than the total number of words in the language. A syllable is a pattern of sounds in words with only one vowel. In English, 'I,' 'it,' 'crunch' 'sling' are one-syllable words and 'table,' 'jumping,' 'forest,' are two-syllable words.

From this point on, the Sumerians began to invent symbols for every sound combination for three types of syllables in their language: CV, VC, and CVC. All new words could be written with syllable symbols alone. So it was that the Sumerian writing system began to accrete symbols that stood for many levels of talk, rather like whales accrete barnacles. Now, you might think, with hindsight, that they should have just thrown out the logographs and the category determiners, and used only the syllable symbols. They couldn't do this right away, just as we have never been able to standardize our spelling system. The reason was that things had gone too far. All the tinkering with the writing system took about 1000 years. The palace archives, temple documents, prayers and sacred myths, laws, case decisions, forms for writs, marriage licenses, etc. were written with the old logographs and couldn't be changed just like that.

This meant that by around 2500 B.C., there were symbols that looked a bit like the old pictures that were used for inventory control, symbols that stood for words you couldn't draw, symbols for words related in meaning, symbols for three types of syllables, and symbols for categories like "water," "mineral," "plant," "animal," "field," or "farming equipment." The reader had to shift gears from thinking about words, to thinking about meaningless sounds in words, to thinking about categories as clues to meaning. Samuel Kramer, the famous translator and popularizer of Sumerian literature, writes that not only was this a major stumbling block in deciphering the Sumerian writing system, but often words were written more than one way in the same document. This made it even harder to crack the code because no one believed a writing system could be so wasteful as to have more than one way to write a word. In the same text, you might find the logograph for "canal," alongside a category determiner for "water," and later, the syllable symbols (CV-CVC) standing for 'ca'-'nal,' depending on the whim of the author.

The Sumerian writing system wasn't the only one with this many levels of complexity. Egyptian writing evolved in the same way and was, if anything, even worse. The "hieroglyphic" script used by priests to carve or paint on temples and tombs (hieroglyphic means "sacred-carving") used the same solutions: pictograms, logographs, category determiners, and sound-based symbols for single consonants (C) and consonant sequences (CC, CCC). The Egyptians, however, were partial to their pictograms. These pictograms were not only very beautiful, but were considered sacred. When the priests designed the symbols for abstract words and sounds in words, they used their favorite pictograms over and over again. The picture of an owl, 𓅓 meaning "owl" (the bird), was borrowed to stand for various prepositions (in, to, for, with), *and* for the consonant sound /m/, *and* for words, like "obedient," where the owl stood for "good bird," a determiner. The consonant symbols weren't consistent either. The symbol for /m/ was an owl, but the symbol for the consonants /ms/ (word for "fan") was written like this: 𓌟

The Egyptian priests had a saying, which roughly translated, went:

"Put writing in your heart so you may protect yourself from hard labor of any kind."[1] They seem to have had a vested interest in keeping the writing system as complicated as possible so only a select few could learn it.

We have learned from this history that what is natural for a spoken language isn't natural for a writing system. In natural speech we are only conscious of words and meaning, but to learn a writing system, we have to be conscious of the meaningless sounds in words.

TEACHING SUMERIAN WRITING

Even though these writing systems are complex, they are highly redundant. There are clues to meaning alongside clues to sounds. From a whole language perspective, once these writing systems have been designed, they should be easy to learn because there are so many context clues. Were they easy to learn? Could a Sumerian child teach himself to read using context clues?

We can answer this question as well, from the thousands of exercise tablets found in schools all over ancient Sumer. We can reconstruct exactly what happened in these schools with remarkable detail. Let's look in on a typical Sumerian school boy in the town of Shurrupak, around 2000 B.C. We are at the Edduba, or tablet-house, which is Sumerian for "school." The room is filled with school masters and boys of various ages. One boy, Enkimansi, is the son of a wealthy farmer, and he's sitting beside his best friend on a bench made of clay bricks. He has been there since dawn and will stay til the light fades at sunset. He does this seven days a week and will keep at it until his late teens, about the same number of years that boys and girls go to school today. When Enkimansi first started school, he learned how to prepare his own clay tablets and to make his own writing implement, a wedge-shaped stylus made out of a reed. Next, he had to copy lists of symbols that stood for syllables, starting with the simplest ones for consonant+vowel (CV).

tu, ta, ti, te (too, tah, tee, teh) ku, ka, ki, ke, nu, na, ni, ne bu, ba, bi, be, zu, za, zi, ze

He did this until his writing was accurate and he had memorized them. Then he learned the symbols for rest of the syllables (VC and CVC). Next he wrote out and memorized about 900 logographs. Each one had the syllable signs written beside it to help him remember them and pronounce them correctly. Then he learned compound logographs, where two logographs are written side-by-side to stand for a different word (mouth+bread = eat). After he had memorized all this, he began copying thousands of words in long word lists organized by categories (plants, trees, animals, fish), in order to memorize which category markers (determiners) went with which words. When he was done with all this and could remember everything, he started copying out and reading short phrases, proverbs and fables. And *finally,* when he was about twelve years old, he got to read something interesting.

Here is an example of a popular school-boy story that Enkimansi was copying. The actual text is illustrated in Figure 3–2.

It was written by a schoolmaster in Nippur. Both the masters and the students must have thought it was pretty hilarious because frag-

FIGURE 3–2

Photo reproduced with permission of the University of Pennsylvania Museum.

ments of this story have been found in cities all over Sumer. Like many of the schoolboy stories, it shows the Sumerians' flare for satire. The stories create images of rowdy schoolrooms, full of boisterous, disobedient pupils who were frequently caned for misbehavior. ("Cane" was written as a compound logograph, combining the symbols for 'stick' and 'flesh.') Here are some excerpts from the story.

The Boredom:

I recited my tablet, ate my lunch, prepared my new tablet, wrote it, finished it; then my model tablets were brought to me, and in the afternoon my exercise tablets were brought to me. When school was dismissed, I went home, entered the house, and found my father sitting there. I explained my exercise tablets to my father. I recited my tablet to him, and he was delighted.

The Danger:

My teacher reading my tablet, said: "There is something missing," and caned me. The man in charge of neatness said: "You loitered in the street and did not keep your clothes straight," and caned. The man in charge of silence said: "Why did you talk without permission?" and caned me.

The caning sequence continues for about twelve more lines and the section concludes: "And so I began to hate the scribal art and to neglect the scribal art. My teacher took no delight in me."

The Bribe:

At this point in the story, the student asks his father whether they might be nice to the teacher, invite him to their home, give him presents, and perhaps some extra salary (students paid fees to their head teacher). The father agrees, and the school master arrives, is seated in the best chair, fed good things to eat, given a new tunic, a handsome ring, and some money. This works wonders. Later in the story the master speaks:

Because you gave me everything without holding back, paid me a salary larger than my efforts deserve, and have honored me— may your pointed stylus write well for you, may your exercises contain no faults—may you walk among the highest of the school graduates.[2]

I think you can see that Enkimansi's experience and his typical school day is anything but "natural," easy, or fun. Something natural comes without effort. Instead, the Sumerian and Egyptian pupils had to work very hard, for very long hours, and for a very long time just to learn to read and write. If you look closely at the photograph of the schoolboy story, there is no way anyone could figure it out by guess-work from "context clues." It looks like a small wading bird had criss-crossed the clay tablet about a thousand times. You probably can't even tell one symbol from another.

By now, it should be clear that writing systems are *inventions* and completely unlike natural language. Even though the Sumerian and Egyptian scholars were eventually able to transcribe talk, it turned out to be monstrously difficult to do. Over the centuries gifted people have invented all sorts of codes. They have transcribed music into a written notation, and numerical quantities and relationships into a code of number and letter symbols called "mathematics." Computer software designers coded the English alphabet into octal, then to binary, and back again, so that computers can store this in memory and, at the same time, represent it on a screen. But there is nothing "natural" about these codes, something that a young child would just pick up by staring at them for a few months. Codes have to be taught.

We learned something else equally important. A whole word (logo-graphic) writing system can't work. There is a *natural* limit on human memory for memorizing codes with too many confusing symbols. This limit, from the evidence so far, is around 2,000 symbols. About now, some astute readers may be saying: "Wait a minute. What about the Chinese? The Chinese have a logographic writing system, don't they?"

CAN THE CHINESE MEMORIZE LOGOGRAPHS?

Whole word, "read for meaning" methods like "whole language," and especially "look-say" which came before it, are based on the premise that children can memorize letter patterns or letter sequences standing for whole words. In "look-say" this was taught in the same way as memorizing thousands of telephone numbers. According to the re-ceived wisdom of educators, English-speaking children can memorize letter patterns for whole words because Chinese children are supposed to be able to do this. Misconceptions about Chinese writing have fos-tered the myth that the Chinese people have a "logographic" or "ideographic" (idea symbol) writing system, and that Chinese children are taught to read symbols for whole words and ideas.

The earliest examples of Chinese writing were found on oracle bones dated to the Shang Dynasty, at around 1500 B.C. Writing was already highly developed with about 4,000 different symbols or "characters," showing it had originated much earlier. At the close of the Shang Dynasty, wars and conquests had divided China into city-states or provinces. Each city-state began to develop the writing system in different ways.

In 221 B.C., Emperor Qin unified China and initiated a writing reform. He appointed the scholar Li Su to develop what is called the "small seal script," which he finished in 200 B.C. Li Su's basic job was to standardize the symbols into one uniform system. He assigned one character each to several hundred words (logographs), to CV and CVC syllables, and to "classifier" signs which stood for categories (determiners). In other words, the Chinese writing system was almost identical to the Sumerian writing system. During the same century, the Chinese invented the brush, and in A.D. 106 they invented paper, allowing Xu Shen to compile the first dictionary in A.D. 120. The dictionary was divided into sections by 540 classifiers organized in a fixed order. The classifiers and their order had to be memorized before you could look up a word. Xu Shen's dictionary included around 10,000 entries.

Over the next 1,700 years, many more characters were created, culminating in the great K'ang Hsi dictionary with nearly 50,000 entries. The classifier symbols were reduced to 214, about the same number there is today. To look up a word in a Chinese dictionary, you decide which classifier sign the word might belong to, you remember the order of the classifiers in the dictionary, and then look up the word based on the number of brush strokes in each character, which occur in a fixed sequence. As you can imagine, this isn't very efficient. Only a few eminent scholars were able to take full advantage of the K'ang Hsi dictionary. In further reforms the number of entries shrank dramatically. The modern Chinese dictionary contains about 12,000 entries.

The Chinese writing system is largely based on the *syllable*. Misconceptions about Chinese writing are due to the syllable structure of the Chinese language. Just under half of all Chinese words are only one syllable long: 'li,' 'chu,' 'kao,' 'chang,' a word *and* a syllable at the same time. Most Chinese syllables consist of only two basic sound sequences: CV and CVC, and most CVC sequences end in one of only two sounds: /n/ (tan) and /ng/ (tang). The Chinese language has very few consonant clusters or "blends" (kwan), and a grand total of around 1,277 "tonal" syllables. In tonal languages, meaning can change by altering the tone or pitch of the vowel. This open, simple syllable structure means that the Chinese language is riddled with homophones, those words that sound alike with different meanings, which makes it necessary to use about 200 classifiers. Ninety percent of all Chinese words are written as compound signs, with the syllable sign and classifier sign fused together.

Due to its lengthy evolution, the Chinese writing system is far from perfect. Sometimes the same syllable is written with two or more different characters. Sometimes two or more syllables are written with the *same* character. Sometimes two characters are joined to fuse parts of two words into a new word. Sometimes a "classifier" symbol can also be a syllable symbol. Figure 3–3 on pp. 48–49 shows some examples.

There is modern research to show whether or not Chinese writing is easy to learn. In the early 1980s, Harold Stevenson and a group of American, Japanese, and Chinese scientists tested over 2,000 fifth-grade children in Taiwan, Sendai, and Minneapolis. The children read text of comparable difficulty, with similar vocabularies averaging around 7,000 words. What they discovered first is surprising. Taiwanese children do not begin by memorizing the 1,277 syllable signs, as whole language teachers might imagine. Instead, they are taught the individual sounds of their language using a Roman alphabet. For example, they learn the CVC syllable/word 'tang' has three sounds: /t/ /a/ /ng/. Once these sounds are mastered, they begin to memorize the syllable characters and 214 classifier symbols. For a while, each syllable character 唐 is written alongside its alphabet equivalent (**tang**), so it can be pronounced correctly. Finally, the alphabet symbols are discarded. Apart from historical tradition, there is a good reason why the Chinese don't use an alphabet. Until the advent of typewriters and computers, they didn't need to. Syllable signs are equally fast, or faster, to read because each symbol stands for more than one sound.

The researchers set a 75 percent pass rate for their tests. They found that more of the Chinese children (69 percent) passed this criterion than either the Japanese (44 percent) or American children (54 percent), but this is just as likely to be a function of their excellent, systematic training as a function of the writing system. This superiority effect, for example, was not observed for first-grade children from Beijing who learn whole words from the beginning, in a study by Shin-Ying Lee and his colleagues. Stevenson's team discovered something

FIGURE 3–3A

唐　　tang

	Classifier		Meaning
cereal	米	糖	sugar
earth	土	塘	embankment
hand	手 扌	搪	to block
water	水 氵	溏	pond

FIGURE 3–3B

Position of the Classifier Can Vary

辟　　pì

Classifier	
亻	僻
言	譬
門	闢
女	嬖

else. The majority of the Chinese children who failed the "pass" criterion, failed entirely because they couldn't understand what they read. There was a discrepancy between the Chinese children's ability to read isolated words (decoding) and their understanding of the meaning of the text (comprehension), a discrepancy not found for either Japanese or American children. It seems that it is relatively straightforward to memorize the sound/symbol correspondences for syllable symbols, but not so simple to remember what they mean when they are combined with classifier signs.

FIGURE 3–3C

The Syllable Is Not Consistent with the Symbol

堯 yāo

Classifier				Meaning
person	亻	僥	jiǎo	lucky
hand	扌	撓	nǎo	scratch
wood	木	橈	náo	oar
water	氵	澆	jiāo	sprinkle

Diacritics indicate "tone" or voicing.

I've written a little story in pseudo-Chinese to illustrate this problem. The story is full of homophones, like the Chinese language. The homophones are spelled the same way, similar to the Chinese writing system. Each homophone is followed by a classifier in parentheses. Try to imagine that each word and each classifier is fused into one symbol.

The Hunter

Frank(name) saw(eye) the bare(animal) in the would(plant). He saw(eye) the marks of paws(animal part) at his feat(body part) and decided to paws(time) and think. He sat on a bare(abstract) rock and looked at the weather(sky) to see(eye) weather(thought) he new(thought) when knight(time) was coming. The sun(heavenly body) was low(position). His sun(family) had already left(movement) to weight(time) by the rode(travel). He decided to leave(travel) too. He rose(position), left(movement) the seen(nature) to meat(greeting) his sun(family) and go home(dwelling).

This doesn't look too "natural" does it? It certainly isn't the way that Chinese people talk.

All writing systems are imperfect transcriptions of talk. They are very difficult to design, and this can take hundreds and even thousands of years. Writing systems are imperfect even after centuries of tinkering, and most cultures have attempted some type of writing reform. Writing systems go through "stages," not because this is a natural progression, but because they are so *unnatural,* people begin with the wrong solution and work backwards to a simpler one.

No culture ever used the *word* as the sole basis for a writing system. Not even the Chinese. A word-based system will always fail. This means there is no such thing as a "logographic" writing *system,* and there never was. What turns out to be "natural" is that ordinary people (including children) can only remember about 1,500 to 2,000 abstract visual symbols. What is also "natural" is that people don't know the sounds of their language, or whether there are more words or more sounds, or how many kinds of sounds. We are not conscious observers of how we speak.

There are two main choices for converting talk into scribbles on a page, and scribbles on a page back into talk. The first choice for the novice inventor of writing is always based on what has the greatest psychological relevance, and that is *meaning.* When this fails, scholars scramble to create symbols that are props for decoding meaning. When this also fails, they discover they must use the *meaningless* sounds in words, simply because there are far fewer sounds than words in all languages. There are many choices about which meaningless sounds to use, and the evidence shows these choices are *critically dependent upon the type of syllable structure or sound-based structure of the language.* The Sumerian language had three syllable types: CV, VC, CVC; the Chinese two: CV, CVC. The Mayans used vowels and CV units. The Egyptians used consonant sequences: C, CC, CCC. There are other units of sound you could choose, and we'll talk more about this in the next chapter.

We have a 200-year historical record to show that writing systems are fiendishly difficult to decipher. This is true even when you have good clues and good information, such as knowing ancient place names, or words remaining in the language of the local people, or even knowing the language itself. The reason for the difficulty in deciphering writing systems is that there are several elements of "talk" the written code can stand for, and some writing systems use them all: whole words, syllables, syllable fragments, and consonant sequences.

These facts explain why the children described in chapter 2 were having such a hard time. They were completely ignorant about which unit of "talk" the letters stood for. Most had either no help whatsoever, or partial and misleading help. Each child came to a different decision, either believing that random letter strings between the gaps on the page stood for a whole word, or by cueing off the first consonant and guessing a real word by its shape, or by combining various fragments of these letter strings: CV, VC, CVC, into nonsense words. For example, here are three children reading "watermelon."

Child Sees	*Child Says*
xntiemspe (random letters)	football?
watermelon	wonderful?

w at ate ter term er erm me lo on.   we-ate-term-me-on?

There's one more question a whole language teacher might want to ask. As the early writing systems were so hard to invent and hard to learn, maybe these *particular* writing systems aren't "natural." Maybe the people who promote whole language are talking about alphabets (so far we haven't seen any alphabets). Maybe an alphabet is the only "natural" representation of talk, and these other writing systems are "unnatural." But if alphabets are natural, why didn't everyone invent an alphabet to begin with, or at least come up with an alphabet in over 2,000 years? And why did people in all these different parts of the world do the *same* thing, in the *same* order? If only alphabets are natural, why are these other ideas so alike?

WHAT TEACHERS REALLY THINK
ABOUT WHOLE LANGUAGE

Let's take a closer look at whole language, because there's more to it than just "natural" language and "natural" reading. If you believe something is natural, this has a number of consequences. The first one is that you don't have to teach something natural in any direct way. The child just needs exposure. Conversely, you would never ask the child to do something *unnatural,* like breaking words up into fragments of sound, and putting the fragments back together again (sounding out and blending). Instead, the child should look at the whole word on the page, notice its shape and overall length and *say* the whole word, or *hear* the whole word pronounced by the teacher or parent. Using this approach, children are supposed to be able to learn to read independently. Context, or meaning is very important, because it helps the reader anticipate which word might come next in a sentence. Using context means knowing what the story is about ahead of time or using picture clues. This is why there are so many illustrations in the books in whole language classrooms.

On the other hand, whole language advocates believe that learning to spell is different. Reading is simple decoding based on context clues, but writing is a direct creative act. The most important thing is not to block creativity. If children do lots of writing, according to the theory, they will gradually discover how words should be spelled by inventing their own spelling system. Children can figure out the relationship between sounds in words and the print code *on their own*. They can do this, because they are supposed to have a natural sensitivity to sounds in their own speech. To quote the leading expert on invented spelling: "Using their knowledge of letter names and in some cases letter sounds, children are able to represent the sounds of words quite accurately and consistently."[3] (This sounds convincing, except it isn't true.)

What happens in practice, in whole language writing activities, is that many children don't learn to spell anything at all, because they can't *hear* the sounds in their speech. Others learn to spell like Donny did in the "Submarine Rtet," using letter names almost exclusively, because that was all they were ever taught. As invented spelling is supposed to be "invented," it is never corrected (no direct instruction is permitted). Children like Donny practice errors over and over again, until these errors are fixed in their brains and become very hard to unfix. It would be just like saying to a beginning piano student: "Never mind about all those mistakes. Just remember the tune, get the feeling of the music and you will learn to read the notes correctly." Anyone who has ever learned a skill, knows that practicing errors over and over again is always a bad idea.

By now, you should be feeling a little uncomfortable with the notion that a six-year-old should discover how a writing system works without any help, when it took great scholars thousands of years to design them so imperfectly. Let's find out what teachers in whole language classrooms really think. Patrick Groff is a professor at San Diego State University, a city where whole language was mandated by the State of California in 1987. Groff read the major books on whole language and pulled together the central ideas expressed in those books.

He then sent surveys to first- and second-grade teachers to ask for their opinions of a list of statements. He got responses from 275 teachers. Here are ten of the most important statements on his list:

1. Children learn to read best the same way they learned to speak.
2. Children can teach themselves to read. Formal instruction is unnecessary.
3. Children should not learn reading subskills in any type of instructional sequence or "hierarchical" order.
4. Children should guess at written words, using sentence context cues.
5. Children should be taught to recognize words by sight as wholes.
6. The length and complexity of words is of little consequence in beginning reading instruction.
7. The intensive and systematic teaching of phonics hinders reading comprehension.
8. Intensive phonics makes it more difficult for children to learn to recognize words.
9. No workbooks or worksheets should ever be used.
10. English is spelled too unpredictably for phonics to work well.

These statements were based upon quotations from books written by top whole language advocates, which Groff reports. These quotes are peppered with hyperbole and unsupported by any scientific research. Absolute certainty in the face of no data is always a dangerous sign. I have italicized words in these quotes to illustrate this.

Children *must* develop reading strategies by and for themselves.

It is easier for a reader to remember the *unique* appearance and pronunciation of a whole word like 'photograph' than to remember the unique pronunciations of meaningless syllables and spelling units. [Whoever said English was written as a syllabary?]

One word in five can be *completely* eliminated from most English texts with scarcely any effect on its overall comprehensibility. [Let's try it: One in five can be completely from most English with scarcely any effect on its overall.]

English is spelled *so unpredictably,* that there is *no way* of predicting when a particular spelling correspondence applies.

And the totally contradictory statement:

Children can develop and use an *intuitive knowledge* of letter-sound correspondences [without] *any* phonics instruction [or] without deliberate instruction from adults.

Sounding out a word is a cumbersome, time-consuming, and unnecessary activity.

Matching letters with sounds is a flat-earth view of the world, one that rejects modern science about reading. [What "modern science" means here is unknown.]

And finally, an extraordinary statement, considering 5,500 years of historical evidence:

There is *nothing unique* about reading, either visually or as far as language is concerned.[4]

What do San Diego teachers believe about the statements that Groff presented to them? Altogether they disagreed overwhelmingly with all but three. They particularly disagreed with those which claimed that any type of direct instruction or phonics instruction was *bad*. On the other hand, most teachers thought the child should "learn to recognize words by sight," and "guess words using context cues." (We'll see they should do neither later on.) The teachers were split evenly (true, false, undecided) on their responses to Statement 1 ("Children learn to read best the same way they learned to speak."), yet were overwhelmingly against Statement 2 ("Children can teach themselves to read. Formal instruction is unnecessary.") Only 4 percent said "true," and 80 percent said "false." Either these teachers hold contradictory beliefs, or they think that children also need direct instruction to learn how to *talk* (which they don't).

Apart from this, teachers were in opposition to the remaining principles of whole language. This is very surprising. They were running "whole language" classrooms, yet they were more likely to *believe* in "phonics." Teachers are no longer trained in phonics. We did not see much phonics in evidence in whole language classrooms we have observed in our research in Florida, yet we also heard teachers *saying* that phonics is important. Phonics instruction took up, on average, only 2 percent of the language arts period, and teachers did not know what they were doing:

Today we're going to learn about long "ee." It's different from short "ee," like in the word 'bed,' because it sounds like "ee" in 'be.'

Something is clearly amiss; teachers doing one thing and believing something else, or thinking that the two approaches are compatible when they are mutually contradictory. When they try to do what they believe, they have no understanding of how or where to begin.

In the final analysis, none of the whole language principles are supported by any evidence, not by the historical record, not by "structural linguistics" which made it possible to decipher writing systems and understand how they work, not by any scientific research on how children actually learn to read which will be presented in section 2 of this book. Furthermore, the type of attack on "phonics" is misguided. There are many problems with phonics, as we saw in chapter 2, but phonics programs are not "wrong" for the reasons whole language advocates claim, that direct instruction about letters and sounds is *bad for you*.

Nor is there any evidence that children should be taught the "stages" in the history of writing as if this was a "natural" linguistic developmental progression. This would mean teaching children to mimic every mistake that was ever made, mistakes which took hundreds or even thousands of years to undo.

In the next chapter, we will take a look at the alphabetic writing system, and how an alphabetic writing system determines the way it should be taught.

Chapter 4

ALPHABETS

Splitting Sounds

The idea that stages of reading development are "natural" and mirror the evolution of writing was based, in part, on the theories of Ignace Gelb, who wrote influential books on early writing systems. Gelb created a myth which still lingers in academic books and encyclopedias. It goes like this:

> All writing systems develop in a fixed order: pictograms, logographs, syllabaries, alphabets. The alphabet is the highest and final stage of this evolution.

One implication of this myth is that Chinese and Japanese writing are archaic (logographic) forms, historical dinosaurs, kept alive by people who stubbornly cling to tradition.

Almost nothing in this myth is true. People used pictograms for accounting and not for a writing system. Pictograms and logographs could not and *never did* suffice for a writing system. Only two major cultures ever used a syllabary: the Sumerians and the Chinese, and this was entirely because the syllable structure of these languages is so uncomplicated.

All other cultures used different sound-based units. The choice of this unit is not governed by an evolutionary progression but by a simple principle: *Use the largest possible phonological unit which is most economic* (fewest symbols).

In other words, it is the phonological or syllable structure of the language which determines how all writing systems are designed. And in every case, when an alphabet could be avoided, it was. This means that *nobody used an alphabet unless they absolutely had to.*

The purpose of this chapter is to show you why we have an alphabet, and to prove the point that the structure of the language directly determines how it can and *cannot* be written, and, therefore, how it must be taught.

If you ask most people what an alphabet is, they will probably tell you that it is a series of letters that stand for sounds in speech, and that the English language is written in an alphabet script with twenty-six letters. Apart from this, most people don't know exactly *which* sounds the letters stand for, nor how many sounds are in our language. There are other things that people vaguely know which are mostly incorrect, like "an alphabet is the simplest writing system to learn," or "everyone today has an alphabet, except the Chinese and Japanese."

Our alphabet is a direct descendant of the Phoenician "alphabet." Until recently, there was another myth that the Phoenician alphabet was the "Great Mother Alphabet." New discoveries have revealed that it was simply one of a long line of "alphabet" experiments in the Middle East. The earliest so far was found in a turquoise mine on the Sinai desert. It was inscribed on a stone sphinx and dated to around 1700 B.C. There were many other "alphabets" to follow. The Phoenician "alphabet" originated much later at Byblos, around 1050 B.C. It became popular, not because there was anything revolutionary about it, but because the Phoenicians were great traders and Byblos was an important port. Plus everybody liked the symbols. They were easy to write and easy to read. The Jewish people borrowed the Phoenician letters for the Old Hebrew writing system and so did the Greeks. The name "alphabet" comes from the Greek, as you can see from the letter names for the old Greek alphabet:

alpha beta gamma delta epsilon

Actually, they are "nonsense" names. They don't make any sense in Greek either. The Greeks borrowed the letters *and* the names from the Phoenicians. Each letter was named with a Phoenician word that started with the same sound. Here are the first six letters in the Phoenician writing system along with their Phoenician names.

𐤀	'alpu	(ox)	𐤃	daleth	(door)
𐤁	beth	(house)	𐤄	he	(not a word)
𐤂	gimel	(camel)	𐤆	zain	(weapon)

The Phoenician letters stood for these sounds:

/'/ a glottal stop made by the soft palate and tongue
/b/ as in "boat"
/g/ as in "get"
/d/ as in "door"
/h/ as in "hot"
/z/ as in "zip"

If we went through all twenty-two of the Phoenician letters, you would see that there are only consonants and no vowels in this "alphabet." That doesn't mean there were no vowels in the Phoenician language. What kind of alphabet is this? Is this an alphabet at all?

To answer these questions, we need to go back to Egypt briefly. By 2700 B.C., the Egyptians had developed several sets of symbols for sounds in their language. One set was for each consonant and one vowel sound. The other symbols were for double- and triple-consonant sequences: CC, CCC. Remember, the picture of an owl stood for the consonant sound /m/, and the funny-looking symbol 𓄟 stood for *two* consonants: /m/ combined with /s/ (/ms/). The Egyptians used pictograms, logographs, determiners, *and* these consonant symbols all at once, so there was absolutely no confusion about meaning (see Figure 4–1).

The Akkadians to the north of Sumer borrowed the Sumerian writing system. They discovered that the Sumerian syllable symbols didn't fit their language. They adapted what they could and created many more symbols. At first they used three syllable types, like the Sumerians, but later they found that two types of syllables (CV, VC) fit most Akkadian words. This meant they could throw away the Sumerian logographs and determiners, and they did precisely this around 2000 B.C. At this time, about 90 percent of the Akkadian writing system consisted of syllable symbols.

The next step was to combine these two solutions. It turned out that there was a simpler way to do it. Old Egyptian and Akkadian were languages of the Hamito-Semitic group, and Semitic languages have a unique property. The most important sounds in Semitic words are the

FIGURE 4–1

Theban Title for "Book of the Dead"

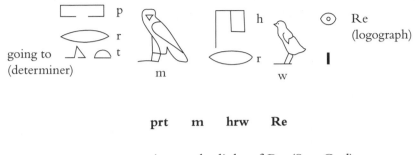

prt   m   hrw   Re

going to the light of Re (Sun God)

to plough   **sk '3**

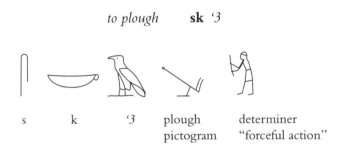

s   k   '3   plough   determiner
                                  pictogram   "forceful action"

consonants. They are so important that you don't need to mark the
vowels at all. It seems the ancient Egyptians had already figured this
out. Most words in Semitic languages have a fixed consonant frame,
called a "root." This consonant frame, or skeleton, is C-C-C, or C-C.
Vowels can change in and out, but the consonant sequence stays put.
Table 4–1 is an example, using the Semitic verb for "to carry." It is
written qbr, but it isn't *read* "qbr." You can see that this consonant
frame is the same for a number of Semitic languages. Only the vowels
are different.

With this kind of writing, if you know the consonant-symbol code,
you can read your own language pretty efficiently and several other
languages as well. This could be very helpful if you are a traveling sales-
man doing business around the Middle East, or a diplomat or emissary
trying to negotiate peace settlements or trade agreements.

In the Phoenician writing system the reader has to *fill in the vowel
sounds* as he is reading. These types of writing systems are known as
"consonantal alphabets," but they are not alphabets as we know them.

TABLE 4–1

qbr "to carry" (Imperative)

	Hebrew	Syrian	Arabic	Ethiopian
		SINGULAR		
Masc.	qebur	qebor	uqbur	qeber
Fem.	qibri	qebor	uqburi	qeberi
		PLURAL		
Masc.	qibru	qebor	uqburu	qeberu
Fem.	qeborna	qebor	uqburna	qebera

They are something quite different. The twenty-two consonant symbols actually stand for a consonant-*plus*-vowel (CV) even though the vowel isn't marked. Consonantal alphabets are a kind of abbreviated syllable system. The reader's task is to figure out *which* missing vowel sounds to supply from context clues. This doesn't always work, and sometimes the meaning is ambiguous. Modern Semitic writing systems, like Hebrew and Arabic, use special "diacritic marks" for missing vowel sounds. These are sloping lines and dashes written above or below the text. These marks are usually omitted in newspapers and books and only appear consistently in sacred texts and in children's primers and books.

INTRODUCING DIPHONES

When babies begin to talk, they babble in CV units: ba-ba, ma-ma, ga-ga-ga. There are hundreds of languages that build on this basic speech pattern, and there are hundreds of writing systems in the world that use CV symbols exclusively. These systems are mistakenly called syllabaries or alphabets. There are so many CV writing systems, I'm going to give them a special name, since nobody else has. I will call them *diphone* systems ("diphone" means "two sounds" in Greek). By "diphone" I am referring only to CV diphones and to no other combinations. In a diphone system, *one symbol* stands for two sounds: C+V. In English, the word "baby" would be written with two symbols instead of four: ▽ ℰ (bay-bee). The word "trap" would be written with three symbols instead of four: ⌇ ∧ ⊂ (ta-ra-pa).

Here's how a diphone system is set up. First, you work out all the consonant sounds and all the vowel sounds in your language and assign each of these sounds a symbol. We'll take an imaginary language as an example. Our imaginary language has the vowel sounds /a/ /e/ /i/ /o/ /u/ and five consonant sounds /b/ /t/ /g/ /s/ /f/. (The slash marks means these are sounds and not letter names.) To create a CV diphone writing system, you set up a matrix:

	a	e	i	o	u
b	ba ↓	be	bi	bo	bu
t	ta ⋛	te	ti	to	tu
g	ga ₒ⊦°	ge	gi	go	gu
s	sa ∧	se	si	so	su
f	fa ʔ	fe	fi	fo	fu

We started out with 10 symbols (an alphabet) and we will have to create 25 new symbols, one for each of the diphone combinations, as I started to do in Column 1. This doesn't seem very efficient, especially as most languages have about 40 consonant and vowel sounds altogether. If you multiplied the 25 consonants and 18 vowels in English to create an English diphone writing system, you would need 450 symbols instead of 43. So why would anybody do this? Is this just another historical milestone, a step along the thorny path to alphabets?

There are three very good reasons. The first reason is that 400 to 500 symbols are well within the human memory limit for abstract visual symbols. The second reason is that diphone systems are just as fast to read as an alphabet. The more sounds you pack into a symbol, the fewer symbols you have to look at to get out the same information.

The third reason is the most important. CV diphones are much easier to *hear* than consonants or vowels alone. We have proof of this from modern scientific research. Computer scientists struggled for decades to generate speech by computer, the robot-like "voice" you hear on some telephone answering systems. They found they had to use the acoustic signals across two adjacent sounds as the *smallest* speech fragment that could be recombined into words. They called this overlapping acoustic pattern a "diphone." Consonants split off from a vowel don't sound like speech at all, but more like chirps and wheezes.

We have proof of a different kind from the historical evidence showing how scholars developed CV diphone writing systems. We can show that an alphabet is not the final stage of the evolution of writing, or a "perfect" solution for all languages, by an example of evolution going *backwards,* from alphabets back to something else. There are many such examples. In India, writing was invented at the same time as in Sumer and Egypt, but no one has ever been able to decipher this script. A completely new type of writing appeared around the 5th century B.C. One script, the "Brahmi script," became the prototype for over 200 writing systems used today throughout India and for most writing systems across southeast Asia, in countries like Thailand, Burma, Tibet, Mongolia, and Kashmir.

The Brahmin scholars set up a matrix of consonants and vowels, like the one in Figure 4–2. Next, they created a separate diphone symbol for each CV pair. The main or primary diphone symbol always stood for a consonant plus the vowel sound /ah/, which was the most common vowel sound in the language. Next, the diphone symbol was modified systematically to mark each different vowel sound.

We have a more precise record of how one of these diphone systems is set up from the Buddhist priests who developed the famous Devanagari script for the Sanskrit language. They designed this script in the 11th century A.D. They had already invented symbols to stand for each of the thirteen vowels and the thirty-five consonant sounds in the Sanskrit language. These were written out in a fixed (alphabetical) order to teach novices to chant mantras and recite sacred texts. They had a complete understanding of the phonetic structure of the Sanskrit language, classifying each sound according to which parts of the mouth move to make it. You can see how clever this is in Figure 4–3.

Next, they set up a matrix and created new symbols for all the CV diphone combinations in the Sanskrit language. It's clear that this system was not designed by accident, or because the priests weren't clever enough to figure out that an alphabet was the "most perfect" writing system. It was done this way on purpose, with the utmost skill. The Brahmi writing system of the 5th century B.C. and the 200 writing sys-

FIGURE 4–2

Brahmi Script 5th Century B.C.

Examples of Diphone Symbols for 2 Consonants and 9 Vowels

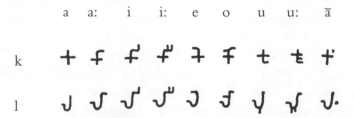

	a	a:	i	i:	e	o	u	u:	ā
k									
l									

FIGURE 4–3

The Devanagari Alphabet for Sanskrit

Vowels

*	+	
अ, अ	—	a
आ, आ	ा	ā
इ	ि	i
ई	ी	ī
उ	ु	u
ऊ	ू	ū
ऋ	ृ	ṛ (or ṛi)
ॠ	ॄ	ṝ (or ṛī)
ऌ	ॢ	ḷ (or ḷi)
ए	े	e
ऐ	ै	ai
ओ	ो	o
औ	ौ	au

Consonants

क	k	gutturals	प	p	labials
ख	k-h		फ	p-h	
ग	g		ब	b	
घ	g-h		भ	b-h	
ङ	ṅ		म	m	
च	c	palatals	य	y	semivowels
छ	c-h		र	r	
ज	j		ल	l	
झ, झ or झ	j-h		व	v	
ञ	ñ				
ट	ṭ	cerebrals	श	ś (or ç)	spirants
ठ	ṭ-h		ष	ṣ	
ड	ḍ		स	s	
ढ	ḍ-h		ह	h	
ण	ṇ				
त	t	dentals	ः	ḥ (visarga)	
थ	t-h		ं	ṃ or ṁ (anusvāra)	
द	d				
ध	d-h				
न	n				

* initial form of letters + medial form of letters

tems related to it today, go *backwards* down the so-called "evolutionary path."

Figure 4–4 shows an example of Indian writing. The long bar across the top means that several words are strung together, like Howard and Ethel's conversation ('wujjadoodaday?'). The bar breaks where people would naturally pause or breathe.

Why didn't the Brahmin and Buddhist priests stick with the straightforward alphabet they had designed? There can be only one possible reason. They knew it was *hard for people to hear consonant sounds separated from vowels.* This is clear from their understanding of the structure of their language, and from the way they linked the symbols to mimic the natural flow of human speech, where words are connected in phrases. They knew how difficult it was to pick out isolated consonants and vowels from a stream of speech sounds. They knew that if something was hard for them, it would be hard for everyone else. And if something is too hard, many people can't use it.

This evolutionary reversal wasn't unique to India. It happened in Korea as well. In 1446, King Sejong issued a writing reform "out of pity for the people." Up to that time, the Koreans had been using Chinese syllable and determiner symbols as logographs for Korean words. They had the same problem memorizing logographs that everyone else did. In the writing reform, Korean scholars analyzed the individual sounds in the Korean language, wrote out a set of symbols for them into an alphabet, set this up in a matrix, and turned the alphabet into a CV diphone system of 140 symbols, called Han'gul. Figure 4–5 shows

FIGURE 4–4

Sanskrit Text in Devanagari Script

व्यवहारान्नृपः पश्येद्विद्वद्विर्ब्राह्मणैः सह ।
धर्मशास्त्रानुसारेण क्रोधलोभविवर्जितः ॥ १ ॥

*vyavahārān nrpah pàsyed vidvadbhír bràhmanaih
saha dharmasàstrānusārena krodhalobhavivarjítah*

The ruler shall examine the trials together with learned Brahmins in accordance with the law, free of ire and passion.

FIGURE 4–5

Diphone Symbols for Combinations of Vowels and Consonants in Han'gul

Vowels

		ㅏ	ㅑ	ㅓ	ㅕ	ㅗ	ㅛ	ㅜ	ㅠ	―	ㅣ
		a	ya	ŏ	yeo	o	yo	u	yu	eu	i
ㄱ	g(k)	가	갸	거	겨	고	교	구	규	그	기
ㄴ	n	나	냐	너	녀	노	뇨	누	뉴	느	니
ㄷ	d	다	댜	더	뎌	도	됴	두	듀	드	디
ㄹ	r(l)	라	랴	러	려	로	료	루	류	르	리
ㅁ	m	마	먀	머	며	모	묘	무	뮤	므	미
ㅂ	b	바	뱌	버	벼	보	뵤	부	뷰	브	비
ㅅ	s	사	샤	서	셔	소	쇼	수	슈	스	시
ㅇ	※	아	야	어	여	오	요	우	유	으	이
ㅈ	j	자	쟈	저	져	조	죠	주	쥬	즈	지
ㅊ	ch	차	챠	처	쳐	초	쵸	추	츄	츠	치
ㅋ	k	카	캬	커	켜	코	쿄	쿠	큐	크	키
ㅌ	t	타	탸	터	텨	토	툐	투	튜	트	티
ㅍ	p	파	퍄	퍼	펴	포	표	푸	퓨	프	피
ㅎ	h	하	햐	허	혀	호	효	후	휴	흐	히

Consonants

what this looks like today. It is beautifully systematic. The vowel symbols and consonant symbols are fused to form unique pairs.

Once you know they are there, diphone systems pop up all over the place. They were the ancient writing systems for Crete, Cyprus, and mainland Greece. They are the modern writing systems in Ethiopia and for the Cherokee nation. The diphone is the basis of the katakana and hiragana scripts used in Japan, introduced from India through Buddhist writings. Each of these two diphone scripts is written with a different set of about 75 symbols each. The diphone turns out to be a perfect fit for the Japanese language, as most words are built out of CV-CV-CV sequences, like "ka-ta-ka-na."

In addition to the katakana and hiragana scripts, the Japanese still use the ancient Chinese symbols as logographs for Chinese loan words and

Japanese words (kanji), though many kanji contain phonological clues. The Ministry of Education has set a minimum target of 1,850 kanji for "an educated person." This puts the upper boundary of abstract visual symbols over 2,000, the highest number for any written language today. Japanese elementary school children learn hiragana first, followed by 1,000 kanji logographs, then katakana plus alphabet symbols for foreign words, making Japanese writing the hardest system in the world to learn. It isn't surprising that many children fail. As we saw earlier, Harold Stevenson's research shows that 56 percent of Japanese schoolchildren failed to meet the 75 percent pass criterion for fifth-grade reading, compared to 46 percent of American children and 31 percent of Taiwanese children. A recent study on first-grade children in Sendai compared to children in Taipei, Beijing, and the U.S., by Shin-Ying Lee and others, shows that Beijing and Sendai children are considerably less likely to have advanced reading skills. Takeshi Hatta and Takehito Hirase tested 871 Japanese 11-year-olds on a standardized reading test, and found that 30 percent were one or more years below age-level norms. The Japanese could solve this problem by standardizing on *one* of their two diphone systems and by eliminating kanji. This would give them one of the easiest writing systems to learn. So far, there has been no successful attempt to do this.

Diphone writing systems, or abbreviated diphone systems like consonantal alphabets, dominate in India and across southeast Asia and Korea. They form the core of the writing system in Japan. They are found everywhere in the Middle East. If all these people can get along without an alphabet, and their scripts are equally fast to read and write, and use a unit of speech that is much easier to *hear*, then why do we have an alphabet?

TRUE ALPHABETS SPLIT SOUNDS

The answer is actually quite simple. It started with the Greeks in the 8th century B.C., when they borrowed those Phoenician symbols. The Greeks already had a writing system borrowed from Crete. It was deciphered about forty years ago and we know it as "Linear B." Linear B is a diphone system, which also includes five vowel letters used only at the beginning of words. The archaeological evidence shows that Linear B was never used for anything more sophisticated than invoices, ledgers, and inventory control. The Greek language cannot be written accurately in a diphone writing system because Greek has too many consonant clusters. Second, Greek is not a Semitic language, so it is impossible to represent Greek with a consonantal alphabet. The vowel sounds in Greek carry as much of the meaning load as consonants do.

Let me show you why neither a consonantal alphabet nor a diphone system could work for the Greek language or for any other European language. The first example is a letter written in a consonantal alphabet, not too different from the Phoenician script the Greeks decided to borrow.

> Dr Sm,
> Wl—gs ths s gdb. Ftr r ft lst nt—n t wnt wrk.—m mvng w t tr t frgt.—dnt nd t b rmndd f ths pls nd l th sd mmrs.
> Pls s gdb t ls fr m.—wl ms hr.
> Sdl,
> ls

The blanks are at the places where one whole word is a single vowel sound.

The letter reads:

> [Dear Sam, Well, I guess this is goodbye. After our fight last night, I know it won't work. I am moving away to try to forget. I don't need to be reminded of this place and all the sad memories. Please say goodbye to Alice for me. I will miss her. Sadly, Eloise]

I think you can see the important "work" that vowels do in the English language, as they did in the old Greek language.

Here's another letter written with a slightly more complex vocabulary. This is transcribed as it would *sound* if it was read *out loud,* from a CV diphone system like Linear B. Linear B had five vowel symbols used in the initial position in a word, plus a symbol for every possible CV combination. When it is read out loud it sounds CV-CV-CV-CV-CV, whether this speech pattern fits the word or not. In this example all the unnecessary vowel sounds are written with the letter <u>a</u>.

> Deara Fareda,
> I, canata parovida U witha caleera paroofa ova the sapeeseesa ova theeza sataraynja palanatas. Ifa I ama correcata ina my asasumapashunasa, they ara a raira bareeda ova davarga karysanathimuma, wuna thata Iva never comma acarossa befor.
> Satumapata,
> Joraja

[Dear Fred, I can't provide you with clear proof of the species of these strange plants. If I am correct in my assumptions, they are a rare breed of dwarf chrysanthymum—one that I've never come across before. Stumped, George.]

Neither of these writing systems works for European languages, although from the last example, diphones might do a fair job with Italian!

The Greeks used the Phoenician letters to create the first "true" alphabet. A true alphabet is a writing system in which each consonant and each vowel is represented by a symbol. These individual sounds (consonants and vowels) are the smallest or finest sounds in speech that people can hear. They are known collectively as "phonemes," which simply means "units of sound." Hence, a *true* alphabet is a "phonemic" alphabet.

To set up their alphabet, the Greeks began by using Phoenician letters that stood for the same consonants in the Greek language. They used left-over letters for vowels and invented some new vowel letters. The Greek alphabet was tailor-made for the Greek language, a perfect fit, one symbol for each "phoneme" or sound. The alphabet was revised as the Greek language changed over time. It was borrowed by the Etruscans, and then by the Romans, who brought it to Britain at the time of the Roman invasion in A.D. 43. The Anglo-Saxons borrowed it for an English alphabet. In Figure 4–6, you can see how the alphabet changed over time as it was modified to fit one language and then another.

This history explodes the myth that an alphabet is the ultimate writing system, and shows instead that *the alphabet is the most unnatural writing system ever designed*. Alphabetic writing is unnatural because it splits sounds in speech in a way they don't normally split. Consonant clusters hang together. Consonants are very hard to unglue from vowels. Many consonants in English are hard to *say* separately from a vowel sound, even when they are isolated from words. Try saying /b/ all by itself without saying 'buh.' This is exactly what you must be able to do to use an alphabet efficiently. This is why Sally's mother wasn't helping her all that much when she taught her "the sounds of letters" incorrectly (buh duh guh). It is even more difficult to split phonemes apart when they are embedded in a word, or when words are strung together in speech. This is what the Brahmin and Buddhist priests understood so well. See if you can hear every sound in these one-syllable words:

FIGURE 4–6

1050 B.C. Phoenician		8th century B.C. Old Greek		8th century B.C. Etruscan		5th–4th century B.C. Classic Greek		Old Latin	
⟨	'	A	a	A	a	A	a	A	a
	b		b	B	b	B	b	B	b
	g		c		c	Γ	g		c
	d	Δ	d	Δ	d	Δ	d	D	d
	h	Ǝ	e	Ǝ	e	E	e	E	e
–	–		f		f	–	–	F	f
I	z	I	g	–	–	–	–		g
	h		h		h		ē	H	h
⊗	th	⊕	th	–	–	⊖	th	–	–
	y		i	I	i	I	i	I	i
	k		k		k	K	k	K	k
L	l		l		l	Λ	l	L	l
	m		m		m	M	m	M	m
	n		n		n	N	n	N	n
	s		ks	–	–	=	ks	–	–
O	'	O	o	O	o	O	o	O	o
⊃	p		p		p	Π	p		p
	ṣ	–	–	–	–	–	–	–	–
Φ	q	Φ	q	Q	q	–	–	Q	q
	r		r		r	P	r	R	r
W	š		s		s	Σ	s		s
+	t	T	t	T	t	T	t	T	t
Y	w	Y	y	V	u		u,ü	V	u
–	–	X	x	–	–	X	chi	X	x
–	–	–	–	–	–	Φ	phi	–	–
–	–	–	–	–	–	Ψ	psi	–	–
–	–	–	–	–	–	Ω	omega	–	–

"strong," "scratch," "shrink," "dwells," "crunch." Each word has five sounds. (The number of sounds doesn't match the number of letters.)

In case you don't believe that many people find it hard to hear phonemes in words, here's an example of what we see regularly in the clinic. This is an early session with eight-year-old Jake.

Teacher: Jake, can you say the first sound in "frog"?

Jake: Frog.

Teacher: You said the whole word. Try to say just a little bit of the word "frog."

Jake: Frog.

Teacher: Now try this. Start to say the word "frog" and stop before you finish.

Jake: Frog.

Teacher: Say /g/.

Jake: /g/.

Teacher: O.K., now say "frog" again but *don't* say /g/.

Jake: Fro——

Teacher: Very good. Now try to make it even shorter.

Jake: Fro——

Teacher: Say "fro" for me.

Jake: Fro

Teacher: Good, now say it again without the /ah/ sound at the end.

Jake: Fr——

Teacher: Terrific. Now listen to me carefully. What is the very first sound in "ffrr"?

Jake: Fr——

Teacher: You said two sounds: /f/ and /r/. Try saying the first sound in "ffffrr."

Jake: Fr——

Teacher: That's still two sounds.

Jake is having a very tough time, but he is by no means unique.

One of the main points of this chapter is to show *why* the English language had to be written in an alphabet and in no other way. Think about what this means. Any teaching method that tampers with the alphabet principle, trying to turn our writing system into something else, like a logographic system (whole language), a diphone, syllable, or part-word system (phonics "word families"), will inevitably cause many children to fail to learn to read. It is difficult to hear sequences of isolated phonemes, and this problem is compounded when children are taught to make the wrong choices about how words are broken down into sounds. This problem is even more critical with the English alphabet, because in our spelling system two or more letters can stand for one sound. Here's what the eyes have to look at to be able to read "strawberry ice cream":

$\boxed{s}\boxed{t}\boxed{r}\boxed{aw}\boxed{b}\boxed{err}\boxed{y}\quad\boxed{i}\boxed{ce}\quad\boxed{c}\boxed{r}\boxed{ea}\boxed{m}$

Despite the fact that alphabets make extreme demands on auditory analysis (ungluing sounds in words), they turn out to have an unexpected bonus. All languages have a small, finite number of phonemes, usually around forty. If alphabets are taught properly, they are very efficient, especially when they are well designed so that only one symbol stands for only one sound. Unfortunately, only Spanish and Finnish come close to this ideal.

Alphabets are "transparent" writing systems in the sense that they directly represent speech and are only as ambiguous as spoken language itself. Ambiguity has been a consistent problem throughout the history of writing. Consonantal alphabets need diacritic marks to indicate vowels. Indian languages also have consonant clusters. The Brahmin priests added little loops to the symbols ("ligatures" or "connectors") to show where vowels should be dropped between two consonants. This makes the writing visually confusing. The Mayans, Cretans, Cypriots, and everybody who still uses a CV diphone system have to remember to drop vowels between consonant clusters or when a word ends in a consonant. The Mayans said "balam" (jaguar) when they read the diphones for 'ba-la-ma'. The Japanese say "kanji" when they see the written symbols for 'ka-na-ji'.

The English alphabet shares all the good features of other alphabets, but has one enormous drawback. *It lacks a one-to-one correspondence between each sound in the language and the symbol that represents it.* This means that learning to read the English alphabet system can be a trap if taught badly or not at all. If there was a simple answer to teaching children to read an English alphabet, we would have found it before now, especially since English schools have been common since the sixteenth century.

Let's pause for a minute and take stock. There are many important lessons from this historical account. Writing systems based on the whole word don't work. Languages have too many words. Because people are limited in their ability to memorize abstract symbols, speech sounds are the basic unit for *all writing systems.* This means that no child should ever be taught to memorize or guess whole words by sight. This will never work, and we now have 5,500 years of evidence to prove it.

All writing systems are designed to fit the syllable structure, or sound-based structure, of the language for which they are written. When the language has an open, simple syllable structure, like Sumerian or Chinese, you can use syllable symbols (a syllabary). When it has mainly a repetitive C-C-C or CVCVCV sound structure like Semitic languages, Indic languages, or Japanese and Korean, then a consonantal alphabet or diphone writing system will work. When the language has a complex syllable structure, riddled with consonant clusters, it must be written with an alphabet. There is no other way.

Individual phonemes embedded in words are hard to hear and disconnect, which is why so many cultures abandoned the alphabet solution. It's hard to detach consonants from vowels and consonants from each other. Many children can't *hear* the units of sound the letters of the code stand for, and if nobody teaches them these sounds, they won't have a clue what the code is about. This means that many children can't learn the code. It's just that simple. The whole language claim that all children will automatically be sensitive to the phonological units of speech simply because they can talk is an erroneous and dangerous assumption. We now have an avalanche of data to show this isn't true.

A final lesson relates to the logic of writing systems. Writing systems are designed to transcribe *talk.* Speech sounds are the basis for the code. It is the sounds in speech that are "real," consistent, and stable. The letters *are the code:* unreal, arbitrary, and, in English spelling, unstable. Of course *all codes are reversible;* you can put something into a code (encoding) and translate it back out again (decoding), otherwise it wouldn't be a code. The alphabet code is no exception. But teachers must understand what the code was designed to do. They must know the *direction* in which the code was written.

If you teach a child that abstract squiggles on the page (letters) are "real," and that these squiggles "have" arbitrary noises (sounds), she won't understand what you're talking about. By contrast, if you tell her that letters on the page stand for specific sounds in *her own speech,* the process of matching letters to sounds will make sense.

DOES PHONICS TEACH THE ALPHABET PRINCIPLE?

This brings us to phonics. In chapter 1, we saw how children can develop reading difficulties in "phonics" classrooms, where teachers are supposedly trying to teach the alphabet code. The word "phonics" simply means "sounds" in Greek, and this term is used by educators as a generic term for any reading method that teaches "sounds" rather than whole words. (The overuse of the word "phonics," and the confusion this creates, will be discussed in the following chapter.) Jeanne Chall, in her famous book *Learning to Read: The Great Debate,* pointed out that teaching methods up to that time (1967) had polarized into "read for meaning/whole word" approaches and "phonics." The "Great Debate" was about which of these two approaches was best. In 1967, the popular "whole word" method of the day was not whole language but "look-say," where children were taught to memorize whole words by rote drill using flash cards, as if each sequence of letters was a logograph.

Look-say was an educational disaster, prompting Rudolph Flesch to write *Why Johnny Can't Read* in 1955. Flesch mounted an attack on the educational establishment that resonated in parents' hearts. Both Flesch and Chall advocated a return to "phonics." Flesch designed a mini "phonics" program in his book, which was accurate in the important sense that he understood how an alphabetic writing system works, that *sounds* in the language are the basis for the code, and that English has forty-two sounds (phonemes). However, Flesch had no access to modern data which show that a large proportion of children can't hear phonemes in words.

For most of this century people believed, and most still do, that there are really only two ways to teach reading. Either you use whole word/read for meaning approaches, or you use phonics. There is supposed to be nothing else. We are still trapped in the whole word/phonics "great debate" mentality. Today, educational publishing houses design reading programs based on one of these possibilities: Teach whole words using good children's literature. Teach phonics. Hedge your bets and teach both (never mind that the two methods contradict each other). This last approach is called "the eclectic method." Watch out! It is coming to a school near you.

Authors and publishers have churned out scores of phonics programs over the years, with different worksheets, different readers, and different vocabularies. People have attempted to classify these programs. Jeanne Chall made a valiant effort in her book. They have been given names like "analytic" or "synthetic" or "intensive" or "structured" or "linguistic." This makes them seem as if they are different, and though some are much more comprehensive than others, they aren't really all that different.

To begin with, all phonics programs teach "the names and sounds of letters." This is even in the dictionary definition of phonics, and this definition fits every phonics program I have seen. This means that *all phonics programs teach the alphabet principle backwards,* as I described above. Phonics programs teach that "letters have sounds," rather than that "speech has sounds" and these speech sounds "have letters." Even when they know better, and confess that really, strictly speaking, "letters don't *have* sounds" (if you put your ear to the page, you hear nothing), teachers like Mrs. Earnest believe it's easier to teach children that they do. It's easier to do it this way because letters seem "real." After all, they are there on the page, visible, concrete, and permanent. Sounds are invisible, fleeting, and ephemeral. We'll see how much havoc this misunderstanding can create when we analyze how the sounds in the English language map onto the English spelling system.

Phonics programs *don't teach the sounds in English for which the code was written.* Of course they don't. They teach the "sounds of letters." But there are twenty-six letters and forty-three sounds. How is this supposed to work? No child is ever told what the alphabet code really is. This is because the teachers don't know what it really is either. No one ever taught them. You can prove this yourself by asking any elementary school teacher how many sounds there are in the English language. Most will tell you twenty-six, or that they have no idea. Today, there are only a few university departments of education in the English-speaking world in which this important secret is revealed.

Here's another thing most phonics programs have in common. They set up a schizophrenic writing system in which they mix up the number of sounds in speech that letters stand for. This makes it impossible for the child to figure out the unit of speech upon which our alphabetic code is based. And it is doubly impossible to learn the code, for those children can't hear the sound units to start with, like Jake in the example.

We saw in chapter 2 that children in phonics classrooms were struggling with this problem. They were taught letters that stand for units of one phoneme: b, t, ch, letters that stand for two phonemes, like the clusters: bl, dw, shr, letters that stand for three phonemes (word families): <u>enth</u>, <u>ond</u>, <u>unch</u>, as if these letter patterns stood for *only one sound.* This is why Andrew decoded 'hated' as "hat–ate–ted," which he thought was three sounds, instead of /h/ /ae/ /t/ /e/ /d/ (five sounds). Children in phonics classrooms can become completely baffled about how our writing system works. If you don't understand what you're teaching, you will mislead your students and risk causing them to fail.

We will be examining these and other problems with phonics programs in the following chapter when we look in depth at the sounds in the English language and how these sounds are transcribed or "mapped" to letter symbols.

Chapter 5

THE ENGLISH ALPHABET CODE

As a child, I remember waiting with bated breath for the closing moments of my favorite serial, when the announcer read a series of numbers that you had to "decode." Only then, could you find out whether the hero or heroine burned to a crisp or was rescued in the nick of time. (I always knew they would be rescued but I wanted proof now.) These messages could be "decoded" with a special device that had to be purchased with wrappers from Ovaltine jars. This kind of code is a *translation* from one symbol system into another. My decoding device translated numbers into letters that spelled words, a "code of a code":

1=p 2=a 3=f 4=s 5=i

Writing systems are also codes of codes. Language itself is a code. Languages are based on an agreement between language users that things, persons, places, actions, intentions, and feelings can be represented by combinations of vocal noises. The noises are utterly arbitrary and have no meaning in and of themselves. Because of the way the vocal apparatus works, there is considerable freedom of choice about the available noises, though not absolute freedom. Our mouth parts and vocal cords can move in just so many ways, and most languages share a number of speech "noises" in common.

All languages are composed of two main kinds of sound: vowels and consonants. Vowels are "voiced," causing the vocal folds or "cords" to vibrate, and vowels pass freely, unconstrained by touching mouth parts. Vowels add volume to speech. When Stephen's Mom calls him for dinner, the vowel carries her voice: "Steeeeeeeephen." A language can't be constructed of vowels alone: eeeeeeaaaaaaaouououououoooooooo. Consonants add "features" to a barren landscape of vowels, separating one group of noises from another into little packets of syllables, words, and phrases. Consonants are made by touching various mouth parts together. Some consonants are "voiced" and the vocal cords vibrate. Some are not. Put your fingers on your neck, near your vocal cords, and feel the vibration at the beginning of the word "dot," but not at the beginning of the word "tot." The sounds /d/ and /t/ are produced by the same mouth movements, tongue tapping behind the front teeth, but only the /d/ is voiced, so they sound quite different.

Until this moment, you probably never knew this. We speak fluently and effortlessly without any conscious awareness of how we do it. This happens because we learn the sounds of our native language when we are too young to be conscious observers of what we do or think. When we learn a second language later in life, it takes months to pronounce the sounds only tolerably well, and even with years of intense conscious effort, most of us will never sound like native speakers.

Perhaps you can imagine how difficult it was for people to design an alphabetic writing system. No one is aware of these speech sounds in the first place, and once you become aware of them, it's still hard to calculate how many different sounds are in your language, especially before you have a way to write them down. Imagine too, how difficult it is for children, who are just as unconscious of how they speak as you are, to analyze the sounds of their own speech and try to figure out which sound goes with which letter or letter combinations.

Most languages of the world have about the same number of individual sounds, or "phonemes." English is pretty much on target with other languages, having approximately forty-three. I say "approximately" because there are endless disputes over this number. Many people are partial to the number forty-four. It does look nicer in print. But this means that you must accept the argument that speakers can hear the difference between the /w/ sound in "witch" and the /wh/ sound in "which," and they can't.

There are 25 consonants and 18 vowel sounds in English, similar to Chinese, or Semitic, or Indian languages. Yet, we saw in the last two chapters that these languages don't need to be written in an alphabet because of the way that consonants and vowels are combined into syllables and words. English must be written with an alphabet because our language is awash with consonant clusters due to its Germanic roots. There are 27 consonant clusters that come at the beginning of syllables (bl, dw, str), and 49 consonant clusters that come at the end (nd, lk, nch, mpt), and only *three* of these consonant clusters occur in both positions. They are /sk/, /sp/, and /st/ as in the words: "skunk," "spoon," "stamp," and "ask," "wasp," and "past."

We have already seen why English can't be written with a consonantal alphabet (the vowels are too important) or a diphone system (too many clusters). Nor can it be written as a syllabary, like Sumerian or Chinese, and here's why. Consonants and vowels can combine to create 15 different syllable patterns:

CV, CCV, CCCV, CVC, CCVC, CCCVC, CVCC, CVCCC, CCVCC, CCVCCC, CCCVCCC, VCCC, VCC, VC, V

The way that the 25 consonants and 18 vowels can combine in these syllables means that there are over 55,000 "phonetically legitimate" syllables, as many syllables as words in common use. And this is the tip of the iceberg. Most English words are two or more syllables long. "Phonetically legitimate" simply means that a word or syllable has consonant-vowel patterns that are recognizable as English. A writing system must be able to represent every legitimate syllable pattern in the language, though not all of them are used at the time. You could read the word "Grinch" in chapter 2 and recognize it as "English," because it obeys the syllable structure of English. If we couldn't use the writing system this way, we wouldn't be able to write new words or people's names. One beauty of an alphabet system is that it is as flexibly expandable as language itself. Without this flexibility, we wouldn't have words like "bonk," "thwack," "nerd," "twit," "doodle," or "scrumptious." Dr. Seuss and Lewis Carroll couldn't have written their books. There would be no Grinch, no Yertle, no Loraxes, grickle grass, or truffula trees, and no "gyre and gimble in the wabe."

New English words can be created by compounding existing words (household, desktop, firefighter, doughnut, baseball) and by compounding with prefixes and suffixes, a trick which exploded when we borrowed thousands of Latin words. We can erect a "statue," draft and ratify a "statute," create an "institute," or "institutionalize" Aunt Dorothy, or complain about the "institutionalizing" of the Arts, or "deinstitutionalize" a bureaucracy, a process known as "deinstitutionalization." (Note that 'instatute' ought to be the correct spelling.)

It is hard to pick individual sounds out of these complex words. Simple arithmetic will show why children can have trouble learning an alphabet right from the start. We have seen that consonants are hard to "unglue" from vowels. There are 22 consonants that begin words, and each can be followed by 18 vowels. This is 396 CV sound combinations that are hard to unglue. Consonant clusters are even harder to unglue, both from each other and from the following vowel sound. There are 27 consonant clusters that come at the beginning of words, and each can be followed by 18 vowels. This adds another 27 + 486 unglueable combinations, a total of 909 so far, and we're only talking about the beginning of words. It is because of these problems that children must be taught the individual phonemes in English, and how to unglue these phonemes from each other, as we saw in the example with Jake. Next, they need to learn how each phoneme is transcribed or "mapped" to letter symbols. We can't teach reading and writing using a minimalist fraction of the code, taught backwards (phonics), because many children will never understand how the code works. Nor can we harbor the delusion that the length and complexity of words are irrelevant (whole language) and expect children to become able, fluent readers and spellers, and sophisticated users of the language. Later on we will be looking in great detail about how to teach children to hear and be able to manipulate sounds in words. Here, I will be addressing the final problem of the English writing system, our formidable spelling code.

WHAT WENT WRONG WITH ENGLISH SPELLING?

In a perfect alphabetic writing system, each of the forty-three English sounds would have *one,* and only one, symbol. But the English alphabet has only twenty-six letters, four of which are wasted. Spelling reformers want them eradicated or put to better use. The letter c doubles for the sounds /k/ and /s/. The letters qu stand for the sounds /kw/ pronounced simultaneously. The letter x is used for the consonant cluster /ks/ when the word *isn't* plural: tax, box, fax (versus tacks, blocks, flicks), and for /ks/ or /gz/ in words like exit and exact. The letter y doubles for several different vowel sounds which already have letters: fly ('flie'), baby ('babee'), yes ('ee-es'). Some argue that the sound /w/ is really a very short /oo/ sound, and the letter w could be thrown out as well: "winter" would be spelled 'oointer.' These ideas have not met with any success.

Too many sounds chasing too few letters creates a major roadblock for the young reader. Instead of designing new letters for these leftover sounds, like the Greeks did, the old letters were *reused* in different combinations. The Romans started this habit by using letter-pairs to stand for one sound. These are called *digraphs.* The missing consonants in English were spelled: <u>ch</u> church, <u>sh</u> shoot, <u>ng</u> ring, <u>qu</u> quit, and <u>th</u>. The "voiced" and "unvoiced" sounds /<u>th</u>/ and /th/ as in "this" and "think" share the same spelling. (Put your hand on your throat again and check this out.) One consonant sound never got its own spelling. This is the sound /zh/ we inherited from Norman French, which usually appears in the middle of words (Asia, azure, pleasure, measure, vision), and is spelled <u>si</u>, <u>z</u>, <u>s</u>, or <u>ge</u> (camouflage).

When something can be classified in two or more overlapping ways, this is known in logic as a "class inclusion problem." Later, we will talk about the difficulty children have with class inclusion logic. Digraphs create a class inclusion problem. For example, the letter <u>h</u> can stand for the sound /h/ when it's beside some letters (house, hear, ahead), but can stand for entirely different sounds when it's beside other letters: <u>ch</u>est /ch/, <u>th</u>em /th/, <u>sh</u>ine /sh/, <u>gh</u>ost /g/, <u>ph</u>one /f/, tou<u>gh</u> /f/. The spellings for ghost, phone, and tough show that the basic idea of using one consonant digraph to stand for one sound, didn't hold up, and <u>h</u> was combined with other letters to stand for sounds that *already had letters,* like /g/ and /f/. This gives you the flavor of the problem, but by no means the substance. The situation is far, far worse with vowels. We will look at the entire structure of our spelling code at the end of this chapter. First, we need to find out what went wrong.

The English spelling system evolved over a period of 1,150 years until it ran up against the mighty pen and intellect of Samuel Johnson. Since that time, in the mideighteenth century, there have only been minor skirmishes of the spelling reformers, which never had any impact. Johnson was not a reformer. He knew he could do nothing to turn back the clock and start again. One of his main objectives was to stop the rot and keep our spelling system from running amok.

It wasn't always thus. The Venerable Bede, who wrote the first history of England, describes how King Oswald of Northumbria worked together with Bishop Aidan from Ireland to translate Irish into English. Bishop Aidan had come from the monastery at Iona to establish the Christian church in Northumbria. He couldn't speak English, but Oswald could speak Gaelic. He had grown up at Iona. Together they developed a written code for English around A.D. 635, borrowing the script that was used in Ireland to write Latin. They taught the boys and novices at the monasteries to read in English, and then Latin by translating from Latin to English. Almost no examples of this writing have survived. The Danes attacked Northumbria in 793, and burned everything in sight.

The Danes marched relentlessly on through most of the next century, attacking by land, river, and sea, finally ending up in the Kingdom of Wessex in the southwest of England. Here they were defeated by King Alfred in 878, after several years and many fierce battles in which Alfred lost his father and three brothers. Alfred was thirty years old when he secured the peace. He not only saved England, but he saved the English language and the English writing system. If it hadn't been for Alfred, we might all be speaking Danish.

Alfred began a campaign of unifying England, building fortresses (burghs), and restoring the spirit and pride of the people. As part of this enterprise, he had major Christian texts translated from Latin into English, a novel idea at the time. He recreated English writing by tracking down any monks or clerics he could find who knew it. Alfred was an intellectual and a Latin scholar and he personally translated many of these works.

Alfred was eager to educate his people to read and write in Saxon English, and he maintained two large scriptoria at Canterbury and Winchester. It isn't known what documents Alfred and his priests used to reconstruct English writing, but their translations survive today. They show that the English spelling system was nearly perfect, and it got a little more perfect over the next 100 years at the hands of Alfric, the greatest English scholar of that time.

A perfect spelling system has no **alternative spellings** for the *same* sound like we have today: b<u>e</u>, b<u>ee</u>n, b<u>ea</u>n beli<u>e</u>ve, dec<u>ei</u>ve, bab<u>y</u>, donk<u>ey</u>, and no "**overlap**" in the code: out, soup, soul, tough, where one spelling pattern (<u>ou</u>) stands for *different* sounds. In Table 5–1, I have illustrated the spelling alternatives and code overlaps in the Old English spelling system. If the spelling system was perfect, this table would be a blank page. At the end of this chapter you can compare this to the tables I have prepared for modern English spelling.

The detour back to Saxon England is of interest, because many spellings today resemble spellings from 1,100 years ago. There isn't space to discuss them all, but you can see in Table 5–2 where some of

TABLE 5–1

Deviations from a 1-to-1 Correspondence in the Old Saxon
Spelling Code

SPELLING ALTERNATIVES

Sound	Spellings		
/i/	ı	y	
/gh/ guttural	h	c	
/k/	c	k	
/s/	s	ſ	ſ
/th/	ð	þ	

CODE OVERLAP

Letter	Sounds		
ı	/i/	or	/ee/
u	/u/	or	/ōō/
y	/i/	or	/ü/
c	/k/	or	/gh/
ſ	/f/	or	/v/
ȝ	/g/	or	/j/
ƿ	/p/	or	/w/

our strangest spellings come from. In the Old English spelling system, all letters in the word were pronounced. There were no "silent
letters." The Old English spellings are on the right, followed by their
phonetic equivalent. Saxon was a Germanic language with two guttural sounds, spelled with an h and a c. In Middle English spelling, the
h was changed to gh. Then the guttural sounds dropped out of the language, leaving their guttural ghosts behind. The /l/ and /e/ sounds in
"sholde" and "wolde" were pronounced, as was the /k/ sound in
"cnawan."

Not long before Bishop Alfric died in 1020, England was invaded by
Canute of Denmark (later King of Denmark and Norway). Skirmishes
between Denmark and England continued until the Battle of Hastings
in 1066, which brought William the Conqueror to the throne. From
this point forward, England and the English language were never to be
the same, and the English spelling system went haywire.

TABLE 5–2

Old Saxon Spellings of Some Familiar Words

Written	Pronounced	Modern Spelling
ſcolðe	sholde	should
polðe	wolde	would
ælmihc	almight★	almighty
brohc	broghte	brought
ſohcɛ	soghte	sought
nohcɛ	noght	nought
meahcɛ	meaght	might
ðohcɛ	thoghte	thought
ðuꝑh	thurgh	through
hꝑıle	hwile	while
hꝑæꝑ	hwar	where
hꝑelcɛ	hwelch	which
hꝑæðeꝑ	hwather	whether
cnapan	cnawan	to know
cnıhc	cnight	knight
ꝼeαpα	fe-ah-wa	few
anðyꝑðɛ	andwyrde	answered

★gh is pronounced as a guttural sound.

William, his barons, relatives, and acquaintances whom he installed in every church and on every estate, farm, cattle and sheep ranch, spoke Norman French, a patois of Danish, Romanz (Old French), and Latin. Everybody who was important spoke French, and the "unimportant" peasants, artisans, and merchants spoke English in the dialect of their region. All affairs of the church, the chancery, and the courts were conducted in Latin, the official language of State. English writing all but disappeared, kept alive by a few obscure monks who did their best to avoid any direct encounter with William or his cronies.

After about 200 years, English writing began to reappear, mainly in sermons and secular poetry. In this brief time, the English language had changed almost out of recognition. The case grammar of Old English, with special endings that marked gender, the subject of the sentence, and the object of the action, had disappeared. Some of the words for "learn" (verb), "learning" (noun), and "learned" (adjective) originally had these forms:

lar lare lareda laera laeren leorn leornian lerne lernan lareo lareowas liornunga geleara geliornod geliornodon geliorn-ode

By the end of the thirteenth century, all that remained of this grammar was a vestigial e left behind on the ends of words, the spellings familiar to us in "Ye Olde English Tea Shoppe." Thousands of French words had entered the language, and strange French spellings (au, ai, ay, ou, oi, eu) were adopted for new English vowel sounds.

Meanwhile, extraordinary events of the fourteenth century helped save the English language from oblivion. The Black Death struck in 1348, and again in 1361 and 1368–1369. Estimates put the death rate at 35 to 50 percent of the population. Farmers and merchants were thrust to the forefront as the only people left in England who could run successful farms and businesses. The severe labor shortage led to skyrocketing wages. As these families began to acquire wealth, they started to buy up land around the deserted villages, and by the fifteenth century, "peasant" farmers were the largest landowners in England. Farmers and merchants became the new aristocracy and they wanted their children educated in English.

Edward the III, who was on the throne from 1327 to 1377, initiated the 100 Years' War with France. It was an unpopular war, and it was hard to rally support, especially when the aristocracy spoke French. In the meantime, Parisian French had become the language of diplomacy, and Norman French was becoming something of an embarrassment. Pressure was felt at all levels of society to speak English. Parliament was conducted in English in 1362. Chancery documents started appearing in English in 1380, and when Henry IV took the throne in 1399, he was the first king in over 300 years to speak English. He spoke in the dialect of London, the state and commercial capital of England.

Here is how he might have sounded. These are the opening lines of "The Vision of Piers Plowman," a fourteenth-century book-length poem in alliterative verse, written by William Langland in the London dialect.

In a somer sesonn, when softe was the sonne
I shop me in to a shrowde as y a shep were,
In abite of an heremyte unholy of werkes,
Wente forth in the worlde wondris to here.
And saw many sellis and selcouth thynges
Ac on a May mornynge in Malverne Hullys

Me bifel for to slepe for weryness of walked
And in a lannde as y lay pened y and slepte
And meruailous lichte me metter as y may gow telle
At the welthe of the world and the woo bothe[1]

[In a summer season, when soft was the sun, I changed me into
a shroud, as I a sheep were, in 'abit of a hermit, unholy of works,
went forth in the world, wonders to hear. And saw many good
and various things. Ah on a May morning in Malvern Hills, me be-
fell for to sleep for wearyness of walking, and in a land as I lay,
pained I, and slept. And marvelous light met me, as I may go tell,
at the wealth of the world and the woe both.]

The words are nearly modern, but the spellings are strange. If you
look closely, you will see that the same sounds have more than one
spelling, the sound /ee/ is spelled: b<u>e</u>, b<u>i</u>fel, sl<u>e</u>p<u>e</u>, sh<u>e</u>p, h<u>e</u>r<u>e</u>, w<u>e</u>ry, the
sound /oe/ is spelled: g<u>ow</u>, w<u>oo</u>, b<u>o</u>th<u>e</u>, h<u>o</u>ly. The variety of spellings
for the *same* sound actually increased over time, despite all the efforts to
stop it.

The English Renaissance is dated from 1476, the year William Cax-
ton brought the first printing press to England. He opened a bookshop
in Westminster called the Red Pale. Cheap books, increasing prosper-
ity, and a renewed interest in the classics of Greece and Rome changed
the language once more and spelling along with it. Scholars became
fascinated by the origins of words and began altering spellings to reflect their Latin, French, or German origins, creating a new discipline
called "etymology." Words about science, philosophy and medicine
were borrowed into the language from the Greek, and got special
"Greek" spellings (etymology, metaphysics, philosophy, phonology).
Authors of books tended to favor the spellings that reflected their idiosyncratic knowledge of word origins, or their special point of view, or
nothing at all.

Three main groups were struggling to standardize the spelling system. These were the Chancery, who drafted documents of state, the
publishers, who needed a "house style" for their type setters, and schoolmasters who had to teach pupils how to write and spell. This isn't easy
to do if there are three or four or five ways to spell the same word.
"Well, John, you can spell the word 'great': gret, grete, great, greate,
greet, grate. Just use whatever looks best on the page."

Here's a letter written by Sir Walter Raleigh's wife, Elizabeth, to Sir
Robert Cecil, announcing news of Raleigh's return from South

America. Elizabeth was an educated woman and had been a lady in waiting at Queen Elizabeth's court.

> Sur hit tes trew i thonke the leving God sur Walter is safly londed at Plumworthe [Plymouth] with as gret honnor as ever man can, but littel riches. i have not yet hard from him selfe. Kepe thies I besech you to your selfe yet; only to me lord ammerall [Admiral]. In haste this Sunday.
>
> Your pour frind
> E. Raleg[2]

Disagreements about spelling created two major factions. There were the spelling reformers, who wanted to scrap everything and design a perfect system, like King Alfred used to have. There were the pragmatic tinkerers, mainly schoolmasters, who said this was impossible, and wanted to tidy it up and agree on one spelling for each word. These groups fought each other in books, pamphlets, lectures, and in the trenches (the classroom). The publishers sometimes paid attention, sometimes not, and went doggedly about trying to standardize their own in-house spelling systems, with marginal agreement between them.

In the meantime, dictionaries were called for as a possible solution. There were no dictionaries of the English language until late in the sixteenth century, and most were written for schoolboys. In a dictionary, each word can have only one entry. Dictionaries standardize spelling by default. That is, if everyone buys the same dictionary. The first dictionary of any merit was published anonymously in 1702 by someone who signed himself J.K. (probably John Kersey), which meant that nobody paid much attention to it. After a succession of mediocre dictionaries appeared on the scene, friends of Johnson, along with several booksellers, urged him to write a dictionary. Johnson was highly regarded throughout England for his brilliant books and essays, and if anyone could make an impact, it would be him.

While this was going on, sounds in the language started changing again, even faster than the spellings. Until Henry IV came to the throne in 1399, the aristocracy could demarcate themselves from the hoi polloi by speaking an entirely different language. Now they sounded just like everybody else, and this would never do. This is speculation, but it answers a very puzzling question: Why did vowel sounds change so dramatically during the fifteenth and sixteenth centuries, a phenomenon called the "Great Vowel Shift"? One plausible reason was a conscious effort on the part of the aristocracy and those who were educated to change their pronunciation of English. They needed to put as much distance as possible between the way they spoke and the "Cockney" English of London and other regional dialects. The major distinguishing characteristic of the English class system today is the way people speak. Later, the accent of the aristocrats became known as "received pronunciation" (RP) or "the King's English."

The whole mess landed in Johnson's lap around 1746: the 700 years accumulation of changing sounds in the language, the conscious efforts to alter vowel sounds even more by the aristocracy and social climbers, the practice of spelling anyway you felt like it, the thousands of French, Latin, and Greek words entering the language, the scholars who zealously created more and more special spellings to mark the "etymological" roots of these words, and the failure of any one person or group to influence *everyone* to agree on a standard spelling system. That Johnson succeeded is nothing short of a miracle.

STANDARDIZED SPELLING

Johnson's *A Dictionary of the English Language* was published in 1755 and was soon on the bookshelf or library table of all the people who considered themselves "literate." It did just what everyone hoped it would do.

Johnson's major goal in writing his dictionary was actually more ambitious than standardizing spelling. He wanted to provide accurate definitions of words and establish a standard *pronunciation* of the English language. He complained about the "nonstandard" and "incorrect" pronunciation of words and thought that fixed spellings would help, though he recognized that it was impossible to fix pronunciation over time.

Linguists know that languages "drift" over time, and nothing can stop them doing this. Yet, since Johnson's dictionary appeared, English hasn't drifted very far. It was as if he tied the English language to a stout oak tree, to which all dialects of English are connected by shorter or longer pieces of rope. Today, over 240 years later, most people of America, England, Australia, New Zealand, Canada, South Africa, Scotland, Wales, Ireland, and India have little difficulty understanding each other's English. Contrast this with the extraordinary changes in the language from 1066 to 1300.

Johnson compiled the words for his dictionary from the vocabularies of Hooker's Bible, Shakespeare, Spenser, and Francis Bacon, plus his own prodigious knowledge of the language. In addition to standardizing pronunciation through phonetic spellings, he also emphasized word derivation as a major source for spelling, and he provides etymological roots (five languages) for many of the words. Other than this, and stating that he found it impossible to work from other people's dictionaries, he provides no further insights, or guiding principles, for why he spelled words in particular ways.

Throughout the dictionary, a few consistencies stand out, and these ideas were not original with Johnson. Words with the sound /j/, previously spelled i, were now standardized to j (iump/jump). The confusion between how to use the letters v and u was resolved (vnless/ unless; heauen/heaven). The letter y was banished from the middle of words (wylle, kyng, hym, eyght), unless the word was Greek (myth, symbol). A long-standing plea to systematize those final es at the ends of words was heeded. The letter e was retained when it signaled a change in a vowel sound: "mate" but not "seeme." Johnson also left a final e on consonant endings to signal pronunciation: ce (fence not fenc), se (dense not dens), ge (barge not barg), the (bathe not bath), and/or when the spelling was originally French: le (table), ve (carve). The ve combination creates problems in words like: above, dove, give, have, love, live, shove (abov, dov, giv, hav, lov, liv, shov), where the e works with the v and not the vowel.

The use of the letter e as a cue or "diacritic" for five different vowel sounds (/ae/ tame, /ie/ time, /ee/ teem, /oe/ tone, /ue/ cute) became known as the "e-control principle." Its effect on spelling is far-reaching, and constitutes one of the few spelling patterns that has any consistency. Basically, the principles are these:

1. e signals the pronunciation of the preceding vowel letter (a, e, i, o, u only) backwards across one consonant but not two: mut/mute/mutter   mate/mated/matted   mar/mare/marked
2. To cancel e-control, you must double the consonant: bat/batter, tin/tinned.
3. Other vowel letters can substitute for e when adding a suffix: whine/whining   shine/shiny

But like all spelling "rules" for English, this doesn't hold up 100 percent of the time: fable, table, maple, paste, waste, haste, are but a few examples. If they followed the "rule," two consonants in a row would cancel e-control, and the words would be read: labble, tabble, mapple, past, wast, hast.

Johnson ensured that most homophones (words that sound alike with different meanings) got a different spelling. He managed to locate over 600 of them. He systematized plural and past tense spellings so they were always consistent, regardless of how they sounded in the word. The plural is always spelled s or es, even when it sounds /z/: trees, chairs, tables, peaches. Past tense is spelled ed, though the letter e may not be sounded, or the d sounds like /t/: pact/packed, past/passed, bold/bowled, board/bored, find/fined.

Perhaps Johnson's changes can be observed most clearly, in comparison to the spellings of one of the most famous of all publications, The First Folio of Shakespeare's plays, published in 1623 by Jaggard and Blount. I have listed the nonmodern spellings from Hamlet's soliloquy and compared them to the spellings in Johnson's dictionary (Table 5–3). Only one of Johnson's spellings has since been changed to reflect its French origin: "unkle" to "uncle" (from oncle), and Johnson made a mistake with "shooes." He should have left it alone. Instead, he removed an o and left the e to reflect its old Saxon spelling, ᵹceo ('sheo') which had a different pronunciation.

Johnson's knowledge of the individual sounds (phonemes) of the English language was incomplete, and he was inaccurate about some of the complex vowel sounds or "diphthongs," which he occasionally confused with "digraphs." He comments on "mute" letters in spellings of words, specifically consonant spellings, but did nothing to get rid of them. His examples were debt, subtle, lamb, gnash, sign, ghost, though, right, sought, damn, condemn, psalm. He says he leaves these "mute" letters in the spelling because of "custom" or because of etymology: debt/debit, sign/signature, damn/damnation, condemn/condemnation.

Johnson was very aware of his shortcomings in tackling this formidable problem. I'll let him speak for himself:

> I have laboured to settle the orthography, display the analogy, regulate the structures, and ascertain the signification of English words, to perform all the parts of a faithful lexicographer: but I have not always executed my own scheme, or satisfied my own expectations. The work, whatever proofs of diligence and attention it may exhibit, is yet capable of many improvements: the orthography which I recommend is still controvertible, the

TABLE 5–3

Changes in Spelling from Shakespeare to Johnson

Hamlet's Soliloquy (1623)	Johnson (1755)
fixt	fixed
selfe	self
seemes	seems
growes	grows
growne	grown
possesse	possess
grosse	gross
meerely	merely
louing	loving
heauen	heaven
shooes	shoes
poore	poor
teares	tears
vnkle	unkle
vses	uses
moneth	month
vnweeded	unweeded
vnprofitable	unprofitable
breake	break
euen	even
mourn'd	mourned
vnrighteous	unrighteous
breake	break
encrease	increase
windes	winds
beteene	between

etymology I adopt is uncertain and perhaps frequently erroneous; . . .

. . . if our language is not here fully displayed, I have only
failed in an attempt which no human powers have hitherto completed.[3]

These spellings are original. "Labour" is correct in England. Nothing has changed.

Johnson's success in standardizing spelling had an unforeseen consequence. Now that there was only one "right" way to spell a word, the
task of every school boy or girl was to memorize that one right way,

otherwise their written work would reflect their ignorance. From this point on, teaching spelling began to diverge from teaching reading and took on a life of its own.

NOAH WEBSTER'S GREAT MISTAKE

Webster was a brilliant linguist who wrote the first American dictionary and is responsible for any differences in American spelling. He borrowed mainly from Johnson, and the changes he made were minor. For example, he decided that words ending in the sounds /ik/ should be spelled ic and not ick: "music" not "musick." He applied this principle religiously to multisyllable words: panic, terrific, atomic, frantic, endemic, septic, etc., but left the one-syllable 'ik' words untouched: trick, stick, flick. He abolished the letter u from words like labour, colour, favour.

Webster studied the classics at Yale and was admitted to the bar in 1781 at the age of twenty-three. He taught school for a while and realized that children were having problems pronouncing English correctly and learning to read and spell. He saw that their books had no accurate or systematic content about pronunciation, spelling, or grammar. At the ripe old age of twenty-five, he set out to change this once and for all, and published Part I of the *Grammatical Institute of the English Language,* in 1783. This became known as *The American Speller,* or *Blue-Backed Speller,* the most popular speller on both sides of the Atlantic for nearly 100 years.

Webster practiced law, founded two newspapers, and wrote and lectured on the English language, politics, history, and other topics. In 1801, he began work on a dictionary. His first dictionary was published in 1806. He wasn't proud of it and wrote later: "I found myself embarrassed at every step for want of a knowledge of the origin of words, which Johnson—and others—do not afford the means of obtaining."[4] Webster took eighteen years to study and compare over twenty languages. These included all the obvious ones, plus Arabic, Hebrew, Chaldee, Russian, Amharic, Persian, Syriac, and Icelandic, to name but a few. Finally, in 1828, he published his magnum opus, a 70,000-word dictionary. He was seventy years old.

It's the *Speller* that created problems in the teaching of reading and spelling in American and British schools, although they may have happened anyway. Some of these problems were due to Webster's emphasis, and others were created by publishers who imitated Webster, but omitted most of the spelling code and his systematic exposition of syllable patterns.

Webster's goal was to reform the teaching of spoken and written English. He saw himself, like Johnson, as a champion of "correct" pronunciation and felt that this could be accomplished by teaching spelling properly, marking syllable boundaries and pronunciation with various diacritic marks. Proper spelling was mainly what Johnson had established. Webster writes: "In spelling and accenting, I have generally made Dr. Johnson's dictionary my guide." Webster devised a set of exercises which gradually took the student through word lists of simple to complex spelling and syllable patterns.

In the Preface to the 1783 edition of the *Speller*, Webster began by outlining the sounds of the English language. First he derived sounds from their "spellings," and then "sounds" independently of spellings. Webster writes as if he is thinking out loud, so it's easy to follow his train of thought. Webster knew that a writing system is an arbitrary code for sounds in the language. As he put it: "Letters are the marks of sounds." After all, he was a student of languages. He was surprised to discover that he didn't know the sounds in his own language. In the Preface he "discovers" thirty-eight sounds. Later, he found one more (/ng/).

In the same edition, Webster wrote out the spellings in two directions: first, from each "sound" in the language to its various spelling alternatives. The sound /ae/ "can be spelled: hate, fair, day, they, vein, gauge." Next, he wrote out the various *sounds* each letter could represent: the letter a "can sound: fate, hat, halt." I described these two patterns earlier as *spelling alternatives* and *code overlaps* (my terms not his). So far, so good. If he had developed both these ideas, he would have revolutionized the teaching of reading and spelling.

Instead he made a mistake. The *Speller* itself consisted of word lists of increasing complexity and syllable length, interleaved with short phrases and little stories. Rather than organizing the lists by sounds (phonemes) in the language, he decided to do this by letters, word families, and syllable length, set out alphabetically. In some ways this is understandable, because it is hard to represent "sounds" in print. Lessons begin with short word lists:

ba ca da fa ga; ab ac ad af ag;
can man pan ran van; brag drag flag stag

The child encounters consonant digraphs (two letters = one sound) almost immediately, mixed together with consonant clusters (two letters = two sounds). On page 3 we find: glut shut smut slut (!), and chub club drub grub (digraphs are underlined). Next come a series of e-controlled vowel spellings: hide ride side wide; face lace pace race, etc. After about twenty to twenty-five pages of these lists, the child is plunged without warning into word lists containing these vowel digraphs: ai, ay, ey, ee, ea, oa, oi, oy, ou, ow, none of which have been seen before.

In succeeding editions, his detailed analysis of the sounds in English along with the various spelling alternatives for different sounds was either abbreviated or put in an Appendix, and "sounds" were explained and organized in the speller as if they were derived from letters. The following quotes are from the 1870 edition.[5]

> The regular long sound of a [meaning the letter] is denoted by a horizontal mark over it, as in āncient, profāne.

When the vowel letters run out, he switches logic from letter to sound, but often this is muddled:

> The short sound of oo in pool is that of u in pull and oo in wool.

Here Webster presents oo as a "sound," when what he actually means is that the *letters* oo represent two sounds, as in "pool" and "wool," and that the *sound* /oo/ can also be spelled u as in "pull." Consonants are presented in the Introduction in alphabetical order (visually) rather than by sound, with sounds derived from letters. When a letter has only one sound, and a sound has only one letter (one-to-one mapping), then this works fine. But look what happens here:

> F has only one sound: life, fever, except of, in which it has the sound of v.

The letter F may stand for only one sound (no code overlap), but the *sound* /f/ has four spelling alternatives: deaf, cliff, phone, rough. If you never introduce the *sound* /f/ to the student, there is no way to get to this information.

When Webster's approach breaks down (as it must), he tries to solve the problem by switching logic, as illustrated with the example for "pool," or by inventing spelling "rules." Here is one of his "rules":

Gh are mute in every English word, both in the middle and at the end, except in words like cough, tough [etc.] when they close with the sound of f.

He should have added: "unless they appear at the beginning of the word, when they have the sound g (ghost)." Yet, Webster (accurately) cautions teachers never to teach rules to children, because they "can't understand them."

If this is getting confusing already, you can imagine that Webster's imitators were only going to make things worse. What happened as a result of Webster's emphasis was that the sounds of the language, which he had carefully worked out, got lost. Today, in phonics classrooms, the alphabet is taught entirely from letter to sound, which destroys the logic of the alphabet code. This will be explained in more detail below.

Webster made other decisions which impacted "phonics" teaching methods. His *Speller* begins with ten vowels, actually five vowel letters, described as being "long" or "short" vowels. The "short" vowels are /a/ bat, /e/ bet, /i/ sit, /o/ hot, /u/ cup, and the "long" vowels are /ae/ gate, /ee/ seem, /ie/ tie, /oe/ toe, /ue/ cute (in other words, e-controlled spellings). Webster actually believed that the word "made" took longer to say than "mad." Webster didn't invent this idea. The terms "long" and "short" vowels were used by Johnson and by earlier writers. No one knows exactly when this practice began. Some people thought that the old Saxon language had long and short versions of the same vowel sound: 'mad' and 'maaad,' but there is no evidence for this.

The long and short distinction is meaningless. It doesn't hold up in terms of duration or in any other way. And it doesn't correspond to what phoneticians call "long" or "short" vowels. There are simply ten different vowel sounds related only because they share the same letters. Children have no idea what the teacher means when she says vowels are long and short. They think she is talking about physical size, a long A and a short A.

Johnson informed his dictionary readers that he was leaving certain "mute" letters in words, which he identified only in consonant clusters (sign, doubt). In Webster's hands, "mute" letters began multiplying like some dreaded virus. They invaded all vowel digraphs, and he marked these "silent" letters with italics so children would be sure to notice them (lif*e*, gr*i*ef, thou*gh*, b*u*ild, pe*o*ple, tau*gh*t, he*a*d, go*a*l).

Later, someone invented the famous phrase: "when two vowels go walking the first one does the talking." This means that when you see a vowel pair, the second letter is "silent" and you say the *letter name* of the first vowel: "beach," "feet," "soap," follow the rule. This is supposed to be a useful mnemonic device for decoding vowel digraphs. Children in phonics classrooms can devote the greater part of their reading time, searching for "silent" letters and blocking them out with a fingernail. Having to do this is bad enough, even if the rule worked, but it only holds up about 40 percent of the time. If the rule was true, you would pronounce the words:

dawn, launch, soil, boy, pouch, cow, bread, touch, eight, thief, grew, group, pear

like this:

dane, lainch, sole, boe, poach, coe, breed, toach, eat, thife, gree, groap, peer

And these are just a few of the *common* spelling patterns that don't follow the rule.

In every edition of Webster's *Speller,* it is clear that Webster was fully aware that sounds in English are the basis for the code. For example, he writes in a footnote: "Children may be much assisted by being told how to place the tongue and lips to make any sound."[6] Perhaps because this was so obvious to him, it got deemphasized over time, and in setting up the lessons entirely from letters to sounds, the importance of the sounds was obscured and then lost.

At the end of the nineteenth century, there was a brief ray of hope in the work of Nellie Dale, a school teacher at Wimbledon High School for girls (six to fourteen years old) in England. She designed the first true linguistic reading program for the classroom based entirely upon forty-two sounds in the English language. Each of the forty-two sounds was taught in highly imaginative lessons in which children "discovered" how sounds are produced, by feeling the movement in their mouth, and sensing the position of lips, tongue, and jaw. When the sounds were mastered, the children learned to match each sound to its letter or digraph. She designed a large "letter frame" that stood at the front of the classroom upon which letters hung in groups according to which parts of the mouth moved to make the sounds. Children copied the letters onto blackboards inside the lids of their desk as they were introduced. Dale was insistent that children should not be taught letter names, as they would interfere with training the automatic connection between sounds and letters. I can't do justice here to the eighty-six lessons she designed or her excellent advice ("never teach anything you have to discard later"), but in view of all we know today, her program would have had an incredible impact. The last edition of Dale's program was published in 1902, and we had to wait over sixty years for anything like it to appear again.

Any innovative left-overs from the nineteenth century were soon to be crushed into oblivion by the universal education movement and the bureaucracy it spawned. Bureaucrats at the district, state, and national levels joined forces with businesses that stood to profit from the economic spinoff of universal education. It is these forces that drive the shifts in curriculum and teaching philosophies. William Bennett, former secretary of education, has aptly christened the education bureaucracy: "the Blob." The function of the Blob appears to be to ensure that nothing useful gets into the classroom, or if it gets in by mistake, it is never allowed to stay for long.

When universal education was introduced at the end of the last century, the structure of the classroom changed. Instead of small classes with lots of individual attention, where children learned Latin and French so they became aware that sounds in speech are the basis for a writing system, hoards of children were herded into classrooms all neatly sorted by age (age-graded) according to the factory model that pertained at the time. Teachers (the factory foreman) directed classes from the front of the room, and everybody did the same thing at the same time. It was impossible for teachers to work with individual children, and so it was decreed that individual attention was unnecessary. Even the analysis of letter-sound relationships was deemed to be a waste of time. Instead, children could learn to read whole words, just like the Chinese, using the "progressive" method called "look-say," where teachers held up flashcards and children chanted in unison, as they memorized each word by sight.

"Look-say" took the English speaking world by storm. It was the dominant method in classrooms from early in this century until after World War II, by which time it had been discovered that hardly any soldiers could read. A "phonics backlash" began to build from the late 1940s, and found its most eloquent advocate in Rudolph Flesch (*Why Johnny Can't Read*). Phonics was gradually reintroduced in the late 1950s, but by now no one was quite sure what phonics was. Phonics basal readers tended to be as dull as the look-say readers, except that the words were more phonetically regular so children could "sound them out." The vocabularies of worksheets, stories, and spelling lists didn't match. Children were taught to spell words they couldn't read, and read words they couldn't spell. Whole language was supposed to be the antidote to this dullness and confusion, and was swept in on a wave of euphoria that good children's literature was back into the classroom at last. As the pendulum swings toward phonics once more, curriculum designers have even less idea what "phonics" should be than they did in the 1950s.

When phonics reemerged after the failure of look-say, it was but a pale imitation of Webster's program. There was no mention of the sounds in English on which the code is based. There was no attempt to teach all possible spelling and syllable patterns in a systematic way. All that seemed to remain from Webster's efforts were his mistakes, particularly his "great mistake" in setting up the code backwards. Let me show you exactly why this won't work. We'll start with the code the right way around.

THE TRUE LOGIC OF THE ENGLISH ALPHABET CODE

There are 43 phonemes in English, which can be represented by approximately 100 letters or letter combinations. In order to teach this you must set up a Basic Code in which each phoneme is represented by only *one* letter or digraph. The remaining structure of the spelling code should be taught as "spelling alternatives" for those sounds with more than one spelling and "code overlaps" for those letters that represent more than one sound. The structure is as follows:

Consonants

24 consonants can be spelled with a total of 50 spellings. 12 consonants have mainly one spelling, or one spelling by position in a word:

/b/ /d/ /h/ /l/ /p/ /t/ /v/ /ng/ /qu/ /sh/ /th/ /th/

The remaining 12 consonants are assigned one spelling (the most probable or least ambiguous) which completes the Basic Code for consonants:

/f/ /g/ /j/ /k/ /m/ /n/ /r/ /s/ /w/ /x/ /z/ /ch/

The 25th sound /zh/ (vision) isn't taught at this stage.

This leaves *26 spelling alternatives for 12 consonants* which must be taught.

Example: the sound /f/ can be spelled: f, ff, gh, ph

Consonant Clusters

76 consonant clusters are simply adjacent consonants and are spelled exactly like single consonants. 73 are spelled in Basic Code (only one spelling). There is no new logic and no new complexity.

Vowels

18 vowels can be spelled with a total of 50 spellings. 3 vowels are mainly spelled one way, and 1 by position in a word:

/a/ cat, /i/ sit, /ar/ car, /oi/ toil/toy

The remaining 14 vowels are assigned one spelling (the most probable), which completes the Basic Code for vowels.

/e/ /o/ /u/ /ee/ /ae/ /ie/ /oe/ /ue/ /aw/ /o͞o/ /oo/ /ou/ /er//or/

This leaves 32 spelling alternatives for 14 vowel sounds that must be taught.

Example: The vowel sound /oe/ can be spelled:

o-e tone, oa goat, o told, ow low

Code Overlaps

There are 21 vowel letter patterns that overlap more than one vowel sound (consonant overlaps are too few to be a problem).

For example: The letters ou stand for five phonemes:

/ou/ out, /o͞o/ soup, /oe/ soul, /u/ touch, /aw/ cough

These 21 code overlaps must be taught.

Notice that this process whittles away at the complexity so that it becomes smaller and more manageable. Beyond the Basic Code level (42 sounds/42 spellings), this is what remains:

26 consonant spelling alternatives
32 vowel spelling alternatives
21 code overlaps

The total complexity = 79.

Outcome. The complexity of the code shrinks. The code can be organized by the probabilities of how likely a letter or letters will be to spell a particular phoneme. The child has a logic to read and to spell. *The code is reversible.* This makes it possible to read (decode) and spell (encode) using the same logic. The child sees that the alphabet is a *code* for sounds in speech. *The code makes sense to the child.*

PHONICS LOGIC

Phonics programs teach from the letters to "sounds" only. Most commercial programs teach a fraction of the code, forcing the child to figure out the rest on his own. The following sets out the complete code if it was taught with "phonics logic."

Consonants

There are 50 consonant letter patterns (graphemes) that represent a total of 62 "sounds."

Consonant Clusters

There are 76 consonant cluster letter patterns that represent a total of 76 "sounds."

Vowels

There are 50 vowel letter patterns that represent a total of 95 "sounds."

Altogether, the total complexity that must be taught is 176 letter(s) representing 233 "sounds."

Outcome
1. You have destroyed the logic of the alphabet code. There are not 233 "sounds" in the English language.
2. You have greatly increased the complexity rather than reducing it.
3. You have taught 76 clusters as if they were 76 new "sounds," instead of combinations of single consonants.
4. You have made it impossible to categorize what you need to teach or to organize lessons on the basis of spelling probabilities.
5. You have created a TRAP from which there is no escape. The code can't reverse and only works to decode but not to encode. You have made it impossible to teach spelling using the same logic, because you can't teach spelling alternatives for 233 "sounds"!

To make matters worse, many phonics programs teach "word families" or "rimes (VC, VCC, and VCCC endings—<u>ing</u>, <u>unch,</u> <u>est</u>), as if they were "one sound." Here's what happens when you do this. There are 1,260 "rimes" in English (over 820 in common English words alone), adding another 1,260 "sounds" to the 233 "sounds" you already have, a total of 1,493 "sounds."

If you really want to make things as bad as they can possibly get, you can also teach syllable fragments from any position in a word: beginning, middle, end. The child is taught <u>est</u> as a single "sound," so that it can be recognized anywhere in a word, even though it may cross over syllable boundaries or change pronunciation: blest, west, establish (establish), destiny (dest–iny), destroy (dest–roy), etc. The number of these syllable fragments in English is likely to come close to infinity, based on the fact that English has over 55,000 syllables to start with.

Today, educators and publishers have no idea what to do after the failure of whole language. In 1986, the Center for the Study of Reading was awarded a grant to evaluate the research on phonics and reading. Marilyn Adams was selected to write the review of the research literature, and her book *Beginning to Read* was published in 1990. Adams maintains a cool and scholarly approach in her assessment of the literature, until she begins to review phonics instructional programs and finds little support for their validity. She writes:

> Given the diffuse and complex nature of English spelling-sound translations, there is no obvious path through the phonic correspondences and generalizations; along that path, there are no obvious landmarks to let the teacher or student know which way it will turn next or how much headway has been made towards its end. (p. 287)

> Experts have invested enormous efforts in finding the most coherent and teachable way to do so [phonics]. Yet chaos prevails. (p. 286)

Adams' frustration is heard in these remarks:

> On scrutiny the notion of phonics first turns into a pedagogical morass. (p. 285)
> The teachers are responsible for teaching this mess. (p. 286)

The problems here are twofold. The developers of "phonics" curricula have never analyzed the structure of the spelling code, so that phonics programs are not only seriously impoverished but chaotic. The second issue is that even if "phonics" programs were complete, as illustrated in the assessment of "phonics logic," they still couldn't work, because phonics logic is backwards and the code cannot be categorized with this logic.

The *word* "phonics" is problematic as well because it is used in two entirely different ways. In Adams' book, "phonics" means anything to do with teaching "sounds" as contrasted to teaching whole words. The other meaning refers to a type of reading program. But there are diametrically opposing ways to teach "sounds." One way, traditional "phonics," is to teach "the sounds of letters." The other way, which doesn't yet have a name, teaches the "sounds of the language" and how these sounds are mapped to letters.

Misunderstanding this fundamental difference has been the major cause of the failure of reading programs probably well before Webster. In this century, it has been the cause of the endless flip-flops between whole-word methods and phonics. As a start on the path to a complete understanding of the "new way," let me introduce you to the code.

THE CODE

This chapter closes with the sounds of the English language and the complete structure of the English spelling code. All codes are based on what is called "mapping" or mapping transformations. When a phoneme is coded with only one letter, this is simplest type of mapping: 1-to-1 mapping. Because there aren't enough letters for all the phonemes in English, letters were combined in pairs to stand for the remaining sounds. These letter pairs, or "digraphs," introduce a more complex variation of 1-to-1 mapping: one phoneme to one letter-pair or 1-to-1(2) mapping. Many phonemes have multiple spellings or "spelling alternatives." Also, a letter or digraph can represent multiple sounds or "code overlaps," creating two further mapping logics, known as 1-to-many, and many-to-1 mapping. The Latin layer of language represents still another mapping relationship, which will be discussed in chapter 10.

These mapping relationships can be seen in the tables at the end of this chapter. The first tables present the spelling alternatives for each phoneme in English, and the second set of tables, the code overlaps for vowel letter patterns only. You may want to compare these tables to the spelling alternatives/code overlaps in King Alfred's spelling system in Table 5–1.

There are few consistent patterns or "rules" in our spelling system, especially for vowels, but there is a way around this problem. The tables are arranged according to spelling *probabilities.* Perceptual learning or perceptual memory occurs by a process called "probability matching." The brain is specially adapted to learn visual and auditory patterns automatically by seeing or hearing them a few times. *If, and only if, the eye is trained to look at specific letter patterns,* these patterns will be coded without effort. The brain searches for "reoccurring regularities." What is frequently encountered will be remembered. What is very strange or discrepant will be noticed.

When a system, such as our spelling system, cannot be easily categorized or classified, the solution is to organize it according to its probability structure, and teach it by systematic exposure to this structure. This probability structure must be based on how the code was written. Phonemes are the *categories,* and letter(s) are the code. This means teaching the child the *most likely spelling* for each phoneme first (Basic Code), the next most likely spellings, and the next. In order to do this, you have to know which spellings are most likely or unlikely. Someone has to work this out ahead of time. The tables present this probability structure for common English words, for the first time.[7] We'll be looking at this issue in depth in chapter 10, the chapter on how to teach spelling so it is consistent with the logic of the English alphabet code.

In the meantime, we'll move ahead to the late twentieth century, where a quiet revolution has been brewing.

HOW TO READ THE TABLES

"Sounds," or phonemes, in English are on the left, spelled in Basic Code, which is the most probable or least ambiguous spelling for that sound, along with a key word as a cue for pronunciation. Spelling alternatives, or multiple ways to spell that sound, are listed separately for beginnings and endings of words.

Vowels are set out in the Tables according to probabilities, from the most likely spelling to the least. The probability order is based upon the number of *common* English words with that spelling, and does not include the Latin layer of the language.

The final set of Tables show the Code Overlaps for vowels only. These illustrate the number of different sounds each vowel spelling pattern can represent.

Very rare spellings, like those that some people love to use to prove our spelling system is totally chaotic (sew, people, yacht, debt), are not included in this probability structure. There are only about 100 of them in common English words.

Single-Consonant Spelling Alternatives

Sound	Key Word	Word Beginning	Word Ending
b	big	b	b
d	dog	d	d
f	fun	f ph	f ff ph gh
g	got	g gu gh	g gue gg
h	hot	h wh	—
j	job	j g	ge dge
k	kid	c k ch	k ck c
l	log	l	l ll
m	man	m	m mb mn
n	not	n kn gn	n gn
p	pig	p	p
r	red	r wr	r
s	sat	s c sc	ce se ss s
t	top	t	t bt
v	van	v	ve
w	win	w wh	—
x /ks/	tax	—	x
z	zip	z	se ze zz s z
ch	chin	ch	ch tch
ng	sing	—	ng
qu/kw/	quit	qu	—
sh	shop	sh	sh
th	thin	th	th
<u>**th**</u>	then	th	the

Spelling alternatives are ordered by most to least likely.

Consonant Clusters

Beginning Clusters	Spelling Alternatives	Ending Clusters	Spelling Alternatives
bl br			
dr dw		dth	
fl fr		ft fth	
gl gr			
kl kr	**cl cr**		
	chl chr	(kt)	**ct**
		ld lf (lj)	**lge**
		lm ln lp lt	
		lch lsh lth	
		mp mpt (mf)	**mph**
		nch nd (nj)	**nge**
		nt ntch	
pl pr		pt pth	
		rb rc rd	
		rf rg (rj)	**rge**
		rk rl rm rn	
		rp rt rch	
		rsh rth rve	
sk	**sc** sk sch	sk sm sp st	
sl sm sn			
sp spl spr			
st str sw			
squ			
tr tw			
		xt	
		(ngk) (ngkt)	**nk nct**
		ngth	
shr			
thr			

Clusters in parentheses are never spelled this way. Optional spellings in bold are either the *only* spelling or most likely spelling.

Vowel Spelling Alternatives

Sound	Key Word	Spelling Alternatives in Order of Most to Least Likely						
		1	*2*	*3*	*4*	*5*	*6*	*7*
a	had	a						
e	bed	e	ea	ai				
i	it	i	y	ui				
o	dog	o	a(ll)	(w)a				
aw	law	aw	au	ough	augh			
u	but	u	o	o-e	ou			
ae	made	a-e	ai	a	ay	ei	eigh	ey
ee	see	ee	ea	y	ie	e	e-e	ey
ie	time	i-e	i	y	igh			
oe	tone	o-e	o	oa	ow	ou	ough	
ue	cute	u-e	u	ew	eu			
oo	look	oo	u	ou				
$\overline{oo}$	soon	oo	u-e	ew	u	ou	ui	
ou	out	ou	ow	ough				
oi	soil	oi	oy					
		VOWEL + R						
ar	far	ar						
er	her	er	ur	ir	or	ear	ar	
or	for	or	ore	oar	our	ar	oor	
e+er	bare	are	air	arr	err	ear		

Code Overlap Chart 1: The Code from Letters-to-Sound

| Letters | Most to Least Likely | | | |
	Sound/Word	Sound/Word	Sound/Word	Sound/Word
a	/a/ cat	/ae/ table	/o/ father	
a+ll	/o/ all			
w+a	/o/ wash			
e	/e/ bed	/ee/ be		
i	/i/ sit	/ie/ find		
o	/o/ dog	/u/ from	/oe/ cold	
u	/u/ but	/oo/ pull	/ue/ pupil	/$\overline{oo}$/ ruin
a-e	/ae/ made			
ai	/ae/ sail	/e/ said		
ee	/ee/ see			
ea	/ee/ meat	/e/ head	/ae/ break	
i-e	/ie/ tie	/ee/ believe	/e/ friend	
o-e	/oe/ tone	/u/ done	/oo/ shoe	
oa	/oe/ boat			
u-e	/ue/ cute	/$\overline{oo}$/ tune		
aw	/aw/ law			
au	/aw/ haul	/a/ aunt		
oo	/$\overline{oo}$/ soon	/oo/ look		
ow	/ow/ how	/oe/ low		
ou	/ow/ out	/$\overline{oo}$/ soup	/u/ touch	/oe/ soul
oy	/oy/ toy			
oi	/oy/ oil			
y	/ee/ baby	/ie/ fly	/ee+v/ yes	/i/ gym
ay	/ae/ day			
ey	/ee/ key	/ae/ they		
uy	/ie/ buy			
ye	/ie/ lye			
ui	/i/ build	/$\overline{oo}$/ juice		
ew	/$\overline{oo}$/ new	/ue/ few		
eu	/ue/ feud			
ei	/ee/ wield	/ae/ vein		
eigh	/ae/ eight	/ie/ height		
igh	/ie/ high			
augh	/aw/ caught	/a/ laugh		
ough	/aw/ ought	/ow/ bough	/oe/ dough	

Code Overlap Chart 2: r-Controlled Vowels

Letters	Sound/Word	Sound/Word	Sound/Word
		Most to Least Likely	
ar	/ar/ far	/or/ war	/er/ dollar
er	/er/ her		
ir	/er/ sir		
ur	/er/ fur		
or	/or/ for	/er/ work	
air	/e+er/ hair		
are	/e+er/ bare	/ar/ are	
arr	/e+er/ arrow		
err	/e+er/ error		
ear	/eer/ ear	/air/ bear	/er/ learn
eer	/eer/ peer		
ere	/eer/ mere	/air/ there	/er/ were
iar	/ire/ liar		
ire	/ire/ hire		
ore	/or/ ore		
oar	/or/ roar		
our	/our/ hour	/or/ four	
oor	/o͞or/ moor	/or/ door	
ure	/ue+r/ pure	/oor/ lure	/er/ measure

Irregular endings used to spell only one or two words are omitted: aigh (/ae/ straight), oir (/ie/ choir), yre (/ie/ lyre), ai /ie/ aisle), awer (/or/, drawer), etc.

A COMMENT ON DIALECTS

The forty-three phonemes in the English language are the basis for our alphabet code. There is an argument against teaching the sounds of English to children learning to read and write because people speak in regional dialects.

In England, an excellent program used in Oxfordshire was withdrawn under orders from a national authority because it advocated teaching sounds using the local dialect rather than standard BBC English. It was believed that this would promote class divisions and be socially harmful to some students.

In the United States, Kenneth Goodman argues that because people speak in different dialects in different parts of the country, children should not be taught the sounds of the language as a basis for learning to read.

These concerns are groundless for several reasons:

People who speak nonstandard dialects understand the standard dialect perfectly (for example, on TV), yet this does not cause them to change their dialect or feel bad about themselves.

England and America share a nearly identical spelling system, yet have different standard dialects and different pronunciations of these spellings. But this doesn't cause any special problems in either country.

Teaching children the sounds in their speech does not mean that there is only one way to pronounce those sounds. A teacher can pronounce them in any dialect, including a local dialect. Using a key word code makes this possible.

SECTION II

A READING REVOLUTION

Chapter 6

SCIENCE TO THE RESCUE

Earlier I introduced you to several children who were having trouble learning to read.

Donny was using letter names to spell words ('full steam ahead' = fl sdm a ked) like whole language experts said he should, and guessing whole words when he read ('the rabbit crossed the road' = "the ranger climbed the rock"), like whole language experts said he should. But he didn't develop into a good reader and speller.

Sally was using letter names to decode text, until her mother taught her "letter sounds" (incorrectly). Sally translated from each letter name to a letter sound slowly and painfully: 'rabbit' = are/ruh ae/a bee/buh bee/buh ie/i tee/tuh: "rabies-it."

Nigel was told by his teacher *not* to sound out words. Instead, he was told to "look at the pictures" and memorize a string of letters standing for a whole word: bdextntk = 'baseball.' Nigel knew this strategy wasn't working, but he couldn't figure out a better way.

Albert was told the same thing, but Albert was more adventurous. Albert, like Donny, noticed that the first letter or letters in each word stood for a sound, and this sound was a clue to the word. Then he used his excellent visual memory to memorize the *shape* of the rest of the word. He could read short words correctly, but he was extremely inaccurate when words got longer: matter = mother, horse = house, swimming = sailing.

Sam was misled by an off-the-shelf "phonics" program into thinking that the alphabet code was about groups of letters standing for lit-tle words or bits of words. This strategy was hopeless for decoding multisyllable words: "hated" = 'hat-ate-ed.'

Donny, Sally, Nigel, Albert, and Sam will not learn to read without help. They are definite candidates for the diagnosis of "dyslexia" or a "learning disability."

Now we're ready to answer the question: If other children can learn to read given the *same* instruction, in the *same* classroom, is there some-thing wrong with these children? Here's where science enters the pic-ture. Scientists and educators alike ask: *"What do these children have in common?"*

What do you think these children have in common? Here is a checklist of possibilities:

Brain damage/brain anomalies
    Language systems of the brain
    Low IQ/borderline intelligence
Genetic predisposition
Delay or deficiency in subskills important to reading
Poor instruction
Inadequate support from parents/family members
Developmental issues
    Logical reasoning
    Language development
    Attentional difficulties
Child's strategy choice
Chance

In the next three chapters I will be addressing these issues. The cen-tral problem in reading research is that there are many "variables" which influence a child's ability to learn to read. It's the scientist's job to control for all of these variables, but that is easier said than done.

In this chapter I will be reviewing the research on brain damage/anomalies, genetic predisposition, and subskills related to reading like auditory processing, visual processing, speech and language, and IQ. Topic headings are provided so that you can read about what is of in-terest to you, but before you start turning pages, wait until I explain how science works.

If everybody learned to read effortlessly, we wouldn't need any sci-entific research on reading. It is because of the "failures" that parents, family members, and scientists alike begin to ask questions. Scientists ask the same kind of questions that parents and family members ask, and then design research studies to answer them. Scientists study *groups* and use a "statistical" model. If each individual case was unique, science wouldn't work. Instead, scientists are searching for *patterns* that fit the majority of poor readers. By contrast, parents, family members, and reading specialists look at the individual. The questions, however, are the same. Parents of a poor reader want to know:

1. Does my child have low intelligence?
2. Does my child have a brain disorder?
3. Is there something wrong with my child's eyesight? Does he see letters upside down and backwards?
4. My husband had a reading problem. Is my son's reading problem genetic?
5. Does a reading problem stay with you for life?
6. Is my child's teacher doing an adequate job?

WHAT SCIENCE IS AND ISN'T

To understand how to assess the research designed to answer these questions, I need to talk about the word "research," one of the most misused and misunderstood words in the English language. Journalists do "research" by telephoning their sources for information. Many academics do "research" by going to the library to read up on some topic. They rely on information published by people who went to the library before they did and wrote a book or paper about it. The first section of this book is partly based on this kind of library "research." Some educational "research" consists of observing children in classrooms and forming subjective opinions about this experience.

None of these activities qualify as *scientific* research. Science can only work when things can be measured and recorded in numbers. If you want to find out if a particular teaching method is good or bad, *ask to see the data* from research on the method. These data should be reported in comparisons of test scores on standardized tests. These kinds of statements don't count: "the children really like it." "Research in Nebraska showed that the teachers and parents report that children are reading 'better' using this method."

In the past few decades, some educators have begun misusing the word "science," calling something "scientific research" when it is nothing of the sort. When people with influence misuse language, this can have dangerous consequences, leading people to believe that a statement is a scientific fact when it is not. In a recent book, *Phonics Phacts,* whole language advocate Kenneth Goodman repeatedly stresses that whole language is based on scientific research, especially his.

On pages 3 and 4, in explaining the purpose of the book, Goodman uses the words "research," "science," and "scientific" ten times:

> . . . show how these misunderstandings [phonics] conflict with scientific realities.

> . . . came to understand the science of how sounds and letters work together in an alphabetic language—. [This] science demonstrates [his] conclusion [that] phonics relationships are between the patterns and systems of oral and written language, not between individual letters and sounds.

> He says he will avoid technical language and

> still keep my explanations scientific.

> This book is—my personal statement of scientific belief.

If you are a scientist, or if you think logically, these statements are strange. There is no "science" of how sounds and letters work together in an alphabet. This is strictly an issue of categorization and mapping relationships. Science doesn't "demonstrate a conclusion." Either the data are there, and replicable, or they are not. In any case, our writing system was designed for individual phonemes and not for "patterns" of sounds. This is simply a fact. As all the evidence is in conflict with his claim here, one wonders where his "conclusion" comes from.

Finally, how can you have a "personal scientific belief"? You can have a model or a theory based on a set of data. But this is not a "personal belief."

Goodman proceeds to discuss rudimentary phonetics and linguistics, leading the reader to believe that they are "sciences." They are not. They are descriptive disciplines and depend on other phoneticians and linguists to agree with you. (Not one of the phoneticians referenced in chapter 5 had the identical list of English phonemes!) Classifying things is not "science." It is the first step to begin to do science.

Be that as it may, let's take a look at Goodman's research. In 1965, 1967, and 1969 (the only peer-reviewed research cited), he reported on errors children make when reading stories, which he calls "miscues." This is similar to the research described in chapter 2 on children's errors in decoding isolated words. Goodman became intrigued about why children don't rely more on context and grammar to avoid making mistakes. In other words, why do children read "nonsense words" or real words that don't make any sense in the context of the story? This is a very interesting question and completely amenable to scientific enquiry. For example, Goodman could have compared the number and type of miscues produced by children taught with different reading methods. Instead Goodman blames this on "phonics" instruction, and simply "talks" about these errors in subjective language:

> Patricia starts out her reading *preoccupied* with getting the words right. — *perhaps* her teacher has been *admonishing* Patricia and her classmates to say the final <t> and <d> ——since that's a phrase that *makes sense* to her. . . . She *seems to be trying* to do two things: get the words right and *make sense* of the story. But *she can't do both,* so she *swings from one way* of reading to the other.[1] [Italics mine]

How does Goodman know that Patricia is "preoccupied," or that her teacher has been "admonishing her," or that she is "trying to do two things," or "swinging" from one way to another? There are ways to find out if you want to do science. Otherwise you can just speculate.

Science is a search for the truth and open to falsifiability. If you never do scientific research, you can never be proven wrong. The truth is reached through the "scientific method." This method is procedural. It dictates the way studies to answer a particular question should be designed.

Another major error in some educational research has been to rely exclusively on average scores of small groups. If Classroom A scores at an average of six years eight months at the end of first grade, and Classroom B, using the new, revolutionary reading program X, scores at seven years, is this a difference that matters? To find out, each child's test score must be submitted to statistical analysis. This will tell you whether a pattern of reading scores could occur entirely by chance (random), or whether there is a consistent effect *caused* by the reading method. Statistics are based on the mathematics of probability. They allow the researcher to *predict* the likelihood that using reading method X would produce consistent effects again and again on different groups of children. This prediction cannot be based on "average" scores alone. The early Head Start research was riddled with this kind of reporting.

Statistics is particularly important in behavioral research because it allows scientists to use small populations (samples) and estimate what would happen if they had access to large populations, such as all the children in the state of New York. In the national literacy survey reported in chapter 1, they didn't need statistics to show our children were in trouble. They tested 140,000 children. With such large numbers, percentages or averages alone are sufficient.

As a point of information, all the research findings reported in this and the following chapters are "statistically significant" unless otherwise stated, meaning that the probability of a particular result is well above chance—nonrandom. A scientific "fact" is established when several research studies produce the same results.

Scientists try to be "objective" in that they accept their results even when the data go opposite to what was predicted. Scientific data are nature's way of knocking at the door and saying: "Hey, there's a real world out here, and it doesn't conform to what you think." This is not to say that scientists never have biases or hunches about their research. But real scientists are not wedded to their theories, and when the data run counter to these theories, they must change them to accommodate the data.

This does not mean that scientists don't make mistakes. Subjective bias can enter into the scientific process, even though scientists do their best to guard against it. It can affect the way you ask a research question. It can affect what you choose to measure and what you leave out. It can affect the way you interpret your data. This doesn't mean that the scientist is "dishonest," but it does mean that the real world has to knock louder and louder to be heard. In other words, it takes more research and a lot more time.

Before we move on to the true scientific breakthroughs in reading research, I need to dispel two powerful myths. One is that persistent reading failure is due to brain damage, and the other is that reading is encoded in genes.

If you have read the first five chapters carefully, you will now be way ahead of the game. You will have more insight into the complex nature of reading and how children fall through the cracks than some scientists working honestly and rigorously in the field right now. Let me explain why. You have seen the list of possible reasons why children might have difficulties learning to read. There are items on this list that most parents are well aware of, but some scientists forget all about, especially if they work from a clinical or "deficit" model. Stripped to its essence, this model relies on only two variables: (1) humans' ability to decode a writing system is determined by their brain and (2) whether or not someone was taught to read.

Thus poor reading is viewed as being a property of the child and as having nothing to do with current methods of reading instruction. The main reason for a persistent decoding problem is that you have something wrong with your brain. To explore the fate of this idea, let's begin with the modern research on "dyslexia."

IS DYSLEXIA A SPECIAL READING DISORDER?

"Dyslexia" is Greek for "poor with words" or "poor reading." "He has dyslexia" sounds medical and scientific. "He has poor reading" doesn't have quite the same impact. Like many medical terms, "dyslexia" merely describes a state of affairs and has no diagnostic validity. "Strabismus" means that your eyes are not properly aligned. But the word "strabismus" doesn't explain *why* your eyes are misaligned.

The term "dyslexia" was coined by a nineteenth-century ophthalmologist who noticed that some brain-damaged patients could no longer read. It was later popularized by Samuel Orton, a neuropathologist, who believed, on the basis of his observations, that severe reading problems were due either to cerebral dominance or to abnormalities of the language systems of the brain. Though Orton was right about the connection between language and reading, unfortunately these ideas led to the belief that poor readers have brain damage.

This belief reflects a serious misconception about the human brain, along with a failure to consider normal variation in traits. We call complex human traits *talents*. An inability to sing in tune is due to lack of musical talent, not to brain damage, and singing is far more natural (biological) than learning to read. Normal variation is on a *continuum*, but people working from a medical or clinical model tend to think in dichotomies: perfect/imperfect, healthy/diseased, intact/damaged.

We have just reviewed 5,500 years of evidence to show that writing systems are inventions, and that humans do not spontaneously and effortlessly develop writing systems or find it easy to learn them. We have seen that the alphabet is a particularly "nonnatural" writing system. Reading is definitely not a biological property of the human brain. If reading problems were due to brain damage, they would be immutable or only partially fixable. Progress would be slow and the client never really "cured." Some reading programs for "dyslexic" children take *years,* a self-fulfilling prophesy.

Of course humans use their brains to learn to read. We need the primary visual system (visual cortex) to see and discriminate letters on the page. We need visual-motor commands (frontal eye fields) to control eye movements to scan text smoothly from left to right. We need language systems to remember the order of words in phrases and to analyze meaning and grammatical structure (posterior left hemisphere). We need auditory analysis of sounds in words in order to use a phonetic alphabet (left-brain auditory cortex). We need speech output and articulatory control to read aloud (left-brain speech-motor systems). We need brain systems that *connect* all these processes (Wernicke's area, parietal lobes, and subcortical white matter). We need to keep our attention focused on what we are doing from one moment to the next (frontal lobes/basal ganglia), and if we're bad at something, it takes more effort (hippocampus) and more brain cortex to do it. Reading engages the entire brain. There is no "place" or "box" for reading in the brain. Only when a child shows a clear and enduring deficit in one of these natural abilities should parents be concerned about a possible "biological basis" for their child's reading problem, but a "biological basis" usually means normal variation, not brain damage.

Do dyslexics have brain damage? Twenty years of data from brain-imaging studies and electroencephalographic (EEG) recordings have shown conclusively that people diagnosed "dyslexic" have no damage to any part of their brain. Studies using modern imaging techniques such as computerized tomography (CAT) and magnetic resonance imaging (MRI) search for anatomical differences between poor and normal readers. So far, nothing has been found. The only result that is even marginally consistent is a tendency for poor readers to have more symmetrical brains. But 35 percent of the population have symmetrical brains. Symmetry is not pathology.

There is research on the microstructure of brain tissue on eight people who had reading problems as determined by school records. But there are serious methodological problems with this study. It wasn't possible to measure reading properly to verify the nature of their reading difficulties before the people died. Many had other brain-related problems that could affect the results, such as epilepsy, severe language disorders, and extreme old age. The researchers found greater brain symmetry and evidence of abnormal cell migration (ectopic nests) in the left hemisphere or in the right or in both. Whether these abnormalities correlate with reading or language or epilepsy is unclear.

There is an even more serious problem than trying to find "dyslexia" in the brain. A number of studies on very large populations of children show conclusively that the diagnosis of dyslexia or "learn-ing disabilities" is invalid. This calls into question all research on "dys-lexia." The diagnosis for many years was based on these assumptions: If a child has a serious reading problem, but normal or above-normal in-telligence, the child must have a special type of reading disability: "dyslexia." Children with low reading scores and low intelligence are supposed to read badly because they have low intelligence.

In 1975, Michael Rutter and William Yule reported their findings from several studies on large populations of children carried out in London and on the Isle of Wight. They were interested in whether there were two types of poor reader: children whose reading test scores were highly discrepant to their age and IQ ("specific reading retarda-tion") versus children with low IQs *and* low reading scores ("general reading backwardness"). They identified a group of children with ex-treme deviations between IQ and age and a reading score. For exam-ple, at age ten, the formula selected children whose reading test scores were thirty months below age and IQ.

Next, they plotted the reading test scores expecting to see a normal distribution predicted by the "bell-shaped curve." Instead, children with reading/IQ discrepancies had reading test scores that were abnor-mally distributed. Too many scores clustered at the bottom end of the curve, forming a "hump," or a discontinuity. In a symmetrical distrib-ution, only 2.28 percent of children should score in the bottom group. Instead, there were 1 percent (ten-year-olds) and 2 percent (fourteen-year-olds) more of the Isle of Wight children than expected, and 4 percent more of the London children (ten-year-olds) than expected. Rutter and Yule pointed out that these results were just as likely to be due to methods of teaching as to any biological factors.

To find out more about these two types of poor readers, they com-pared them to a control group of normal readers on a battery of tests. More of the low-IQ children had neurological and motor problems. However, poor readers, regardless of type, differed from the controls on these measures: family history of reading difficulty, family history of speech delay, first word spoken after eighteen months, first phrase spo-ken after twenty-four months, and current speech/articulation prob-lems. These language problems occurred in both groups of poor readers at three times the rate of normal readers. It is clear that speech delays are a predictor for subsequent reading problems. However, this does not mean that reading problems are always caused by speech de-lays *or* that speech delays are due to organic brain damage.

Rutter and Yule did not believe they had identified "dyslexia." They argued strongly against the vague definitions of "dyslexia" currently in vogue, and the idea that "dyslexia" is a unitary disorder with a high genetic component. Instead, they cite additional evidence to show that they also found strong environmental effects on reading, such as large family size, the child's temperament, and teacher turnover rate at the school. They also point out that if dyslexia was a true genetic "syndrome," then the heritability should be identical in different geographic regions. Yet the poor readers scoring in the bottom range were four times greater in London than on the Isle of Wight, evidence for an environmental effect.

They conclude as follows:

> In short, there has been a complete failure to show that the signs of dyslexia constitute any meaningful pattern. It may be concluded that the question of whether specific reading retardation is or is not dyslexia can be abandoned as meaningless.[2]

Rutter and Yule's clearly stated arguments were ignored, and instead, educators decreed that at last proof for "dyslexia" had been found. For almost ten years, no one even challenged their results. Everybody used a discrepancy measure to select subjects for research on reading disabilities, and to identify children for special reading services. The "discrepancy" model underpins U.S. federal guidelines for the diagnosis of learning disabilities in Public Law 94-142. This law provides funding to school districts for special education. The discrepancy measure is taken so literally in some school districts that a child with a high IQ, around 130, with an average reading test score of 100 (normal reading), would be diagnosed as LD and qualify for special services, but someone who had a very poor reading score, around 85, with a normal IQ of 95, would not. (Both sets of scores are standardized so that 100 is "average." Scores in the range 92.5 to 107.5 are normal.)

The first study to challenge Rutter and Yule's findings was carried out in Australia by David Share and his colleagues in 1987. After testing 1,037 children, they found no evidence for two types of reading disorder. They concluded that Rutter and Yule's results occurred because of an artifact of scoring in the reading tests they used. They argued strongly that a diagnosis for a "special" reading disorder must be based on other tests besides a reading test.

The remaining studies date from 1992. Jack Fletcher is one of the team leaders of the Connecticut Longitudinal Study which began in 1983. He and his colleagues reported on 199 poor readers, seven to nine years of age. They were divided into four groups on the basis of different statistical methods of computing a "discrepancy" between IQ and reading. A fifth group (controls) had no reading problems. All children were given a battery of nine tests, some of which were known from previous research to be related to reading. The discrepancy model did not hold up. Children with reading problems, regardless of IQ, all scored badly on one particular test which measures the *ability to hear individual phonemes in words,* a skill required by an alphabetic writing system, but by no other writing system. Children with low IQs did worse on a memory test, but otherwise all poor readers scored normally on the remaining tests.

Fletcher and his colleagues concluded that there is no evidence for any special type of reading disorder like "dyslexia" and that reading scores are on a continuum from good to bad. They comment that if children with lower IQs and reading problems were included in the LD diagnosis,

> this would mean that 25% of the population could be defined as reading impaired, a figure that would probably frighten policymakers and state-federal funding sources.[3]

(The national literacy survey data for Connecticut schoolchildren showed that 34 percent are below basic skills in reading.)

Fletcher was also a collaborator in a Canadian study with researchers at Windsor, Ontario. They tested 1,069 children referred to a clinic for reading problems. Children were between the ages of nine and fourteen years. The children were divided into four groups based on different calculations of IQ/reading discrepancy scores, and were given a battery of ten tests by the Canadian psychologists. All children with poor reading scores, regardless of IQ, regardless of group, did badly on the same two tests. One test measured the ability to blend isolated phonemes into words, and the other, the ability to decode letters into phonemes. Once again the results were the same, and the conclusion was that there is no basis for any special category of reading disorder.

Sally Shaywitz, project director, and other researchers on the Connecticut Longitudinal Study, followed children over time to see if the discrepancy diagnosis of "dyslexia" was constant from one grade to another. They tested the same children many times from first to sixth grade. Twenty-five children were diagnosed "dyslexic" in first grade, and 31 in grade 3, but only 7 were classified as "dyslexic" in both grades. The same thing happened at fifth grade. Of the 24 children classified as "dyslexic" at fifth grade, only 14 were also "dyslexic" in third grade. The chance of being diagnosed "dyslexic" in sixth grade as a function of being diagnosed "dyslexic" at first grade was only 17 percent.

Similar findings are reported by scientists Keith Stanovich and Linda Siegel, at the Ontario Institute in Toronto. They reanalyzed data from a data base of over 1,500 children, fitting poor readers into various groups based on discrepancy scores. They could find no differences in the performance of types of poor readers on a wide variety of tests, except for tests requiring the child to read phonetically spelled nonsense words. All poor readers had the same problems with these tests regardless of their IQ. Stanovich and Siegel conclude as follows:

> If there is a special group of children with reading disabilities who are behaviorally, cognitively, genetically, or neurologically different, it is becoming increasingly unlikely that they can be easily identified by using IQ discrepancy as a proxy for the genetic and neurological differences themselves. Thus, the basic assumption that underlies decades of classification in research and educational practice regarding reading disabilities is becoming increasingly untenable.[4]

Finally, a study on twins has been carried out by Bruce Pennington and his co-workers at the University of Denver. They tested 538 pairs of twins, dividing the children into four groups based on age, IQ, and reading scores. They had the same results. All poor readers, regardless of group, IQ, or age, had problems reading phonetically spelled nonsense words and nothing else. The authors concluded that there is no evidence for any test that can identify groups of poor readers who do or do not have a discrepancy between IQ and reading scores.

These studies sound the death knell of "dyslexia" and "learning disabilities" as a category of specific reading retardation. The truth is simply that if a child scores badly on a reading test, he or she has a reading problem and needs to be taught to read. There is no evidence from any of the studies or any of the tests that most poor readers have anything wrong with them, except the inability to read an alphabetic writing system, and this in turn is related to a difficulty in accessing the phonemic level of speech. In other words, children with reading problems have a hard time "ungluing sounds in words," exactly what the Brahmin priests must have predicted 2,500 years ago when they opted not to use an alphabet. Humans have no reason to "unglue" sounds in words unless they have to learn an alphabetic writing system. So whether or not this ability is brain-based or "genetic" is really moot.

A GENE FOR BAD READING?

The demise of the dyslexia diagnosis is a serious blow for heritability studies and genetic models of "dyslexia." These studies use a formula to diagnose "dyslexia" based on discrepancies between reading scores, age, and IQ. In family studies, a discrepancy score is used to identify children, their parents, and other family members. If scores are not discrepant, you are not included in the study.

Three scientists, Bruce Pennington, John DeFries, and Richard Olson, are studying heritability and genetics of "dyslexia." They have carried out a number of studies on families and twins. Their findings seem impressive. Thirty-five to forty percent of first-degree relatives of very poor readers also have a reading problem. Sons of affected fathers have a 40 percent risk, sons of affected mothers, a 35 percent risk. Daughters of affected mothers or fathers have a risk of only around 18 percent.

Studies on twins are a more powerful research design because monozygotic twins (one egg splitting) have 100 percent genetic inheritance, and dizygotic twins (two eggs) only 50 percent inheritance. Comparing the heritability of "dyslexia" in populations of the two types of twins, it was found that with IQ controlled (subtracted from the equations), "dyslexia" is 30 percent "heritable."

What does this actually mean? Superficially it means that you can predict a reading problem with 30 percent accuracy knowing the family history (30 percent genetic/70 percent environmental). This means, also, that the miss-rate in this prediction is 70%. However, there are two other factors to consider. Now that the diagnosis of dyslexia has been shown to be invalid, what would happen if all poor readers, regardless of IQ, were included in the heritability and twin studies? What, exactly, is being inherited, the reading problem, the discrepancy effect, or the inability to unglue sounds in words?

The second issue is that 43 percent of American fourth-grade children are below basic-level skills. You could predict that a child would be reading poorly in any household in America with 43 percent accuracy, knowing nothing about the family member's reading skills. There are 40 percent of children "below basic" skills in reading in Colorado, where many of these family and twin studies occur.

Nevertheless, something very interesting came out of these studies. In a twin study by Richard Olson and others reported in 1989, they found that "dyslexics" had difficulty ungluing phonemes in words and manipulating them. They couldn't use "pig latin." In pig latin, you remove the first consonant in a word, put it at the end, and add /ay/. 'Cat' in pig latin is "at-cay." The pig latin score was almost as powerful in estimating heritability as the reading score. Subsequent research on twins showed that "phonological decoding" had a heritability of around 80 percent, evidence for a genetic role in a *normal variation of a trait.*

Pennington, in his book on learning disabilities, reports on the efforts to discover what kind of gene mechanism or type of genetic transmission can explain how "dyslexia" is inherited. Here are two of his conclusions:

> It was estimated that dyslexia is linked to chromosome 15 in about 20% of families.

> Existing data support genetic heterogeneity in the transmission of dyslexia, and the recent analyses provide support for a partially dominant major gene or genes.[5]

In 1996, Pennington told a conference audience that there is a linkage of "dyslexia" to chromosome 6, but that dyslexia is complicated and we are unlikely to find only one gene.

Genes for Bad Reading?! If reading is a biological property of the brain, transmitted genetically, then this must have occurred by Lamarkian evolution. (In Lamarkian evolution, what parents learn during their lifetime is transmitted to their offspring, a theory for which there is zero scientific support.) A genetic model for reading cannot work by Darwinian evolution. *Homo sapiens sapiens* has been illiterate for more than 40,000 years, and universal education is only about 100 years old, much too short a time span for such a complex behavior to evolve.

Reading cannot be coded in genes anymore than other highly skilled behaviors. For example, skateboarding might be found to have high heritability. Obviously, what is inherited is not "skateboarding," it is the necessary aptitudes to *be able to skateboard.* It is these skills that are properties of brains, such as *balance* and *visuomotor* integration. If skateboarding was as highly valued socially as reading, it would be no more nonsensical to look for a skateboarding gene than a reading gene. Here are other possibilities of disorders that might be genetically transmitted:

dysmechanica: the inability to repair machines
dysmusia: the inability to read musical notation
dysmobilia: the inability to drive a car
dyscarpenteria: the inability to build things out of wood

Pennington doesn't really mean "dyslexia" is inherited, because he says: "—the final common pathway in most of developmental dyslexia is a deficit in phonological coding."[6]

In other words, Pennington recognizes that it is "phonological processing" (the auditory skill to hear and manipulate sounds in words) that might be inherited, and not reading. Pennington's use of habitual language trails behind what he actually thinks and knows. The problem here is that the layman, not familiar with twenty-five years of research, is confused by this habit. Parents or family members of poor readers need to know that there is no valid diagnosis of "dyslexia," no such thing as a "reading gene," and no such thing as "inheriting bad reading." Nor is a weakness in discriminating phonemes caused by organic brain damage.

Although it is meaningless to look for a "reading gene," subskills or aptitudes that are important to learning reading may be heritable, just as balance and visuomotor skills may be heritable. It is the *natural* abilities of people that are transmitted genetically, not unnatural abilities that depend on instruction and involve the integration of many subskills. This does not mean that these subskills are untrainable, or that they would spontaneously be brought to bear on a task when instruction was misleading. There is now an enormous literature on subskills related to reading. These studies will be considered next.

PHONOLOGICAL AWARENESS AND READING

Subskills important in learning to read were first studied using correlational research designs. Correlational research is used at the outset of scientific enquiry. It helps determine what things or events go together or "predict" each other. Here is an example of a simple correlation: The speed at which you drive to the supermarket is highly correlated to the time it takes to get there. Here is an example of a more complex relationship: Weight loss is correlated to the intake of total calories and fat calories, *and* to the amount of exercise you get, *and* to your basal metabolism or "set point."

Correlations don't allow you to determine *causes* of the relationships. You can get the flavor of this problem and the complexity created by correlational patterns if you ask these questions: Does metabolic rate cause eating which causes exercise which causes weight? Does weight cause exercise which causes eating which causes metabolic rate? Or, does exercise cause metabolic rate which causes eating which causes weight? I think you get the point. You can't discover causes just by calculating what goes together. The only way to answer these questions is to do an experiment: Change fat calorie intake, while you hold everything else (exercise, total calories) constant.

With these reservations in mind, correlations are a powerful tool for any initial inquiry. Experiments are only practical when all possible connections have been mapped out. You wouldn't want to waste time training poor readers' eyesight unless vision was correlated to reading. In the early stages of research on reading, scientists began by looking at simple relationships: does a single test score predict a single reading score? Many different tests were tried: eye-movement control, visual acuity, auditory discrimination, memory, vocabulary, IQ, and so forth. This was followed by more ambitious studies using several of these tests at once. Next came the "kitchen sink" phase, in which batteries of tests were given to large populations of children to find out what the tests had in common (which tests are redundant), and which test was the most *powerful* predictor of reading, the next most powerful, and so on. Finally, there is the "fine-tuning" period, which is where we are right now. Fine tuning can go on until everybody gets tired of it, or another breakthrough takes place.

In the research presented so far, we have seen that one subskill consistently predicted reading scores, and that is sensitivity to sounds in speech. "Phonological awareness" and "phonological processing" are major buzzwords in reading research today. The term "phonological" is broad and means any kind of analysis of sounds in words: syllables, syllable fragments, and phonemes.

During the mid-1960s/early 1970s, four important scientific discoveries took place. That these "discoveries" were, in fact, major breakthroughs has only been recognized for about ten years. This is an example of the real world knocking and only a few people listening. The research came from different parts of the country, conducted by people who had never met, and who were in entirely different disciplines.

Jerome Rosner was working at the University of Pittsburgh at the

Learning Research and Development Center. Rosner and his colleague Dorothy Simon began a quest to develop a test of auditory analysis that would correlate with (predict) reading test scores. They reasoned that as children needed to learn a phonetic alphabet, they would do this efficiently *only* to the degree that they could hear and manipulate sounds (phonemes) in words. Up to this time, simple auditory tests did not correlate well with reading.

They designed the Auditory Analysis Test (AAT) in which the child has to mentally "remove" a sound from a word he hears, close up the remaining sounds, and then repeat back the word that's left.[7] The simplest part of the test uses compound words. The tester reads the statement: "Say cowboy. Now say it again without the cow." The child must respond with the word that remains: "boy." The test has various levels of difficulty including removing the initial consonant ("smile without the /s/" = mile), removing a consonant from a cluster ("steam without the /t/" = seam), or removing an inner syllable ("continent without the /in/" = content).

Rosner and Simon gave this test to 284 children in kindergarten through sixth grade. The children were also tested on the reading subtests of the Stanford Achievement Test and the Otis Lennon IQ Test. Rosner and Simon found that the AAT was too difficult for kindergartners, but for the other children, the AAT scores were highly correlated to reading at every grade, with correlations ranging from .59 to .84. (A perfect correlation is 1.0.) The AAT was also correlated to IQ. This relationship was statistically subtracted to get a pure measure of the correlation between AAT and reading, independent of the children's intelligence. When this was done, the AAT and reading scores were still strongly correlated, with values ranging from .40 at first grade to a high of .69 at third grade. You can estimate the accuracy of predicting one score from another by squaring these numbers (.40 x .40, .69 x .69). These values range from 16 percent to 38 percent predictibility between scores on the AAT and scores on a reading test.

The order of difficulty of the forty items on the test was calculated:

1. Remove a word from a compound word
2. Remove the initial phoneme from a CVC word
3. Remove the final phoneme from a CVC word
4. Remove the initial phoneme from a cluster: CCVC
5. Remove an inner phoneme from a cluster: CCV or VCC
6. Remove an inner syllable from a multisyllable word.

Performance on this test was highly dependent upon the age of the child. The test was too difficult for most of the kindergarten children, and 60 percent of the first and second graders got only about half the items correct. After this age, the scores fit a normal distribution.

Rosner and Simon demonstrated that there was a powerful connection between the ability to *hear* and manipulate sounds in words (to unglue sounds) and the ability to read and comprehend text. But they were left with the tantalizing question: does some innate ability to hear sounds in words *cause* a child to be able to learn a phonetic alphabet, or does learning a phonetic alphabet *cause* a child to be able to hear sounds in words? "The logical position is that the two are completely interwoven," Rosner and Simon concluded in their discussion of the data.

Meanwhile, in a small university town halfway up the California coast, Pat Lindamood had another breakthrough. Armed with two masters degrees, one in reading and one in speech and hearing sciences, Lindamood opened a clinic for children in the sixties. Despite her extensive training, she found that most of what she had been taught was irrelevant, and nothing really worked at all for the serious cases of reading disability or speech disorders. Because she had two kinds of clients and two types of training, this allowed her to make connections that someone else might not have made. She observed that people with speech disorders had reading problems as well. Her initial insight came from an unanswered question: Does the person with a speech disorder suffer from a motor disability (an articulation or output dysfunction), as she had been taught, or do they also suffer from an auditory processing deficit (a perceptual or input dysfunction)? Could it be that the reason people with speech difficulties speak in such a peculiar manner, is because that's the way *they hear other people speak?* And could an auditory processing problem explain their inability to use a phonetic alphabet? Given these questions, how could you ever find the answer? All the tests and materials she had at her disposal required a spoken response from the client. This made it impossible to tease apart a motor dysfunction from an auditory processing dysfunction.

Lindamood pondered on this problem for months. One day she was working with a young girl with a severe speech disorder who was clearly in a state of despair and who could scarcely make eye contact. Lindamood's sense of frustration at her inadequacy was overwhelming. That night she awoke around 3:00 A.M. with an image of a row of colored blocks. She roused her husband Charles, a linguist, and together they worked until dawn on the basic elements of a test of auditory discrimination. This eventually became the LAC test (Lindamood Test of Auditory Conceptualization). Lindamood's reasoning was identical to Rosner and Simon's, that a valid test of auditory processing had to involve the manipulation of phonemes in words. Unlike Rosner, she couldn't use a vocal response to answer her particular question. Instead, she had clients represent sequences of phonemes *silently* as rows of colored blocks, first individually: /b/, /b/, /v/, and next in nonsense words in a sequence or chain. The tester says: "If that is /i/, show me /ip/. If that says /ip/, show me /bip/. If that is /bip/ show me /bop/" and so forth. Each sound is represented by a different color (any color will do) and blocks are added, exchanged, or removed as the chain proceeds.

This basic tool became the foundation of a new method not only for remediating speech disorders but for reading disabilities as well. Her initial insight was correct. Children and adults with speech deficits failed this test. They cannot speak clearly because they cannot *hear* speech clearly. Children who speak normally can also have serious reading problems, and many of these children, it turned out, also had weak phonemic processing skill but to a much milder degree.

In a team effort with Robert Calfee at Stanford University, the Lindamoods gave the LAC test to 660 normal children in kindergarten through twelfth grade. The children were also tested on the reading and spelling subtests of the Wide Range Achievement test. There were high correlations between the LAC scores and reading and spelling, ranging from .66 to .81. The average correlation between LAC scores and reading for the 660 children was .73. These values would be lower if the relationship of IQ to reading had been subtracted, but they are very similar to Rosner and Simon's results. They are also subject to the same criticism: there is no way to confirm the direction of causality based upon simple correlations.

On the opposite seaboard, in New Haven, Connecticut, research was being conducted at the Haskins Laboratory on the perception and production of speech by Alvin Liberman and Donald Shankweiler and their colleagues. Isabelle Liberman, a psychologist, and wife of Alvin Liberman, joined the faculty at the University of Connecticut and began an important collaboration on the relationship between the perception of speech and reading. Isabelle Liberman reasoned that there must be a connection between the ability to hear individual sounds in words and reading an alphabet writing system, but that this relationship was not obvious. Most poor readers speak normally and can recite the alphabet fluently. To decode an alphabetic writing system, you must be consciously aware of the order of phonemes in words. This aptitude is not essential to understanding speech which is produced in coarticulated chunks of sound, like syllables, words, and phrases. A. Liberman and Shankweiler proposed in 1967, on the basis of their extensive research on speech perception, that the language systems of the brain reorganize to process speech at the level of the syllable and not the phoneme. This topic will be revisited in the chapter on children's language development.

In research published by Isabelle Liberman, Donald Shankweiler, and their students, they attempted to discover which kinds of phonological processing were critical to learning to read. They explored sensitivity to rhyme, the ability to segment by syllables and by phonemes, the ability to remember the order of words in word lists, and the order of sounds in words. Their results revealed that children do not spontaneously learn to segment words into their constituent parts just because they are exposed to an alphabetic writing system. Many children are not even aware of a "word" as a separate unit of speech. Syllables (counting beats) are easier to segment than phonemes, and the ability to segment phonemes is predictive of subsequent reading skill. Liberman found that at the end of first grade, approximately 30 percent of children had *no understanding that words can be segmented into phonemes.*

Their research also indicated that poor readers had more trouble repeating back lists of letters or words in the correct sequence (spoon, tree, floor, dog, sheet, etc.), but no problem remembering sequences of environmental sounds (animal calls, bird calls, various noises), or visual patterns. The researchers concluded that children with reading problems have difficulty in one or more aspects of phonological processing. Liberman's extensive research and the number of graduate students she inspired to carry on this work are responsible for putting "phonological processing" on the map. These early studies have been supported by hundreds more from countries around the world.

In addition to the phonological processing and verbal memory difficulties in poor readers, there was one other discovery from this period that has stood the test of time. Patients with brain damage to the left hemisphere can have word-finding or "naming" problems. Martha Denckla, a neurologist at Columbia University's College of Physicians and Surgeons, reasoned that reading difficulties may be due to a language-based dysfunction. Therefore, children diagnosed "dyslexic" may also have problems in naming similar to those of brain-damaged patients. In particular, she was interested in "naming fluency" for well-known, overlearned ("automatic") words. In 1972, she published a test called Rapid Automatic Naming (RAN) along with test scores for children aged five to eleven years. The children had to name fifty squares of colors as rapidly as possible. The colors were red, green, blue, yellow, and black, arranged in rows and repeating randomly. The norms were used to compare children referred for reading problems. Ten percent of these poor readers were found to have abnormally slow naming times.

In 1976, Denckla and Rita Rudel expanded the test to include naming of pictures, letters, and digits. They tested 128 children, seven to eleven years old, diagnosed with "a learning disability" (LD) (either reading or math), and 120 average readers. Charts of pictures, letters, and digits were prepared in the same way, five different items repeated randomly for a total of fifty items. Denckla and Rudel found that the poor readers had the slowest naming speed, the low-math LD children were faster, and normal controls faster still. There was a strong developmental trend for children's naming speed to increase with age, and the naming fluency measure did not level out by eleven years.

More recent studies on naming speed, particularly the work of Maryanne Wolf, have shown that letter and digit naming speeds are more highly correlated to reading skill (correlations ranging from .50 to .57) than naming speeds for objects or colors, which correlate to reading at around .35 to .38, about a 10 percent prediction rate, which is what Denckla originally found. Naming objects and colors is a truer reflection of natural or biologically based ability than naming letters and digits, and though these correlations are low, they are consistent across many studies.

We now have evidence of the following tests correlating to reading scores: auditory analysis of phonemes, verbal short-term memory, sensitivity to rhyme, ability to segment syllables and phonemes, naming or word-finding speed.

These initial breakthroughs prompted other researchers to begin investigations of a variety of language-related abilities. There are now hundreds of such studies and it is only possible to summarize the findings. Tests that involve an analysis and manipulation of phonemes (phonemic awareness) correlate with each other. These are tests like Rosner and Simon's AAT, Lindamood's LAC test, tests of sounding out words (segmenting), combining individual phonemes into words (blending), pig latin, and so forth. All of these tests are measuring some aspect of the same skill, and any one of them is a powerful predictor of reading ability in absolutely everyone's data. This is the real world knocking with a sledge hammer.

The developmental aspects of children's ability to hear and discriminate phonemes in words have been worked out in detail by Margaretha Vandervelden and Linda Siegel, in Toronto. They tested children in kindergarten and first and second grade, and developed simpler tests for the younger children. They found that the sequence for being able to hear individual phonemes in simple, one-syllable words was initial consonant first (what's the first sound in 'bat?'), then final consonant, then vowel, and last, separating consonant clusters (what's the first sound in 'frog'?), which was the most difficult task of all. The most powerful predictor of reading and spelling for the younger children is a test of segmenting, and the most powerful predictor for the second graders was Rosner and Simon's AAT. This single test predicted second-grade reading scores at .85 and spelling scores at .78.

Sensitivity to rhyme has not been shown to be a powerful predictor. The Belgian psychologist José Morais found this was true for adults as well. He tested illiterate poets, none of whom had any difficulty rhyming, but who were unable to read. Other research has shown that neither simple rhyming tests nor syllable segmenting is a good predictor of reading test scores.

Tests that combine rhyming and memory are correlated to reading, but the data are conflicting. The first evidence for this effect was a study by Donald Shankweiler and Isabelle Liberman. They found that good readers were more susceptible to "rhyming confusion" when they were asked to repeat back letters that "rhymed": D C P G B, versus letters that did not: L H J F K. Later, Virginia Mann and Isabelle Liberman found the same effect with lists of rhyming words. However, David Share, Anthony Jorm, and their colleagues in New Zealand, using a much larger population of children, found that good readers were consistently *better* than poor readers in remembering sentences that rhymed. My students and I replicated this effect on ninety-four first graders who were asked to repeat back lists of rhyming words. Good memory for rhyming words was strongly correlated to reading skill but *only for girls*. The scores of the boys were uncorrelated.

The studies reported so far measure relationships between subskills and reading in real time. They measure what "goes together" now and not whether a particular test can predict reading scores *later* in time. This would involve measuring phoneme awareness in the first grade to see if it correlated to reading when children were older. A prediction over time provides tentative evidence for "cause," on the assumption that time does not go backwards. Several studies of this type have been carried out in the United States, England, Australia, Denmark, and Norway. They all report more or less the same result. The major predictor of reading skill from first grade (independent of reading scores themselves) is a test of phoneme analysis. These are tests like the AAT, the LAC, and segmenting and blending phonemes. Simple rhyming and syllable segmenting are not good predictors of reading scores over time.

However, while these predictions hold up well for about a year or two in the early grades, they do not hold up well over longer periods. For example, we found that LAC test scores at the beginning of first grade predicted reading test scores with about 40 percent accuracy at the end of the year, but did not predict reading scores when the same children were tested in third grade. This is a function of the rapidly changing skill in phoneme awareness in young children, and also of correlational research designs. As time goes by, *reading predicts reading* more than anything else. When two measures are nearly perfectly correlated, no other test score can contribute further to the relationship.

This does not mean that phonemic awareness becomes less important for poor readers as they grow older. Phoneme processing deficits of adult nonreaders were found in a landmark study by José Morais and his colleagues in 1979. They tested adult illiterates in Portugal who had never been taught to read, and compared them to other former illiterates who had been taught to read. They measured the ability to segment words into phonemes. The people who had been taught to read were superior on the phoneme segmenting tasks. Charles Read and three Chinese colleagues found that Chinese people who had originally learned to read by memorizing whole characters had poor aptitude to segment by phonemes. Those who learned with the aid of a phonetic alphabet had good segmenting skills.

Ilana Ben-Dror, Ram Frost, and Shlomo Bentin tested two groups of adult bilingual speakers of Hebrew and English. One group had learned to read and write English as children, and the other group had learned the Hebrew consonantal alphabet, where letters represent CV or VC units (diphones). They were asked to "delete the first sound" from spoken words. The group who had learned English writing first, deleted the initial consonant—/b/ in 'bat.' The group who had learned Hebrew first deleted CV diphones instead—/ba/ in 'bat.'

These studies show the strong impact of the type of writing system and type of instruction on the development of phonemic awareness—an environmental effect, and restates the point that you do not acquire this aptitude unless you need it. So far the evidence could support four possible conclusions:

1. The ability to access the phoneme level of speech is heritable. Phoneme awareness is on a continuum of innate ability (normal variation), and good/bad phoneme awareness runs in families, just as musical talent runs in families.

2. Phoneme awareness is acquired through learning an alphabetic writing system.

3. Phoneme awareness fails to be acquired in learning to read because the instruction is poor.

4. Phoneme awareness is excellent but never applied by the child as a decoding strategy.

I want to close this section with a cautionary tale to explain the fourth point. Having good phonemic awareness is no guarantee that someone will automatically use it. This connection is not a given.

Let me introduce you to Alice.

Alice was a subject in one of our research projects. At the age of six she scored at the top of almost every test we gave. Her vocabulary score placed her in the highly gifted range with a score of 140 (comparable to a 140 Verbal IQ). She was the only child we tested to score 100 percent on the LAC test of phoneme awareness. Her verbal and visual memory were excellent. Her reading score placed her a full year ahead for her age. By third grade, Alice was the second worst reader in two third-grade classrooms and was making no further progress. I also discovered that she got 100 percent correct on spelling tests on words she could not read (like Donny in the opening story).

When I retested her at third grade, I looked in detail at both sets of transcriptions of her errors on the reading test. It was almost as though no time had elapsed. Alice succeeded in reading only ten more words on the test. She made exactly the same mistakes on many of the same words that she made nearly two years before, reading 'grade' for *garage,* 'curl' for *cruel,* 'rake' for *wreck,* and 'incure' for *inquire.* When Alice got to a certain point on the test, she turned to me and said: "I can't read any more of these words because I have never seen them before."

Translated this means: "I can only read words that I have been individually taught. I have no understanding of the principles of a phonetic alphabet and cannot use these principles to decode unfamiliar words."

Alice was using a combination of two strategies. Most of her errors were whole word "guesses." Occasionally, she decided to slow down and "sound out" chunks of words (word-part assembling), but this didn't work much better. How could this have happened to someone who was predicted to be the best reader in the class, according to all her scores in first grade? Meanwhile, Alice had become a total nuisance in class, disobedient, disruptive, and sometimes rude.

I asked to work with her to discover more about the nature of her processing strategy. Before I report on what transpired in our sessions, I want to emphasize how important this case is for understanding the reading process. Since working with Alice, we have seen many "Alices" in our clinical research.

1. Children who are taught by the same teacher in the same classroom with the same method will, unless carefully monitored, adopt their own strategies for learning to read.

2. Children are surrounded by print. Many begin to try to read at very young ages. Letting them drift along using their invented strategies, without intervention, may harm them for life.

3. Children with high verbal intelligence and good visual memory can score in the normal or even superior range on reading tests in the early school grades, *despite* using a "whole word guessing" strategy. These children will go undetected until the second or third grade, when their memory capacity becomes overloaded.

4. When children begin to fail, their behavior deteriorates. Alice's parents had been asked to "think about whether she might be better off in a public school." (This private school prided itself on excellent SAT scores and college admissions.) Her misbehavior was an added impetus to get her out of the classroom. In a public school, Alice would be reading "at grade level" (according to test norms) whereas the children in this school were reading well above grade level. For Alice, "grade-level" (score of 100) is 40 points below her verbal IQ of 140.

5. Possessing *all* the talents to be an expert reader is no guarantee that you will use them if the teaching is inappropriate or inadequate. Alice's outstanding ability in phoneme analysis had never been engaged at any point in her reading instruction.

Alice's story continues. I became curious about what had become of her phenomenal ability. Had her phoneme analysis skill deteriorated over the past two years, withered away with disuse, or was it still intact? I got permission from her parents to work with her during the lunch hour. We used the Lindamood program, and as I proceeded through the step-by-step exercises, Alice continued to surprise me. Having worked for hours with poor readers, I knew how long it took for some of these exercises to be mastered. Alice mastered them immediately. After about six hours of work, she was reading (decoding) multisyllable nonsense words (pseudo-words) up to twenty sounds long ('pre-rauncherchoidingly') with no difficulty whatsoever, that is, as long as we were working with the movable alphabet tiles which had digraphs ch clearly demarcated from single letters. c

c	a	t
ch	a	t

Alice could even *create* these complex nonsense words and check me to see if I read them correctly. I couldn't trick her. But the moment we tried to move back to print on a page, she began to experience difficulty and promptly fell into her old routine of guessing whole words and assembling word parts. It was a habit reinforced by many years of practice and was now imbued with a visible sense of panic. This panic forced her on through the text at an ever-increasing pace, misreading word after word. To try to solve the problem, I forced her to stop at every misread word and represent it in the movable alphabet. This allowed her to experience a direct relationship between how the word looked on the letter tiles and how it looked on the page. But this activity was frustrating and took much longer to complete than the initial training. It provided me with keen insight into how difficult it is to shift a habit that had become so ingrained, even for a child of remarkable intelligence who could effortlessly decode phonetically, and who now had a complete grasp of the logic of the alphabetic code.

This story answers one more question raised at the beginning of this chapter. Yes, a child can fail to learn to read entirely by chance, unless the teacher is careful to monitor what each child is doing, *and* knows how to prevent bad habits from continuing. This makes it all the more important to teach reading correctly in the beginning, the focus of Section III. (A strategies test is included in chapter 11.)

The remaining topics in this chapter cover three areas of research that may be of concern to many parents and teachers. These are speech and language delays and their link to phonemic awareness and reading, the relationship between IQ and reading, and between vision and reading. The findings from these studies will be summarized briefly at the end of the chapter. If these topics are of little interest, you may want to skip ahead to the conclusions.

SPEECH AND LANGUAGE AND READING

We have already seen from Pat Lindamood's discovery that speech problems can be due to the inability to hear speech accurately. It is not surprising that children with speech and language delays have trouble with an alphabetic writing system. Severe and persistent inability to hear and reproduce speech sounds is a candidate for a possible biological marker for potential reading problems in some children. This does not mean that biology is destiny or that these problems are due to organic brain damage, because speech problems are remediable. It does mean, however, that if a child has speech difficulties, these could impact on reading if uncorrected.

So far, science has not resolved all the important issues on this topic. Research on language and speech development has been ongoing for decades, and the different types of disabilities have been well documented. Unfortunately, tests used to measure these types of disabilities are poorly designed and unreliable, and this makes it hard to determine which kinds of language and speech problems impact on reading and which do not.

Speech perception and production in early childhood is highly variable from one child to another. My students and I tested nearly 200 children aged three to seven years. The children were asked to repeat back forty nonsense words (in "Martian") which conformed to the syllable structure of English, gradually increasing in length and syllable complexity. They had to hear the sounds accurately and reproduce them. Three-year-olds performed erratically, scoring as low as one or two correct to over 75 percent correct. By the age of four the average was around 50 percent correct. At age five, the average was 75 percent correct. At age six, 80 percent of the children scored 75 percent correct or higher, and nearly half of the seven-year-olds scored at or above

90 percent. Table 6–1 illustrates the range of scores for each age group, as well as the fact that high individual variation in speech analysis and production is common throughout the period that children are beginning to read. (The nonsense word repetition test is in chapter 11.)

Accuracy in speech production continues to improve until adulthood and perhaps beyond. In 1971, Hull and others published the National Speech and Hearing Survey on 38,800 children, each individually tested on various measures of speech production by trained specialists. These data are illustrated in Figure 6–1. The children's speech was rated as "acceptable," "moderate deviation," and "severe." The figure illustrates a tradeoff. The number of children with "acceptable" speech increases with age, while the number in the other two categories declines. Severe speech problems dip sharply between the ages of six and eight. Girls have a consistent developmental edge in speech production and clarity, which may explain why fewer girls have severe reading problems, and also why reading difficulties have not been found to be "heritable" for girls.

Taken together, the findings show that the developmental path for speech and language is rapid in early childhood, that speech clarity continues to improve over very long periods of time, that speech perception and production varies *within* age groups until around age eight, and this is partly determined by sex. These complex factors make it difficult to predict language development from an early age. Dorothy Bishop and her group in England have found that just under half of the children referred at ages three and four for speech and language problems (those with normal IQs) spoke normally when they were retested

TABLE 6–1

Percentage of Children Scoring at Five Levels on the Nonsense-Word Repetition Test

	Range of Scores				
Age	Below 25%	25–49%	50–74%	75–89%	90–100%
3	27%	27%	36%	9%	0%
4	0	29	51	15	5
5	0	0	38	50	12
6	0	3	17	45	35
7	0	0	16	37	47

FIGURE 6–1

Articulation Development

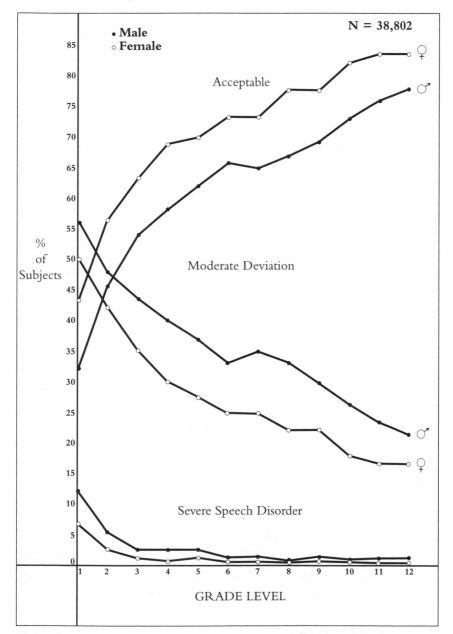

Adapted from F. M. Hull et al.(1971), The national speech and hearing survey, *ASHA, 3*, 501–9.

at five and a half years. When the children were tested again at eight years, only the children who still had speech difficulties at age five also had reading problems.

Research has been carried out on children with reading problems to see if they also have speech or language difficulties. The major finding has been that some poor readers have speech abnormalities. There is not a strong connection between learning to read and vocabulary skills. The relationship of reading and grammatical accuracy is much less clear. William Tunmer and his group found that if reading skill was matched in *older poor* readers to that of *younger good* readers, the poor readers performed significantly worse in tests of syntax (grammar), even though, being older, they had more experience with spoken language. They were less able to correct errors in word order: "The boy home goes," or to supply the correct missing suffix: "Sally went swim———," or supply the correct missing word: "Peter was born a long time ———." On the other hand, Donald Shankweiler and his colleagues found that what appeared to be a problem with syntax might actually be due to something else. They gave 353 children a number of tests of syntax, such as saying whether a picture matched a spoken sentence. The poor readers had trouble on only one test, which involved adding suffixes to words: four/fourth, five/fifth, courage/courageous, especially when the root word has to change: five/fifth. They found that scores on the suffix test were almost entirely predicted by phoneme awareness skill, whereas none of the other tests of syntax related either to reading or to phoneme awareness test scores. Obviously, the verdict is still out on this issue.

Lynn Snyder and Doris Downey studied thirty children, 8 years and 6 months to 13 years and 6 months of age, who were at least two years below grade level in reading. They were compared to normal readers on the Rapid Automatic Naming test, discussed earlier. They measured how long it took to initiate and execute each word in milliseconds. Poor readers as a group paused longer between words and took longer to pronounce each word. They were less efficient both in word finding and in speech production itself. However, there was no difference in *accuracy*.

Janet Werker and Richard Tees discovered that poor readers had weaker "categorical perception" of consonants. This is measured by varying consonant contrasts using a speech synthesizer, slowly changing a /ba/ into a /da/ in eight equal steps. Fourteen children, reading at least two years below grade level, were asked to make various comparisons of these consonant patterns. (Are the sounds the same or different? When you hear a change, press this button, etc.) They had more difficulty than normal readers comparing contrasts when the consonants were very similar to each other.

An extensive series of studies on children with speech problems has been carried out by Paula Tallal and her colleagues over a period of twenty-five years. She began with the question: What exactly do children with severe speech problems have trouble *hearing?* Using computer technology and a speech synthesizer, she was able to control the exact timing of various consonant-vowel combinations. She has now produced evidence for the following:

Children with severe speech problems cannot hear rapid transitions between patterns of sounds. They have particular difficulty telling consonant contrasts apart, such as noticing whether the sounds /ba/ and /da/ are the same or different. (Whether this problem is unique to speech or not is the topic of considerable debate.) These children perform normally with vowel contrasts. Their problem is restricted to an inability to hear rapid temporal patterns in complex sounds. The critical information in consonant contrasts like /ba/ and /da/ lasts only about forty milliseconds. When Tallal artificially slowed down these components tenfold by computer, the children could hear the difference easily, just like normal children.

Tallal also studied twenty children, eight to twelve years old, who were one to five years below grade level in reading, and attended a private school for "learning disabilities." Forty-five percent of these children were found to be worse than normal readers in discriminating rapid contrasts of complex speech-like sounds. The score on the auditory test correlated at .81 to a nonsense word reading test, and .64 to word recognition.

This problem does not appear to be due to a developmental delay. Even infants have little trouble discriminating between consonant contrasts. In fact, most children can tell consonants apart far better than similar vowel sounds, such as in the words /bet/ and /bit/. Tallal concluded that children with severe speech difficulties may have abnormal development of parts of the brain responsible for processing sounds with rapid transitions, areas in and around the auditory cortex of the left hemisphere.

The ability to detect finer and finer contrasts ("discrimination") is something our brains learn easily, and at all ages. Discrimination is highly trainable. People can learn to tell wines apart by developing their sense of smell. Artists, decorators, and others can discriminate very fine shades of the same color. The discrimination of musical pitch improves dramatically with learning to play a musical instrument, especially those you have to tune (guitar, violin). Recently, Tallal, in collaboration with Michael Merzenich, developed a computerized training game for children with severe receptive speech problems. The game artificially slows down acoustic components of consonants in connected speech until the child can hear them clearly. The speech sounds like it was recorded under water. During practice, the contrasts are gradually speeded up in a series of trials. With about sixty hours of training, the seven children in the study made two years of developmental gains in speech perception, and these gains held up at retesting three months later. Standard methods of speech therapy had failed. However, there is *no evidence* that there is any connection between this type of training and reading, despite a media blitz making this claim. Severe speech disorders affect a very small number of children, 3 percent or less according to the National Speech and Hearing Survey.

The final story is not yet in. So far, there is no definitive breakdown on exactly which children with which kinds of speech and language difficulties will have reading and spelling problems. In clinical observations, perhaps the most common auditory problem of poor readers is an inability to hear similar vowel contrasts: bit, bet, bat. Yolanda Post reported that very poor readers had difficulty hearing vowel contrasts and no difficulty at all with consonant contrasts. We have also observed in our clinic that children who appear delayed in speech development often learn to read just as quickly as children with no speech delays. These are children who are still saying "wabbit" at age six. Tallal reported that over 55 percent of the extremely poor readers at the school for LD children performed normally on her auditory tests.

The main issue for parents is that if their child's speech problem persists past the age of four, they should have the child tested and have speech therapy if necessary. Speech difficulties predict problems learning an alphabetic writing system. Equally predictive are the teaching methods currently used in most classrooms. If your child has a speech problem, he or she is in double jeopardy. The earlier the child is taken to a good reading clinic and taught to read *correctly,* the better. Information on how to find one is presented in chapters 12 and 13.

INTELLIGENCE AND READING

A major concern of parents and of researchers has been whether or not low intelligence leads to reading difficulties. The short answer is "no," unless a child is mentally retarded. Children with low or marginal IQs may be slow in word finding because of poor vocabulary or poor verbal memory, but although they may be slow in matching print to a word, they can still learn to read, if they are taught the code.

Intelligence is moderately and positively correlated to reading. Keith Stanovich and his colleagues compiled results from studies comparing Total IQ scores to reading ability, carried out during the years 1955 to 1982. Here are the median values for these correlations for each grade level: grade 1 = .45, grade 2 = .47, grade 3 = .45, grades 4 to 8 = .60 and grades 9 and above = .66. This tells us that IQ becomes more closely connected to reading with age. This would be expected, as IQ scores are impacted by what you learn at school, and what you learn is related to how well you can read. A major problem with these studies is that reading tests at the higher grades include measures of comprehension, verbal reasoning, and spelling. This makes it difficult to know which intelligence subtest is correlated to which kind of reading test.

The IQ subtest with the highest correlation to Verbal IQ is a vocabulary test. For this reason, vocabulary tests are often substituted for Verbal IQ in research on reading. The most reliable vocabulary test is the Peabody Picture Vocabulary Test (PPVT). In this test, the child hears a spoken word and must point to one of four pictures that matches the word. Tests that require the child to *read* are, of course, invalid as a measure of vocabulary for a poor reader or a nonreader.

Stanovich and his group presented data on forty-nine first graders, who were tested individually on a variety of tests, including the PPVT. Vocabulary was correlated to reading comprehension (Metropolitan) at a very modest .34, showing only about a 12 percent connection between the two skills. Further, they found that vocabulary scores were unrelated to performance on any other reading tests or phonological processing tests.

Recent longitudinal studies show little support for the impact of Verbal or Performance IQ on reading scores. In 1989, Hans-Jorgen Gjessing and Bjorn Karlsen published their results on 3,090 children in Bergen, Norway, who had been tested since 1977. These children carried out hundreds of tests over that period. Gjessing and Karlsen, along with various collaborators, focused most of their efforts on a group of severe "dyslexics," who constituted 6.6 percent of the sample. This group was compared independently to another group classified as "mentally retarded" (1.6 percent of the population) and to normal readers. Correlations for the dyslexic group were computed between intelligence tests (Total score, Verbal and Performance subtests) and reading and spelling. The correlations ranged around a low .30 (9 percent of the variance).

The Norwegian children identified as "dyslexic" in grades 1 and 2 were given remedial instruction and followed on to grades 3 and 4. The authors looked closely at every measure in order to determine the best predictors for successful response to remedial help. The IQ score showed no prediction whatsoever. Furthermore, they also found no support for a special "dyslexic" type based on a discrepancy measure, confirming the research cited earlier. The highest predictors for successful response to remediation were tests classified as "complex phonological functions," in other words, tests of phoneme awareness.

Richard Wagner, Joseph Torgesen, and Carol Rashotte studied 244 Tallahassee school children from kindergarten to second grade. One of their measures was the vocabulary subtest from the Stanford-Binet IQ test. Vocabulary correlated to reading in kindergarten at .26, in first grade at .36, in second grade at .48. However, they found that vocabulary scores did not predict reading later in time either from kindergarten to first grade, or from first to second grade. The strongest single predictor was a test of phoneme awareness similar to the AAT.

My students and I tested ninety-four first-grade children on a battery of reading predictors including the Peabody Vocabulary test. The Peabody test scores were uncorrelated to reading scores, nor did vocabulary predict reading ability in a group of forty-two children who were followed over the year.

By contrast, Lynette Bradley and Peter Bryant in Oxford, England tested children between four and five years of age and followed them for three years. They found that vocabulary was *the* strongest predictor of reading skill, and IQ added even further to this prediction. These robust effects have not been found in most other countries and may be due to something different about the English educational system, or the English tests. In another study by the same group, children were followed across the ages of four to seven years. As mentioned earlier, the mother's education predicted 40 percent of the score on a reading test, and IQ added another 15 percent to this prediction.

Apart from the findings in England, most studies show that intelligence impacts marginally on reading skill. Vocabulary does not predict early reading skill, but is more highly correlated to reading in older children and adults, probably because reading a lot improves vocabulary. Nevertheless, as we have seen, a child or adult can have high intelligence and an excellent vocabulary and still have a serious reading problem.

VISION AND READING

Research on vision and reading has been extensive because reading begins with visual perception of letter forms. One impetus to the study of vision and its connection to reading was due to technical advances in eye-movement recording devices in the 1960s. It was soon discovered that poor readers had erratic eye-tracking patterns when they read. They did not scan the text smoothly, they repeated fixations, their eyes frequently jumped backwards, and so forth. Today, everyone agrees that eye movements do not cause reading problems, but that reading problems cause erratic eye movements. In 1985, Keith Rayner did a simple but elegant experiment to prove this point. He had poor readers read very simple text, well within their ability level. Their eye-tracking patterns were completely normal. Next, he had good readers read very difficult material. Their eye-tracking patterns became erratic and looked just like those of the poor readers.

Let's be clear about what is and is not important in this research. To see objects in the normal world, eyes scan in multiple directions. Scanning in straight rows from left to right, down one line, etc., is unnatural and must be trained in a child learning to read. Smooth and efficient scanning develops slowly over childhood.

Reading therapists report that a small minority of poor readers have serious trouble scanning print from left to right. These children are unable to maintain binocular fusion (both eyes consistently in focus) while the eyes are scanning rows of print. This sends the print in and out of focus. Research support for this clinical observation has been provided by J. Stein and M. Fowler at Oxford University. Older children with severe reading problems were compared to younger good readers, matched for reading ability. The older poor readers had poorer binocular control, and visual training *alone* improved reading test scores for these children.

Children with serious problems in binocular control tend to telegraph this in noticeable behaviors. They frequently rub their eyes, squint at the page, cover one eye or turn sideways to read, or move their head from left to right instead of their eyes. Any one of these behaviors, if persistent, is an indication that parents should have their child tested by an optometrist specializing in diagnosing and treating visuomotor problems. Binocular fusion and controlled scanning are highly trainable.

Most of the time, when children show erratic, unplanned or unsystematic eye movements as they read, they do not necessarily have something wrong with their eyes. It's not the eye-movement control that's the problem, reading is the problem. Poor readers, like Albert, who look at the first letter of the word (in focus), and then globally scan to estimate word shape and length (out of focus), also have strange eye-movement patterns. These are caused by a *strategy* problem and not an eye-movement control problem.

Scores of studies on the relationship of vision and reading were based on the popular belief that "dyslexics" see letters upside down or backwards. Young children sometimes write letters backwards or in mirror image transformations, because they look at visual patterns globally and not in a sequence. But they do not confuse letters when they are asked to compare them. They can tell you that **b** and **d** are different. Robert Calfee and his group at Stanford, discovered that young children rapidly outgrow any tendency to confuse the orientation of visual symbols. Nevertheless, this belief spawned surveys on children's eyesight and its connection to reading.

In the study on Norwegian children, H. Aasved reports on visual screening of 2,590 children. Children were classified into five groups according to reading ability. There was no difference between the groups on any of the visual tests, which included stereopsis, measures of strabismus, convergence, and central suppression. A group of 259 children classified as "dyslexic" were compared to a group of normal readers. There was no difference between the two groups in the incidence of abnormal eye conditions. Included were measures of acuity, refraction error, strabismus, squint, convergence, accommodation, fusion, stereopsis, eye dominance, and reference eyedness. This was true even when the dyslexics were separated into subtypes. Visual problems were no more evident in the "visual subtype" than in any other subtype. When Aasved measured the progress of dyslexic children in remediation compared to their visual sensory function, no prediction was found between a prior eye condition and reading progress. He concluded: "Dyslexic children did not differ from other children with regard to eye characteristics. Most children with eye problems do not have dyslexia. In general, there appears to be no particular causal relationship between eye characteristics and reading and spelling difficulties."[8]

In the same study, Gjessing divided poor readers into categories or subtypes based upon a battery of tests. He found a small group of children with particular problems in visual memory and visual processing. They had trouble on various spelling tasks, difficulty in copying and identifying letters, and appeared to have visual confusions when they read text. They were normal on auditory/phonological tasks. This group consisted of only 10 percent of the "dyslexic" population, who, in turn, constituted only 6 percent of the entire sample. Ten percent of 6 percent is less than 1 percent of all schoolchildren. If only a fraction of the population has visual problems, they aren't going to be observed very often.

These findings cast strong doubts on claims that poor readers as a group have problems fixating, controlling vergence movements of the eyes, and abnormal occulomotor dominance. I would be just as cautious of any statements that reading upside down and wearing colored lenses "cures dyslexia." There is little research support for these claims.

CONCLUSIONS

Here is a summary of the findings so far.

Children with reading problems do not have brain damage.

There is no diagnosis and no evidence for any special type of reading disorder like "dyslexia."

There is no logic to the notion of a gene for "bad reading." Genes do not code complex skilled behaviors that have to be taught. Genes code natural subskills which are combined to produce that behavior.

Of all the subskills measured by the hundreds of tests that have been given over the past twenty-five years, tests of phonemic analysis or phonemic awareness are consistently the most predictive of reading skill. No other type of test comes close in predictive power. Yet, phonemic awareness is also enhanced by learning to read an alphabetic writing system (an environmental and not a biological effect). We will see in chapter 8 that phoneme awareness is also highly trainable.

Children with severe speech problems have trouble hearing rapid transitions between individual speech sounds (and other sounds). In some cases this is not caused by a developmental delay, because even infants can hear these transitions. This problem is remediable with proper training. Children with more minor speech problems generally grow out of them. In the Hull study illustrated in Figure 6–1, 13 percent of boys and 7 percent of girls were classified as "severe" in speech production at age six. Yet only 3 percent of both sexes were found to be "severe" at age eight.

Most children with reading problems do not have speech or language problems.

In general, IQ does not predict reading skill unless the IQ is so low that memory and vocabulary are severely impaired. If a child with a low IQ has reasonably intact language skills, the child can be taught to read. It may take a little longer, or the child may read a little slower, but fluency will improve with time.

Visual problems are not a factor in the vast majority of children with poor reading skills. However, maintaining binocular fusion while scanning from left to right is unstable in early childhood, and a small minority of children will have problems focusing as they read. This is easy to spot because it is accompanied by noticeable behaviors. Visual scanning and binocular control are trainable by optometrists specializing in this problem.

In the following chapter we look at developmental research which provides important clues for curriculum development and setting up a sequence of instruction.

Chapter 7

THE CHILD'S MIND AND READING

A friend related this experience at a scientific meeting. Jim was attending a three-hour symposium on child development. On the stage were several leading experts in the field of child psychology seated at a long table. The room was packed with eager listeners. After hearing the first speaker, Jim began to feel slightly uncomfortable, because he couldn't quite see the connection between the speaker's point of view and his own extensive experience with his four children. His feeling of discomfort didn't go away. Instead, it mounted with each speaker, until at the end of the symposium, Jim was in a state of bewilderment and confusion. The experts seemed to be doing research on robots, making all sorts of assumptions about children that were simply untrue, such as believing that kindergartners can be tested for one to two hours at a stretch and produce reliable data. He wondered if any of these speakers had ever actually met a child.

At question time, Jim put up his hand. He had one question for all of the speakers on the platform: "Do any of you have children?"

To his amazement, not one of them did!

In the last chapter, I mentioned that in research on reading, the child is often left out of the picture. Sure, children are given batteries of tests, on auditory perception, eyesight, IQ, memory, reading skill, and so forth. But there is rarely any mention of what might be going on in a child's mind, or how children *think* when they are learning to read.

In chapter 2, we saw that children were using different strategies in response to the *same* instruction. Sally did what her mother told her to do, basically ignoring what the teacher was saying. In the same class, Nigel faithfully adhered to the teacher's advice: guess words in context as if random letter sequences were "logographs." When an unfamiliar letter sequence standing for a new word appeared on the page that wasn't stored in Nigel's brain, he couldn't read the word. He had no way to begin and he didn't even try. He just got mad.

Albert liked to figure things out for himself. He discovered, completely on his own, that beginning letters stood for the beginning sounds in words. Albert was actively problem solving. Nigel was not.

Sam interpreted his basal-reader phonics lessons absolutely literally. He thought that various short letter sequences like 'ing' (two sounds) and 'unch' (three sounds) stood for only one "sound" in words, and that the number of these letter patterns and sounds was likely to be infinite. He could never have put it this way, because children are very bad at explaining how they think. At the rate he was going, Sam probably thought that learning to read could take a lifetime.

Our research on children's strategies showed that whether the child was using an effective or ineffective strategy was not caused by an inability to analyze sounds in words, or weak vocabulary skills. In fact, children with the *worst* strategies, had the highest vocabulary scores. These children seemed to be relying on their excellent vocabulary to *guess* words in context. When reading instruction is inadequate, incomplete, or misleading, children can adopt a particular strategy by relying on their most efficient skill or more or less by chance. Children can follow blindly, but most actively try to figure out what to do.

Children are not empty vessels waiting to be filled. Children have expectations. My son, age five, announced at breakfast one morning that he was quitting school. As he put it: "I have been in school a whole week. It seems like a hundred years, and I haven't even learned to read." In first grade, when he did learn to read, he informed us again that he was quitting school. Now that he had learned to read he could teach himself what he wanted to know. Nothing would convince him that his teachers might teach him something interesting he hadn't thought of yet.

Children are not robots. They are active and inquisitive learners. They do not all do exactly what the teacher is telling them to do, especially when what she is telling doesn't work. Children go home to families at the end of the day. Moms and Dads, as well as reading tutors, say many things about learning to read that can directly contradict what the teacher is trying to teach. From these various pieces of information, plus their own analysis of the problem, children try to "make sense" of their experience and what they are being taught. After all, it's what they have been doing almost since the day they were born.

In this chapter we will be examining those developmental issues which directly impact on learning to read. The way skills develop over childhood determines the appropriate sequence of reading instruction.

MAKING SENSE OF THE WORLD: INITIAL STEPS IN A SYSTEM OF LOGIC

There is a consensus in developmental psychology that children have different patterns of thought and process information differently at different ages. Children learn some things much better at younger ages than they do when they are older, something that Maria Montessori observed and called "sensitive periods," and scientists now call "critical periods."

According to Jean Piaget (who did have children), a child's first task is to develop an inventory of his body and his motor capabilities, and then learn how to integrate movement with sensory impressions in order to create perceptual "schemas." Schemas are concepts, or frameworks, for building knowledge about the world. Piaget called this first phase the "sensorimotor" period. By "motor" he did not necessarily mean physical action. You can learn about an object by *moving* your eyes around it. In fact, if you don't move your eyes you can't "see" it. Experiments have shown that when eye movements are temporarily stabilized, the world disappears. Blind children "see" objects by *moving* them around in their hands.

Piaget carried out extensive research on the performance of children in tasks of logical-mathematical reasoning, such as understanding the properties of objects and object relations in the physical environment. The importance of his work to teaching a writing system is that every code also has a logical structure. This is called a "mapping relationship," as described in chapter 5. For this reason, Piaget's discoveries are important in understanding the child's emerging skill in discriminating sensory elements and written symbols, and her ability to fathom the logical structure of the spelling code.

Piaget has been under attack from experimental psychologists for about forty years. There is no space here to enter into this debate, except to say that there are problems with Piaget's estimates of the average ages at which his tasks could be solved. In cross-cultural studies, ages vary by as much as four years, and this is strongly determined by the type of education the child receives. Piaget developed a stage model, arguing that stages remain invariant, regardless of age or culture. That is, stage 1 comes first, stage 2 next, and so forth. In a paper by myself, Karl Pribram, and Miriam Pirnazar, we reviewed evidence to suggest that Piagetian "stages" (meaning levels of skill and understanding) are reinvoked every time you learn something completely new, even if you're an adult. The difference is, you run through the stages much faster.

A related difficulty for Piaget's model is shown in studies where children (and adults) can use higher levels of logical reasoning when tasks are based upon something *familiar,* but use lower levels on unfamiliar tasks. No doubt this debate will continue for decades to come, unfortunately without Piaget's brilliant participation. Despite the debate and the problems with aspects of Piaget's model, no one has been able to come up with a better one, and no one has done more to provide an analysis of the different types and levels of children's logic, such as their understanding of reversibility, transitivity and class inclusion.

What does any of this have to do with a writing system? Earlier, you met the Sumerian boy Enkimansi. In the Sumerian school the children copied symbols from clay tablets and then recited the words or sounds that they had written. Each day was spent in exercising this reversible process: copy-recite, recite-copy. This provides a concrete understanding of the basic logic of a writing system: reversibility. It works in two directions: decoding/encoding.

But Enkimansi's story teaches something more. While I was doing research for this book at the Bodleian library in Oxford, I had my first encounter with authentic Old Saxon writing. Figure 7–1 shows an example of it, from Alfric's "Grammar" circa 990 A.D.

I had a little paperback book which allowed me to translate each Old Saxon letter to its modern English equivalent, along with a pronunciation key. I memorized this without much trouble, because many of the letters are the same. However, I found that I was completely unable to read Old Saxon phonetically from text. I literally couldn't *see* where one letter stopped and the other began when they were combined into words, especially as words wrap around lines and are often joined together. I found this very frustrating.

Fortunately for me, the Bodleian Library doesn't permit readers to make photocopies of ancient documents. If you want to study the documents, you order photographs (which are expensive) or you copy

FIGURE 7-1

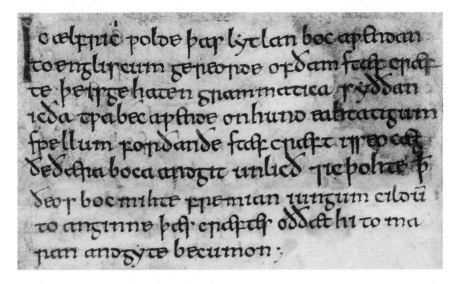

Photo reproduced with permission of the President and Scholars of St. John's College, Oxford.

Ic aelfric wolde thas lytlan boc awendan to englishum geweorde of tham staef craefte the is gehaten grammatica sythan ic tha twa bec awende on-hund eahtatigum spellum forthan the staef craeft is seo caeg the thaera boca andgit unlicth and ic thohte that deos boc mihte fremian iungum childum to anginne thaes craeftes othaet hi to maram andgyte becumon.[1]

[I, alfric would this little book to translate to English words of the letters craft that is called grammar since I (into) two books translated eighty ser-mons, because the letters craft is the key which these books understanding unlocks and I thought that this book might help young children to begin this craft until they to great understanding come.]

them by hand. To my surprise, once I began copying text, I was able to "see" each letter clearly. It didn't take long before I could read Old Saxon fluently, though not with the correct accent, or much under-standing of the words.

This is a perfect example of sensorimotor integration. It was the *movement* I made with my hand combined with the visual comparison of my writing with the print on the page (eye movements scanning the letters) that forced me to really look, and allowed me to "see" the let-ters. I became aware of how the letters were formed by the writer, and that there was an efficient and an inefficient way to write them, such as a vertical stroke first, horizontal next, or vice versa. In a fairly short space of time, the individual letters seemed to pop off the page, rather than being blurrily wedged in words. This is what Piaget would call a "transformation," the creation of a new schema. And it doesn't go away. Even though I don't look at Saxon script for months at a time, the moment I look at it, I "see" it just as vividly.

What this experience shows is that "sensorimotor" learning can occur at any age, and that it is a necessary first step to learn any task with which you are completely unfamiliar. Remember when you first learned to drive, and every movement and every perception was completely (overwhelmingly) conscious? Once the individual movements are mastered, and the timing of those movements with the perception of landmarks, stop signs, and other moving vehicles is integrated, a "transformation" takes place. When this happens, everything appears to run off automatically, without the need for conscious reflection. It's only when the road conditions become dangerous that you suddenly become acutely conscious, and you realize that "something" in your brain had been monitoring everything all along, otherwise you never would have noticed the danger.

This transformation of an acquired skill into a semiautomatic process has been measured in the brain. A skill that has become automatic uses fewer neurons and the brain needs far less glucose ("brain food"). When scientists first began to use positron emission tomography (PET), which measures glucose uptake in various regions of the brain, they were amazed to find that if you are "good" at something, reading for example, fewer brain regions are active, and neurons need less glucose to do it. If you are bad at something, huge areas of the brain gobble glucose. The brain lights up like a Christmas tree. Previously, people thought that the better you are at something, the more neurons in your brain are involved and specialized for that task. Instead, it turns out that the better you are at something, the *less of your brain is actively involved*.

It makes sense when you think about it. The neurons of the brain reorganize through facilitating new connections into efficient neural networks. This is just as Piaget suggested by his concept of higher-order schemas. Computer programmers call these schemas "subroutines." You can drive a car along a highway, listen to music on the radio, carry on a conversation with your passenger, and drink coffee at the same time. Some people shave and talk on a cellular phone while they negotiate heavy traffic! This is because all of these activities have been turned into semiautomatic subroutines through practice. When this happens, the brain can handle multiple subroutines at the same time and switch attention from one task to another almost instantaneously.

Here is the main message of this section. If you want a child to be a good reader, a good speller, and a creative writer, then your first goal is to create efficient and automatic subroutines in the sensorimotor skills that should not require overt attention, such as encoding and decoding. An efficient reader looks at text and does not see letters, nor does she see words; she experiences *meaning* directly. An efficient writer puts *meaning* on a piece of blank paper, not letters and words. He has to stop and think only when he is unsure of a particular spelling or is seeking for a particular word to convey a special meaning. You can't get to meaning unless everything else is efficient and automatic. This is why whole language doesn't work. The important subskills are never put in place.

Let's look at the subskills a young child needs to master even the simplest type of writing system:

Sensorimotor Processing

1. Auditory discrimination of the exact sounds in speech which the letters represent. Occurs by listening and through kinesthetic or motor feedback from articulation of speech sounds. "Say /m/. Watch my mouth. Feel your lips close to make this sound."
2. Visual discrimination of letter shapes. Occurs by eyes moving around the shapes and by hands copying them.
3. Putting letter shapes in a left-to-right sequence across the page. Occurs by copying or writing letters in a left-to-right sequence, training eyes to move from letter to letter.
4. Cross-modal association. The integration of these new skills, one auditory, and one visual, into a cross-modal schema. Sounds are matched to letters; letters are matched to sounds.

Logic

1. *Symbolization*. Know that an abstract symbol can stand for a sound in speech.
2. *Transitivity*. Know that this symbol can stand for that speech sound in all words and *anywhere* in the word: beginning, middle, end. <u>b</u> stands for /b/ in 'big' 'boy' 'cab' 'about.'
3. *Reversibility*. Know that the code is reversible. You can "read" (decode) letter sequences into sounds in words, and write (encode) the sounds in words into letter sequences.

The more that these new sensory units are anchored in something *already known,* the better and more efficient the learning. An alphabet script uses abstract visual patterns to represent phonemes in speech. The primary sensory components of the task are the *sounds the child already makes when he talks.* For the adult with a severe reading problem, these sensorimotor schema are missing and must be put in place. It is never too late to do this.

So far we have only discussed the simplest level of logic. We have introduced a writing system that involves 1-to-1 mapping only, which is *concretely* reversible. The letter b̲ *always* stands for the sound /b/, and the sound /b/ is *always* spelled by the letter b̲. The English alphabet code, however, is not this simple, and the reversibility of the code can get lost unless great care is taken.

LOGICS FOR THE ADVANCED CODE LEVEL

Young children have difficulty handling more than one sensory dimension at a time. A child may be able to sort objects easily by color alone, or by shape, or by size, but cannot solve the task: "put the largest red squares in the box." "Red squares" as a portion of "all squares" represents what is known as a class inclusion problem, a type of problem that Piaget studied extensively. One of Piaget's class inclusion problems goes like this: "Imagine I have a lot of flowers. Some of my flowers are yellow. Do I have more *flowers* or more *yellow* flowers?"

This problem can be diagrammed like this:

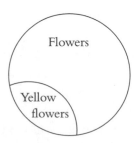

Piaget found that Parisian schoolchildren couldn't solve this problem until around the age of nine. Others have found that by changing the wording ("larger number" instead of "more"), this problem can be solved at younger ages.

Categorical language is also slow to develop. Eleanor Rosch showed that during language acquisition children first learn "basic level" category words. Children notice and remember words like "dog" but not "collie," "tree" but not "oak." Stephen Pinker points out that basic level category words also contain the maximum amount of information. They are not too general ("plant") or too specific ("dwarf rhododendron"). Children also learn names for category members. "This is my dog. His name is Rover." They don't learn words that represent complex categorical relationships and cannot fathom these relationships, such as "Rover is a cocker spaniel, a breed of dog, and member of the animal kingdom."

As children start to master simple category relationships, a system of logic begins to develop. Logic in the Piagetian sense means an understanding of "the way entities are put together." Francis Richards and Michael Commons have continued the analysis of logic based upon Piaget's model. They emphasize Piaget's important point that subsequent abilities are *always* based upon preceding abilities.

> Learning is possible if you base the more complex structure on simpler structures, that is when there is a natural relationship and development of structures.[2]
>
> —Piaget, 1964

This means that to handle the complex logic of our alphabet code, the child must have mastered each level of complexity in carefully sequenced steps. It does *not* mean that the child needs to know the logic in any formal sense. However, as Richards and Commons note, "Each of these logics is based on abilities to detect, measure, and relate the features of an environment." Children must be able to *hear* phonemes, *see* letters and letter patterns, know their extent (how many/how much), and relate these "features" to one another. When there is a one-to-one match between these features, this is known as an "equivalence" relationship. The relationships are perfect and mutually imply each other (1-to-1 mapping).

The more advanced levels of logic in our alphabet code are known as the logics of "classes" and "relations." "Classes" simply means categories where objects or events that share similar properties are grouped together ("all the red ones"). Relations refer to relationships within and between categories. In relational logic, objects share certain features but not all features: Most birds have beaks, feathers, wings, and fly. A penguin has a beak, furry feathers, wing-like flippers, and doesn't fly. Is a penguin a bird? Is a penguin a "kind of" bird? Is a penguin something else?

An analysis of the complex "relations" between sounds and letters in the English spelling code is illustrated in Table 7–1. The chart shows one example: using the *sounds* /i/ (sit) /e/ (bed) and /ie/ (tie), the *letters* i and e, and how these units are related across several transformations.

These complex patterns of relations occur with most vowel spellings and some consonant spellings. Nearly half of the sounds in English are mapped to digraphs. Digraphs *reuse* two letters to stand for a different sound. This means that a letter can be in two categories at the same time. In one category the letter exists by itself: t, and in the other category it can only function as a member of a pair: th.

The digraph problem fits a higher level of logic called "propositional logic." Propositional logic involves *integrating* the logics of classes and relations, the ability to simultaneously think of the same entity in two or more combinations. In formal statements of propositional logic, these combinations are connected by relational terms such as **"and,"** **"not,"** **"or,"** **"if—then,"** and **"if and only if."** The digraph problem is stated accurately as:

If the letter t is followed by an h, **then** say /th/ (thank); but **if** the letter t is followed by any other letter or no letter, **then** say /t/ (tank, bent).

Here is a more familiar problem in the same type of propositional logic:

1	This is one
2	This is two
12	This is ??
21	This is ??

TABLE 7–1

Mapping Complexity for a Set of Sounds and Letters

Sound	Spelling Alternatives			
/i/	i (bit)	y (gym)	ui (build)	
/e/	e (bet)	ea (head)		
/ie/	ie (bite)	i (find)	igh (sigh)	y (cry)

Letter	Code Overlap		
i	/i/ sit	/ie/ find	
e	/e/ bet	/ee/ be	
ie	/ie/ tie	/ee/ believe	/e/ friend

Richards and Commons point out that an understanding of relations that are governed by propositional logic typically emerges around the age of eleven to twelve years! And while propositional logic may present no problem whatsoever to adults, it is simply unavailable, qua logic, to a child learning to read. This means that children cannot sort out the systems of complex relationships between patterns of letters and sounds, because they haven't the logical capacity to do this on their own. Nor should we be surprised—curriculum designers can't either! But we'll see shortly that someone else can do it for them.

We're not done yet, because there are still two more types of relational logic structures in our spelling system as shown in Table 7–1. There are multiple spelling alternatives for the *same* sound. This is true of almost all vowels. The sound /ie/ (tie) can be spelled: i̲e̲ **or** i̲ (find) **or** i̲gh̲ (high) **or** y̲ (cry), a relationship expressed by the logical term "**or**." There is also *code overlap,* where a letter(s) can stand for more than one sound. The *letter* i̲ can stand for the sounds /i/ (sit) **or** /ie/ (find); the letter /e/ can stand for the sounds /e/ (bet) **or** /ee/ (be), and the letters i̲e̲ can stand for the sounds /ie/ (tie) **or** /ee/ (believe) **or** /e/ (friend). This is also expressed by the logical term "**or**."

Think how difficult arithmetic would be if a child had to learn that the number 1 could stand for 'one' in 81, but stood for 'three' in 91! This is not too far off from the way our alphabet code is set up.

The level of complexity produced by digraphs, plus the unstable and shifting relationships between sounds and letters and letters and sounds, means that accurate and automatic sensorimotor processing becomes even more critical. A child absolutely must notice which letters work together and which do not as they scan across rows of text. These complex relations in our spelling system must be sorted out *by an adult* (curriculum designer, teacher) before they are taught to a child. Although some children may be able to grasp our spelling system "intuitively" and ultimately become good readers and spellers, most children cannot do this on their own. Remember that children actively seek to "make sense" of everything they do. When adults fail to "make sense" of what they are trying to teach, children will struggle to impose some kind of logic on how a writing system works. More often than not, this will be the wrong logic.

Formal descriptions of logical operations are complex and formidable, and neither the child nor the teacher needs to understand them as formal descriptions. Nevertheless, these complex logics are embedded or *implicit* in the code and *someone must understand them* because they dictate how the code should be taught.

According to Richards and Commons, the types of logical reasoning essential to mastering the English alphabet code are not available to children learning to read. If we followed their timetable to the letter, children should not be taught to read our alphabetic writing system until they are around nine to eleven years old. Recent research has shown that this timetable doesn't always apply in real-world contexts. The key lies in the difference between "real problems" and "abstract problems." If reading is taught as a real problem: "How do letters represent sounds in *your* speech?" then we have an opportunity for success. If we are aware of the logical pitfalls that are created by our complex spelling code, we can avoid confusing the child by careful sequencing of the learning process. This means starting with a real problem, stabilizing the first step (1-to-1 mapping/simple logic) so that it in turn becomes "real" (in Piaget's terms: creates a "structure") before moving on to the second step (digraphs—1-to-1(2), mapping—propositional logic), and so on.

Research on some dramatic examples of the importance of context in making problems "real," has been described by Stephen Ceci and Antonio Roazzi. If problems in class inclusion logic were presented in a familiar real-world context, they could be solved expertly, whereas when they were presented in a different context, or in their abstract form, they couldn't be solved at all. Experienced racetrack gamblers couldn't solve a familiar problem presented in a "stock market context," until they were told that a "price-earnings ratio" was similar to predicting "post-time odds."

Illiterate street urchins selling fruit and vegetables in Brazil could solve class inclusion problems related to the sale of fruit and vegetables they couldn't solve in other formats. They could add up the costs of fruit and vegetables with ease ("a small coconut is 50 cruceiros, a large coconut is 76 cruceiros; if you buy both, you pay 126 cruceiros"), but couldn't add up the identical numbers given to them verbally: "How much is 76 + 50?" In their own setting, they were actually better at certain types of mathematics than children the same age with several years of schooling, with 60 percent solving a context-specific class inclusion problem (involving different flavors and quantities of chewing gum) that only 27 percent of the educated children got right.

If you mislead the child into thinking that the alphabetic code is completely abstract and arbitrary and ignore the complex logic in the way our spelling code is structured, you will inevitably fail to teach most children to read and spell efficiently. Seen this way, you can understand why whole language approaches are actually "antireading" methods, because they actively discourage teachers from presenting consistent information about the exact units of speech and letter patterns that constitute our alphabet code. This effectively blocks the child from using his emerging skill in categorizing because there is nothing to categorize. There is only chaos.

You can see also why most phonics instruction will fail for a large number of children. First, phonics never establishes a "real" problem; *sounds in the child's speech* are never taught as the basis, or key, to unlocking the code. Second, phonics confounds the logic of digraphs (1-to-1(2) mapping) with the logic of consonant clusters (1-to-1 mapping). Third, phonics never addresses the most complex level of logic at all: 1-to-many and many-to-1 mapping (spelling alternatives and code overlaps). In most phonics classrooms, children are given spelling lists containing words that have no relationship to what they are reading or are able to read. No chance for learning "reversibility" here. In many phonics classrooms, children are taught to spell with "word families" ('unch'=one sound), introducing a relational logic that doesn't even exist in our spelling system or in anyone else's: i.e., "everything in the word except the first letter is one sound."

THE DEVELOPMENT OF LANGUAGE AND LEARNING TO READ

In the preceding chapter, we learned that phonemic awareness is one of the most critical skills in learning to read and spell. Is there a developmental time course which impacts this ability?

Young infants babble in most sounds of every known language. Even deaf children babble just like hearing children. If this wasn't the case, then Chinese babies couldn't learn Chinese, or French babies learn French. Over time, sounds in the native language increase in frequency and foreign sounds drop out, because only the native sounds are heard again and again in "conversations" with the infant. At one stage in language development, an infant has complete ability to hear (discriminate) any consonant or vowel in any language with great accuracy.

Janet Werker has carried out research on what happens to this early skill as language develops. Infants' ability to discriminate (tell apart) speech sounds that are absent in their native language starts to disappear during the first year of life. At around ten to twelve months children act as if they are "deaf" to nonnative speech sounds, and hear them instead as the most similar sound in their own language. This skill doesn't disappear entirely, but declines slowly over childhood. Young children are much less likely to speak with a foreign accent if they learn a different language. Older children and adults can only learn to pronounce foreign speech sounds after years of consistent drill and conscious training, and rarely ever sound like native speakers.

Once the infant has learned which sounds of her language to notice, her next task is to hear them clearly enough to be able to produce them. Toddlers only gradually develop a more acute sensitivity to complex combinations of sounds. The most difficult of all are consonant clusters. A toddler will say "poon" for 'spoon' and "wing" for 'ring' because the beginning /r/ sound is actually *two* sounds produced simultaneously: /wr/. The most difficult of all, both to hear and to reproduce, are triple clusters. Preschoolers say "teet" for 'street' and "plash" for 'splash.'

What happens when children change languages at an early age? Do sensitivities to the phonemes in their first language disappear? Richard Tees and Janet Werker did a fascinating study on American college students learning Hindi, a language with several phonemes that are completely absent in English. They compared students with five years of training to two types of beginner: those who had spoken Hindi until the age of one or two years, but not since, and those who had never heard the language before. From time to time, the students were given a test of their ability to discriminate (tell apart) various Hindi sounds that don't exist in English. At the end of the first year of training, the group never having heard Hindi before were still performing badly. But after only two weeks, the students with early childhood exposure were as good as the students with five years of training. This shows that the awareness of the phonemes in one's native language is permanently stored in the brain. Even if these sounds have never been heard since early childhood, they can be recovered with relative ease *provided they are taught.* This means that everyone can be trained to become aware of the individual phonemes in his or her language.

This raises the question of why these phonemes are not immediately accessible when the child needs them, when he or she begins to learn to read an alphabetic writing system. There is another developmental milestone that impacts on phonemic awareness. As speech accuracy and clarity improve over childhood, the brain begins to reorganize the basic unit of speech production. Speech output increases in speed with

FIGURE 7–2

Co-articulation

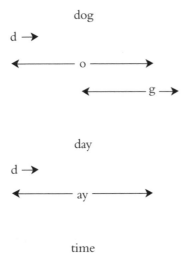

age, so that a continuous flow of sounds becomes effortlessly and flu-ently connected in a phrase or sentence. Children repeat words and phrases over and over again to exercise this skill and increase fluency. We saw earlier that naming fluency increases with age. To accomplish this, a reorganization takes place in the brain. The simple speech seg-ments produced in infancy, ba-ba-, da-da, bi-bi, are incorporated into larger units of speech: syllables and words.

Research at the Haskins Laboratory under the direction of Alvin Liberman and Donald Shankweiler showed that from about the age of four or five years, we speak so rapidly that the final phoneme in a word alters the way phonemes coming earlier in the word are physi-cally produced. The acoustic patterns of the phoneme /d/ in the word "dog," as shown on a speech spectrogram, are noticeably different from the patterns in the phoneme /d/ in the word "day." This is because the movement of the tongue to make the /d/ is controlled by where the jaw and tongue move *next,* and next, and next. Phonemes in words *overlap* each other in speech, a process Liberman and Shank-weiler called "co-articulation" (see Figure 7–2). This, incidentally, is why it is so difficult to program computers to process and analyze nat-ural speech. When this reorganization takes place, the primary speech

units are syllables or words, and phonemes are lost to conscious awareness.

Fortunately, human speakers, unlike computers, do not *hear* these
variations as different sounds or misperceive them. Through another
process called "categorical perception," anything approximating a /d/
will be perceived as a /d/. Nevertheless, as speech becomes fluent,
consonants and vowels become perceptually glued together, and it
becomes difficult for the auditory system to unglue them. Individual
phonemes become embedded in the flow of coarticulated speech.
The auditory system "hears" them as shifting sets of overlapping
sounds in syllable "chunks," and not like individual beads strung on a
necklace.

These major developmental milestones in speech production are always preceded by similar changes in speech perception. This means
that for a child learning a phonetic alphabet, just at the point when he
begins to master his native tongue effortlessly and fluently, his ability to
hear individual phonemes within words or syllables declines, sometimes to zero. The phonemic level of speech is unavailable to conscious
awareness because it is inefficient to be aware of it. The only reason
you would ever need to hear phonemes is if you have to learn an alphabetic writing system.

For these reasons, a child must be taught to hear individual
phonemes in speech, because he doesn't know they're there. To create
a "real problem," something that is tangible and concrete for the child,
a familiar context for learning the rest of the code, children must be
made aware of what the letter symbols stand for.

CONTROL OF ATTENTION

Attentional control has become an important issue in American
schools due to the belief that "deficits in attention" are causing learning failure, which usually means "reading failure." This overly simplis-
tic notion seems immune to twenty years of scientific research
showing conclusively that children diagnosed with "attention deficit
disorder" (ADD) have no attentional problems, at least none that can
be demonstrated in controlled laboratory conditions. Instead, research
has shown the opposite: Learning failure causes an inability to attend.

The worse you are at something, the more brain cells you need
to do it, the harder it is to keep doing it, and the harder it is to keep

your attention focused on what you're doing. As we saw earlier in this chapter, when we're bad at something, our brain burns more glucose in more brain regions. Burning glucose uses "energy," and a high, continuous expenditure of mental energy is exhausting. Frustration also reduces mental energy, because it interferes with concentration.

The attentional systems of the brain operate in two major ways to facilitate efficient information processing. One set of brain systems controls distractibility. They regulate the degree to which you are interruptable or distractible when you're doing something. If you aren't doing very much (nature walk, washing the dishes), then being distractible is fine, and the attentional control systems go into standby mode. If you're doing something difficult (studying for finals), then distraction is bad, and the control systems go to work to partially shut out the world. Activating these systems takes effort: energy. Studying for finals is exhausting not so much because what you are learning is difficult, but because of the mental effort to shut out distracting noises and thoughts and stay focused.

The second type of attention involves the amount of information that can be "held in mind" at any one time, variously called "attention span," "span of awareness," or "conscious awareness." Both types of attention have a strong developmental time course. Young children are highly distractible. When everything is new, "newness" or "novelty" is compelling. Distractibility has a purpose. It alerts the young mind to what is novel and possibly important. The young brain has to code everything important into memory, and until this coding has continued for some time, there is no yardstick to measure what is and is not "important." One reason that adults seem less distractible than children is because to them, everything is "old" and predictable. If adults were suddenly transported to an alien planet, they would become as distractible as children.

Children vary in their level of distractibility. Some children can focus attention on a task and stay focused until they finish what they're doing. Other children, at the same age, cannot. Noises interrupt them. Sudden movement across a room attracts their attention. Curiosity (the pull of the novel or the explained) engages them and they leave what they are doing to watch others. There are maturational differences as well as individual differences underpinning these behaviors. In general, the older the child, the more he is able to sustain attention to a task, and girls seem to have a developmental edge. This is not to say that distractibility is "bad" or even "childish." We all know highly curious people who stay excited about life in a way that we might envy. Furthermore, distractibility can be useful. Teachers who find novel ways to engage children keep their interest.

The ability to hold information "in mind" (attention span) varies from one individual to another depending upon a number of factors. Some children can keep several requests in mind at once: "(1) Take your shoes upstairs, (2) put them in the closet, (3) wash your hands, and (4) come down to dinner." Girls are more likely to rely on the verbal channel than boys, and so do a better job of remembering requests. Boys are more attentive to visual information and more likely to remember only one request at a time: "Take your shoes upstairs." Children can have difficulty storing all these requests in memory in the first place, or they can lose information because something distracts them. Jimmy, heading upstairs to put his shoes away, might notice his Nintendo game on the way to the closet, drop his shoes on the bed, neglect to wash his hands, and forget all about dinner. (These sex differences, incidentally, explain why 80 percent of so-called "ADD" children are boys. When sex ratios for an alleged "brain disorder" are so lopsided, this is extremely suspicious.)

Attention span *and* the ability to focus and keep from being distracted are obviously connected. Both are affected by temperament, interest, motivation, and *competence* in a particular skill. When a child is good at something, she can perform with less effort, be aware of more elements in the task, and stay focused for longer periods of time. That is, she can hold more information in mind (greater attention span) and find it easier to avoid being distracted. The brain is working efficiently and this is a function of ability as much as a function of maturation. When a child is bad at something, she can only perform with great effort, will find difficulty staying focused, and is more likely to become distracted.

Many children with reading problems exhibit behavior problems due to their inability and unwillingness to stay focused and "on task." Being asked to do something you can't do for six hours a day, for hundreds of days a year, year after year, knowing that your peers are fully aware of your shortcomings, must be the most distressing experience imaginable. It is scarcely surprising that children fail to stay on task and cause trouble for the teacher, their classmates, and their parents.

There are scores of studies which show that the majority of children diagnosed with "attention deficit disorder" have serious reading or other learning problems, and most of the rest of these children have serious emotional problems, or both. This means that the inability to pay attention in classrooms is a *symptom* and not a cause. True attentional deficits caused by neurological damage occur in less than 1 percent of the population.

Another reason for acting out is to get attention paid *to you*. Peter Williamson writes that for some children any attention is "good" attention, and whether it takes good or bad behavior to get it doesn't matter. Any attention is purely rewarding. While this may be true for some, most children are more subtle than this. There are limits to the kinds of rewards that children will accept. Praise or "tokens" for good behavior are not always as effective as people once thought. It turns out that children are more likely to maintain interest in a task and accept praise when they have done something that merits it, just like most adults. They respond best to praise when it provides some feedback in the form of what Lilian Katz has called "a tribute." A tribute is a statement that tells a child what is "competent" about his performance. Reinforcement works to create or maintain interest when it is deserved and informative. Reinforcement for the sole purpose of manipulating a child so he stays "on task" Katz calls an "inducement" and is ineffective once it is withdrawn.

Stephen Ceci and Richard Ryan did a fascinating study which proves this point in another way. They observed children and discovered what it was that each one liked to do. Then they gave the children "rewards" (smiley faces) for doing something they had already chosen and were enjoying. The reward caused them to stop preferring this activity. The children interpreted this experience as follows: "Smiley faces are only given to get you to do something you don't want to do. Therefore, I shouldn't like doing this."

A reading program should be good enough to make every child competent. Because teachers are never provided with the training and skills to teach reading correctly, their classrooms are filling up with children who are "dyslexic" because they have a "brain disorder," or "don't pay attention" because they have a "brain disorder," or "aren't motivated," or are "emotionally handicapped." We are blaming the victim because our teachers aren't properly trained to do their job.

We need to stop and think what would happen to attention, to behavior, to emotional stability, if every child was *competent* in the skills he is supposed to be learning in the classroom, where he spends over 1,200 hours per year, year after year.

CONCLUSIONS

Understanding the mind of the child is critical to our attempt to teach anything in a classroom, much less a complex skill like reading. To summarize the key points, here is what must be considered in setting up a curriculum that works for the young child about to begin to learn to read.

Children and adults alike reenter a sensorimotor phase every time they learn a new skill. In learning to drive, every movement of each part of the body has to be made completely conscious until the movements become integrated. Each important sensory and motor component of the task must be identified and the integration of the sensorimotor elements must be trained. In a sensorimotor phase of learning, competency is the primary goal. Competency stems from practice (repetition). Children willingly practice or repeat actions to obtain mastery. Just because repetition may look boring to an adult doesn't mean it's boring to a child.

Children in the early elementary grades can't process more than one or two perceptual dimensions simultaneously. When children begin to be able to classify objects and events, they can only handle one or two categorical levels. Children can't learn new skills that involve complex logics unless the categorical relations in these logics are worked out ahead of time and taught in a carefully sequenced way. Understanding complex relations, like those in our spelling code, is made simpler and more accessible when a child is working on a "real" problem. Real problems are tangible and concrete, and anchored in a familiar context. Learning gets easier (automatic) when a problem has become familiar.

Children are unaware of phonemes in speech, and it is easier for them to become aware of syllables or whole words. If a child can only hear words or syllables, she won't understand how to use our writing system. For this reason, *no reading method should ever teach children to read whole words, syllables, or syllable parts like 'rimes.'* These are the wrong sensory units for our writing system. These incorrect sensory units will be stored in memory, programming the brain, becoming more automatic with time, and making it harder to learn to read correctly. Children must be trained from the start to become aware of the individual phonemes in speech. The earlier this is done, the easier it will be for a child to learn to read.

When children are highly distractible, overly disruptive, and unable to stay "on task," this usually means they can't do the task. Most children diagnosed ADD have reading problems. Drugs may work in the short term to calm a child down so he produces more "seat-work," but drugs can't teach a child to read or do math. Twenty-five years of research shows that true academic performance, measured by standardized tests, is unaffected by medication.

Children appreciate praise or rewards when they are deserved (a "tribute") and inform them about their level of competence. Don't bribe children to keep them "on task." Tell them something good about what they are doing, and be sure that you're accurate.

This chapter has answered most of the remaining questions raised about the potential causes of reading problems listed in the last chapter. These were questions about causes of reading failure due to developmental issues like logic, language, and attentional control in the normal child. Children's language development precludes them from being able to use a phonetic alphabet unless the phonemes are specifically taught. Phonemic awareness can be recovered at any age, but for children learning to read, the earlier the better. At the time when children learn to read, their logical development makes it nearly impossible for them to grasp the complex structure of our spelling code. Some children may figure out 1-to-1 mapping logic *by themselves,* but the remaining levels of the code must be explicitly taught. Furthermore, each step must be grounded in something that has already become "real" (familiar context). Only then can learning proceed evenly and effectively.

Children, like adults, have problems paying attention to something they can't do or don't understand. They have a limited capacity to hold information in mind, and this capacity shrinks to zero when that information makes "no sense."

Just about everything I have talked about in this chapter is directly or indirectly connected to instruction. It is only in the absence of clear, appropriately sequenced, and unambiguous instruction, that these developmental issues can cause problems in learning to read. This is a normal consequence of the child's developmental level and not due to something wrong with the child.

In the next chapter we will be looking into the future at new methods to teach reading that are based on the research discussed so far. These studies provide the ultimate answer to the most important question: Can every child be taught to read?

Chapter 8

THE PROOF OF THE PUDDING

Reading Programs That Work

U ntil now, we have looked at the world as it is. In this chapter we're going to look at the world as it could be. Most of the research on reading presented so far has been descriptive or correlational. Descriptive research counts things and calculates averages, percentiles, or standard deviations. Correlational research tells you precisely what things go together, and whether a particular skill will "predict" another skill, either now or later on. Tests of phoneme awareness correlate with reading skill. So far, we have no proof that phoneme awareness plays any *causal* role in reading skill. It is just as likely that learning to read an alphabetic writing system *causes* phoneme awareness.

No matter how clever and how thorough correlational studies are, they will never tell you whether reading skill can be caused by something you do or do not do. Only an experiment can tell you that. In an experiment, a researcher introduces a new teaching method to one group of children, while another group of children (the control group) are taught in the usual way. Children are tested both at the beginning and at the end of training. A significant difference in gains between the two groups is a positive indication that the new method had an effect. In other words, the researcher *caused* something to change.

Experiments on real people doing real things in the real world aren't easy to carry out. All sorts of unforeseen things can interfere with your results. One of the most powerful effects discovered in reading research over this century is known as the "teacher effect." If the teacher doesn't

understand or believe in what you are asking her to do, she will sabo-
tage your most carefully planned experiment day after day. This can
happen even when teachers sincerely think they are doing what they
were trained to do. The "teacher effect" tells us that teachers need to
be given a clear rationale for being asked to change their teaching
methods. The new method has to make sense and be designed so that
it works in the classroom, with curriculum materials and lesson plans.
The teacher must be thoroughly trained, so that she feels confident and
comfortable with the new approach.

As young readers lack the ability to unglue and manipulate phonemes in words, an obvious component in an effective reading program is training in phonemic awareness. This is assuming it can be
trained, or that the training will impact on reading. The impact of
phoneme training on reading test scores would be direct evidence for
a *cause* of reading success. Another important experimental question is
whether children must be taught the alphabet principle directly (that
phonemes in words are represented by letter symbols), or whether they
can discover this principle without instruction. Another issue concerns
the best way to teach our formidable spelling code so that a young
child can learn it.

Training studies fall into two main types. In the first type, the research team is directly involved in teaching the children. This type of
study has high "internal validity," which means that it has the highest
level of control, because at all times, the researcher proceeds according
to a strict plan.

The second type of study has high "external validity." In this type,
the classroom teacher is trained and monitored. This shows that the
training can be transferred to the real world: the classroom, where it
matters most. If teachers can train skills that help children learn to read
effectively, we could dramatically reduce the number of children referred for special education. There would be no more children diagnosed "dyslexic" or "learning disabled." This would put an end to the
enormous suffering of these children and their families. It would create a nation of readers, a new literate America, saving the taxpayer billions of dollars into the bargain. I think you can see how incredibly
important these studies are.

Hundreds of studies on reading methods have been carried out over
the past century. For the most part, these studies suffer from serious
methodological problems, like missing control groups, or the absence
of baseline testing. I have already discussed the fact that most reading

programs in today's classroom are deficient and misleading. For these reasons, this chapter focuses on studies where teaching methods are in line with the research findings. These studies meet most of the following criteria:

1. Teaches phonemes in words as the basis for the code
2. Includes a phoneme awareness training component
3. Includes instruction in phoneme-to-letter and letter-to-phoneme correspondences.
4. Uses appropriate methodology
5. Presents clearly described procedures
6. Includes control groups when possible
7. Measures outcomes with objective or standardized tests

Surprisingly few studies pass muster by these criteria. Because of this, it is difficult to organize them into a coherent sequence. Each study has a slightly different focus. The children are of varying ages, sometimes trained individually, sometimes in groups, sometimes in the normal classroom, or in a pull-out program, or in a private clinic. Each study has its own story to tell because of these differences, yet the overall picture is one of remarkable agreement. A list of commercially available programs and where they can be obtained is included in the Appendix to chapter 9.

TRAINING STUDIES AT PRESCHOOL AND KINDERGARTEN

We're going to start in Australia with an important series of studies by Brian Byrne and Ruth Fielding-Barnsley. They began with a basic question: what is the minimum amount of information you need to teach young children for them to understand that phonemes in words are represented by letter symbols? Preschool children, three to five years old, participated in a series of five studies. None of the children knew any letter names or "sounds." Different groups of children were taught various tasks ranging in difficulty and complexity. The simplest was word-symbol association. The children were taught words like 'dog' and 'house' and that each could be represented by a "word token" (colored shape). These word tokens could be combined into compound words: 'doghouse.' Another task was to listen for the first sound in a word and match a picture of this word to another picture that started with the same sound: 'bag' 'bat'. Next, children had to match these words to "word tokens" that stood for words starting with the same sound. Another group of children were trained in the same way, only using *letters* instead of tokens. At each stage of the training, the children were tested for their ability to *transfer* what they had been taught to similar tasks in order to discover if the child could generalize her knowledge about the relationship between sounds in words and symbols for those sounds.

The researchers found that many children had great difficulty with these tasks. For those who could be trained, the results were clear. Letter-sound knowledge alone and phoneme awareness alone were not enough for the child to comprehend the alphabet principle. For a complete understanding of how an alphabet writing system works, the child must have a thorough grasp of this information:

1. The ability to analyze words into phonemes.
2. The knowledge that these phonemes occur in all words.
3. The knowledge of which letter symbol represents which phoneme.
4. The understanding that there is a consistent relationship between each phoneme and a letter across all positions in a word and across all words (transitivity). The letter <u>b</u> stands for the phoneme /b/ in the word 'big,' and *also* for /b/ in the word 'bat,' and *also* for /b/ in the word 'tub.'

What seems so obvious to an adult is not obvious to a child. Each of these four elements must be taught because children this age cannot figure this out on their own.

Byrne and Fielding-Barnsley also carried out a study in which they trained preschoolers in small groups to listen and identify beginning and final phonemes in words. The children had only twenty minutes a week of this training for twelve weeks. Another group of children spent the same amount of time learning to categorize on the basis of shape, color, animate/inanimate, etc. One year later, at the end of first grade, the children were tested on various reading and spelling tests. The children with the phoneme training were superior on a test of decoding regularly spelled nonsense words. These children could use the alphabet principle to decode unfamiliar words significantly more accurately than the children without any training.

Children in these studies were trained for short periods of time. What happens when there is a more consistent and extensive training program for this age group? Eileen Ball and Benita Blachman devised a training program for kindergarten children in Syracuse, New York. For Group I, they designed various games, such as having the child manipulate blank squares to stand for the number and order of phonemes in a word, which was cued by a picture, an exercise first developed by Elkonin in 1963. Most of the training was devoted to segmenting each phoneme in words: /b/-/a/-/t/, blending them back into words, and training in listening for beginning, middle, and final phonemes in words. The children were also taught letter names and letter-phoneme correspondences. They restricted the training to nine phonemes and letters:

a   m   t   i   s   r   f   u   b

The children worked in groups of five, twenty minutes daily for seven weeks (eleven to twelve hours altogether).

There were two other groups of children in this study. Group II spent twenty minutes a day learning letter name/letter sound correspondences (phonics) on the same letters, plus general language activities, such as vocabulary development, listening to stories, and categorizing things. Group III remained in the normal kindergarten program.

At the end of training, the children were tested on phoneme awareness and reading tests. Group I, who had both phoneme awareness *and* letter-sound training, was superior on the phoneme tests to the other two groups. Groups I and II, who had the letter-sound training, were superior on this task to the group with no training. All three groups were equally accurate in knowing letter names.

The most important results were on the reading test which the authors developed. The test consisted of 21 two- and three-sound, regularly spelled words using the same nine letters (mat, sub, at, fit). Group I could read five times more words correctly than Group III (ordinary kindergarten group), and three times more words correctly than Group II (letter names/letter sounds only—phonics). Group III could read, on average, only two of the 21 words.

These results confirm what Byrne and Fielding-Barnsley report, that teaching phoneme awareness *and* the letter-phoneme connections are equally important. Further, these results show that knowing *letter names* is not much help in being able to read, and that standard "phonics" training is much less effective.

Since this study, Blachman and Darlene Tangel have developed an 11-week program for kindergarten. They reported on the first test of

this program in 1992. There were 77 kindergarten children who received phoneme awareness training using various activities and games,
plus training on letter-names and letter-sound relationships. They were
taught only 9 letters in two- and three-sound words. They were taught
by their regular kindergarten teacher or teacher's aide, who had 14
hours of training. Another group of 72 children participated in the
usual kindergarten program. The children were all from low-income,
inner-city families in Syracuse, New York.

At the end of kindergarten, the children with phoneme awareness
training and letter-sound training were superior on tests of phoneme
segmenting, letter-name knowledge, letter-sound relationships, and
reading two- and three-sound real and nonsense words. They were also
well ahead in spelling skills, using more developmentally advanced
spelling strategies on measures of "invented spelling."

The entire study was replicated in 1994 with identical results. Children were followed into first grade, where they continued to receive a
first-grade program designed by Blachman. The training was expanded
to include reading and writing exercises along with a continuation of
lessons in phoneme awareness. The control group worked with the
Scott-Foresman reading and spelling programs, which were phonics-
based.

The phoneme training group was superior at the end of first grade
on phoneme awareness and on every measure of reading and spelling
accuracy on both specially designed tests and standardized tests of reading and spelling. These children maintained their superior performance on all measures when tested again, one year later, at the end of
second grade.

Another program in this group is "Reading Fundamentals," an adaptation of the clinical program "Phono-Graphix™" developed by Carmen McGuinness at Read America. (Phono-Graphix is reviewed in
more detail in the last section and in chapter 12.) Reading Fundamentals was designed for small-group instruction for four- and five-year-
olds. It teaches oral phoneme segmenting and blending, sound-to-
letter/letter-to-sound correspondences, reading, and spelling. It includes a comprehensive set of curriculum materials (exercises, letter
cards, word cards, worksheets, stories) for eleven units, beginning with
five vowels and nineteen consonants organized in subsets, followed by
consonant clusters, and ending with consonant and vowel digraphs.

Forty children attending preschool centers in central Florida were
divided into two experimental and two control classrooms of ten chil-

dren each. The average age in the experimental groups was 61.5 months (range 50–71 months), and the average age in the controls was 58.2 months (range 56–64 months). The control groups received a "language experience" program with no direct instruction in reading. Teachers of the experimental groups were trained in Reading Fundamentals for twenty-four hours, and were supervised on site for two hours each.

All the children were tested during the second week of school in the fall of 1996, on segmenting, blending, code knowledge (child sees a letter and is asked, "What sound is this?"), reading, and spelling. The reading test consisted of three words taught in the program plus ten words from the Woodcock Reading Mastery Word Recognition subtest that had not been taught. The spelling test consisted of five CVC words from the reading test; a child scored one point for each letter placed in the correct sequence. The groups did not differ in pretraining test scores:

Segmenting .64 out of 15   Blending .46 out of 5
Code knowledge 1.15 out of 8   Reading .20 out of 13
Spelling 0 out of a possible 15 points

Reading Fundamentals children were taught in groups of three to four for approximately twenty minutes a day, four days a week for eleven weeks, totaling to about fourteen hours of teaching. At the end of this time the children were retested. They scored on average:

Segmenting 11.6   Blending 3.5
Code knowledge 6.9   Reading 5.0
Spelling 10

For Woodcock words only, the average reading score was 3.0, which is equivalent to 6 years 1 month. The control groups made no gains except on code knowledge (.37 vs. 1.68), and reading and spelling scores were both zero for *all control children*.

This study shows that four- and five-year-old children can be taught oral segmenting and blending, and how to read and spell simple words, and that this knowledge transfers to words that have not been seen before.

The last kindergarten study was carried out in Denmark, by a Swedish team led by Ingvar Lundberg. They used two groups of children in different geographic regions of Denmark, matched for socioeconomic class. Kindergarten in Denmark begins at age six, and parents are encouraged to refrain from helping their children learn to read until the age of seven. One group of 235 children received training on a number of phonological tasks, and the control group of 155 children did not.

The training consisted of fifteen to twenty minutes daily for fourteen weeks of rhyming games (what rhymes with or "sounds like" 'fish'?), segmenting words in sentences (wunssaponnatime—once-upon-a-time), and segmenting syllables in words (ta-ble, flow-er). This was followed at week 15 by training in listening to initial phonemes in words (**b**ig, **b**at, **b**ug), and at weeks 17 and 18 (month 5) by phoneme segmenting and blending tasks of increasing complexity. At the end of the school year, the children were given various tests of their phonological ability. The only real difference between the groups was in segmenting and blending phonemes, and *not* in the ability to rhyme or segment sentences and syllables.

The children were retested eight months after the start of first grade when they were about seven and a half years old. Children were asked to read individual words and match each one to a picture. They also were tested on spelling dictation. The trained group was only marginally ahead on reading, but did much better on the spelling dictation test, scoring an average of 10.7 correct to the control group's 6.7 correct. Here is an example of phoneme awareness training working *independently* of direct instruction in letter-sound relationships.

This study shows that training in parsing sentences into words and words into syllables and playing rhyming games had no real effect. The groups did not differ in these skills after training. None of these skills were found to correlate to reading and spelling scores later in time. These activities took up 50 percent of the training, time that was essentially wasted. This finding was replicated by Barbara Foorman and her colleagues in Houston. When they compared children trained in this program to a control group, the only significant difference was on the phoneme awareness tasks.

PREVENTIVE PROGRAMS FOR AT-RISK CHILDREN

Before reviewing the studies that meet the requirements outlined at the beginning of this chapter, I want to discuss one program that has become common in special education instruction. This is "Reading Mastery," part of a curriculum called "DISTAR." It was developed by Wesley Becker and Siegfried Engelmann for small-group instruction for disadvantaged children, and not as a remedial program. Englemann subsequently developed "Corrective Reading" for poor readers in fourth to twelfth grade, taught in small groups. Despite this, we see many children at our clinic who are being taught the Reading Mastery classroom program in special ed, obviously unsuccessfully, otherwise they wouldn't come to us. Also, parents were advised by the school to purchase the parent version of Reading Mastery.

Research from "Project Follow-Through" carried out in the early 1970s showed that Reading Mastery–trained children scored higher on a standardized reading test than children taught in either whole word or eclectic reading programs, and gains were maintained over time. However, Robert Slavin and his group reviewed twelve classroom and tutorial intervention programs and report that DISTAR was the *only* program that had *no success*. S. J. Kuder found no differences between learning-disabled children trained in DISTAR and those trained in a phonics-based program. Elsa Bartlett reports that poor readers and disadvantaged children had particular difficulty with the transition from the coded text, which is a feature of Reading Mastery. So far, research on Corrective Reading has serious methodological problems. These conflicting results indicate either that Reading Mastery is ineffective for remedial purposes but effective in the classroom (which seems unlikely), or that there are methodological problems with these studies.

Reading Mastery consists of 100 scripted lesson plans along with words printed in coded text. This text is visually confusing and represents many letter-sound correspondences incorrectly or inconsistently. The text marks "long vowels" with a heavy line over the vowel letter. "Short vowels" are unmarked. "Silent letters" in "long vowels" are written in tiny type.

mēat çāke hat hāte

Dots are printed below each letter that is sounded. Letters in tiny type have no dots and children are supposed to ignore them. As a result, children don't learn that vowel letters *work together* to stand for one sound, such as e-controlled vowel spellings, where the e works with the preceding vowel across a consonant, as in the words 'cake' or 'hate.' (However, this *is* an emphasis in Corrective Reading.)

When the child moves to real text, the special cues are missing, and he has no true understanding of how to differentiate between fat and fate, bat and bait, got and goat, etc. The coding system makes it impossible to code some vowels at all: 'cow' is coded as: çọẉ. Every letter with a dot is pronounced, making 'cow' have three sounds: /k/ /o/ /w/ or "kahw-" instead of two: /k/ /ou/. Alternative spellings are introduced as "new sounds," coded incorrectly as: 'ṣạịd' 'ẉạḷḳ' 'away'(*four* sounds instead of three: /s/ /e/ /d/—/w/ /o/ /k/—/u/ /w/ /ae/). Clusters receive minimal attention, and those that do appear are underlined in some places and not in others. Lessons give the child the impression that clusters are "one sound." The teacher introduces 'bring' as 'br-ing' (two sounds) instead of four (/b/ /r/ /i/ /ng/).

At the end of 100 lessons, the child knows little or nothing about English phonemes or the spelling code. There is no training in segmenting or in other types of phoneme analysis. Instead, children are asked to "say a word slowly" keeping sounds connected ('mmmmeeeetttt'), or to "say it the fast way," blending sounds quickly ('meet'). To teach segmenting properly, sounds must be isolated: /m/– /ee/– /t/. Only this way can children learn where each phoneme starts and stops.

The remaining studies in this section all correspond to the guidelines set out at the beginning of this chapter.

One of the most famous training studies in the literature was carried out in Oxford, England by Lynette Bradley and Peter Bryant. The children in this study were at risk for reading failure due to extremely poor scores on a phoneme awareness test. Altogether there were sixty-five children, average age of six years, who were divided into four separate groups matched for reading and IQ. The children were trained individually in pull-out sessions across a two-year period, for a total of forty sessions, averaging seven hours per child. The rest of the time they were in the main classroom. Group I was given phoneme awareness training using three-sound words. They were taught to listen and compare words that did or did not match in initial, middle, or final phonemes, as well as to listen for rhyming patterns in words. Words were cued by pictures or generated by the child. It is unclear whether segmenting, blending, or digraphs were taught. Group I was also given training in letter-phoneme correspondences.

Children in group II were given phoneme awareness training only (no letters). Group III spent the same amount of time doing language-related tasks, such as sorting the pictures into linguistic categories: pets, people. Children assigned to Group IV remained in their regular classroom (control group).

At the end of this period, children in group I were the only ones to be at grade level in reading and spelling. They were over one year ahead of group IV on the Schonell and Neale reading tests, and two years ahead on the Schonell spelling test. They were also significantly ahead of group III, the categorizing group. Group I was one year ahead of group II (phoneme awareness and no letters) in spelling. The authors concluded in much the same vein as the research reviewed above. An understanding of the alphabet principle has to be based on two separate skills: the ability to be able to hear and manipulate sounds in words, and knowledge of which sounds are connected to which letters of the alphabet. The evidence shows that phoneme awareness training *by itself* does not automatically transfer to an understanding of letter-sound correspondences. Nor do children spontaneously "pick up" this extra knowledge in the classroom.

Lynette Bradley carried out follow-on testing when the same children were thirteen years old. Group I was about one year ahead of the control group (no treatment) on the Schonell and Neale reading tests, and one and one-half years on Schonell spelling. Group II (phoneme training only) fell in between. However, *all groups were well below age norms.* Group I was now two years *behind* their normal peers in both reading and spelling, despite the early training in phoneme awareness and letter-sound knowledge. Although the results show a strong positive effect for only 7 hours of early training, the program is not sufficiently comprehensive to allow the children to maintain their grade-level standing over the long term.

Other studies have been designed to teach reading to at-risk children in the classroom. These studies were carried out either by the classroom teachers or by specially trained tutors working in the classroom.

One of the first studies of this type was carried out in Chicago in the early 1970s, in two inner-city schools, using a program designed by Michael and Lisa Wallach. The children were beginning first graders who had scored below the 40th percentile on the Metropolitan Reading Readiness Test. There were thirty-six children who received special tutoring and fifty-two children who were taught in the usual way in the main classroom. The tutors were adult volunteers from the community who were trained to use special materials and lesson plans designed by the Wallachs. The tutors saw each child for about one-half hour each day.

Children were initially taught about phonemes in words by matching a sound they heard to the beginning sound in a word. A wide range of materials and games were used to teach this. Children learned to trace letters and to match letters to phonemes. Phonemes were taught in alphabetical order, and only those that matched the twenty-six letters were taught.

At the next step, children learned to blend and segment three-sound words, first just by hearing them, and then by using a movable alphabet. When the children had completed these lessons, they began to read simple books. Through reading, they were supposed to discover the remaining phonemes in English and the more complex phoneme-letter relationships such as consonant clusters, digraphs, and alternative spellings for the same sound.

At the end of first grade, children in the two groups were given a variety of tests of reading, comprehension, and letter-sound knowledge. The tutored children were superior on all of them. This is not to say that all children in the tutored group were equally successful. About one-third still scored at beginning first-grade level or worse. The main difference between the groups was that nearly two-thirds of the control group had made no gains. A problem with this study was the lack of a balanced research design. To prove the effectiveness of the program, a control group should also have had the advantage of thirty minutes of daily individual instruction. These results also show that teaching only twenty-six letters/twenty-six sounds, and letting the child figure out the rest of the code on his own, is not enough and doesn't help about one-third of the children.

Another study on at-risk inner-city children was carried out by Benita Blachman in New Haven. She developed a program for small-group instruction for first-grade children that could be delivered by the classroom teacher. She created a variety of materials for teaching phoneme awareness, including picture cue cards for segmenting and blending sounds in words. The children were given daily practice in thirty-minute lessons in various exercises for segmenting and blending syllables and phonemes. Children were also taught letter-sound correspondences. The teaching extended to consonant clusters, vowel digraphs, and e-controlled vowel spellings. Children were given graded reading material largely drawn from basic phonics book series, and were also given spelling dictation lessons on the same kinds of words they were learning to read. Later, another school joined in and the project was extended.

Much later, at fourth grade, the children participated in schoolwide testing on the Iowa Test of Basic Skills. The children with the special training scored well above national norms, whereas previously the children from these two schools had scored either seven months or one year below national norms. Both schools with the special training program were now close to the top in citywide ranks, whereas before they had been close to the bottom. This shows the persistence of appropriately sequenced training in phoneme awareness and letter-sound decoding, and the advantage of a more in-depth program which held up over a three-year period.

There are important findings from the studies reviewed so far. Children can be taught to "unglue" sounds in words and learn the alphabet principle in kindergarten or earlier. These skills orient the child to the correct strategy for decoding and spelling, and this persists over time. However, teaching *only* the basic twenty-six letters/twenty-six sounds formula, without teaching the remaining twenty-one sounds or extensive work on clusters, digraphs, e-controlled vowel spellings, or any elements of the advanced spelling code, is not sufficient to keep at-risk children at grade level over the long haul. It is important that there is consistency in methods and careful sequencing of skills training across the early school grades until reading and spelling are secure.

Undoubtedly the most ambitious program for at-risk children has been developed by Robert Slavin and his group at Johns Hopkins University. Slavin was approached in 1986 to design a reading program for inner-city children in Baltimore, Maryland. These are mainly black children, and most qualify under Chapter 1 for federal aid to disadvantaged children. The initial work has expanded, and a curriculum was designed for prekindergarten through sixth grade, and includes a tutorial component. The program is called "Success for All" (SFA). The overriding philosophy is that everyone can learn to read. The goal is to teach everybody to read, write, and spell, and ultimately to do away with special education altogether.

In 1996, Slavin and his group published a detailed report on the structure of the curriculum, its programmatic aspects, teacher training, and so forth. It is only possible here to touch briefly on the components of reading instruction, and the results of their research over a six-year period.

There are many innovative components to this program, and perhaps the most notable is how lessons for reading instruction are set up. They use "The Joplin Plan" in which reading groups cut across three grade levels. The entire school reassembles in different classrooms based upon each child's reading skill, which is assessed every eight weeks.

The reading/literacy period lasts for ninety minutes each day and is directed by a trained reading specialist. The specialist spends half her time in the classroom and half in one-on-one tutorial sessions with the poorest readers. In addition, there is a parent involvement component to the program, in which parents participate in school-related functions and are encouraged to listen to their child read for at least twenty minutes each night.

The prekindergarten and kindergarten reading exercises involve lots of rhyming activities, training in awareness of the first sound in words, and syllable segmenting. Children are also taught letters of the alphabet. (Recall that research has shown rhyming, syllable segmenting and learning letter names have no direct impact on reading skill.) In late kindergarten or early first grade, children begin a reading program which includes phoneme awareness training plus components of phonics and whole language. There is a strong emphasis on story analysis and story comprehension, as children lack experience with print and have limited vocabularies.

The phoneme awareness training is comprehensive. It begins with listening for initial consonant sounds in short words and expands to include extensive work in sounding out and blending three or more phonemes in phonetically regular words. Children are also taught to be aware of how they produce phonemes in speech by listening, feeling, and watching the teacher's mouth. Children match sounds they hear to pictures of objects containing those sounds. They do "tracking" exercises, which involve changing one sound to make another word: fat, fast, fist, fit, fin, fun, sun. At the same time, they begin to apply this new skill when reading specially written stories with phonetically regular words mixed with short and long "sight words." As well, children learn to write letters in the air, trace letters, write letters on paper, and spell words from dictation by sounding out phonemes in words and writing each "sound" one by one on the page.

Complete information about the reading curriculum is not provided in the report. It appears from the examples that twenty-six letters are taught and, presumably, twenty-six "sounds." It is unclear how consonant clusters are taught initially. There is no mention or example of how digraphs are taught, except when reading text, nor of any elements of the advanced spelling code.

SFA is an example of an "eclectic" reading program where training in phoneme awareness and phonetic decoding is combined later with training in whole language and phonics. Children work at thinking about meaning based on story context and grammatical structure: "Does what you just read make sense?" When a child encounters a difficult word in a story, the teacher reads the word instead, *or* the child is told to look at the pictures and guess using context cues. Children read and reread and reread the same story until it is memorized. "Word family" (part-word) drill is borrowed from phonics. A story about "Fang" is used to teach 's-ang,' 'b-ang,' etc.

Examples of tutoring lessons provide a vivid illustration of how "eclectic" reading programs combining incompatible logics will fail many readers. Tim is a beginning reader in first grade. He is up to Story No. 11, which is about a costume party. Tim has obviously seen this story many times before. The story contains many phonetically regular words, plus several "sight words" that are well beyond a beginning reader's skills. As Tim begins to read, he first has trouble decoding the word "Nick," which he sounds out connecting all the sounds: "Nnnnniiiiicccckkkk," instead of segmenting them /n/—/i/—/k/. As he never learns the individual phonemes *or* which letters represent them (n̲ i̲ c̲k̲), he has the same trouble each time this word appears. He consistently confuses 'cat' and 'cot,' and 'sad' and 'says,' and corrects himself by *context cues.* On the other hand, he has *no trouble whatsoever* reading: 'baseball,' 'player,' 'dragon,' 'pirate,' 'policeman,' 'jacket,' and 'badge' (the "sight words" in the story). When Tim has read the story, he is shown isolated words from the story on cards. He still has to laboriously sound out 'Nick' once more. He reads the word 'in' as "on." He is told to spell it with letter names: 'oe'- 'en'. He reads 'be' as "did." A note tells the reader that 'be' and 'did' are "sight words" (?) which Tim consistently confuses (why?). Tim sounds out the word 'Fang' as if it had *four* sounds, /f/ /a/ /n/ /g/, instead of *three,* /f/ /a/ /ng/, and the teacher says this is "very good."

In another example, Terrell is shown the story of Fang. The teacher asks if he remembers the story and asks for the title, which Terrell supplies without hesitation. He has seen this book before. Later, when he encounters 'Fang' in text, he can't read it and has to laboriously sound it out, again incorrectly, with four sounds instead of three. This causes him to read it as 'fan' several times, because 'fan'-'g' isn't a word. Terrell reads 'in' as "on," and 'fast' as "fat" and then "far." The teacher tells him that the word 'off' is a word "that you can't sound out" and must be memorized by sight. ('Off' is perfectly phonetic.) When he reads: "The ball is off the fence," the teacher responds: "Does that make sense?" (It does to me!) Then she asks him to look at the *picture* to see if there *is* a fence. The correct word is 'field.' Terrell has not been taught the spelling option u̲e̲ for the sound /ee/, so he learns that this is another "sight word." The story of Fang is peppered with final triple clusters like 'nts,' 'mps,' 'sts' which the child is supposed to "sound out" as 'nnnnttttsss' rather than segmenting into individual phonemes: /n/ /t/ /s/. Triple clusters are the most difficult sound combinations of all to *hear* and "unglue" and come last in speech development. They should not be taught to a child having this much trouble with simple decoding.

These examples show that SFA actually encourages children to become "whole word guessers" and abort the phonetic strategy the teachers had been working so hard to establish. They also show why a whole word strategy would be preferred by the child. It has a much higher initial success rate and is far less laborious. This is especially true for children like Tim and Terrell who haven't yet mastered the Basic Code, and don't know how to segment phonemes in words to apply that code. It is never made clear to the child why he is asked to sound out some words and not others. He learns that little words and long words/funny words must be memorized by sight, but that medium-sized words are sounded out. *This is the only logic he has to work with.* The examples show that "whole word guessing" is less effective for "little words" (too visually similar) than for longer words which are visually distinctive and highly contextual. Remember that a whole word strategy will break down completely later on.

Another source of confusion is that most of the "little" sight words the child is told to memorize, are phonetically regular in spelling: in, on, did, be, she, me, off, up, etc. Telling the child these are "sight words" sends the message: "You might think you can sound out these words, but, trust me, you can't." This hidden message undermines his fragile knowledge of the code.

Success for All is a powerful example of what is wrong with eclectic reading programs, and how the best intentions can go awry. This is a terrible pity, because the authors have worked hard to develop an excellent program structure for all the right reasons.

The research findings reflect the good and bad elements of the program. It is consistently more effective than anything going on in the control classrooms. It has more impact than Reading Recovery and has been subjected to more rigorous experimental research (see last section, this chapter). Unfortunately, it still fails too many children.

By 1996, Success for All was in classrooms in over 300 schools in 70 school districts in 23 states. Thousands of children have been tested (8,000 for grade 1 alone) and so data are extremely robust. The Woodcock Reading Mastery subtest scores for Word Identification (real words) and Word Attack (phonetic nonsense words) for grades 1 through 5 were compiled and are shown in Table 8–1.

Table 8–1 presents *average grade-equivalent scores* for children taught with SFA and for the control groups. Controls were matched for Chapter 1 eligibility, ethnic group, and/or socioeconomic status. Data from the lowest scoring 25 percent are shown on the right side of the table.

Two things stand out in Table 8–1. SFA-trained children combined are more on track than controls, and are close to grade level over the years. They are at least one year ahead of the control group from grade 3 on. On the other hand, the lowest 25 percent of SFA-trained children are in serious trouble. On the Word Attack test (nonsense word decoding), both SFA and control children are stuck at first-grade level

TABLE 8–1

Success for All: Average Grade-Level Equivalent Scores for Grades 1 to 5

| Grade | All Groups | | Lowest 25% | |
	SFA	Controls	SFA	Controls
WOODCOCK READING MASTERY: WORD ATTACK SUBTEST				
1	1.82	1.50	1.53	1.16
2	2.42	1.86	1.74	1.34
3	2.91	2.32	1.87	1.57
4	3.35	2.35	1.68	1.27
5	4.50	2.61	2.15	1.51
WOODCOCK READING MASTERY: WORD IDENTIFICATION SUBTEST				
1	1.79	1.60	1.45	1.28
2	2.52	2.15	1.93	1.63
3	3.24	2.64	2.30	1.88
4	4.13	3.21	2.62	1.87
5	4.79	3.74	3.12	2.24

Note: This program is cumulative. Children in higher grades had more years in the program.

Source: Data were compiled from tables presented in Slavin, Madden, Dolan, and Wasik (1996)

for four years. The SFA children break through to second-grade level only by fifth grade. It should be noted that SFA is a cumulative program and fifth-grade children have been in the program for several years.

Although SFA children in this lowest group are consistently superior to the controls, this is not very heartening when children score three years below grade level in decoding. The suggestion that this program is promoting a whole-word strategy is confirmed by a comparison of the Word I.D. and Word Attack test scores. In competent readers, these two scores are similar, and for the SFA groups combined, they are reasonably close. However, in the lowest 25 percent, the scores begin to deviate noticeably at third grade. By fourth grade, SFA children score one year *higher* when reading real words than when reading nonsense words. A discrepancy this large is a telltale sign that children are using visual memory as their main strategy. It also shows that the effort spent in tutoring sessions in "sounding out" (rather than segmenting properly) has largely been a waste of time. (Note, too, that this discrepancy occurs with the controls.)

The issue remains as to whether a program with such an innovative structure and so many good aspects could be dramatically improved by incorporating a more logically consistent reading program, one which would never mislead any child.

SCHOOL-BASED STUDIES USING NORMAL CHILDREN

Earlier, I introduced you to Pat Lindamood, who was one of the pioneers in recognizing the importance of phonemic awareness to reading skill. She developed a reading method for one-on-one training in a clinical setting. In the late 1970s, Marilyn Howard began a project in Arco, Idaho to teach first-grade children to read by adapting the Lindamood program: Auditory Discrimination in Depth (ADD) for the classroom. The first-grade classroom teacher was trained in the method, and a special assistant was also in the classroom for an hour or so each day to work with individual children.

We will be discussing this program in greater detail in chapter 12. The ADD program is a *true* linguistic program which follows the correct logic throughout. Briefly, the children are taught forty-four phonemes by a process of discovery, feeling movements of the mouth, and watching these movements in a mirror. They are trained to manipulate sounds in words using colored blocks, pictures of mouth postures representing the way sounds are produced, and subsequently using movable alphabet tiles. The movable alphabet represents forty-four sounds, and digraphs are printed together on the same tile so the logic is clear.

Phonemes are taught in categories based upon their similarity in place and manner of articulation. Sixteen consonants are grouped into voiced and unvoiced pairs, or "brothers," /b/ /p/—/d/ /t/, etc. Nasals are taught as a group: /m/ /n/ /ng/, aspirants as another: /h/ /w/ /wh/. Phoneme sequences are taught both in isolation and in "tracking" exercises, or chains. The child is asked to make changes to rows of colored blocks, or mouth pictures, or letters, when told: "If that says /ip/ show me /pip/, if that says /pip/ show me /sip/," and so forth. The program includes extensive work on consonant clusters, taught correctly as sequences of single consonants. There is also training at the multisyllable level and some spelling alternatives are taught. Thus, the ADD program goes well beyond most of the training methods described so far.

Howard's work in Arco has produced dramatic increases in first graders' reading performance on the Woodcock Reading Mastery test. The trained children were one year ahead of the control group after only seven months of training. This has persisted over time. Children in Arco used to score close to national norms (50th percentile). With the new reading instruction, they now scored at the 92nd, 91st, and 86th percentiles at grades 2, 3, and 6, respectively.

Reading specialists from the Lindamood reading clinic in San Luis Obispo carried out a similar project in a nearby school district in Santa Maria, California. A first-grade classroom teacher was trained in the method, and a clinician/aide was in the classroom for about an hour each day. The goal was to teach forty-four phonemes, their letter correspondences, as well as how to manipulate, segment, and blend phonemes in words, prior to reading any text. The ADD children received *no books* until January of the school year. A control class was selected by school administrators, taught by a teacher who consistently had the best test results in the district. So the cards were stacked against success. These children were taught in the usual way. Many of the children in this school district were sons and daughters of migrant farm workers with poor English language skills.

The ADD program was enormously successful. On the Woodcock Reading Mastery test, children could read real words at an average of two years above grade level at the end of first grade. On nonsense word decoding, they were six years above grade level. They were one year ahead in spelling. On nonsense word decoding, even the *lowest-scoring child* was one year above grade norms, reading at a third-grade level going in to second grade.

These children have been followed for a number of years and are still well ahead of their age group on national norms, and for the school district as a whole. At fifth grade, the scores for reading comprehension, nonsense word decoding, and spelling for the rest of the schoolchildren range from 39.4 to 56.5 percentile points. The ADD-trained children scored in the range 63.6 to 81.7. There is no overlap in these scores. This shows the powerful effect of appropriate training using a consistent logic which persists long after the training has been discontinued.

Despite the fact that there were control classes in both of these studies, the children in the control groups did not receive any individual training. This design flaw was remedied in a study my students and I carried out using the Lindamood method. Instead of one-on-one training, the program was adapted for the classroom teacher who used the program during her normal language arts period. There were two classes using the method in two different schools at first grade. There was also a control classroom where the teacher taught children for the same amount of time, using a combination of phonics, whole language, and invented spelling. Children were matched for ability, and all three teachers had produced consistently good reading test scores over the years. Teachers had small classes and worked with small groups of 5 to 8 children for about 30 to 40 minutes a day on reading and language arts. After eight months, children were retested on the Woodcock Reading Mastery Test, for real word reading and for nonsense word decoding. The two ADD-trained groups gained 11 and 14 months in reading real words, and 19 and 36 months in decoding nonsense words. The control group made exactly the gains in reading they were supposed to, based upon time elapsed (8 months gain) but actually fell behind expected gains (+4 months only) in decoding nonsense words, again suggesting that many children were drifting into a whole-word strategy.

These results show that this highly structured clinical program can be successfully adapted to work in a normal classroom situation, and that first-grade teachers can be trained to use this method effectively. Obviously, the gains are not as spectacular as when children receive one-on-one training, but they are remarkable and consistent nonetheless.

REMEDIAL PROGRAMS

Clinical studies on children who are falling behind at school, or diagnosed with a "learning disability," or "dyslexic," provide the final test to answer the one remaining unanswered question: "Are poor readers, poor readers for life?" We certainly have evidence that this is true when children are left to the mercy of the school system.

In the late 1970s, Jack Fletcher and Paul Satz tested 426 boys in five counties in Florida at the end of second grade and again at the end of fifth grade. On the basis of standardized reading test scores, they classified each child as: superior, average, poor, or severe. What they found was astonishing. Not only do poor readers never catch up, but a large percentage of children actually got *worse* over time: 38.5 percent of the "poor" readers became "severe" readers, 30 percent of the "average" readers became "poor" or "severe," and 51 percent of the "superior" readers became "average" or "poor." The number of children in the ranks "severe" and "poor" *increased* from second to fifth grade by 14 percent, while the proportion of "superior" readers increased by only 6 percent. This shows that there is a strong tendency for good and poor readers to become more discrepant in reading ability over time. These results are illustrated in Table 8–2.

Since this study, the general finding has been that differences in reading skill stay rather more static over time. For example, Connie Juel found that first-grade reading scores correlated to fourth-grade reading scores at .88. In the Connecticut Longitudinal Study discussed in chapter 6, Bennett Shaywitz and others followed 445 children from first to sixth grade. Children who were behind their peers in first grade tended to improve at the same rate as good readers, but they never caught up.

Any reading program that can impact on a poor reader's skill, bringing him up to the level of his peers, is obviously of great importance. Steven Truch, and Robert Slavin and his colleagues, report that the vast majority of children in special ed classrooms make no progress whatsoever. In the remedial reading literature, there is a general finding that it is easier to remediate poor readers when they are young, at six to seven years, than when they are older. This could happen for several reasons. First, the intervention process is easier at the earliest grades. The training studies on very young children showed that they could grasp the alphabet principle quite well by being taught sounds in

TABLE 8-2

CONSISTENCY OF READING SCORE RATINGS
FOR 426 BOYS FROM 2ND TO 5TH GRADE

	Ratings at 5th Grade			
Ratings at 2nd Grade	*Severe*	*Poor*	*Average*	*Superior*
Severe	82%	12%	6%	0%
Poor	38.5%	43.5%	13%	5%
Average	8%	22%	49%	21%
Superior	0%	3%	48%	49%

PROPORTIONS OF CHILDREN IN FOUR READING
CATEGORIES AT 2ND AND 5TH GRADE

	At 2nd Grade	At 5th Grade
Severe	12%	20%
Poor	15%	21%
Average	59%	38%
Superior	15%	21%

Source: Adapted from Fletcher and Satz (1980).

three-sound words and how these sounds are mapped to letters. This early training tends to persist over time *if* classroom reading instruction is not counterproductive. Teaching at this basic level doesn't work for older poor readers, because many of them read simple words as wholes, by "sight." The more that these bad habits become ingrained, the harder they are to shift. The brain sets up the wrong perceptual units for decoding print. Maybe it becomes impossible to shift them.

A second possibility is that if children can't learn to read by age eight or nine, they have something "wrong" with them. This is the crux of the "dyslexia" model, which proposes that children will never be "truly" expert readers because they have a brain disorder.

Finally, older children may not be able to learn to read as well as younger children simply because the remedial program isn't effective for this age group. In other words, this is an instructional issue. Fortunately, we now have the answers to these questions.

We will be looking at three programs of remedial instruction, all of which contain a phoneme awareness training component. However, before I begin, I need to point out that there may be other good reading programs I am unaware of because they lack research support. Many well-known remedial programs *do not* train phonemic awareness, or if they do, do not integrate this appropriately into the main program. These programs fall into three main groups.

The first is the "tutorial" method where the child reads and the tutor corrects the mistakes by supplying the correct word. Sometimes the tutor may also help the student "sound out the word," but does not provide any information that allows the student to be independent and to self-correct his errors. This method is completely ineffective. Most parents can do this, and it is a waste of time and money to get somebody else to do it. (It's also a waste of time for the parents to do it.)

Reading Recovery is a popular remedial program which targets 20 percent of the poorest readers at first grade. It combines reading practice (à la whole language) using a graded book series, along with training in sound to letter correspondences in creative writing and spelling. It was developed by Marie Clay in New Zealand, is used in many schools around the world, and in forty states in the United States. In the United States it is more likely to function as a preventive program. In Great Britain, New Zealand, and Australia, it is "remedial," because children are taught to read one year earlier. It's a pull-out program for one-on-one training for thirty minutes daily, delivered by highly trained, expert teachers. Children in the United States receive about sixty hours of training to produce any gains.

Reading Recovery has had an enormous amount of research devoted to it; much of it is unpublished. Recently, Timothy Shanahan and Rebecca Barr published a detailed critique of this research. Because this is an expensive program and is so common worldwide, I want to review some of the methodological problems with the research and report on two studies that are methodologically sound.

1. A major methodological weakness is that only the Reading Recovery children get daily one-on-one help. What would happen if the control group (the children left back in the classroom) also had one-on-one help with their reading?

2. Shanahan and Barr could find only two studies where there were pretest scores for the control children. This makes it impossible to know whether the children left in the classroom were *really* better readers, or what kind of gains they had made over the school year.

3. Few studies measure gains using standardized tests. Instead, the children are tested on the same book series and exercises *on which they have been trained and on which they had practiced during remediation*. The book levels have been found to be uneven in difficulty, with greater "gains" occurring in the lower levels than in the upper levels.

4. The failure to use standardized tests leads to another problem known as "regression to the mean." Without proper test construction, people who score badly on a test usually get better at the second testing, and people who score very well usually do worse. This would make the Reading Recovery group look better at second testing *without any intervention at all*.

5. Reading Recovery teachers are better teachers. They are specifically selected for training on the basis of their teaching skill. Plus, they receive one year's training in how to teach reading that most classroom teachers never receive.

6. There is a huge attrition in the population of children assigned to Reading Recovery groups. Estimates in both New Zealand and the United States are comparable: 7 percent are referred to special ed programs and an additional 25 to 30 percent fail to complete the program. They are either returned to the classroom for lack of progress, or they don't finish the sixty hours of training. The National Diffusion network, which tracks children going through Reading Recovery programs, reports that of 22,193 children, only 62 percent successfully completed it—an attrition/fail rate of 38 percent.

7. The children who fail to complete the program for whatever reason *are never included in the statistics to measure student gains.*

In view of these serious methodological problems, it is not surprising that in properly controlled studies using standardized tests, the gains for Reading Recovery children are not impressive. In one large-scale study by Gay Sue Pinnell and others, involving forty schools in ten school districts in Ohio, the standard Reading Recovery method was compared to three different programs plus a control group. One was a Reading Recovery program in which the teacher training was compressed into two weeks. Another was a small-group version. Another was a teacher-initiated one-on-one tutoring approach. The only children to make gains were the Reading Recovery children with the highly trained teacher (possible evidence for a teacher training effect). They gained seven standard score points (about six months) during one semester four months). The other groups made no gains. However, when the children were retested in May, these gains had disappeared.

Yola Center and her colleagues tested 296 children in ten schools in Australia. They compared the standard Reading Recovery program to two groups: poor readers in the classroom, and children who were scheduled to receive Reading Recovery, but who had not yet been tutored. At the first posttesting and at a retesting fifteen weeks later, the Reading Recovery children were superior on a standardized reading test. However, eight months later, there was no difference between any of the groups. One-third of the Reading Recovery children failed to learn to read, while one-third of both control groups *did* learn to read.

Reading Recovery is expensive and was estimated to cost local U.S. taxpayers over $4,600 per child *in addition to* the $5,938 per child the taxpayer already pays. This estimate was based on average teacher salaries, teacher training costs for one year, travel to training centers, teacher benefits, etc. The average Reading Recovery teacher is estimated to train only about ten children a year.

There is another large group of remedial programs most of which tends to lack a phoneme-awareness training component and have either little research support or research with similar methodological problems. Diana Clark wrote an excellent book reviewing these programs, and this work was updated by Joanna Uhry in 1995. These programs are best described as "sophisticated phonics," and most are derived from the Orton-Gillingham or Slingerland model. This model is based on the premise that there is a brain condition causing "dyslexia." This premise tends to limit expectations and slow down progress. These programs are often highly structured with extensive curriculum materials. They are found in the school system for normal or low reading groups, in special ed classrooms, in the clinic, and in private schools for "dyslexics." Like all phonics programs, most emphasize learning letter names and letter sounds, and letter names are used as a primary decoding strategy at all levels of the curriculum. (Letter names are particularly problematic for poor readers and consistently get in the way of learning automatic connections between print and sound, and sound and print.)

I call these programs "sophisticated phonics" because they make a genuine attempt to teach most letter patterns of the spelling code. Unfortunately, they teach the code backwards, as all phonics programs do, from letters and letter patterns *to* "sounds." This can lead to the problem described in chapter 5, where the child is taught as many as 200 "sounds of letters." Once this "reverse logic" is set up, spelling cannot be taught with the correct logic. To try to solve this problem, some sophisticated phonics programs have developed scores of elaborate spelling rules that must be mastered and memorized. Some programs take an inordinate amount of time, often two to three years or more to see minimal gains. They tend to work better with younger children, perhaps because they are too young to get bogged down in memorizing rules. The published research on these programs shows that it is difficult to get gains after the age of eight or nine years.

There is no space here to review the individual characteristics of every program derived from this model. An appendix to this chapter lists the problems common to sophisticated phonics programs which will slow down or block remediation. Programs vary widely in the number of these problems.

The Wilson Reading Program is better than most. It is a streamlined version that includes intensive training in phoneme awareness via segmenting and blending exercises. It teaches all 44 phonemes, has an extensive curriculum and research support, and has achieved good gains with children on reading nonsense words in 55–100 hours (unpublished data) and with young adults on spelling (improvement by 13 standard score points in 32 hours).

Like many programs in this group, the Wilson program switches logic from phonemes (sound) to letter patterns (visual) in an attempt to categorize the spelling code. Words are classified into six syllable types. Two of these types are "closed" (CVC) and "open" (CV) syllables, both phonetic categories. English spelling tends to vary systematically in closed and open syllables. This is useful knowledge if it is taught with the correct logic using accurate language:

> The vowel sound /ah/ can be spelled o̲ in 'hot,' 'clock,' 'shop' (closed syllables). The vowel sound /oe/ is *also* spelled o̲ in 'go,' 'potato,' 'hero' (open syllables).

This is an example of "code overlap," where a letter can represent more than one phoneme.

Instead, the Wilson program teaches a visual logic using the terms "long" and "short" vowels: The letter o̲ says its "long vowel" sound (/oe/) in open syllables (go) and its "short vowel" sound (/ah/) in closed syllables (hot). The logic is letter driven, and this makes the statement inaccurate, because the letter o̲ *also* sounds /oe/ in "closed syllables" (most, host, told, sold) and /o͞o/ in "open syllables" (do, to, who).

There are further problems with the remaining syllable types, which are classified as follows: "vowel + e" (bake), "vowel diphthong" (bait), "vowel + r" (pork), and "consonant + le" (table). In a classification system, categories must be mutually exclusive. A syllable should not be in two or more categories at the same time. If you say the words "bake," "bait," and "pork" out loud, you will hear that all three are "closed syllables" (CVC). The vowel sounds in "bake," "bait," and "table" are identical: /b/ /ae/ /k/——/b/ /ae/ /t/——/t/ /ae/ /b/ /u/ /l/. All contain the diphthong /ae/. This means, for example, that the words "bake" and "bait" are *phonologically* in two categories at once—"closed" and "diphthong"—and "bake" is *visually* in a third—"vowel + e." These problems are inevitable when you classify the spelling code by letter patterns rather than by phonemes.

There are three remedial programs that include a phoneme awareness component, use the correct logic to teach the code, and also have research support. Bear in mind that these programs teach the children that other programs like Reading Recovery, Success for All, and most special ed programs *can't teach*. So, in one sense, the "control groups" for these studies consist of millions of poor readers making no progress in special ed classrooms or other remedial reading settings.

ABDs of Reading

The first program, ABDs of Reading, was developed by Joanna Williams of Columbia Teacher's College for small-group instruction in special education classrooms. The other two programs are used in 1-on-1 sessions in private clinics.

Williams developed a program called the ABDs of Reading for children in the age range seven to twelve years who had been referred for extremely poor reading skills. The children were in Title 1 schools in Harlem, New York City. In the first year of the project, children in twenty-one special ed classrooms were tested and divided into experimental and control groups, comprising a total of 127 children. The ABD-trained children were taught in groups of about four children. The control children were taught in special ed classrooms. Lesson plans were written for the teachers who were trained in workshops. Teachers were supervised by staff on the project.

A phonological training component began with syllable segmenting and blending exercises up to and including three-syllable words.

Following this, phoneme segmenting and blending exercises began. Children were also taught letter-to-sound and sound-to-letter correspondence and how to decode simple words and nonsense words. Children were trained on a restricted segment of twelve consonants and three vowels. Children spent about thirty minutes daily on these exercises.

At the end of twenty-six weeks, the children were retested. The ABD groups were significantly better on the phoneme tests, but no differences were found at the syllable level. Unfortunately, these results tended not to hold up well over time when subjects were retested in January of the following year. Williams reasoned that the syllable work had taken up too much time. In a second study, much of the syllable work was dropped, and the main emphasis was on phonetic analysis, focusing more on single-phoneme segmenting and blending. Six new sounds were added and training was expanded to include teaching clusters up to the CCVCC level, along with decoding two-syllable words. Teacher feedback led to a revision of the manual and some of the materials.

In the second project, new children were tested, assigned to the ABD or control groups, and taught in groups of four children (total 102 children). After nineteen weeks (fifty-eight half-hour sessions) children were retested. There was now an overwhelming superiority of the trained children compared to the controls on all measures of phoneme analysis. When children were tested on reading simple words and nonsense words composed of the letters they had been taught, the trained children could read four to five times as many words. They could read real words and nonsense words equally well, whereas the control children read real words twice as well as nonsense words, evidence that they were using a sight-word strategy.

This study provides important information on what does and does not work for teaching poor readers. First, just as for beginning readers, extensive training in syllable segmenting is a waste of time. The control groups could segment by syllables just as well without any special training. Readers' problems are at the level of phoneme analysis. Second, the more time that is spent teaching children the phoneme segments in words, their order, and their connection to letters, the faster their progress in learning to read.

Williams's study used a subset of the sounds in English (twenty-one), and we still don't know whether this new knowledge would transfer to the rest of the alphabet code. Even after nineteen weeks of training, the children in the experimental program could read less than half of the words on a reading test composed of the letters and sounds they had been specifically taught.

Lindamood ADD

We have already discussed the Lindamood method (Auditory Discrimination in Depth). This program is notable for the consistency with which the *phoneme* is used as the organizing principle throughout all lessons, and unlike Williams's program, forty-four phonemes in the language are taught (including /w/ /wh/). The results on the thousands of children who have been remediated at the Lindamood-Bell clinics have never been published, but there are two research studies in the literature that used this program.

One was carried out by Steven Truch and included every child and adult (281 people) who were remediated over a two-year period at the Reading Foundation clinic in Calgary, Alberta. Clients were taught in "intensive" sessions of four hours daily, five days a week, for four weeks, totaling about eighty hours of instruction. Truch states that he expanded the multisyllable component of training beyond the teacher's manual. Clients were taught some alternative spelling patterns for various phonemes and required to read text as part of the training sessions.

Measures were taken both prior to and following training, on the Woodcock Word Attack (nonsense word decoding), the Wide Range (WRAT) reading and spelling tests, and the Gray Oral Reading Test. Everybody gained on all measures, with the possible exception of some of the youngest children on spelling. The greatest gains were on nonsense word decoding, ranging from several months to four years or higher. Seventy-two percent of the older children (ages thirteen to seventeen years) and 84 percent of the adults made gains of four or more years on nonsense word decoding, much greater gains than those of the younger group (ages six to twelve years). Across all age groups, the majority of clients had gains in the range of 16 to 30 standard score points on the WRAT reading test and 8 to 15 points on spelling. The overall gain for all clients, regardless of age, was 17 standard score points for WRAT reading (approximately 1 to 1.5 years, depending upon age). Truch comments that these results are the reverse of what is commonly reported, where older children and adults either cannot learn to read or make much poorer gains than younger children.

Another remedial study, using the same program in the same format, was conducted by Ann Alexander and her colleagues at Gainesville, Florida. They report on ten children, ranging in age from seven to twelve years. All had a diagnosis of "dyslexia" based on extreme discrepancies between reading scores and IQ. The children averaged sixty-five hours overall of training (range 38 to 124 hours). They gained about 1 year on average in reading real words, and over 1½ years in decoding nonsense words. The actual gains per hour of clinical time in reading test scores were identical to those in Truch's study.

Read America: Phono-Graphix™

The last remedial study is our own research carried out in Orlando, Florida at the Read America clinic. The reading program is called Phono-Graphix, a program designed from the bottom up to take advantage of all the research to date. It includes phoneme awareness training, plus a complete curriculum based on the structure of our spelling code, sequenced to match the child's developmental level. The lion's share of the program and the curriculum was developed by Carmen McGuinness, a psychologist and former Montessori school principal.

Two primary goals propelled the development of Phono-Graphix. First, we asked the same question that Brian Byrne and Ruth Fielding-Barnsley asked: What is the *minimum* amount of information a child needs to be taught in order to be fluent and an accurate reader and speller? Second, C.M., in particular, was interested in how fast a child could be taught to read. We began with pilot studies in a Montessori school, testing each component of the program against the response of the child, so that the exercises at each level are aligned with the child's developmental capacity.

A more detailed analysis of this approach will be provided in chapter 12. The basic framework is set out below. The platform for the program was built upon a complete analysis of the English spelling code. I classified 3,000 common English words on the basis of how each phoneme is spelled depending on where it is located in the syllable. These words were then organized from the most to least probable spelling patterns for beginning, middle, and ending sounds in syllables. This was compiled into a spelling "dictionary" called "Allographs," which is reviewed in depth in chapter 10. Carmen assessed spelling patterns in text. This gave us an indication of probability and frequency. For example, the spelling e for the sound /ee/ is a low-probability spelling (doesn't happen in many words), but is seen frequently in print because it is the spelling for common words and prefixes: be, he, me, she, we; be-, de-, re-, pre-. This foundation made it possible to organize a sequence of instruction that would work for everyone from five years old to the adult level. The program proceeds in this order:

1. Teach phonemes (sounds in words) as the basis for the code. Introduce by phoneme alone, and then immediately connect this to a letter symbol.
2. Teach that phonemes in words are written from left to right across the page.
3. Teach three types of phoneme awareness: auditory analysis (manipulating sounds in words), segmenting (isolating phonemes from each other), and blending (joining isolated phonemes into words) using real and nonsense words.
4. Start with phonemes that obey simple 1-to-1 mapping: one sound–one letter symbol. For younger children start with a subset of sounds.
5. Teach segmenting and blending of all possible phoneme combinations within a syllable, including consonant clusters at the 1-to-1 mapping level only. Most clusters obey 1-to-1 mapping.
6. Introduce five remaining consonants each written with a digraph (1-to-1(2) mapping).
7. Teach remaining vowel sounds, using the most probable spelling (Basic Code), and transition immediately to spelling alternatives for each vowel sound (1-to-many mapping).
8. Teach overlaps in the code when they appear. (Children from about seven to eight years can learn steps 7 and 8 concurrently.)
9. Teach multisyllable words, the remaining spelling alternatives, and Latin suffixes.

There are common elements at each step of the program. First, a complete curriculum was designed for each of these steps, using different story vocabularies for three age groups (young child, older child, adult). The curriculum includes manipulatives, worksheets, games, and stories in specially coded text which helps the child see which letters work together to represent one phoneme. Digraphs and phonograms are bolded to show they are a "sound picture" for an individual phoneme. **ough** is a "sound picture" for the phoneme /o/ in 'thought,' the phoneme /ou/ in 'bough,' and the phoneme /oe/ in 'dough.' Stories were written to emphasize a single phoneme and its various spellings. The curriculum is "foolproof" so that it is difficult to use incorrectly.

Teach reversibility. The code works in two directions. The child should copy words he reads, write words he hears (spelling), and read what he writes.

Teach *fast*. Let the child do the work and the thinking. Keep verbal instructions or questions absolutely clear and to the minimum. Never use misleading or meaningless language like "long" or "short" vowels or "silent letters." Avoid "adult logic," such as training in complex categorizing exercises. Leave out *everything* that would have to be discarded later, like learning special mnemonic devices or labels for sounds ("tappers"), or funny script that has to be unlearned. Eliminate everything that gets in the way of automatic decoding and encoding, *especially letter names.*

Teach the *whole code,* including useful examples of consistent spelling patterns, *by exposure.* Never teach "rules," as children cannot remember them, and most will be broken anyway ("when two vowels go walking").

We researched and designed a diagnostic test battery to ensure that the client starts at the appropriate level in the curriculum and doesn't have to waste time being taught something he can already do. (The diagnostic test battery is presented at the end of chapter 11.) Finally, a parent or adult mentor is brought into the process. The mentor receives a book containing over 250 worksheets and stories for all levels of the program. These materials are used in weekly homework. Worksheets are assigned to reinforce what was taught at each session. Worksheets are designed so that the mentor and child must use the correct strategy.

We analyzed the test scores of *every child* who enrolled in the program over a two-year period. There were 87 children ranging in age from 6 to 16 years. The program was set up in one-hour sessions, one hour per week, for 12 weeks. Some children did not need 12 hours; some needed more. The average time in the program was 9.33 hours. Minimum time was 3 hours and maximum time 18 hours. All children were tested at intake and again at 12 hours or earlier if it was their last session. Forty percent had been diagnosed with a "learning disability" and were in special ed programs. Four children had IQs in the 70s. Nineteen had large discrepancies between IQ and reading scores ("dyslexic"). Some children were in speech therapy. We referred four children for vision therapy. Several children couldn't read a single word.

Averaging gains to a constant 12 hours, the children gained 1½ years on the Woodcock Reading Mastery test for reading real words, and over two years in decoding regularly spelled nonsense words. Nearly all of the children were at ceiling (100 percent correct) on tests of phoneme analysis, segmenting, blending, and knowledge of 50 letter-sound correspondences.

Children who met the criteria for "dyslexia" made nearly twice the gains of children who did not, averaging an increase of 2.5 years in reading real words and nonsense words, in 12 hours. The four children with IQs in the 70s made the same gains in phoneme awareness as everyone else, along with a two-year gain in nonsense word decoding, within 12 hours. An update on 217 clients shows that average gains are 1.7 years for real words, 4.3 years for nonsense words, and average hours were 9.65.

These gains are similar to those of Steven Truch and Ann Alexander in almost every respect. The difference is that they happened *seven times faster* per hour of clinical training. We interpret this as due to a number of factors: no loss of time in memorizing categories and category names or teaching the client what he already can do; the extensive curriculum, which provides appropriate sequencing and novelty; the analysis of the entire spelling code and the incorporation of all elements of the code into the curriculum; the high involvement of parents.

An anonymous survey was sent to parents at the end of the second year. Fifty percent responded. It's impossible to know why the remaining 50 percent did not respond, except to note that surveys sent by mail have a response rate of around 10 to 15 percent. Children previously diagnosed LD were no longer LD. The lowest grade in language arts was now a C instead of an F. Grades prior to remediation had been Cs, Ds, or Fs. Now nearly everyone was getting As and Bs. One-third of the children were now on the honor roll where none had been before. Parents reported that 100 percent had increased self-esteem, and any behavioral problems had disappeared (87 percent reported improved behavior). One hundred percent of parents reported that they were still using the worksheets with their children each week.

Taken together, these studies provide overwhelming evidence that there is no such thing as "dyslexia" or a "learning disability." If there was something wrong with these children's brains, the remedial instruction wouldn't work, and certainly not in twelve hours. Children fail to learn to read in school because *they aren't being taught correctly.* They fail to learn to read in remedial programs because *they aren't being taught correctly.* Everyone, it turns out, can be taught to read unless they have such deficient mental and/or linguistic skills, they can't carry on a normal conversation. Note that the Lindamood ADD program and Phono-Graphix *teach everyone to read,* including adults, *and* the 90 percent who never escape special ed classrooms, *and* the large percentage of children that other remedial programs fail.

The most important message from the research reviewed in this chapter is that *a good reading program looks the same whether it is in the classroom or the clinic. There is only one right way to teach an alphabetic writing system.* The evidence from other research, particularly the Success for All Program, suggests that not only is there one right way, but that this right way can be subverted if it is mixed up with "wrong ways," such as trying to teach a linguistic-phonetic approach combined with phonics and whole language. The Santa Maria study also shows that *no books* is preferable to the *wrong* books until children are secure in phoneme awareness, segmenting, blending, and phoneme-letter correspondences.

Overall, the evidence in this chapter points to some inescapable conclusions. The earlier children are taught to decode our alphabetic writing system correctly, the less likely they will be to have reading problems and the sooner they will be able to read stories and books accurately and fluently. Progress in learning to read, either in the classroom or in the clinic, is determined first by the quality and consistency of the program, and second, by the *amount* of one-on-one time each child receives. Children learn much faster in one-on-one sessions than they do in small groups. This finding was reported by Slavin and his colleagues, and is also evident in the comparison of the greater effectiveness of the ADD program with individual help (Arco and Santa Maria) versus our study using small-group instruction.

Finally, our clinical data show that if the entire spelling code is worked out (*all* spelling alternatives and code overlaps), so that this structure controls the sequence of instruction, you will get much greater gains in much less time. One of the major discoveries in our clinical research is that poor readers of all ages do not understand the alphabet code. *They do not know it **IS** a code.* Over and over we have heard children and adults say: "Oh, it's a code! I never knew that!"

We can now answer our last question. No, poor readers don't have to stay poor readers for life. They don't even have to stay poor readers for more than twelve weeks. If your child, or a family member, is languishing in a "remedial" reading program, or in a school for "dyslexics" and making no progress, then he is in the wrong program or the wrong school.

In the final section of the book, I outline the correct way to teach reading and spelling from the beginning for the parent and for the teacher. An in-depth analysis of the remedial reading process and remedial programs are also provided in chapters 11 and 12. Information on where to find materials and curriculum will be found at the end of each chapter.

APPENDIX: PROBLEMS WITH PHONICS REMEDIAL PROGRAMS

1. Take too long. For children sixty hours (one-on-one), or one year (small-group), is the absolute maximum.
2. Fail to teach all 43/44 phonemes.
3. Fail to teach phoneme manipulation, segmenting, and blending. All three must be taught.
4. Are visually driven instead of phonemically driven.
5. Use letter names extensively, forcing the child to translate from letter name to sound.
6. Reading and spelling are taught as separate processes (two codes) instead of as a reversible process (one code).
7. Teach lots of decoding and spelling "rules."
8. Use misleading and incorrect language: "silent letters," "long" and "short" vowels, etc.
9. Train the wrong perceptual units. Consonant clusters and word families are taught as "one sound."
10. Teaching sequence is organized by *letter* patterns rather than by phonemes.
11. Programmatic features are incompatible with child's cognitive level.
12. Teach spelling from code overlaps only. No attempt is made to teach the spelling alternatives for phonemes.

SECTION III

PRACTICAL SOLUTIONS

Chapter 9

BEGINNING READING RIGHT

What does a reading program look like that is based on all of the information presented so far? This is the topic of this final section. We will be looking at a detailed analysis of a good reading program in the classroom and in the clinic. The first two chapters are about the beginning reader. They are for the classroom teacher, reading curriculum specialist, elementary school principal, and for parents who are home-schooling a child, or who just want to ensure that their child will learn to read.

Let's recap the important points from the analysis of writing systems, the English alphabet code, and the scientific research on reading. This knowledge dictates the overall structure of a good reading program.

1. Phonemes are the basis of our writing system. Don't teach larger phonological units, such as sight words, word families, or analogies. This can create reading and spelling problems.

2. The alphabet is a letter code for phonemes in speech, not a "sound code" for letters on the page.

3. When you teach the code the way it was designed, it is *reversible,* as shown in chapter 5. Spelling, writing, and reading can be integrated at all levels of the curriculum.

4. Reading, spelling, and writing are skilled behaviors and, like all skills, must be taught from the bottom up, from the simple to the complex.

5. The English alphabet code contains four mapping logics that are beyond the understanding of most young children (see chapter 7). Solve this problem by making the simple logic "familiar" first, then the next most simple, and so on.

6. The ability to analyze and manipulate phonemes in words, to segment and blend isolated phonemes in words, is the basis for unlocking an alphabetic writing system.

I will guide you through the basic mechanics and sequence of instruction, but you need to do something too. Most importantly, you need to hold the firm belief that all children can be taught to read. Clear your mind of notions like "dyslexia," "learning disabilities," and "developmental delays." The research data are overwhelming that these concepts are invalid. If you base your thinking on a deficit model, this will mean you won't expect rapid progress. If a child has a reading problem, you must do something about it fast. Don't hope the problem will self-correct. It won't.

Most teachers lack proper training in reading instruction. Teachers have told me over the years that they discovered they had no idea how to teach reading when they faced their first class in their own classroom. Often teachers are taught nothing more than how to manage a sequence of "language" activities over blocks of time.

In order to teach reading effectively, you must have adequate phoneme awareness yourself and be fully informed about the sounds in the English language. Teachers and parents alike have little awareness of phonemes in speech, even though they may read and spell adequately. Almost no one knows the structure of our spelling code. I can teach you about the code, but I cannot help you develop phonemic awareness if you do not have it. If you mispronounce words or are unable to decode unfamiliar words in print, you need to receive special help or remediation yourself before you try to teach anyone to read. On the other hand, if you feel confident about your reading ability, have a good "ear" for speech patterns, such as being able to tell dialects apart, then all you will need is the phoneme charts in this chapter and a good audiotape of English phonemes (see Appendix).

Never forget that the teacher of the young reader is the custodian of that child's destiny. Be alert. Many things can go wrong. Don't assume that a first grader is reading with the correct strategy even if he seems to be a fluent reader. The evidence shows that children are much more likely to adopt an inefficient strategy than an efficient one. Many children do not change their strategy no matter how inefficient it becomes. Highly intelligent children, like Alice and Donny, can go for years before anyone is aware that they have a serious reading problem. Teachers must monitor each child's strategy and know how to keep the child on the correct path. This can't happen unless the teacher has time for one-on-one interactions with each child. (A strategy test and other diagnostic tests are included in chapter 11.)

Teachers and parents must also be aware of other problems that will impact on reading. Children with severe speech disorders will have difficulties with an alphabetic writing system. By the time these children begin to read, most will be in speech therapy, but some may not. Teachers should (and most do) request testing for children whom they suspect need help with their speech.

Visually scanning across rows of text from left to right, down one line, etc., is an unnatural act, and this aptitude is slow to develop. For a small minority of children, it is nearly impossible without special help. These children will fall into the habit of guessing "whole words" because they can't see each letter in a word. If a teacher suspects that a child has a visual problem, she should reread the section on vision in chapter 6, and notify the child's parents. They will have to get outside help from an optometrist specializing in vision therapy. This kind of training is not part of special ed.

Due to the fact that there are many ways a child can fall through the cracks, this makes the first three years of school the most important in the child's life. It also means that kindergarten, first- and second-grade teachers are the most important teachers in the entire system. Yet in many schools they are paid less money than teachers in higher grades, when, if anything, this should be just the reverse.

This chapter is about teaching the "Basic Code," the forty-two phonemes in English and their most probable spellings. (/zh/—'vision' isn't taught at this level.) The Basic Code includes two types of logic. The first is where a phoneme "maps" to a single letter symbol (1-to-1 mapping) : /b/ = b in 'big' and 'cab.' The second level of logic is a byproduct of having two few letters for forty-two sounds. At this level, a phoneme "maps" to a letter pair or "digraph" (1-to-1(2) mapping) : /ch/ = ch in 'church.' The advanced levels of the code involving spelling alternatives and code overlaps (1-to-many mapping/many-to-1 mapping) are dealt with in the following chapter.

I will be presenting the overall structure and sequence of a good reading program, rather than a detailed curriculum and lesson plans.

There is simply no space for this here. At the end of this chapter there are word lists to help you get started and information about how to obtain good curriculum materials.

Here is an overview of the major components of a good beginning reading program.

1. *Phoneme awareness.* Training in awareness of phonemes in speech and the ability to segment (separate apart) and blend isolated phonemes in words.
2. *Alphabet principle.* Teach the alphabet code the way it was written: from sound to print.
3. *Sound-to-symbol association.* Teach how to connect phonemes in words to individual letters and letter combinations.
4. *Logic.* Instruction is sequenced in a logical order from simple to complex and conforms to the child's developmental level. It should include the entire spelling code, not just a fraction of it.
5. *Curriculum.* Materials should cover all possible skill areas: phoneme analysis, segmenting, blending, reading, writing, spelling. Materials must be related in *content*. Reading and spelling are reversible.
6. *Pedagogic style.* Teach by exposure and example, using brief, clear explanations. Make sure the child is actively problem solving and not passive.
7. *Fail-safe.* Monitor the child's model of the reading process and his performance at frequent intervals.

Parents have the advantage of working one-on-one with their child. Teachers have to manage a class of twenty to thirty youngsters. Some exercises can be carried out with the whole class, but the bulk of teaching must be done in small groups and with individual children who are slower to learn. Four children per group is about the maximum. This will allow the teacher to monitor each child at some time during the week. Small-group instruction should take from ten to twenty minutes daily depending on the age of the child. Kindergarten teachers usually have an aide, making life much easier. Most first-grade teachers aren't so lucky, and they will have to accommodate the rest of the class while working with groups. Here are some suggestions:

1. Assign the rest of the class some activity.
2. Arrange with other teachers to trade off time by sharing some teaching activities that involve larger groups.

3. Ask for parent volunteers to help in your classroom.

4. Ask the principal for an aide who can be shared among teachers.

The lessons in this chapter are designed for the beginning reader starting at age five. This chapter is oriented to children who have not had much exposure to formal training in reading and presents an overview of lessons that would continue to the middle or the end of first grade. Working in small groups helps to keep track of who is having problems. These children should be given one-on-one sessions of five or ten minutes, preferably daily. It is important to ensure mastery at each level before children move ahead. Over time, it can be seen who is moving quickly and who needs more help.

KINDERGARTEN

As a first principle, skills training in mastering the phonemes of the language and the alphabet code does not preclude other language-related activities going on at home or in the kindergarten classroom. These activities are just as important as learning to read and write. They include story time, building new vocabulary through stories or lessons, and discussions of topics of interest. Whole language did not invent good children's literature. There is no reason why good skills training cannot coexist with quality literature, nor, as you will see later, why good skills training can't employ *materials* of good literary content.

It's important to be aware of what is or is not helpful in teaching reading and spelling. The studies reviewed in the preceding chapter show conclusively that extended training in rhyming and clapping out beats for syllables in words does not impact on learning to decode an alphabetic writing system. As part of early skills training, these activities are simply a waste of time. That does not mean that rhyming should not be included in other activities. Children love rhymes and rhyming games, and a sense of rhyme and meter (patterns of strong and weak syllables) is important for an appreciation of poetry and song.

The issue about teaching letter names is more problematic. Some studies show that knowledge of letter names correlates to reading scores in first grade. But in the systematic studies reviewed in the last chapter, knowledge of letter names did not promote good reading skills, whereas the knowledge of phoneme-to-letter correspondences did. Reading specialists working with poor readers, report that letter names get in the way of training automatic decoding skill and recommend that they not be taught until the child has a clear understanding of the fact that phonemes are the basis for our writing system. I would recommend that letter name teaching form no part of the skills training I am about to describe. I would even suggest that it form no part of any training at kindergarten or first grade. Memorizing the alphabet sequence of letter names has one major purpose, and that is to assist you in looking up words in a dictionary. But you don't really need letter names to do this, the child can memorize the "sounds" they represent.

Another issue concerns capital letters. If capital letters were just larger versions of lower-case letters this would present fewer problems, but most capital letters look entirely different from lower-case letters: A a B b. Lower case is used far more often and should be taught first. Learning two sets of symbols with entirely different visual appearances adds an unnecessary memory load. Capital letters can be introduced later during lessons in creative writing.

The four skill areas involved in learning to read in kindergarten are: awareness of phonemes and sequences of phonemes in words, the logic of the alphabet code, fine-motor control, and visual scanning and analysis of visual detail. All are equally important and reinforce each other.

Sounds and Symbols

Isabelle Liberman discovered that children had to be able to hear and understand the concepts of sequence and number in order to be able to segment and blend sounds in words. She used a simple task where children listened to someone knock under the table and tell how many sounds they heard. The knocks could vary from one to three. ("Close your eyes and tell me how many sounds you hear.") This can be turned into a game played by the children. It provides a good first step in learning about sequences. The teacher or children can make different kinds of sounds, using a bell, a triangle, or a woodblock. Once a child can count a series of sounds accurately, or represent them with a row of cards or blocks, she is ready to work with sounds in words.

When children can count sound sequences correctly and show they understand the concept of a word, then more formal reading instruction can begin. For parents and teachers, I will use the word "phoneme" as an accurate representation of a particular kind of sound in words. For children, use the word "sound" instead. All preschool and

kindergarten programs reviewed in the preceding chapter began training with a subset of phonemes, around six to eight, and kept word
length to two to three sound words only. It is not particularly important which phonemes you choose, except to avoid digraphs and restrict
the choice of vowels to this group: /a/ /e/ /i/ /o/ /u/ (bat, bet, bit,
hot, but). There are lists of two- and three-sound words at the end of
this chapter. Some kindergarten children will not get beyond this level,
if they get that far. If a child makes rapid progress, she can move ahead
to the lessons for first grade (see next section).

An important finding in the research is that the first phoneme in a
word is the easiest to hear, the last phoneme next easiest, and the middle phoneme the hardest. For this reason, the kindergarten programs
reviewed in chapter 8 begin training with the first "sound." Some introduce the last and middle sounds in that order. But the main goal is
for the child to be able to segment, or separate apart, each phoneme in
a word in the right sequence and blend *separate* phonemes back into
the word. Some programs begin with listening exercises. The child sees
a set of simple pictures each representing one object or animal. She says
the word in the first picture and listens for the first sound. As she iden-
tifies each picture in turn, she is asked to put them into groups depending on whether they start with the same first sound: cat cub cap
or big bat ball. Next, pictures can be sorted on the basis of the last
sound (cap map top), and then the middle sound (hot dog top).

The next step is to introduce the concept of a "sound picture." This
term was developed for the Phono-Graphix™ curriculum and solves a
number of problems. Children learn that letters are "pictures" for each
sound they have been learning. This makes it clear what is being symbol-
ized. Just as *real* objects can be drawn in pictures, so can *real* sounds be
drawn as "pictures." This terminology also makes it clear later that some
"sound pictures" have more than one letter. The child's task is to represent each sound in a word in the correct order with its "sound picture."

"This is the "sound picture" (**b**) for the sound /b/ in the word
'bat.'" Show the child the letter, or point to it. Do not use letter names.

Some children will need a lot of practice at each step: sounds alone
and then sound to matching letter. Others will move ahead quickly.
Detailed lessons on how to introduce phonemes and letters are provided in the next section on first-grade reading instruction. Information on where to get materials for teaching these skills is provided in
the Appendix to this chapter. Read America's kindergarten program
"Reading Fundamentals," was discussed in chapter 8.

Logic

The child should learn the logic that governs this level. This is that the *same* phoneme, no matter where it appears in the word—first, middle, last—is represented by the *same* letter symbol. Children may be able to learn a phoneme sequence in a particular two- or three-sound word, but won't be able to generalize to another word containing one or more of those sounds. Exercises should involve words where the same phoneme occurs in different positions: bag/cab, mad/dam, pit/top. You can use nonsense words as well: bip/pim, etc. The teacher or parent needs to point out that no matter where a sound is in a word, it is spelled with the same letter, and no matter where a letter appears in a word, it stands for the same sound.

Fine-Motor Control

The children's section of most bookstores has books for tracing, joining dots, copying shapes, etc. These are good exercises for training a child's ability to control a pencil or pen and to notice visual detail. When a child begins to learn to read, she should also trace and copy letter shapes. *Copying letters helps you see them.* Copying letters in a left-to-right sequence helps the child organize his thinking about the order of sounds in words and the order of words on the page. Once tracing and copying skill is fairly good, children can write some words from memory: **cat dog pig,** and once they can do this, they can write *sound sequences* using the letters they are learning about, saying each sound out loud as they write. They can copy what you say from segmented sounds: /c/-/a/-/t/, and from sounds blended into the word: 'cat.' Use standard wide-lined paper or notebook which you can purchase from a stationer.

Don't waste classroom time letting children scribble, color in a coloring book, or write pseudo-letters. If a child wants to do that at home on his own, that's fine. The children should learn early on that letters have special and constant forms, and that letters are "sound pictures" that stand for sounds in words.

Visual Discrimination and Scanning

These skills will improve the more the child copies letters and words (not scribbles), especially if he sounds out each letter as it goes on the page, as shown above. The movement of the hand, the sound of the voice, trains the eye where to look. The sound of the voice, the place where you look, trains the hand where to move. As an aside, "sky-writing," or writing letter forms in the air (a feature of some reading programs), doesn't work. To create cross-modal connections like the ones I'm talking about, *two or more* modes must be connected: writing is movement made *visible.*

Some children may not get far with these skills, and that's perfectly OK. Children are highly variable in their perceptual and motor development at this age, and most will improve noticeably when they are six. What you have done is put them on track, so that when reading and writing begin in earnest, they will have the right logic, and some of the right skills.

FIRST GRADE: TEACHING THE BASIC CODE

Good reading programs use materials that correspond to the child's developing expertise in mastering the alphabet code. This does not mean that the teacher should not read interesting stories, teach poetry, or invite children to invent stories that she can transcribe. One innovative teacher I observed published a weekly "magazine" of individual children's stories. These were not stories the children wrote in undecipherable invented spelling, but stories composed *verbally* that the teacher recorded. The children experienced the power of writing directly, as a true method of preserving their thoughts and ideas. These transcriptions transcended time and space because they were completely intelligible to the whole family. They faithfully preserved what the child *meant* to say.

Teaching the beginning reader is accomplished by keeping to materials and exercises that are mutually reinforcing and complementary. If a child is just beginning to master 1-to-1 mapping of consonants and simple vowels:

a pig sat in mud

he or she should not be expected to read text written at a more complex level of logic:

Fido was a friendly dog until he saw a stranger in the yard.

The more compatible the materials (games, readers, stories, worksheets, spelling words) across all three skills: reading, writing, spelling, the *faster* children will learn and the less likely they will be to develop reading difficulties. The text of traditional children's literature is peppered with digraphs, consonant clusters, phonograms, and irregular spellings, and should be off limits for the child reader at this stage. This does not mean that children's literature is off limits for the teacher or parent at story time. Nor am I proposing that "big books" should be banished from the classroom. However, the sooner the child masters the alphabet code, the sooner she will be able to read anything in print.

In this section, I have adopted a pragmatic approach. I am assuming that children have not had the advantage of skills training in kindergarten as described above. For most teachers, and for parents who have discovered that something is amiss with their six-year-old's reading skills, this section outlines how to begin from the beginning. Traditional kindergarten instruction will usually guarantee that the child has learned precisely what he does not need, and precisely what he should not know. Children entering first grade have usually memorized letter names, which can interfere with learning to read and spell. Many of them have been taught lots of "sight words," setting them up for failure. These children have learned two things:

1. Letter names are something you chant in sequence and don't help you read.
2. The way you learn to read is to memorize whole words by sight.

The goals of beginning reading instruction are identical to those for the kindergartner. The difference is that most six-year-olds understand the logic of sequencing and symbolizing. Working in small groups, or with one child, the first step is to begin introducing each phoneme, first by sound alone, and then with its accompanying letter. Consonants and vowels should be interleaved, so that children can begin to read, write, and spell simple words. The order in which these sounds are introduced is governed by the difficulty of the mapping logic.

For the Teacher

Because the teacher or parent needs to know how to produce each phoneme correctly, Tables 9–1 and 9–2 are for adults, so that you can organize your thinking. Next, I illustrate how these sounds should be introduced to the child. To help understand how English phonemes are produced, they have been set up in linguistic categories. The categories are based on which parts of the mouth move to make each sound and how the air is released. Consonants can be "plosive" or "stopped" (airflow is interrupted, held, and "exploded"), "fricative" (expelled with force or friction), "aspirated" (breathy), or "continuous" (voicing can

TABLE 9–1

Classification of English Consonants

Parts of the Mouth	Voiced	Unvoiced	Air Type
bilabial	b	p	plosive
alveolar	d	t	plosive
velar	g	k	plosive
labial/palatal	j	ch	plosive
labial/palatal	zh	sh	fricative
palatal/dental	z	s	fricative
dental/labial	v	f	fricative
lingual/dental	th	th	fricative
pharyngeal		h	fricative
labial/velar		w	fricative
alveolar	l		continuous
velar	r		continuous
AIR VIA THE NOSE			
bilabial nasal	m		continuous
palatal nasal	n		continuous
velar nasal	ng		continuous
COARTICULATED CONSONANT			
labial/velar		qu (kw)	plosive/ fricative

Latin terms: labial-lips, alveolar-upper gums, velar-soft palate, palatal-hard palate, dental-teeth, lingual-tongue, pharynx-throat, nasal-nose.

be extended). Sixteen consonants can be categorized into pairs because they are produced by the same mouth movements and vary only because one of the pair is voiced and one is not: /b/ (bat) and /p/ (pat). Stand in front of a mirror, put your hand on your throat, and say each pair of sounds.

All vowels are "voiced" (vocal folds vibrate). Vowels differ from one another due to the position of the lips, the jaw, and the tongue. Linguists have organized the vowels into a "vowel circle" based on the position of the jaw, lips, and tongue. Vowels adjacent on the circle are harder to tell apart. We have found in the clinic that children have trouble discriminating the adjacent vowels in the sequence /i/ /e/ /a/ /u/ /o/ (bit, bet, bat, but, hot), set out here in order from the jaw most closed/mouth most smiling/tongue most forward, to the jaw and

TABLE 9–2A

Classification of Simple English Vowels

Sound	Jaw Position	Word	Lip Posture	Tongue
ee	close	see	smile	forward
i		sit	smile	forward
e	to	get	smile	forward
u	↓	but	unrounded	mid
o	open	hot	unrounded	back
aw	open	law	rounded	back
oo	to	look	rounded	raised
o͞o	close	soon	rounded	raised

TABLE 9–2B

English Diphthongs (Double Vowels)

Sound	Word	Combines Vowel Sounds:
ae	ate	/e/ + /ee/
ie	die	/o/ + /ee/
ue	cue	/ee/ + /o͞o/
oe	toe	/u/ + /o͞o/
ou	out	/a/ + /o͞o/
oi	oil	/oe/ + /ee/

VOWEL + R

Sounds	Word	Combines Sounds:
ar	far	/o/ + /er/
or	for	/oe/ + /er/
er	her	/er/

mouth most open/tongue flat (see Table 9–2). You might want to check this in a mirror. You should be able to pronounce each of these vowels accurately, with slight differences in the position of the mouth and jaw, so that children can hear *and see* the difference between them. Because vowels with similar postures (/i/ and /e/) sound alike, introduce the vowels further apart on the chart first. /i/ (bit) and /o/ (hot) are the widest contrast, /i/ and /a/ (bat) make the most three-sound words (see Appendix.) Diphthongs are combinations of two simple vowels produced in rapid succession, and count as *one* vowel sound in a syllable.

Getting Started

The Basic Code presented at the beginning of this book is illustrated in Table 9–3 on p. 223 in a more convenient form. The teacher should begin by asking the children if they know how they produce speech. Ask them to close their eyes and feel how their mouth parts move when they talk. Draw their attention to particular movements, like what the lips are doing at the start of these words:

'mut' 'but'
'mit' 'pit'

Feel the teeth touch the lower lip:

'fat' 'vet'

Feel where the tongue goes at the start of these words:

'dog' 'log'
'tag' 'nag'

These exercises can be done with the whole class, and then repeated in small groups.

Working in small groups, tell the children you are going to teach them how each sound is made in *their speech,* and how each of these sounds is written. Start with a set of consonants that obey 1-to-1 mapping (*no digraphs*) and choose those that are easy to model, and easy for the children to feel and hear. Model each sound clearly and insist that the children watch your mouth. The sound /m/ is a good beginning because the children can see your mouth posture, feel this in their own mouths, and hear it easily when it is extended /mmmmmmmmmmmmmmm/.

Hints for ungluing sounds. When you introduce *one* of these voiced consonants: /b/ /d/ /g/ /j/ /w/ say it *with no or minimal vowel attached to it.* Say /b/ and not /buh/. Voicing obviously adds sound beyond the consonant, but keep it as short as possible. Nor should a vowel sound ever be connected to an unvoiced consonant, like /h/ /k/ /p/ /t/. Say /p/ (a puff of air) and not /puh/. Only this way can the child learn how to "unglue" sounds in words. This is the key for using a phonetic alphabet. (The voiced consonants /m/ /n/ /ng/ /l/ /r/ /th/ /v/ /z/ can be extended without a vowel, and so can the unvoiced consonants /f/ /s/ /sh/ /th/.)

When all the children can make the sound you have introduced (/mmm/) both at the beginning and at the end of several three-sound words, introduce the letter that represents it in print. You can do this with a movable alphabet, or use a small white board and marker. A complete movable alphabet is useful for teaching the Basic Code level. If you purchase one, make sure the the digraphs are printed together on the same card, felt, or tile (see Appendix). You can make your own movable alphabet out of card stock and laminate the letters.

The word charts at the back of this chapter list two- and three-sound words with 1-to-1 mapping only. You can use them to set up a sequence of instruction, or purchase curriculum materials organized in this sequence (see Appendix). It's a good idea to introduce the sound /k/ with both spellings k and c because more words are spelled with c than with k.

You should move quickly through the introductory process. Be sure to make it cumulative by incorporating previous information into new lessons. Children will learn this 1-to-1 logic rapidly and should be able to master a new phoneme/letter combination about every other day or faster. They should have practice, however, to make this stick, at least one hour over a two-day period.

When the child has memorized a subset of phoneme/letter relationships, she can begin to learn the important elements of an alphabetic writing system. These are how to segment or separate phonemes in two- and three-sound words into isolated sounds: /c/ /a/ /t/, how to blend sounds back into a word: 'cat,' and how to listen for changes in sounds in a series of words, a process called "tracking" or "chaining." Some of the exercises are described below. The child should also write at every step, copying letters in sequence, saying the sound aloud (not the letter name) while copying each letter, and spelling words you dictate, sound by sound (no letter names).

Reading materials can be purchased that will complement these early lessons and are listed in the Appendix. Read America has stories

TABLE 9–3

Basic Code and Letters for a Movable Alphabet

VOWELS			CONSONANTS	
			Sound and letters are the same.	
Sound	Key Word	Letter(s)	Sound/Letter	Key Word
a	sat	a	b	bed
e	set	e	d	date
i	sit	i	f	fun
o	dog	o	g	get
u	but	u	h	hot
ae	ate	a–e	j	jump
ee	seem	ee	k	kin
			<u>c</u> as option for <u>k</u>	
ie	time	i–e	l	log
oe	tone	o–e	m	mat
ue	cute	u–e	n	not
oo	book	oo	p	pan
o͞o	soon	oo	r	red
oi	oil	oi/oy (optional)	s	sit
ou	out	ou	t	top
er	her	er	v	vet
/ah/er/	far	ar	w	wet
/oe/er/	for	or	x /ks/	fox
			z	zip
			ch	chip
			ng	song
			qu	quit
			sh	ship
			<u>th</u>	them
			th	thin

for the Basic Code level. Some phonics readers are good because they stay with simple three-sound words, like the early books in the "The Bob Books" and "Primary Phonics" series. This is also true of some of the older phonics readers which may be in your library. A list of them is included at the end of this chapter. Stay with materials that are consistent with 1-to-1 mapping first before moving on to digraphs.

The child will learn a few "sight words" *in the context of reading.* These are words that are not easy to decode because their spellings are irregular. Several irregularly spelled words are hard to avoid in stories: a (uh), the (thuh), was (wuz), one (wun), once (wunce), says (sez). If the child encounters one of these words, simply tell him what it says. Don't explain anything or give a lecture on "sight words" or insist that he memorize them. There are so few of these words, children will learn them without difficulty. Be sure that he *does* read all the words that are consistent with the Basic Code to this point. *Do not ask children to read books containing a lot of clusters and irregularly spelled words,* no matter how pretty the pictures nor how much "fun" they are to read.

Actively discourage letter names. If a teacher asks the class: "What sound does this letter stand for?—b?" she'll get a chorus of "It's a bee!" She must insist that "bee" is a letter name they *will have to forget for now.* Children should be told that letter names do not help you read or spell. What is important is the *sound* each letter stands for in a word. *Show* them the letter b—don't say its name—and tell them it is a "sound picture" for the sound /b/. No matter where that sound comes in a word, it is *always* spelled with this "sound picture": b.

Lessons should begin with a review of what was done during the previous lesson. This means keeping a record book, especially if you are working with several different groups. The teacher needs to make certain that all children learn to do these exercises independently. Children can gradually be identified as to who is going to need more time versus those who "get it" immediately.

During this first level, children can practice using a variety of materials. The letters can be traced, copied, or written from memory. Montessori teachers can use sandpaper letters, first traced by movement of a finger and then copied onto paper while saying the sound. Pictures or objects can be used for cue matching of the initial, final, or middle sound, and then the letter for this sound can be printed on paper or in a workbook. Children should copy words, and "say each sound" as they are writing each letter.

When these exercises become familiar, the teacher or parent should introduce the terms "consonants," little short sounds that come and go quickly, and "vowels," sounds that last longer. Children should be told that you can't have a language with just consonants. Tell a story in an imaginary language made up of consonants so they get the point.

Vowels add volume to speech. You can sing and shout with vowels and not with consonants. Use an example of calling a child for dinner, first with the consonants of his name: "John"—/j/-/nnnnnn/, and then say the vowel sound /ah/ elongated. Ask the children which sound John would be likely to hear if he was down the street. If we only had vowels, we couldn't have a language either. Illustrate this by telling a story using only vowels. The point of this exercise is to give children a vocabulary to talk about the two types of sounds in words. This lesson should make it clear that most words have both vowels and consonants (exceptions are: I, you, a), and ALL WORDS HAVE A VOWEL, no exceptions.

This information is very helpful for spelling in creative writing. Children tend to leave vowels out of words when they write. 'The nd' is a common mistake. The child uses the *letter name* "en" for the vowel+consonant sounds. If children are taught accurate sound-letter relationships, plus the fact that all words have vowels in them, they would never make these kinds of errors.

Segmenting, Blending, and Tracking

After a few vowels and several consonants, along with their accompanying letters, have been introduced, various exercises can begin. Simple CV, VC, or CVC words and nonsense words can be constructed with the movable alphabet in small-group exercises with the teacher. Children should watch and listen while the teacher makes the sounds as they are separated and joined into words using the movable alphabet. This is also available in transparencies (see Appendix). Begin with very short patterns, and make certain each child can see as you model the changing sounds, left to right (child's view). Next the children can make the sounds as the teacher moves the letters apart and together:

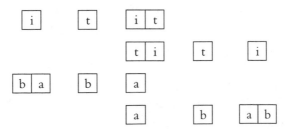

Hundreds of combinations can be made using real and nonsense CV, VC, and CVC patterns. Showing children how these patterns can be connected and disconnected helps them to understand how sounds are represented in print. During exercises with the child, she should "touch and say" each letter and its sound, both when the letters are apart (segmenting) and when they are side by side (blending). This technique is very powerful because it focuses the child on left-to-right sequencing as she decodes words and trains the eye to look at every letter.

Few children have difficulty hearing isolated phonemes (/b/ /m/ /v/) or making comparisons between them (is /d/ the same as /g/?). The trouble begins when phonemes are embedded in words. "Tracking" or "chaining," a technique developed by Pat Lindamood, allows the child to hear that there has been a change made *somewhere* in a sound sequence and to begin to identify where in that sequence the change took place.

The rules of tracking are as follows:

a. Only one phoneme changes at a time
b. Phoneme changes occur in one of five ways:
   1. *Addition.* A new sound comes in   tip/stip
   2. *Deletion.* A sound went away   tip/ip
   3. *Substitution.* One sound went away and another
      took its place.   tip/top
   4. *Repetition.* Two sounds in the word are the same.   tip/pip
   5. *Reversibility.* Sounds change places   tip/pit

A tracking sequence can extend anywhere from a single phoneme to a multisyllable word. Sample sequences are set out below and in the word lists starting on p. 236. The teacher begins by putting out a letter from the movable alphabet facing the child. For groups, each child should have his own set of movable alphabet cards, tiles, or felts. The child is told: "If that is /p/, show me /pi/" (say /i/ as in 'it') and the child should bring the letter i̱ into position to the right of the p̱. The chain proceeds: "If that is /pi/ show me /pip/," the teacher repeating the last word each time before the next instruction. The child, and not the teacher, is responsible for manipulating the letters according to the instructions. For each tracking exercise give the children only the letters they will need for the sequence. In the first example below left, they will need

a i o b h p p s t

Real Words	Nonsense Words
p	p
pi	pi
pip	pim
pop	pom

hop	dom
hot	dop
hat	dup
at	tup
bat	tut
bit	ut
sit	sut
sip	tus

When children make an error or become confused, simply back up and repeat an earlier simpler pattern. Keep the sequencing simple if the child has difficulty with complex transformations. The child should "touch and say" the sounds in left-to-right order to keep the sounds in mind. A child must work just at the margin of his level of competence.

When children write a word, or spell it with a movable alphabet, using spellings that have not yet been taught or discussed, these should correspond to the Basic Code. For example, "duk" or "duc" is acceptable for "duck" until the child has learned the ck spelling for the sound /k/.

Consonant Clusters

When a child is secure with simple CV, VC, and CVC patterns, and most letters for 1-to-1 mapping have been taught, consonant clusters can be introduced. The consonant clusters that begin words and end words are provided in Table 9–4. Lists of words with consonant clusters are provided at the end of this chapter. Consonant clusters are *two or more sounds* and must never be confused with digraphs (one sound). At this point in learning to read, consonant clusters must be restricted to those spelled with single letters, those the child has already learned. *Most clusters have only one spelling.* This means the children can take the knowledge they have so far and expand this using the same logic into hundreds of new words.

When children move on to clusters, also make it clear that double letters stand for only one sound. The double letters **ff ll ss** occur often at the ends of common words.

Start with two-sound clusters in the initial position: /s/ /l/ 'slat' (CCVC). When children are reasonably secure on several different CCVC clusters, move on to two-sound clusters in final position: /s/ /t/ 'last' (CVCC), and finally to clusters in both positions: 'blast' (CCVCC). When you use nonsense words in tracking exercises, be sure to keep to the clusters that are legitimate in English, that is, those

TABLE 9–4

Consonant Clusters

Beginning Clusters	Spelling Options	Ending Clusters	Spelling Options
bl br			
dr dw		dth	
fl fr		ft fth	
gl gr			
kl kr	**cl cr** chl chr	(kt)	**ct**
		ld lf (lj) lm ln lp lt lch lsh lth	**lge**
		mp mpt (mf)	**mph**
		nch nd (nj) nt nth	**nge**
pl pr		pt pth	
		rb rc rd rf rg (rj) rk rl rm rn rp rt rch rsh rth rve	**rge**
sk sl sm sn sp spl spr st str sw squ	**sc** sk sch	sk sm sp st	
tr tw			
		xt	
		(ngk) (ngkt) ngth	**nk nct**
shr thr			

Clusters in parentheses are never spelled this way. Optional spellings in bold are either the *only* spelling or the most likely spelling.

that are likely to appear in real words. In English, /mp/ is a legitimate final cluster ('bump'), /np/ is not, even though it can be pronounced.

As a rule of thumb, some clusters are much more common than others. Consonant plus /l/ or /r/ is common in initial consonant clusters and is fairly easy to hear, especially by extending or exaggerating the /l/ or /r/ sound in the word. These two consonants follow a limited number of initial consonants: /b/, /f/, /g/, /k/ (c), and /p/ (brim, flat, grip, glad, clap, plan). The /r/ can also follow /d/ or /t/ (drop, trip). The initial /s/ blends with more sounds than any other: /k/, /l/, /m/, /n/, /p/, /t/, /w/ (skip, slam, smell, snap, spin, stop, swim), as well as in triple clusters: /spl/, /str/ (split, strap). However, triple clusters are very difficult for young children to master, especially in final position ('tempt'), and come late in speech development. It is not important to teach triple clusters at this stage. Leave them for later.

Final consonant clusters begin with a limited number of consonant sounds, mainly /l/, /n/, /r/, and /s/. Most of these sounds *precede* the following consonants: /d/, /p/, /k/, /t/. Examples for /l/ are 'old,' 'alp,' 'elk,' 'melt,' for /n/ 'and,' 'bent.' The sound /r/ does double duty in a final cluster. It functions as part of the vowel and as part of the cluster: /f/ /or/ /t/—'fort.' Save these /r/ clusters for later, when the child has mastered vowel+r spellings.

The same kinds of activities described earlier should be used for learning clusters. These include sorting words cued by a picture containing initial or final clusters or both, copying words with clusters, filling in missing letters in a cluster on worksheets (c—ab = crab), writing stories that contain certain words with clusters, and "tracking" exercises with clusters. As a caution, don't get digraphs (ch, ng, sh, th, ck, etc.) mixed up in these exercises.

When students begin to show facility in mastering clusters in both initial and final positions in a word, they are ready to move on to consonant digraphs.

Consonant Digraphs

Consonant digraphs introduce a completely new logic. The teacher should not begin to work with digraphs until the child is comfortable manipulating, reading, and spelling sounds with single letters. The children have so far learned a particular logic, which says: Sounds can be represented by one letter: one letter–one sound. For young children, a switch to a logic that says: "Sometimes two of *these same letters* will represent a new sound" creates a problem in logic in which a symbol is simultaneously in two categories at the same time (see chapter 7). When the simple logic of 1-to-1 mapping is secure, then teaching digraphs will go smoothly and quickly.

The remaining consonant sounds in English are:

/ch/		chair
/ng/		ring
/sh/		shut
/th/	(voiced)	them
/th/	(unvoiced)	thing
/qu/		quit (qu is /kw/ pronounced simultaneously)

Introduce the ck spelling alternative here also. It is a common spelling for /k/ in the final position in a syllable.

Digraphs need a special introduction to explain that two letters make a "sound picture" that stands for one sound. If the children are receptive, they may enjoy hearing the story about the people who invented our alphabet. The monks borrowed the letters from the Latin alphabet and ran out of letters because English had a lot more sounds than Latin. Instead of inventing new ones, they just stuck two of the old letters together to stand for the leftover sounds. The two letters are *a* "sound picture" for one sound. This is an interesting story and makes the important point that letters are assigned to sounds, rather than sounds being assigned to letters.

To understand that a digraph represents *only one sound,* children have to go back and explore mouth movements, and do listening exercises, to make this point stick. Once the child has become aware of the *sound* /ch/, the teacher can introduce the "sound picture" (letter pair) ch written on a *single* letter tile, or card, or felt, on the movable alphabet. Do not teach this with two separate letters pushed together. This same procedure is used for the remaining consonants spelled with digraphs. Practice with digraphs proceeds in exactly the same way as discussed earlier. Lists of words spelled with digraphs are found at the end of this chapter.

If you introduce the spelling alternative ck, explain that this is another "sound picture" for the sound /k/ at the ends of words.

Redundant Consonant Letters

The letters c, x, and qu are redundant in English spelling. They stand for sounds that can be spelled with other letters. This is important information for the teacher, but the children do not need to know this.

Just teach them as "sounds." Children will already have learned that the letter c stands for the sound /k/. Later, they will be learning that c is also a spelling alternative for the sound /s/ when it is followed by the letters e, i, or y: cent, city, cypress (the only spelling rule that is completely consistent). The letter x stands for /ks/, spelled in the singular as x (fox) and in the plural as ks or cks: (sharks, socks). The spelling x is also used in the Latin prefix ex, as in "exit" and "exact," for /ks/ (eksit) or /gz/ (egzact), and rarely as /z/ at the beginning of Greek words (xylophone). The letters qu stand for the consonant sounds /kw/ pronounced simultaneously, and this spelling is always used. You may have a child who notices that /ks/ is "two sounds," and that's OK. Just tell her that she is a very good listener to notice this.

Plurals

Introduce plurals after consonants are secure. Plurals are always spelled s or es even though they sound /z/ or /ez/ most of the time. In fact, the only time that the letter s sounds /s/ is when it follows the phonemes /f/ /k/ /p/ /t/ (cliffs, bricks, caps, cats). Children will need to be taught about plurals (spelled s but sound /z/) so no one gets confused. Most children have no trouble with this in reading because it doesn't "sound right" to read words incorrectly: 'treess,' 'trainss.' In creative writing, however, they might write a z, which is incorrect: 'treez,' 'trainz.'

Vowel Digraphs

So far, the children have learned five vowel sounds and five vowel letters. There are eighteen vowel sounds in English. The children should have practiced enough consonant digraphs to be comfortable with the fact that double letters are "sound pictures" for one sound. The teacher must be aware that apart from poor phonemic awareness *vowel digraphs are the single most important cause of reading and spelling problems.* There are so many of them spelled so many different ways. The children must be taught consistent spellings for these vowels (Basic Code) and stay with this long enough for the sounds to be firmly embedded in memory. The key to mastery of English spelling is being absolutely secure on the sounds of the vowels. Some vowels are hard to tell apart and vowel spellings cannot be constantly shifting when these sounds are introduced.

As the teacher proceeds, *introducing one vowel sound at a time,* she should continue to use all of the techniques described earlier. Children should learn the vowels in the same types of exercises, segmenting, blending, copying, tracking, reading, writing, spelling. Teach the remaining vowels in this order.

e-Controlled Vowel Spellings

Five vowel letters combine with e̱ to stand for five different vowel sounds. There is no satisfactory way to classify the eighteen English vowels. Vowels aren't "long" or "short," so that's no help. Vowels *are* "simple" or "complex" in terms of their sound patterns. Complex vowels, or "diphthongs," are two simple vowel sounds pronounced in rapid succession: /oe-ee/ 'toil,' but our spelling code doesn't mark vowels this way (toeeel). So this is no help either. As there is no solution to this problem, don't try to classify vowels for children, especially do not use the terms "long" and "short." This makes the child believe that he should have noticed something about these vowels that he cannot see or hear.

The e-controlled vowel spellings are introduced next for several reasons.

1. They reuse all five vowel letters the children just learned.
2. They all use the same spelling feature (an extra e̱).
3. The e-controlled spelling is the most probable spelling for the vowel sounds: /ae/ /ee/ /ie/ /oe/ and /ue/. In other words, they are ideal for the Basic Code.
4. They introduce a new principle, in which a digraph can be split apart by a consonant and still work together. The e̱ can "control" the pronunciation of the preceding vowel *at a distance*. These are the only digraphs like this.

The teacher needs to know that all but one (/ee/) is a diphthong, so she can pronounce them correctly. She needs to know that the splitting off of the e̱ occurs very rarely for the sound /ee/ (seen, queen, theme), *always* for the sound /ae/ (came), and mainly for the rest: time, tone, cute. For these reasons, the movable alphabet should reflect these common spelling patterns:

a-e   ee   i-e   o-e   u-e
same, seem, time, tone, cute

Be sure not to confuse the vowel sound /ue/ with /o͞o/. 'Cute' is not 'coot'; /ue/ is a diphthong (/ee-o͞o/) and /o͞o/ is a simple vowel.

The children should be taught that even though the <u>e</u> is separated from its vowel letter, the sound is the same as if the letters are side by side. *Do not teach this as "the <u>e</u> is silent."* Instead, simply say that these letters work together as a "sound picture" for a vowel sound. To illustrate how the <u>e</u> can move to the right, make up lots of these vowel pairs on card stock and then cut the letters apart, inserting the consonant to spell a word:

$$\boxed{c}\;\boxed{ae}\;\boxed{k} \qquad \boxed{c}\;\boxed{a}\;\boxed{k}\;\boxed{e}$$

Let the children use scissors to cut off the <u>e</u> from its companion vowel, and reassemble the letters in the correct order. Words with e-controlled spellings are listed at the end of the chapter.

Another way to teach the impact of the <u>e</u> on antecedent vowels is to transform one word into another using the letter <u>e</u> from the movable alphabet: subtracting and adding it back to make words like: bit/bite, hat/hate, win/wine, pin/pine, etc. There is a list of these words at the end of this chapter.

Vowels Spelled with O

The next group of vowel digraphs all coincidentally use the letter <u>o</u> for no particular reason. These are the vowel sounds /o͞o/ "soon," /oo/ "book," /ou/ (/a-o͞o/) "out," and /oi/ (/oe-ee/) "oil." The first two are simple vowels; the last two are diphthongs. The difference between the vowel sounds /o͞o/ (soon) and /oo/ (book) is hard to hear, which probably explains why they are spelled the same way. Both vowel sounds are produced by an exaggerated rounding of the lips. The /o͞o/ has the smallest opening. The teacher should ask children to say word pairs contrasting these sounds and listen carefully: soon/soot, boon/book, loot/look, and so forth. Teach these vowels one at a time using all the previous exercises.

Vowel+r (Growl Vowels)

The last vowel group, and one of the easiest for most American children to hear, is the vowel+r group. In some U.S. dialects and in England and Canada, final /r/ is softened to /ah/ or /eh/ 'motheh' instead of 'motherrrr'). One of the vowels in this group is an extended /r/ by itself, spelled <u>er</u>, <u>ir</u>, or <u>ur</u> to distinguish it from a consonant: 'furry'—'free'. There are two other major vowel+r sounds (and six minor ones).

All of them combine a vowel with the sound /r/. These are /ah-er/ always spelled ar (car), and /oe-er/, which can be spelled: or, oar, ore, our, ar, oor (for, soar, tore, four, war, door). The teacher needs to understand that the r alters the way the vowel *letter* in front of the r would sound in Basic Code (cat—car), in just the same way that the e changes the vowel sound in e-controlled spellings. Stand in front of a mirror and say these word pairs slowly, listening to the vowel:

hem her   cat car   fob for

The Vowel Sound /aw/

The sound /aw/ is a problem and can be taught as a separate sound. Say 'dog' then say 'law' with lips rounded, and see if you hear any difference. In most parts of America these two vowel sounds have "fallen together" which means they sound alike. In some regions and other English-speaking countries, however, they are still two distinct sounds. Depending on where you live, you can teach this as a new vowel sound *or* as a spelling alternative (aw) for the sound /o/ (hot). If you can't hear the difference between the vowels in 'hot' and 'law,' it probably doesn't exist in your region.

Y Vowel Letter

Y is not a consonant, as many people think. Y is a spelling alternative for several vowel sounds, mainly /ee/ (baby), /ie/ (cry), and /i/ (gym), the most common substitution being for the final /ee/ in multisyllable words (lucky, plenty, mainly, vicinity). The beginning sound in the word 'yes' is also a *very* brief /ee/ sound (so brief, some people can't hear it), but it can't be spelled with an ee, or else 'yes' would be spelled: eees, 'yellow' eeellow, and so forth. The teacher might want to introduce the letter y here because it appears frequently. She should explain that sometimes this letter is a "sound picture" for vowel sounds the children already know. Y can be introduced informally when a child asks how to spell a word like "yes," or "baby" during creative writing.

Once the children have learned one symbol for every sound in English, they now know the Basic Code, the most common spelling for forty-two sounds of the English language. They will also know the alternative spellings c, ck, and y. This sets up an "Initial Teaching Alphabet" but without any funny letters that must be unlearned. Children can now spell hundreds of words correctly, *and nearly every word in English phonetically.* When this initial alphabet or Basic Code is secure, it is time to move on to the next step in the logic of learning the alphabet code. Children are now ready for training in mastering the spelling alternatives of English orthography which are introduced in the next chapter.

This chapter provided a brief overview of the sequence in which the sound-to-letter and letter-to-sound code of our alphabet should be mastered. Depending on the age and aptitude of the child when lessons begin, this sequence should take from about four to eight months. If this doesn't happen, you're either doing something wrong, or the child has a problem you haven't discovered, like a difficulty with visual tracking. If you're using this approach correctly, any problem a child might have with phoneme awareness should disappear.

The approach outlined here is compatible with most types of language arts instruction that are ongoing in the classroom. If taught properly, the children can read stories written in simple prose by the second semester of first grade. This method is not, however, compatible with invented spelling, where children are allowed to misspell words without correction and to invent and practice spelling patterns that don't exist in English. This will undo everything the teacher is trying to accomplish.

This does not mean that children should do no creative writing. By the middle of first grade, children should have a good grasp of the Basic Code, which means they can write most words in English they want to and be able to spell them phonetically. They can do lots of creative writing. Any errors in their "invented" spellings can be checked for confusion they may have about the code so far, and turned into an individual spelling lesson. Spelling lessons should be based on words that the child uses and that he can read, and not on unrelated word lists.

WORD LISTS

CV/VC/CVC Words

VOWELS: a, e, i, o, u
CONSONANTS: p/b, t/d, k/g, f/v, s/z, j

a	e	i	o	u
at	bed	bib	Bob	bug
bad	beg	bid	dog	bus
bag	bet	big	dot	but
bat	fed	bit	fog	dug
fat	get	did	got	Gus
gap	jet	dig	job	jug
gas	keg	fib	jog	jut
pat	peg	fig	jot	pup
sad	pep	fit	pop	sub
sag	pet	if	pot	tub
sap	Ted	it	sob	tug
sat	vet	kid	top	up
tag		kit	tot	us
tap		pig		
zag		pit		
zap		sip		
		sit		
		tip		
		zig		
		zip		

c as option for k. c sounds /k/ when not followed by e i y.

cab			cob	cub
cap			cod	cup
cat			cop	cut
			cot	

Words ending in x /ks/

ax	ex	fix	ox	tux
fax	hex	mix	box	
lax	Rex	nix	fox	
max	sex	six	lox	
sax	Tex		pox	
tax	vex			
wax				

Nasal consonants: m, n

am	Ben	bin	Mom	gum
an	den	dim	mop	gun
Ann	men	din	not	mud
can	met	fin	on	muff
Dan	mess	kin	Tom	mutt
fan	net	kiss		sum
jam	pen	miss		sun
mad	ten	mit		
man		nip		
map		pin		
mat		tin		
nap				
pan				
ran				
Sam				
tan				

Aspirated consonants: h, w

had	hem	hid	hog	hub
ham	hen	him	hop	hug
hat	wed	hip	hot	hum
	wet	hit		hut
		win		
		wit		

Continuant consonants: l, r (final l usually doubled)

lad	bell	Bill	log	gull
pal	fell	fill	lot	rub
ran	led	hill	rob	rug
rat	leg	Jill	rod	
	red	lid	rot	
	well	lip		
		lit		
		mill		
		pill		
		rid		
		rim		
		will		

Avoid these types of words for now:
1. Sight words
2. "<u>all</u>" endings where vowel sounds /o/ ("ball")

CVC Consonant Digraphs

VOWELS: a, e, i, o, u

/ch/sh/th/<u>th</u>/

a	e	i	o	u
ash	mesh	chin	chop	chum
bath	shed	chip	gosh	much
cash	shell	dish	moth	rush
chap	them	fish	shop	such
chat	then	ship		shut
dash		thin		thug
mash		this		
math		wish		
sash		with		
shall				
than				
that				

/ng/

bang	ding	dong	hung
fang	king	long	lung
gang	ring	gong	rung
hang	sing	song	sung
rang	thing		
sang			
tang			

/kw/ always spelled <u>qu</u>

quack	quell	quick
		quip
		quit

E-Controlled Vowel Spellings

e–e	a–e	i–e	o–e	u–e
eve	age	bike	bone	cube
even	ape	bite	choke	cure
here	ate	chime	code	cute
theme	bake	dice	cone	fume
	base	dime	dome	mule
	cage	dive	dope	mute
	cake	file	dose	pure
	came	fine	dove	Yule
	case	fire	doze	
	chase	five	hole	
	date	hide	home	
	face	hike	hope	
	fade	hive	joke	
	fake	ice	lone	
	fame	kite	mole	
	gale	life	mope	
	game	like	nose	
	gate	lime	note	
	gave	line	poke	
	hate	live	pole	
	jade	mice	quote	
	lace	mile	robe	
	lake	mike	rode	
	lane	mine	rope	
	late	nice	sole	
	made	nine	tone	
	make	pine	vote	
	mane	quite	whole	
	maze	rice	zone	
	name	ride		
	pale	ripe		
	race	shine		
	rake	side		
	rate	tide		
	sale	tile		
	save	time		
	shade	vine		
	shake	while		
	shame	whine		
	shape	white		
	take	wide		
	tale	wife		
	tame	wine		
	vase	wipe		
	wade			
	whale			

Vowel Transformations

e–e	a–e	i–e	o–e	u–e
her–e	at–e	bit–e	cod–e	cub–e
them–e	fad–e	dim–e	hop–e	cut–e
	gal–e	fin–e	mop–e	mut–e
	hat–e	fir–e	not–e	
	mad–e	hid–e	rob–e	
	man–e	kit–e	rod–e	
	pal–e	pin–e	ton–e	
	rat–e	quit–e		
		rid–e		
		rip–e		
		shin–e		
		tim–e		
		win–e		

Consonant Clusters: Vowel Sound /a/

CCVC	CVCC	CCVCC
blab	band	bland
brag	bank	blank
bran	bask	blast
clad	camp	brand
clam	can't	clamp
clan	cask	clasp
clap	cast	craft
class	daft	crank
crab	damp	draft
crag	fact	drank
cram	fast	flank
drab	gasp	flask
drag	lamp	gland
dram	land	graft
flab	lank	grand
flag	last	grant
flap	mask	grasp
flat	mast	plank
glad	pact	plant
glass	pant	prank
grab	past	scamp
gran	raft	scant
grass	ramp	slant
plan	rank	spank
scan	rant	stank
scat	rapt	swank
slab	rasp	tract
slam	sand	tramp
slap	sank	
slat	tact	
snap	tank	
span	task	
spat	vast	
stab		
stag		
tram		
trap		

Consonant Clusters: Vowel sound /e/

CCVC	CVCC	CCVCC
bled	bend	blend
bred	belt	blest
clef	best	cleft
dress	deft	crept
dwell	dent	crest
fled	desk	slept
flex	fend	spend
fret	held	spent
sled	help	trend
smell	jest	swept
sped	kept	
spell	left	
swell	lend	
	mend	
	nest	
	next	
	pelt	
	pest	
	rent	
	rest	
	self	
	send	
	sent	
	tend	
	tent	
	vent	
	vest	
	weld	
	wend	
	went	
	west	
	zest	

Consonant Clusters: Vowel Sound /i/

CCVC	CVCC	CCVCC
brim	dint	blimp
cliff	disk	blink
clip	film	brink
crib	fist	brisk
drip	gift	crimp
flip	gild	crisp
flit	hilt	drift
frill	hint	drink
glib	jilt	frill
grid	jist	frisk
grill	kiln	glint
grim	kilt	primp
grin	kink	print
grip	lift	skimp
grit	lilt	spilt
prim	limp	stilt
skid	link	stink
skiff	lint	stint
skill	list	twist
skim	milk	
skin	mink	
skip	mint	
skit	mist	
slid	rift	
slim	rink	
slip	risk	
slit	sift	
sniff	silk	
snip	silt	
spill	sink	
spin	tilt	
spit	tint	
stiff	wilt	
still	wind	
swim	wink	
trill	wisp	
trim		
trip		
twin		

Consonant Clusters: Vowel Sound /o/

CCVC	CVCC	CCVCC
blot	bond	blond
clog	cost	frond
clot	fond	frost
crop	golf	stomp
cross	honk	
drop	loft	
frog	lost	
slot	pomp	
stop	pond	
trod	romp	
trot	soft	

Consonant Clusters: Vowel Sound /u/

CCVC	CVCC	CCVCC
blub	bulk	blunt
bluff	bump	brunt
club	bunk	crust
drug	bunt	drunk
drum	bust	flunk
fluff	cult	grump
glum	cusp	plump
grub	duct	skulk
gruff	dump	skunk
plug	dunk	slump
plum	dusk	slunk
plus	fund	spunk
scuff	gulf	stump
scull	gulp	stunk
scum	gust	trump
slug	hump	trunk
slum	hunk	trust
smug	hunt	
spud	husk	
spun	jump	
stub	junk	
stuff	just	
stun	lump	
	mump	
	musk	
	must	
	pulp	
	pump	
	punk	
	punt	
	rump	
	runt	
	rusk	
	rust	
	sulk	
	sunk	
	sump	
	tuft	
	tusk	

Examples of Tracking Sequences

Teacher begins by setting up the chain, or by the statement "Show me ——" followed by: "If that is ——, then show me ——": Example for the simple chain: "Show me /ip/. If that says /ip/, show me /bip/."

Simple	Complex
ip	ab
bip	tab
bep	bat
ep	bit
up	it
vup	et
vut	te
vuz	tek
suz	ket
siz	kat
diz	kap
dip	kop
fip	sop
fap	sap
hap	tap
hag	pat
bag	pet
bug	pe
bog	ep
fog	up
dog	ups
dig	us
dif	tus
if	stu
it	stuf
sit	stup
zit	step
zip	stap
zap	sap
gap	pas
gop	past
top	vast
op	vest
po	vet

APPENDIX: BEGINNING READING PROGRAMS AND CURRICULUM MATERIALS

READING PROGRAMS FOR SCHOOLS

Preschool/Kindergarten

SOUND FOUNDATIONS. Authors: Byrne and Fielding-Barnsley. Sydney, Australia: Peter Leyden Educational.

READ RIGHT. Authors: Blachman, Ball and Black. Contact National Center for Learning Disabilities. 381 Park Ave. South, Suite 1420, New York, NY 10016.

PHONO-GRAPHIX. McGuinness, C. and McGuinness, G. *Reading Fundamentals.* Read America Inc. Tel. 1-800-READ-TO-U.

SUCCESS FOR ALL. Kindergarten program. Contact Drs. Slavin or Madden at Johns Hopkins University, Baltimore, MD. Available to schools only.

First Grade and Up

AUDITORY DISCRIMINATION IN DEPTH. Lindamood and Lindamood. To inquire about classroom adaptation contact Lindamood-Bell Clinic. Tel. 1-800-233-1819.

WALLACH AND WALLACH. See Book: *Teaching All Children to Read,* 1976. Chicago University Press.

PHONO-GRAPHIX. McGuinness, C. and McGuinness, G. Classroom. Grades 1 to 3. Read America. Tel. 1-800-READ-TO-U.

READING PROGRAMS FOR PARENTS AND HOME-SCHOOLING

McGuinness, C. and McGuinness, G. *Reading Reflex.* New York: Free Press, 1997.

EARLY BOOKS FOR HOME AND CLASSROOM

ALLOGRAPHS. McGuinness, D. Sound Search and Spell Search Story Books. Sea Gate Press, P.O. Box 563, Sanibel FL 33957. Fax 941-472-4513.

PHONO-GRAPHIX. Coded Text Readers. Published by Read America: Tel. 1-800-READ-TO-U.

BOB BOOKS. Books Series 1. Book Series 2. Bob Books Publishing. P.O. Box 633. West Linn, Oregon 97068. Tel. 503-567-1883.

PRIMARY PHONICS. B.W. Makar. Educational Publishing Service, 1990. *Readers only.* Recommended sequence: Books 1, 3, 4, 2, 5.

Old phonics readers. Try the library. The following have controlled vocabularies and spellings.

1. *Reading with Phonics.* Hay and Wingo. J.B. Lippincott, 1954.
2. *Lippincott Readers.* McCracken and Walcutt. J.B. Lippincott, 1963. (Recently rereleased by Macmillan.)
3. *Let's Read.* Part 1. Bloomfield and Barnhart. Self-published. 1963.
4. *Merrill Linguistic Readers.* Fries, Fries, Wilson & Rudolph. Merrill Books, Inc., 1966.
5. *Carden Reading Method.* Grade 1. Book 1. Mae Carden Inc., 1967.
6. *The Royal Road Readers.* Book 1. Daniels and Diack. London: Chatto and Windus, 1962.

CURRICULUM MATERIALS

Movable Alphabet. 42/44 sounds in Basic Code.

AUDITORY DISCRIMINATION IN DEPTH. Lindamood and Lindamood. Program Kit includes Alphabet Tiles. Tiles may be sold separately. Pro-Ed or Riverside Publishing.

ALPHABOXES. Card stock or felt. Overhead transparencies. Read America. Tel. 1-800-READ-TO-U.

Audiotape. 42 sounds.

READ AMERICA. Tel. 1-800-READ-TO-U.

Games

READ AMERICA. Tel. 1-800-READ-TO-U.

"Sound Bingo." Graded levels.

"Sound Memory." Graded levels.

Activities pack. Eight reading and spelling games.

Publications

Phono-Graphix Magazine. Membership subscription. Articles. Activities and stories for children. Read America. Tel. 1-800-READ-TO-U.

Chapter 10

MASTERING THE ADVANCED CODE IN READING, WRITING, AND SPELLING

O nce the child has mastered the Basic Code, as described in the previous chapter, he has learned the *most probable* spelling alternative for every sound in English. The next step is to add the remaining less probable spelling alternatives to this code. A child cannot understand the logic of our spelling system unless and until the foundation of the Basic Code is secure.

Spelling is more difficult than reading because it is entirely a sound-to-print activity. First, you have to think of the words you want to write, hear the order of each individual sound (phoneme) in those words in your mind, and then transcribe those sounds into a letter-by-letter representation on the page. This is opposite to reading, where the translation is from print back into sound. In reading, the printed text provides reminders or "clues" of how to decode, and the context of the story adds further information. In spelling there are no clues. You begin the task of writing facing a blank page. Initially, the process is tedious, sound by sound by sound. Ultimately, it becomes automatic, and words and phrases are mentally regrouped and transcribed onto the page as units or "chunks" of sounds.

If every English word was spelled according to the Basic Code, this chapter would not need to be written. But as English spelling has multiple spelling alternatives for the same sounds, this adds a further processing step. Images of letter patterns have to be stored in memory in such a way that the reader and speller knows *which* pattern fits with *which* sound into *which* word. Unless there is some type of probability structure stored in memory about these patterns, every spelling of every word would have to be memorized separately—in other words, randomness or chaos.

Certain types of information help organize memory and reduce the memory load. This is information about how words and word parts can be classified so that there are clues about which spelling alternatives are more or less probable. This classification process is known as "orthography." For example, the final /ee/ sound in multisyllable words is spelled mainly y (baby) and sometimes ey (monkey) and almost never ee (jamboree). This does not mean that children should learn this as a "spelling rule," because memorizing rules is not only inefficient, it doesn't work. Even when children can memorize rules, research has shown that they never apply them when they read or spell. Instead, spelling "tendencies" or "expectancies" must become part of tacit knowledge through *use*, so that they are stored in memory effortlessly.

The structure of our spelling system is set out in a spelling program I designed, called Allographs™. Allographs was developed in response to a client's insistence that "spelling is completely random." Mike's story is informative. He had suffered injuries in a car crash leaving him permanently disabled. He could not continue in his job because of its heavy physical demands, so he returned to college to train for another career. Mike is highly intelligent but suffered incredibly in his courses because he couldn't spell. He couldn't take notes that he could read. He couldn't write exams that the professor could read. He came to every exam with a bulky electronic spell-master that dramatically slowed down his performance, as he had to feed every third or fourth word into the machine. When Mike wrote a term paper he always got A's. On essay exams he usually got C's, not because he couldn't remember the material, but because he ran out of either time or patience.

Mike heard about the work I was doing with poor readers and came to ask for help with his spelling problem. But Mike had more than a spelling problem: He had an attitude. He protected his self-worth with an unassailable defense about why he couldn't spell. At every session he would arrive with a list of words that he had heard the previous week that were spelled irregularly. He became more and more expert at this as we began to work together. The more he improved in his awareness of spelling patterns, the more he noticed spellings with rare patterns. I told him that experts had determined that over 80 percent of English spellings were regular. He was convinced this was incorrect and started compiling more and more lists of irregularly spelled words to prove that the experts were wrong. Mike was deaf to my argument that in order to learn to spell, you must focus first on what is regular. By paying attention *only* to what is irregular, you have to remember every word as a unique visual pattern.

Memory is efficient when it is organized on the basis of what is most likely rather than what is most unlikely. The human brain is particularly adept at storing recurring patterns, and very inefficient at remembering randomness, one of the primary differences between the human brain and a computer. Mike's strategy, however, blocked his brain from organizing predictable, recurring spelling patterns so that nothing could ever be retrieved from memory.

I took this as a challenge and decided to prove to him that spelling patterns were nonrandom. I began by looking at all the spelling books that were available in classrooms or in the library. Everything I saw was indeed random (Mike was right!), and I had to abandon this effort and start from scratch. If spelling was nonrandom, the only way to demonstrate this would be to find every spelling alternative for each of the forty-three phonemes and phoneme combinations in English. Next, I had to find every common word that was spelled with each particular spelling alternative. Although the task was clear, the way to execute it was not. There is no simple way to look up this information either in a dictionary or anywhere else (see note 7 of chapter 5).

After several months of work compiling a sound-to-print "dictionary," I had a basic framework sufficient to demonstrate the probability structure of the code for English spelling. (The final version of the spelling dictionary took much longer.) Mike was convinced, and as he became less defensive and began to learn to spell, we could even joke about his dogmatic belief system. One day I asked him if he knew when his spelling problems began. He remembered vividly that during second grade, he saw that most of the spelling words he was given each week did not "play by any rules." That is, they did not fit with any rudimentary "phonics" he was being taught in reading lessons or any other kind of logic. He pointed this out to the teacher and was not given a satisfactory explanation. At that moment, he decided that as spelling "made no sense," he would not bother learning to spell at all. Instead, he became an "antispeller," committing about twenty-five years of his life to a belief system created by a seven-year-old! If there is any doubt that a child's logic is important to learning, Mike is living proof to dispel that doubt.

Shortly after my work with Mike (who learned to spell and completed graduate school with honors), my students and I began doing observational research in first-grade classrooms. These transcriptions illustrate why so many children have problems learning to spell. Here are minute-by-minute notes from a first-grade classroom exercise in spelling:

> The lesson begins at 8:32 A.M.
>
> "Today we're going to learn a new spelling list which has words that share the sound /ee/, like long /ee/ or short /ee/. [Writes on the board e-a-t.] Some of you might spell this /ee/ /tee/ [writes on board e-t] which is O.K. for your spelling, but now you should remember that it's /ee/ /ae/ /tee/. Next, we're going to learn the short /ee/ sound, like in the word /hed/. [The word head goes on the board.]" Asks a student to write the word bean on the board. Asks another student to write the word instead on the board. Next, introduces the bonus word leprechaun. Children get a list of spelling words. They chant in unison. They spell words out loud in unison with letter names: /ar/ /ee/ /ae/ /dee/-read.
>
> The lesson ends at 8:44 A.M., twelve minutes later.

This example is by no means unusual. The children will have spent twelve minutes in an entire day, and perhaps an entire week, with this so-called "spelling" exercise. This may be the only explanation they will ever get about the vowel sound /ee/ or the vowel digraph ea.

Let's dissect what the teacher was actually doing:

1. She begins by telling them a lie, that everything in their spelling list has the sound /ee/, when half of the words contain the sound /e/ (bed).

2. She makes the sound /ee/ and writes the digraph ea with no explanation about why the sound /ee/ is spelled this way, or why two letters are used for one sound instead of one letter. She is actually introducing a letter pair (digraph) and not a sound. The letters ea, in and of themselves, do not "sound anything."

3. She says and writes that e t (letter names) is an "O.K. way to spell." In fact, she uses letter names instead of phoneme sounds to

"spell" <u>ea</u>t to the class: "ee-ay-tee." This gives them the impression that "eat" has *three* sounds (actually there are *four* in her version:—/ee/ /ae/ /t/ /ee/) instead of two (/ee/ /t/), and that it is spelled this way by chance.

4. She tells them that they are going to learn a "short /ee/ sound." There is no such thing as a short /ee/ sound. She then uses an example of a word containing the vowel sound /e/ ("head"), which is *not* the sound /ee/.

5. She alternates back and forth between words that contain the sound /ee/ and /e/, the only common denominator between them being the vowel digraph <u>ea</u>. This destroys any chance for the child to infer a connection between a phoneme and its spelling.

6. Next comes "leprechaun," presumably because they heard a story about one. The word does not contain the sound /ee/, does not contain the vowel digraph <u>ea</u> as a spelling for /e/, but *does* contain the main way to spell the sound /e/ (which is <u>e</u>), something she didn't teach. Further, this word is much too difficult for first graders, and reinforces visual memory as a way to learn to spell.

7. Students end the lesson by spelling the words out loud using letter names. This reinforces learning that letter *names* is the most important thing to remember. Letter-sound correspondences are never mentioned.

We have many examples like this one, taken from three different schools and seven different classrooms. It is obvious when reading through these notes that this teacher has no idea what she is doing, no idea how to teach a phonetic alphabet, and that the children would probably be better off if she didn't even try. The only thing she has succeeded in doing in this lesson is to confuse the children about how to spell words. She gives them the impression that everything must be memorized visually, because this is the only coherent perceptual experience that connects with what she described.

Teaching spelling with the correct logic, from sound to print, avoids this kind of confusion. The lesson just described should have been three separate lessons. The first lesson should have gone like this: "There are two main ways to spell the sound /ee/. One you will already know because it is the Basic Code spelling: <u>ee</u> (feet). Now we're going to learn a second way to spell the sound /ee/, which is <u>ea</u>

(each)." Next, children need practice in using this information. They can write stories using words that sound /ee/, fill in worksheets with this sound and spellings, and so forth. The second lesson should have been that there are "two main spellings for the sound /e/." One they already know as the Basic Code spelling: e̲ (bed) and the second is: e̲a̲ (head). They also learn that the spelling e̲ is used most of the time. Again, the children engage in activities using this information. When this foundation is established, the third lesson begins. The teacher points out that the digraph e̲a̲ is used for *both* the /ee/ sound and the /e/ sound (an example of "code overlap"), and that the e̲a̲ spelling is used much more often to spell the sound /ee/ than it is to spell the sound /e/.

These three steps make the logic clear. There is no confusion about what is being taught. The child's task is clear as well. He knows that he must learn which spelling alternative is used for a particular sound in a particular word. He *does not learn* that he has to memorize the spelling for every single word in the English language separately.

For the remainder of this chapter I want to outline how reading and spelling should be taught at this level, and show along the way how learning to spell can be fun.

ALLOGRAPHS™ IN PRACTICE

Allographs consists of a child's spelling dictionary, a manual with more than fifty partially scripted lesson plans and activity guide, plus worksheets and stories for most lessons. In the spelling dictionary "all graphs" (all possible spellings for all common English words) are organized by phoneme sounds. The information is sequenced by initial and final consonants and vowels. Allographs Book I contains one- and two-syllable words. Allographs Book II contains multisyllable words, information about compounding, prefixes, suffixes, and spelling patterns for words we borrowed from Latin and Greek. In this chapter I discuss Book I, which is suitable for children from the end of first grade through third grade. It is also suitable for anyone, up to and including adults, who has not learned the code.

The major goals of learning to read and spell with Allographs are as follows:

1. Must use a phonetic strategy to look up sounds in words. This has the important function of reinforcing the correct strategy.

2. Connects spelling to the sound-based strategy used in learning to read. Reading and spelling are integrated.

3. Learn which spelling alternatives are most or least probable. When in doubt about spelling a word, start with the most probable spelling first (Basic Code). Check the result with visual memory to see if it "looks right." If it doesn't, try the next most probable, and so forth.

4. Isolate which spellings are irregular and must be memorized by sight.

5. Learn all this effortlessly via *controlled exposure,* by the correct sequencing of spelling training and by being able to *look up sounds in words.* The Allographs "dictionary" contains over 3,000 words (about seventy pages) and can be used easily by many first graders and all second graders as a reference resource. It is far easier to use than a children's dictionary.

Allographs is organized in three sections, which are color-coded. The book begins with color-coded summary charts for all the spelling alternatives for initial and final consonants, consonant clusters, and vowels, as shown in chapter 5 and reproduced here for convenience. After the charts containing sounds come color-coded sections that list the words that have alternative spellings. There are separate word lists for consonants that begin words and consonants that end words or syllables. This is followed by the vowel section, which is the largest section. Each page (or pages) is devoted to one vowel sound. All common words with that sound are set out in columns under each spelling alternative. The different spellings are ordered from left to right in order of probability (most to least common), and the words are organized alphabetically down and across the page.

Initial Consonants

To begin, children are told that sometimes there are different spellings for sounds than the ones they have learned so far, and that these are called "spelling alternatives" or "spelling options." Children begin with the twenty-two *initial* single consonants in the following order:

1. Consonants with only one spelling (twelve) (review)
2. Consonants with two different spellings (six)
3. Consonants with three different spellings (four)

Most consonant spelling alternatives are *digraphs.* New consonant digraphs in this group are: /f/ ph (phone), /g/ gh (ghost), gu (guard),

TABLE 10–1

Single-Consonant Spelling Alternatives

Sound	Key Word	Word Beginning	Word Ending
b	big	b	b
d	dog	d	d
f	fun	f ph	f ff ph gh
g	got	g gu gh	g gue gg
h	hot	h wh	—
j	job	j g	ge dge
k	kid	c k ch	k ck c
l	log	l	l ll
m	man	m	m mb mn
n	not	n kn gn	n gn
p	pig	p	p
r	red	r wr	r
s	sat	s c sc	ce se ss s
t	top	t	t bt
v	van	v	ve
w	win	w wh	—
x /ks/	tax	—	x
z	zip	z	se ze zz s z
ch	chin	ch	ch tch
ng	sing	—	ng
qu/kw/	quit	qu	—
sh	shop	sh	sh
th	thin	th	th
<u>th</u>	then	th	the

Spelling alternatives are ordered by most to least likely.

/k/ <u>ch</u> (chaos), /n/ <u>gn</u> (gnat) <u>kn</u> (know), /r/ <u>wr</u> (write), /s/ <u>sc</u> (scene), /w/ <u>wh</u> (which). [Rare digraphs <u>pn</u> <u>rh</u> aren't taught.]

In a sequence of lessons, corresponding to the level of difficulty, children create their own spelling notebooks with words they choose. Every lesson has activities, worksheets, and stories to allow the child to practice new information.

TABLE 10–2

Consonant Clusters

Beginning Clusters	Spelling Alternatives	Ending Clusters	Spelling Alternatives
bl br			
dr dw		dth	
fl fr		ft fth	
gl gr			
kl kr	**cl cr** chl chr	(kt)	**ct**
		ld lf (lj) lm ln lp lt lch lsh lth	**lge**
		mp mpt (mf)	**mph**
		nch nd (nj) nt nth	**nge**
pl pr		pt pth	
		rb rc rd rf rg (rj) rk rl rm rn rp rt rch rsh rth rve	**rge**
sk sl sm sn sp spl spr st str sw squ	**sc** sk sch	sk sm sp st	
tr tw			
		xt	
		(ngk) (ngkt) ngth	**nk nct**
shr thr			

Clusters in parentheses are never spelled this way. Optional spellings in bold are either the *only* spelling or most likely spelling.

TABLE 10–3

Vowel Spelling Alternatives

Sound	Key Word	Spelling Alternatives in Order of Most to Least Likely						
		1	2	3	4	5	6	7
a	had	a						
e	bed	e	ea	ai				
i	it	i	y	ui				
o	dog	o	a(ll)	(w)a				
aw	law	aw	au	ough	augh			
u	but	u	o	o-e	ou			
ae	made	a-e	ai	a	ay	ei	eigh	ey
ee	see	ee	ea	y	ie	e	e-e	ey
ie	time	i-e	i	y	igh			
oe	tone	o-e	o	oa	ow	ou	ough	
ue	cute	u-e	u	ew	eu			
oo	look	oo	u	ou				
o͞o	soon	oo	u-e	ew	u	ou	ui	
ou	out	ou	ow	ough				
oi	soil	oi	oy					
		VOWEL + R						
ar	far	ar						
er	her	er	ur	ir	or	ear	ar	
or	for	or	ore	oar	our	ar	oor	
e+er	bare	are	air	arr	err	ear		

Initial Consonant Clusters

Following lessons on single-consonant spelling alternatives, children move on to review the twenty-seven initial consonant clusters. They learn that clusters are adjacent *single* consonants, spelled just the same, in Basic Code, which they already know. The exceptions are rare and mainly involve Greek words. Spelling alternatives are c̲l̲ c̲h̲l̲ (clap/chlorine), c̲r̲ c̲h̲r̲ (cream, chronic), and s̲c̲ s̲k̲ s̲c̲h̲ (scum/skunk/school). Children do not use many Greek words at this stage, and so only the last group is important: s̲c̲ s̲k̲ s̲c̲h̲.

During these lessons the child has a copy of Allographs and can check the spellings on the charts or in the word list sections, depending on the task he is assigned. For example, children are taught that words that begin with the sound /r/ can be spelled two ways: r and wr. Later, a child may be writing a story about the time he fell and broke his wrist. If he can't remember how to spell "wrist," he can check the Initial Consonants Chart at the front of Allographs and find that there are two ways to spell words beginning /r/, either r or wr. At this point he can write this both ways to see what "looks right" (rist or wrist). If he is still uncertain, he can turn to the "Word Beginnings" section (color-coded) and look up the words that begin with sound /r/. The Word Beginnings section is *only two pages* long, as it only lists alternative spellings (see Table 10-4). Most initial consonants and consonant clusters are consistent with the Basic Code.

TABLE 10–4

Word Beginnings

Sound /s/	Key word: see. Spell s except:

ce	cease, cedar, cede, ceiling, celebrate, celery, celestial, cell, cement, cent, centennial, center, centi—(100), central, century, ceramic, cereal, ceremony, certain, certify
ci	cider, cigar, cigarette, cinch, cinder, cinema, cinnamon, cipher, circle, circuit, circulate, circus, cite, citizen, citrus, city, civic, civil
cy	cycle, cyclone, cylinder, cymbal, cynic, cypress, cyst
sc	scene, scent, science, scepter

Sounds /sk/	Key word: skip. Spell sc except:

sk	skate, skeleton, skeptic, sketch, skew, ski, skid, skiff, skill, skim, skimp, skin, skinny, skip, skirt, skit, skull, skunk, sky
sch	schedule, scheme, scholar, school, schooner

Sound /w/	Key word: wet. Spell w except:

wh	whale, what, wheat, wheel, wheeze, when, where, whether, which, whiff, while, whim, whine, whip, whir, whirl, whisk, whistle, white, whiz, whoa, why

Sound /r/	Key word: rug. Spell r except:

wr	wrack, wrap, wrath, wreath, wreck, wren, wrench, wrestle, wretch, wriggle, wring, wrinkle, wrist, writ, write, writhe, wrong, wrote, wrung, wry

Table 10–4 is an illustration of page two of Word Beginnings. Under the sound /r/, the child learns that all words beginning with this sound are spelled r, *except* for the words listed. The child knows that if he *doesn't* find the word "wrist" here, it will be spelled with the letter r. Note that while the child is looking up 'wrist,' he is also systematically searching through every common word that starts with wr. There are only twenty-two of them and only about fourteen that the child is likely to use. Looking through this list increases his familiarity with the words spelled wr, so his brain will begin to memorize them without practice or conscious effort.

Final Consonants

There are twenty-one final consonants and forty-nine final consonant clusters that close syllables as seen in the previous chapter. Final consonants are different from initial consonants and need some extra lessons. All but three of the forty-nine final consonant clusters are different from initial consonant clusters. Final consonants should be taught in the following sequence:

1. Consonants with only one spelling (ten) (review).
2. Consonants with two spellings (three). The alternative spellings are rare: /g/ g gue (bag/vague), /n/ n gn (rain, sign), and /t/ t bt (bet/debt)
3. Consonants with more than two spellings (four). One is rare: /m/ m mb mn (sum/dumb/autumn), and three need extensive practice: f ff gh ph (gulf/cliff/laugh/graph), s ce se ss (gas/race/mouse/dress), and z s se ze zz (quiz/his/rise/freeze/buzz).
4. Consonant spellings controlled by the preceding vowel sound (four). An example is final /ch/, which is spelled ch unless it follows the vowel *sounds* /a/ /e/ /i/ /o/ /u/, when it is spelled tch (branch/brooch/batch/botch).
5. Final consonant clusters. All have only one spelling (Review).

The forty-nine final consonant clusters are all spelled only one way (Basic Code) with no spelling alternatives. It helps a child enormously to know this, because there is no way to misspell them. There is one source of confusion. Six final consonant clusters can be confused with the spelling for the past-tense verb ed in all clusters ending in the sounds /d/ or /t/. They sound exactly alike: pact/packed, past/passed, bend/ penned, etc. There are about 230 words in this group. You can spell these words correctly if you know whether or not the word is a past-tense verb. This can be turned to good advantage by teaching final clusters simultaneously with a lesson on past-tense verbs.

During these lessons, children also begin to learn about multisyllable words. They learn, for example, that initial and final consonants and clusters are "initial" and "final" for single-syllable words and can also appear in the middle of multisyllable words. For example, the sound /f/ spelled ph, can appear at the beginning of a word: "phone," in the middle: "dolphin," and at the end: "graph."

Multisyllable work continues in the last lessons in this group. The final consonants section ends with the introduction of the "schwa" + /l/ words. A "schwa" is an unaccented /uh/ sound in multisyllable words. This is a perpetual problem in English spelling, because the "schwa" can be spelled so many ways: about confuse important benefit, sensitive. About 250 multisyllable English words end in the sounds /ul/, as in: table, uncle, symbol, tribal, gavel, terrible. The spellings are not consistent, but they are predictable by the consonant that *precedes* the schwa. For example, words that end in the sounds /bul/ are much more likely to be spelled ble than any other way: table, but **not** tabul, tabel, or tabol. Words ending in /vul/ are more likely to be spelled: vel: marvel, novel, travel, etc. For this reason, this group of words is organized alphabetically by the consonant sound that precedes the schwa+l. A page from this group is shown in Table 10–5.

VOWEL SPELLING ALTERNATIVES

Vowel spellings cause the most difficulty in both reading and spelling. Using Allographs avoids confusing the child and reinforces both of these skills and integrates them. The vowel sounds are set out in four major groups.

First come the sounds spelled with the five vowel letters, followed by the e-controlled spellings for the sounds: /ae/ /ee/ /ie/ /oe/ /ue/, the remaining vowel sounds /o͞o/ /oo/ /ou/ /oi/, and vowel+r. This is the same order in which the vowels were learned originally. The "optional" vowel sound /aw/ (law) is listed under the vowel sound /o/ (hot).

In Allographs, every vowel sound is represented on a page or a series of pages. Words containing that sound are listed under each spelling alternative from left to right across the page in order of the most to least probable spelling. Words are listed in alphabetical order down and across the page. The order of the alphabet is highlighted in

TABLE 10–5

Word Endings

Sounds /ul/   Key word: apple.

Sounds/ Spellings	Words
/b/	
bal	tribal
bel	label, libel, rebel
bol	symbol
ble	able, amble, babble, bauble, Bible, bramble, bubble, bumble, cable, cobble, crumble, double, dribble, edible, fable, fumble, gable, garble, gobble, hobble, horrible, marble, mumble, nibble, noble, ogle, pebble, possible, ramble, rumble, rubble, sable, scribble, sensible, stable, table, terrible, treble, trouble, tumble, wobble, visible
/c/	
cal	rascal
cle	miracle, uncle
kle	ankle, sprinkle, wrinkle
ckle	buckle, chuckle, cockle, crackle, fickle, knuckle, pickle, tackle, tickle, trickle
/d/	
dal	bridal, medal, pedal, scandal, tidal
dle	bridle, bundle, candle, cradle, cuddle, curdle, dawdle, fiddle, fondle, girdle, griddle, huddle, hurdle, ladle, meddle, middle, muddle, noodle, paddle, poodle, puddle, saddle, straddle, swaddle, swindle, trundle, waddle
/f/	
fle	baffle, muffle, rifle, ruffle, sniffle, shuffle, truffle, waffle
ful	awful, bashful, beautiful, careful, dutiful, faithful, graceful, grateful, hateful, helpful, hopeful, restful, wonderful
/g/	
gle	beagle, eagle, gaggle, gurgle, jiggle, struggle, wiggle, wriggle
/ng/	
ngle	angle, bangle, bungle, dangle, jangle, jingle, mangle, mingle, shingle, single, tangle, tingle, triangle
/nj/	
gel	angel
/m/	
mal	formal, mammal, normal, thermal
mel	camel, caramel, enamel, trammel
/n/	
nal	abdominal, cardinal, eternal, final, journal, signal, spinal, terminal
nel	channel, flannel, funnel, kennel, panel, tunnel

bold in the margin, so the child also learns about alphabetical order and must use this order to look up words and how they are spelled. When children reach this stage in Allographs, it helps to have an alphabet chart on the wall (lower–case letters only).

A particular advantage of this method is that the spelling alternatives that overlap two or more sounds (code overlap) don't get mixed up. This avoids the confusion that the teacher created in the example. Allographs shows the child clearly where and how often the <u>ea</u> spelling alternative (and any other spelling alternative) is used. A page for the sound /e/ (bet) is shown in Table 10–6. The child can see immediately that <u>ea</u> and <u>ai</u> are less likely spellings for the vowel sound /e/ and that <u>e</u> is the *most* likely spelling for this sound.

The parent/teacher manual has three or partially four scripted lessons for every consonant or vowel sound that is spelled more than one way. These lessons involve children in "thinking about sounds in words," using this information to solve interesting puzzles or problems, and reading and writing exercises. One of the tasks children most enjoy is called the "Sound Search Game." The child has a worksheet or story which has lots of words containing a particular sound. The child's task is to locate all the words with that sound and underline them. Next, she copies these words onto a worksheet, and beside each word, writes out the spelling for the target sound in that word. Here is an example of a Sound Search Story. I will let you decide which sound is featured and figure out how many times it appears. (Answer at the end of the chapter.)

Nigel the Nice

Nigel the Nice was a knight. He was quite a sight in an iron suit that was too bright. Nigel was mild. He was kind. He was nice. But Nigel takes flight when the other knights fight.

"Fie on you Nigel," said King Idle the Wise. "Get out of my sight. Fly to the wild and find Sir Guy. He might die from tiger's bite."

Nigel had on too much iron to climb or hike, so he had to ride his bike. He cycled miles under the hot sky to Igo-Ego in Bye-um-Byes, with his visor over his eyes. He began to cry. He felt he'd die, and never arrive alive.

Byron the Lion heard his sighs.

"Sire, you must be on fire. You're about to fry. I'll get some pliers. We'll pry open your fine bright iron, so you can survive."

Nigel, free at last, saved Sir Guy and got a prize. He took a wife and stayed in Bye-um-Byes for the rest of his life.

(Who said that controlled curriculum materials had to be boring?)

TABLE 10–6

Vowel Sheet 2

Sound /e/	Key word: bed	
Spelling Alternatives		
e	*ea*	*ai*
a		again
b		bargain
bed		
bell		
belt		
bench		
bend		
bent		
best		
bet		
better		
bled		
blend		
bless		
blest		
	bread	
	breast	
	breath	
bred		
c celery		captain
cell		
cent		certain
check		
chest		
clef		
cleft		
clench		
clever		
crept		
crest		curtain
d	dead	
	deaf	
	death	
debt		
deck		
deft		
den		
dent		
desk	dread	
dress		
dwell		

There are many activities and games in the Parent/Teacher Manual to Allographs. Briefly, here are some examples:

1. Search real text for a target sound.

2. Look up words in Allographs, using the game "I Spy." ["I spy words ending in the sounds /ie/–/t/ (ite)."]

3. Sound search: Look for a particular sound or sounds that have more than one spelling, such as "find all the words that have the two final sounds /o/ /l/ in them and write each one under its spelling alternative: **al ol awl**" (all, doll, crawl, etc.). This provides a concrete example of the probability of a particular spelling.

4. Spell sort: Children sort a list of scrambled words with the same vowel sound into separate spelling alternatives:

o	oa	oe	ow
go	goat	note	blow
no	boat	tone	grow
most	foal	hole	mow

5. Vowel-controlled sort: This is used to teach final consonant spelling alternatives that are controlled by the preceding vowel sound, such as ch/tch, ge/dge: branch/batch, huge/hedge.

6. Creative writing: A writing task or poem based on a sound. Allographs is organized so that words that rhyme or start with the same initial sound can be easily located in the lists.

7. Parent or teacher writes little stories based on a sound, like "Nigel the Nice," which couldn't have been written without the Allographs Dictionary.

8. Games using the Allographs tables and charts:

a. How many words can you think of starting with the sound /f/? Is there any other way to spell words starting with this sound? What are some of these words?

b. How many words can you think of that end in the sound /ch/? How many ways to spell this sound? After several words have gone up on the board, children can look up some more words in Allographs to see how many they missed.

c. How many words have the spelling <u>ie</u> for the sound /ee/? What are those words?

9. Spelling: Individual spelling exercises can be developed based on a child's spelling errors in creative writing. Children can correct their errors by looking them up.

10. Spell check: Children can use Allographs to write stories and poems, and to check spelling as they go.

11. Children can help each other spell by showing other children how to look up sounds in words. Children with good phonemic awareness can easily help those with weak phonemic awareness.

In addition to the child's own copy of Allographs, it is helpful for classroom teachers to have a large chart containing the vowel spelling alternatives on the wall, similar to the one shown in Table 10–3. The children can glance at the chart when they write and immediately try out various spellings to see how they look in a word.

These spelling materials and exercises make it possible for a child to write creatively and at the same time avoid practicing spelling errors or spelling patterns that don't exist.

Reflecting back on what the teacher said to her class, that <u>et</u> was OK as an option for "eat," this is not OK. If the child had been taught correctly and in the proper sequence, he would know that <u>et</u> would be a highly unlikely option to spell "eat," and further he would also know that <u>eat</u> was a highly likely option for "eat." Why withhold this information from the child and cause him to make errors?

CODE OVERLAP

Code overlap refers to letters that stand for more than one sound: <u>ou</u>— in 'soul' 'soup' 'out' 'touch.' Code overlaps create a problem in decoding (reading) more than in spelling. They need to be addressed, however, and should be taught as new vowel spellings are introduced. Code overlaps occur less often with consonants and can be dealt with easily: ie., <u>gh</u> stands for /f/ in 'tough' and /g/ in 'ghost.' Vowels are a problem in reading, because the reader must decide which phoneme a particular letter pattern stands for.

Here is an illustration of an exercise to teach a code overlap. The sound /oe/ has the alternative spellings: <u>o-e</u> 'tone,' <u>o</u> 'go,' <u>oa</u> 'goat,' <u>ow</u> 'slow,' <u>ough</u> 'dough,' and there are multiple overlaps in this group. The first spelling, o, overlaps with the Basic Code spelling for the sound /o/ (dog). There are games and exercises the parent or teacher can use to sort words and spell words with letter patterns that overlap two, three, or more sounds. Here is an example of an overlap exercise.

Sort the words into two groups based on the sound that the letter o stands for in these words. (This can be done on worksheets or with word cards.)

hot   sold   dog   block   ghost   roll   across   hello dolphin   stroll   told   profit   post   radio   robin   yolk

A more complex exercise adds a third way to sort words that are spelled o, but which sound /u/ (cut). This would expand the list to include words like:

from   front   brother   ton   wonder   other   son   month

SIGHT WORDS

Sight words were originally defined as words with such irregular spellings they had to be memorized "by sight." Later, memorizing *all* words by sight became the major mode of learning to read in whole word approaches, especially "look-say." Phonics programs and most reading textbooks also advocate teaching a large group of "sight words." Here, the rationale shifts to the "getting started' theory. Children should learn sight words, it is claimed, because they can start reading "right away," and this is motivating. Thus, sight words are taught prior to learning the alphabet code or concurrently with learning the code. Teaching sight words this way can have profoundly negative consequences on the child's fragile understanding of the alphabet principle.

All reading programs have to deal with sight words, in the original meaning of the term. I am advocating two things: teach only "real" sight words, words that are undecodable, and teach them in the context of reading stories or in creative writing. Children readily accept that some words have "funny spellings" (especially if you tell them), which they will learn easily by sight. This does not mean that special drill and practice should be devoted to sight words.

When children reach the advanced level of the spelling code, they will be exposed to certain words that cannot be classified into a spelling category because there are too few words in the group to constitute a category. In Allographs, on the final page of the vowel sheets for the sound /e/ are the "exception words" 'friend' and 'leopard.' If you create two new spelling categories for two words, the child must remember that e<u>i</u> and e<u>o</u> are possible spellings for the sound /e/ *and* that they are rare. It's easier just to memorize the spellings in <u>friend</u> and <u>leopard.</u>

It is interesting that children up to about the age of eight don't agree with this solution. Bear in mind that young children are concrete thinkers and actively categorizing everything. They think that *everything* can be and should be classified, even if a category contains only one of something. Thus, there should be a spelling alternative <u>ei</u> for the sound /e/ in 'friend,' a spelling alternative <u>eo</u> for the sound /ee/ in 'people,' and <u>cht</u> for the sound /t/ in 'yacht,' and <u>ew</u> for the sound /oe/ in 'sew,' etc. They don't like it when things are left ambiguous.

The goal in Allographs is to establish a balance between the number of spelling alternatives the child needs to master and the number of "exception words" where certain sounds can be memorized by sight.

I want to spend some time discussing "sight words" as they are typically presented in most classrooms. I will take as an example a list of sight words from a well-known reading textbook for teacher training (see Table 10–7). The list was compiled from sources dating back to the famous Dolch sight word series published in 1936. This list also contains about 100 "high frequency words" with "irregular spellings," plus another group of common words. The children are supposed to memorize these words by sight so they could say them automatically "within a second." The teachers are instructed to "concentrate on teaching these words during the first two or three grades" (ages six to eight).

There are 165 words in the list. I will eliminate the word "wanted" because the root word "want" is already in the list, and also the abbreviations for Mr. and Mrs. Of the remaining 162 words, 57 (35 percent) are spelled completely phonetically in Basic Code. Examples are: that, it, for, with, made, at, or, out. Decoding these words should be effortless if the child has been taught correctly. Why, then, should these words be memorized by sight when they can be decoded in the usual way? This gives the child the impression that these words are somehow different and are "spelled funny" when they're not.

Another large group of words, forty-eight of them to be exact, are all spelled with a common spelling alternative. In other words, these are *highly probable* spellings. These words are set out below with an explanation about how and why the spellings are common.

TABLE 10–7

Sight Words

anything	give	great	Mrs.	says	very
and	at	when	about	time	than
a	could	group	night	should	want
because	do	have	nothing	some	water
in	be	can	out	has	first
again	does	head	of	something	was
is	this	use	then	look	called
almost	done	knew	brother	the	were
another	door	heard	on	sometimes	wanted
that	or	an	them	more	oil
always	buy	know	off	their	what
it	had	each	these	write	its
any	enough	light	one	they	where
are	four	only	long	who	thought
he	by	which	so	go	now
been	from	dog	other	there	father
for	but	she	her	see	down
both	friend	many	own	through	goes
brought	full	might	people	to	work
as	words	how	make	number	day
house	don't	money	put	together	you
with	not	if	like	no	did
city	live	mother	right	today	would
come	gone	Mr.	said	two	your
his	all	will	him	way	get
year	they're	school	our	there's	once
I	we	up	into	my	find
made	may	part			

"about." The "schwa" (unaccented /u/ sound) in the initial position in a word is almost always spelled a (again, around, above, amount, ahead). The spelling ou is the Basic Code spelling for the sound /ou/.

"all, almost, always, call." This is an example of an "l-controlled" vowel spelling where the vowel letter l causes the vowel letter a to sound /ah/. Exceptions are 'half,' 'calf.' *These* are sight words but don't appear on the list.

"another, brother, among, from, mother, other." The spelling o is a common spelling for the sound /u/ (cup), as you already saw above.

"come, done, money, some, something, sometimes." The spelling o-e is the third most common spelling for the sound /u/.

"by, buy, my." Final sound /ie/ is commonly spelled with the letter y, especially in one-syllable words (cry, fry, fly).

"almost, both, don't, go, most, no, only, so." The spelling o is the second most common way to spell the sound /oe/.

"know, own." The spelling ow is the third most common spelling for the sound /oe/ (low, grow, blow, show).

"find, I." The spelling i for the sound /ie/ is the second most common spelling (mind, child, kind).

"first." The spelling ir for the vowel /er/ is one of the three common spellings for this sound (er, ir, ur).

"full, put." The sound /oo/ (book) is spelled two ways. This is one of them (pull, bull).

"head." The sound /e/ is spelled two main ways. This is one of them.

"knew." The spelling ew is a common spelling for the sound /o͞o/ (dew, flew, grew). kn is always pronounced /n/. There are fourteen words with the kn spelling.

"light, might, night, right." (The author forgot 'sight,' 'tight,' 'fight,' etc.) Most words that end in the sounds /ie/-/t/ are spelled ight. The spelling igh is the third most common spelling for the sound /ie/.

"more." The spelling ore is the second most common spelling for the sound /or/.

"school." The spelling oo is the Basic Code spelling for the sound /o͞o/. The digraph ch is one of three possible spellings for the sound /k/ and is used only for "Greek" words beginning /k/ or /sk/ (chlorine, scheme).

"these." The spelling e-e is the fourth most common spelling for the sound /ee/ (theme, eve, recede.).

"they, way." When a word ends in the sound /ae/, it is spelled one of two ways. These are the two ways.

"brought, thought." The phonogram <u>ough</u> usually stands for /ah/ or /aw/. (The author left out the nine other common words spelled this way.)

"want, water." (The author left out 'wad,' 'waffle,' 'wan,' 'wand,' 'wander,' 'wash,' 'watch.') This is a w-controlled vowel spelling. When <u>w</u> precedes <u>a</u> (but not <u>ar</u>) this usually makes the letter <u>a</u> stand for the sound /ah/.

"as, has, is, his." Final <u>s</u> sounds /z/ in these words, which is very common. Final <u>s</u> is pronounced /z/ in *all* plurals that don't follow the consonants sounds /f/ /k/ /p/ /t/: bees, days, words, bags, tables, chairs, cars, trains, etc. In a child's vocabulary, this would be about 2,000 words.

"be, because, he, she, we." (The author forgot 'me.') This is a less common spelling alternative for the sound /ee/, but it is also the spelling for very high frequency words (those that occur often in print), and includes a group of common prefixes: pre-, be-, de-, e-, re-, tre-.

We have now eliminated about 70 percent of the sight words. This brings us to the next group, those with less probable spellings.

"four, your." This is a less common spelling alternative for the sound /or/. But six other words are spelled this way, like 'pour' and 'source,' and <u>our</u> should be a spelling alternative for /or/.

"they're." This is a contraction of 'they are.' It is unusual but phonetically regular.

"heard." This is the least common spelling alternative for the vowel sound /er/. This group includes eight common words: 'pearl,' 'search,' etc., and <u>ear</u> should be a spelling category.

"work" This represents another group of w-controlled vowel spellings. When the letter <u>w</u> precedes <u>or</u>, this changes the pronunciation to /er/, as in 'world,' 'worry,' etc. There are no exceptions to this pronunciation or spelling.

"you, group." The initial letter y *always* sounds /ee/ when it precedes a vowel (yes, yellow, etc.), and the digraph o͟u is a spelling alternative for the sound /o͞o/.

This leaves us with thirty-nine of the original words. Here are the words:

a, are, again, been, could, do, does, door, enough, father, friend, give, gone, great, have, into, live, of, once, one, people, said, says, should, the, their, there, through, to, together, today, two, very, was, were, what, where, who, would.

The children would argue that these can be classified, and the list reduced further. The words with the sound /oo/ spelled o͟u ('could,' 'should,' 'would') could be a category, as could 'great,' plus 'break' and 'steak,' and 'door,' plus 'floor,' and 'poor.' They would also argue that 'to,' 'do,' and 'who,' should be a group where the letter o͟ represents the sound /o͞o/. Also, there is no need to memorize the word 'to' and then memorize it all over again in compound words like: 'into,' 'together,' 'tomorrow,' and 'today,' and so forth.

If we follow the children's thinking, this eliminates eleven more sight words from the list.

This reduces the list to very few *true* sight words, in the sense that the spellings are so irregular and unpredictable that they cannot be decoded. But the point of this exercise is to show something else. IF it was a good idea to teach sight words because of "irregular spellings," then *most of the true sight words are missing from this list.* Furthermore, if the words 'I' and 'kind' are supposed to be "sight words," then what about the words that are left off the list, like:

behind bind blind child Christ climb find grind iron lion mild mind pilot pint quiet sign silent triangle vibrant wild wind—and about 100 more.

If all words ending in the sound /z/ spelled s͟ are "sight words," then about 50,000 plural words are missing.

I hope this exercise has not been too tedious. The purpose is to illustrate that "experts" in the field of reading, those who write the textbooks that many classroom teachers try to rely on, *do not know the English spelling code.* They have never bothered to work it out. Teachers all over the world teach "sight words" based on lists like this one. This is very scary, because if authors of textbooks don't know the code, then teachers can't learn the code, and if teachers don't know the code, then the child can't learn the code. If the child can't learn the code, the child can't learn to read or spell.

Multisyllable-Word Level

Over 80 percent of English words are multisyllable words, though the most common Anglo-Saxon and French words are only one syllable long. As was seen from the examples, children get introduced to many two-syllable words in Book I of Allographs. In Allographs Book II, they learn words built from smaller meaningful units. These are compound words (doghouse), root words which take prefixes and suffixes (unhappy, happier), and words we have borrowed from Latin and Greek (information, symbol).

The multisyllable level needs considerable attention and there isn't space here to discuss this in any depth. Two auditory skills are involved:

1. The ability to segment words into syllable units or "chunks of sound." This is easy for everyone, as we learned from the research cited in chapter 8.
2. The ability to decode phoneme-by-phoneme *within* each syllable unit and remember the phoneme sequences in the right order, and to encode (spell) each syllable chunk by chunk. This is hard for everyone.

Children can become overwhelmed at the multisyllable level because they see a very long word and don't know how to attack it, break it apart, and reassemble it. At the multisyllable level, everything must slow down. The children need to practice verbally isolating syllables in words and putting syllables together into words. Start these lessons with children's names, because this is motivating: Jenn-i-fer, Al-ex-an-der, Jon-a-than.

These lessons are followed by a two-step process: isolating the first syllable in a word, analyzing its phoneme components, going on to the next syllable and doing the same thing, keeping track of the *order* of sounds across all the syllables in the word. Let the child decide where the syllable boundaries come. There is no absolute right or wrong way, despite what the style manuals say. Thus, a child could tackle the word **comforting** in one of two ways:

/k/ /u/ /m/——/f/ /or/——/t/ /i/ /ng/
/k/ /u/ /m/——/f/ /or/ /t/——/i/ /ng/

The final stage of multisyllable work introduces the last level of logic which cannot be taught using a strict phonetic approach. These are the Latin suffixes which don't conform to any of the English spelling patterns introduced so far. Latin prefixes, by contrast, are usually spelled phonetically (un, in, re, de, sub, ab, ad). Latin suffixes must be taught as a special group in which a set of letters (a phonogram) represents more than one sound. The suffix /shun/ tion is a case in point. There are thousands of words ending in the three sounds /sh/ /u/ /n/. There are over 500 words spelled ation alone, such as 'nation,' 'information,' 'investigation,' 'abomination,' and so forth. The suffix /shun/ is spelled four ways, tion (nation), cian (musician, electrician), cion (suspicion), and sion (aggression, tension). The phonemes /sh/ and /u/ in these Latin suffixes can each be spelled several ways. The sound /sh/ can be spelled: ti (nation), ci (musician/suspicion), sci (conscious), ch (machine), and the vowel sound /u/: o (tion), a (cian), and ou (ous). It is more practical to use phonogram spellings than to memorize these seven spelling alternatives.

The child learns simply, that tion, cian, cion, and sion are the four ways to spell /shun/ when these sounds come at the end of a multisyllable word. And there are further clues. tion is the most probable spelling of the four, cian is for an occupation or person, cion is practically never used, the tion/sion distinction is often determined by the spelling of the root word: vacate/vacation, aggress/aggression. This approach also works well with code overlaps, because an entire phonogram can "overlap" more than one sound: sion stands for /shun/ in 'aggression' or /zhun/ in 'vision'. Programs for teaching the Latin layer of language and Latin suffixes are listed in the Appendix to this chapter.

COMPREHENSION

There are no special comprehension exercises at this level. Standard comprehension approaches will work fine with this program (finding the story line, getting the main idea, retelling the story in the child's words, etc.). It turns out that comprehension exercises during early reading instruction matter less than one might think, though, of course, interpretation of text is critical for enjoyment of reading.

The highest predictor of a child's comprehension score on a standard reading comprehension test is a measure of decoding skill, the ability to read one word at a time *out of context*. This means simply that if you can understand the meaning of spoken language, you should be able to understand the meaning of written language. And the only way you can understand the meaning of written language is to be able to decode it accurately and fluently.

According to the Brian Byrne and A. Gates, reading comprehension could be predicted completely by two measures; *nonsense word* decoding accuracy and speed. They followed 159 children in grades 2 and 3 over one year. Accuracy was more important than speed, because slow but accurate decoders could still comprehend what they read, whereas rapid, inaccurate decoders could not. Most reading textbooks that teachers rely on say just the opposite.

The truth is that fluency *follows* accuracy and does not precede it. So the teacher who says: "Don't sound it out, don't slow down, read it faster or you won't understand it," isn't helping the student who has decoding problems, and this student won't understand what he reads. Simply "reading faster," or practicing to be "fluent," without understanding the code, doesn't improve comprehension at all.

Similar findings were reported by Connie Juel and her colleagues in Austin, Texas. They followed 129 children over the first two years of school, from early first grade through second grade. They measured the children's phonemic awareness, decoding skill, listening comprehension, IQ, and various measures of writing, reading, and spelling. Reading comprehension across the two years was strongly predicted by reading and spelling *isolated words,* and these in turn were predicted by decoding accuracy, which was predicted by phoneme awareness. The reading and spelling test scores correlated to reading comprehension across the age range at .69 to .84. By contrast, listening comprehension, the ability to understand the meaning of what someone said, was not highly predictive, nor was vocabulary (correlations around .37 to .44), which is a very interesting finding. This means that in order to understand what you read, you must be accurate and fluent in decoding it, *more than* whether you understand the meaning of natural spoken language (opposite to what whole language advocates claim).

Research showing the connection between comprehension and decoding is now substantial, and studies like these have been replicated many times, using different subject groups and different tests. The Connecticut Longitudinal Study recently published data on the correlations between decoding accuracy and reading comprehension. The correlations are large and consistent across all grades, with ninth-grade comprehension scores being predicted by decoding accuracy from second grade onward at around .60. The correlation between decoding accuracy and comprehension in first grade is .89.

The research clearly shows that accurate and fluent decoding skills underpin everything that follows. And while traditional comprehension activities, such as "finding the main ideas," answering questions about specific information, and writing summaries, are important and useful activities, they will not have any impact on a child's comprehension unless the child is reading accurately and efficiently.

WRITING

When children start to feel confident with the mechanics of writing, it's helpful, and equally interesting for the child, to copy sentences or passages of printed stories. This gives the child a feeling of pride and accomplishment, and begins to train the various technical aspects of writing itself, such as manual left-to-right sequencing, leaving spaces between words, capitalizing, and punctuation. The children need this experience, otherwise their creative writing will not be legible.

When children write stories on their own, the teacher should be watchful about how words are spelled. This does not mean that everything needs to be corrected, but rather, misspelled words can provide important information about whether the child is progressing appropriately in learning sound-to-letter correspondences. Words that the child should be able to spell based on what has been taught, or misspelled words that are "impossible" nonphonetic transcriptions, can be circled or underlined. These provide a useful list for spell checking in Allographs. The spellings can be corrected on the same page. This is the *only spelling test* the teacher needs to give at this level. Children should not be taught to spell from word lists unrelated to the stories they are reading, and should never be asked to spell words they cannot read, or at a more advanced level than their current knowledge of the spelling code.

Once the child has succeeded in presenting a reasonable approximation to a correctly spelled piece of creative writing, this should form the basis for an Anthology Book of that particular child's work. The selection by the teacher of the child's best work, again, motivates the child to want to succeed. Work that is chosen for an anthology should have all spelling errors corrected. Whether the child chooses to recopy the story or leave the corrected spellings on the copy is unimportant and should be the child's decision.

INVENTED SPELLING

Before ending this chapter, I want to say a few words about invented spelling. Recall that this is a method of teaching creative writing which is supposed to allow the child to "discover" our spelling system on his own. When invented spelling is used in conjunction with whole language, the teacher believes she should never interfere, or never ask the child to correct anything that is written. Children are supposed to develop an awareness of the alphabet code through a process of discovery, and if you interfere, this isn't "discovery." There is no evidence that it's *better* for a child to "discover" the code unaided than to be taught the code directly, and considerable evidence to the contrary (see chapter 8).

This does not mean that children should never do creative writing until they can spell every word they need correctly—far from it. Beginning readers should be encouraged to write freely and to spell words they don't know by the closest approximation. Once they know the Basic Code, they can spell everything phonetically, so that anyone can read it. However, this doesn't mean that their spelling errors are off limits to the teacher. These errors can be very helpful in providing feedback to the child.

Unfortunately, this is not the way that invented spelling is used in most classrooms. In fact, we have never seen it used this way in any public school classroom we have observed. Instead, the teacher teaches nothing and the child "invents" his own version of a writing system. This "invention" is so unstable that it changes from word to word, and from line to line, except for those words that have been memorized by sight.

Inventing nonexistent phoneme-grapheme combinations is one thing, but spending valuable time practicing them is quite another. The main thing that "pure" invented spelling offers the child is the certainty that he will spend hours practicing errors, because there is no way the child can self-correct his mistakes. Further, our observations also show that one of the claims for invented spelling isn't valid either. This is the claim that children are "free" to be creative if they are never taught to spell, and that even if adults cannot read what a child writes, the child can. When we asked first graders to "read" to us what they had *just* written, minutes earlier, many of them made up completely different words (assuming we could translate it in the first place). Let's take this example which was written sufficiently clearly for us to transcribe: "I just love mukes speshle babesg uus." Notice first that the child is practicing writing letter sequences that do not exist in English: <u>shle</u> <u>sg</u> <u>uu</u>. The first three words were learned by sight, so the child gets the first words correct, but reads: "I just love cats because they are nice." Children frequently stared up at the ceiling as they "read" to us. If the teacher wants the children to be "creative," before they know enough of the spelling code to write something that can be read, then why not have them tell stories out loud which she could transcribe (as I suggest above)? Why let children write misspelled gibberish they cannot read?

In the following chapters we take up the issue of remediation, the emotional consequences of reading failure, and what programs look like that can bring a child up to grade level in a short space of time and allow an illiterate adult to read on his own for the very first time.

In "Nigel the Nice" (p. 263) the sound /ie/ appears sixty-six times.

APPENDIX: SPELLING PROGRAMS, HOME OR CLASSROOM

Allographs I. McGuinness, D. Grades 2–4. Ages 7–9. Phonemic spelling patterns for the English and French layers of the language, up to two-syllable words:

Child's spelling dictionary
Teacher manual and lesson plans
Worksheets
Sound-search stories books 1, 2, 3

Published by Sea Gate Press, P.O. Box 563, Sanibel, FL 33957. Fax: 941-472-4513.

Allographs II. McGuinness, D. Grades 3–5. Ages 8–10. Morphemic spelling patterns for multisyllable words, prefixes, suffixes, compounding, and the Latin and Greek layers of the language. Available late 1997.

Teacher manual and lesson plans
Worksheets and exercises

Published by Sea Gate Press. See above.

Words. Henry, M.K. Excellent component for teaching spellings for the Latin and Greek layers of the language. Published by Pro-Ed, 8700 Shoal Creek, Austin, TX 78757-6897; 1-800-397-7633.

Patterns for Reading and Spelling Success. Henry, M. K. and Redding, N. C. Published by Pro-Ed.

Chapter 11

HELPING THOSE WHO
DIDN'T MAKE IT

The saying "an ounce of prevention is worth a pound of cure" is more relevant to reading instruction than to any other sphere of endeavor. Reading impacts on almost everything we do. It determines how we learn, what we learn, whether we can graduate from high school, gain entrance to college, or hold down a job. Reading skill impacts on every school subject, including mathematics. This chapter is about that "pound of cure" and the emotional consequences of reading failure for adults, for children, and for their parents. It is written mainly for parents of children with reading problems, adults with reading problems, and reading specialists who work with poor readers.

To understand the plight of the child or adult who has problems learning to read, imagine that your child has joined a Little League ball club. The coach is a local Dad, who doesn't know much about the techniques of the game, but who has some very strong opinions about how to coach batting. He tells his young charges to be certain to keep their weight on the back foot as they strike the ball and, for good measure, to close their eyes just before they swing the bat. He has developed numerous exercises for teaching these techniques. His reasoning sounds plausible to the children and even to most of the parents. For instance, he tells them that "anchoring your weight on the back foot keeps you balanced, while moving into the ball and shifting to the forward foot alters the plane of the bat." Furthermore, he has read somewhere that the ball moves too swiftly for the eye to track it all the way to the bat. Thus, closing your eyes makes you more accurate than leaving them open. He can produce a very convincing set of arguments for these beliefs. Of course, they are simply nonsense, as anyone who has ever played baseball can tell you.

Most children who are instructed in these ridiculous exercises will be miserably inept at batting. Staying on the back foot means that you are off balance and can't transfer your weight into your swing and produce any power. Taking your eye off the ball means that you are likely to miss a curve or a fade. How will the children respond to this kind of training? Take those who have some innate natural talent. Some may have marginal success when following these instructions, because their bodies can compensate even when off balance. More independent children will just ignore what the coach is saying, because it "feels so wrong," and because they observe that great players on TV do neither of these things. Others, less assertive and anxious to please, can have their talent temporarily derailed and lose interest in the game.

After a couple of years these children may get a new coach, or join the school ball club. Now they will have to learn to do the exact opposite of what they had been taught. This involves unlearning the habits they have developed and acquiring new habits. Because the two physical actions are mutually incompatible, this is a difficult and frustrating experience.

Here, in a nutshell, is the predicament of every child or adult with reading problems when they come for remedial help. For many poor readers, their inadequate skill has been *caused* directly by bad methods in the same way that the well-meaning Dad taught bad batting habits. Others may have developed their own strategies or "habits" by themselves. In contrast to the baseball example, however, these "habits of mind" cannot be visually inspected like the physical act of hitting a ball. Chapter 2 reviewed the various "habits" or strategies that children typically adopt when reading instruction is absent or confusing. Remedial reading instructors must always test for strategies before training sessions begin and be certain to monitor this throughout remedial training.

In this and the following chapter, I will be dealing with several issues involved in remediation. This chapter assesses the motivational and emotional aspects of the problem for adult, child, and parents. Next, I look at the remedial environment for the school and for the specialist in private practice. Diagnostic testing and how this is communicated to the client or parent is the final topic for this chapter. In chapter 12, the characteristics of the remedial process are set out in terms of goals and sequencing of activities directed toward those goals.

MOTIVATIONAL AND EMOTIONAL ASPECTS IN REMEDIATION

Parents as Motivators

The motivation and determination of parents of children with severe reading problems are critical to the success of the remedial process. Hopefully, this may change when teachers have more knowledge and better training. Parents often have to fight the system to get testing and help for their child, monitor this help on a daily basis to judge its worth (assuming they get it), and fight the system once more when they find it's not working, which is frequently the case. Their next task is to locate a reading specialist or therapist who knows what he or she is doing. This is especially true for those children with specific processing deficits that must be remediated *before* the child can learn to read. Unfortunately, there are few places across the nation where such special treatment can be obtained.

Parent motivation continues to be vital to the success of any remediation while it is ongoing. Children have to be delivered to the place where training is conducted. This must take precedence over tennis lessons, gymnastics, horseback riding, family holidays, and so forth.

This is a problem for parents to recognize when they begin a series of sessions for their child. When the child is changing bad habits and developing new perceptual skills, the training must be ongoing and consistent. One solution to maintaining gains, used by the Lindamood-Bell clinics, is daily "intensives," where the child rotates through various teachers for several hours each day for about a month. Intensive training makes it possible to introduce new techniques at the same time as preventing the recurrence of old bad habits. The child doesn't have days or weeks to slip back into what he was doing before. Another solution, adopted by Read America, is to involve parents in the training process itself and to provide fail-safe homework materials so that progress is maintained from one weekly session to the next and can continue long after sessions have been completed. An hour a week is a minimum, and interrupting sessions for a few weeks can put the child back to where he was before sessions began.

Parents' Emotions

Parents' emotions are sometimes even more important than the child's in producing a successful outcome. Parents come to a clinical setting with a variety of mixed feelings. These are largely the result of the lack of knowledge about the complexities of reading and frustration with the school or with the child. It is important for a remedial teacher to be aware of parents' thinking and feelings about their child's situation. Sometimes people can hold quite incompatible beliefs.

One implicit belief is that "reading is easy because it's something everyone does," especially when the parent is an expert reader. If a parent has had trouble learning to read, she will have much more sympathy with her child. This implicit belief is in conflict with the reality that the child isn't reading. "If reading is easy and everybody can do it," this means that her child is failing at something "easy." Parents search for reasons to explain how this could happen. Maybe their child has low intelligence or has something wrong with his brain. Another possibility is that their child is too lazy to learn to read. This belief can be reinforced by teachers who tell parents that their child "isn't trying" or "isn't paying attention."

At a school conference or private clinic, the first job a reading specialist has to carry out is to find out what the parents believe about their child's reading problem. Sometimes they may have to convince parents that many of these beliefs are in error. For example, reading is *not* easy, as the preceding chapters have shown. Most children, even those reading at grade level, do not read phonetically. Contrary to what the classroom teacher was saying, children with reading problems have often tried very hard. Every child wants to learn to read. If children stop "paying attention" or stop "trying," it's because reading is too difficult for them, not because they don't care. We know that reading is not a biological property of the brain and so there cannot be damage to a "reading center in the brain." Furthermore, if there was damage to such a center, rapid remediation would never work!

Parents have a range of emotional reactions to this new information. Some experience a sense of profound relief that their child isn't brain-damaged or "stupid." Often this information confirms what they already know about their child, that he is intelligent and highly motivated. This relief can sometimes turn into anger that is directed to the school system or to the child's previous teachers. The anger grows in proportion to the number of years they have spent trying to get help from the school and is fueled in proportion to the child's progress in learning to read during reading therapy. Parents have said to us: "If you can teach my child to read, why can't his teacher?" "If you know these methods that work, why doesn't the school system know them?" These are legitimate questions that are hard to answer because they involve a discussion of experimental research, a detailed background about the remedial method we're using, and a brief historical account of why we are where we are. (Parents' questions and concerns have been one of the major motivators for writing this book.)

Sometimes parents lose faith that their child can be helped. My colleague had the following exchange with parents who had recently moved into town. The parents had been visiting various schools in the district. My colleague ran a private school that specialized in both class-room and remedial treatment for children with reading problems. The program had a documented history of success with children with severe reading problems. Children's lives had literally been turned around at this school.

The parents stated that their child had a serious reading problem and they were looking for the right school. My colleague assured them that their child would learn to read, and that she specialized in teaching children with severe reading problems to read. She said to the parents: "Don't worry, we will teach your child to read." This appeared to make the mother furious. She responded with words to the effect that their child "would never learn to read, that he was 'dyslexic' " and that my colleague didn't know what she was talking about because "our child had been tested by experts." They left the school abruptly, never to be seen again. In psychological terms, this reaction is known as "cognitive dissonance," in which the amount of time, effort, and money spent to accomplish something (in this case the diagnosis "incurable dyslexia" from "experts") is in direct proportion to the intensity in defending one's opinion against contradictory information.

This brings us to another common misconception on the part of parents and also many reading specialists. This misconception derives from a "nominal fallacy," the belief that naming something explains it. Many people hold the belief that you can "have dyslexia" as if it was a brain disorder or disease. I have already discussed the fact that "dyslexia" simply means "reading poorly" and has no valid diagnosis. But there is a reason why the notion of a "brain damaged" model of reading failure, such as that implied by the term "dyslexia" is comforting to parents. Many of them have been searching for years for answers to why their child has a reading problem. It is often more acceptable to believe that their child is "unique" and has a special reading disorder than to face the fact that their child has lost years of education because of poor reading instruction.

THE CLIENT'S EMOTIONAL REACTION TO READING FAILURE

People have various reactions to reading failure. These can range from outbursts of highly aggressive behavior and subsequent hospitalization to mute passivity and depression. The reading specialist has to be able to deal with every type of emotional reaction to reading failure, otherwise she cannot convince the child or adult to trust her, and nothing can be accomplished. Making the client feel safe and establishing trust is the first step toward a successful remedial intervention.

Reading problems cause major emotional problems which increase in intensity the older the child becomes and which continue throughout adult life. This is because reading is unavoidable, and the poor reader believes that "everyone else can read except him." Children are reminded of their shortcomings on a daily basis and there is no escape. When the object of loathing cannot be avoided, there is intense distress. All children want to learn to read. When they come up short in comparison to their classmates, this causes an incredible sense of failure. What children want most is to show that they are competent in all areas in which their age mates are competent. When a child cannot do this, there are four main ways to respond to the distress.

Anger/Acting Out

Frustration causes anger. If someone is repeatedly teased, he ultimately retaliates by losing his temper. If you are required by law to sit for five to six hours every day in a classroom where you cannot do the work, this is the ultimate frustration. Because anger against an adult, especially in classrooms, is unacceptable behavior, only the very daring or desperate will actually display overt aggression. Children can redirect their anger into more covert ways of getting back at the teacher or getting even with the school, which they blame for failing them (with some justification).

All sorts of minor misdemeanors can be perpetrated which contribute to making the teacher's life miserable. A youngster can wander around the room at inappropriate moments and feign surprise when reprimanded: "I was just looking at the rabbit!" They can throw spit wads, tell jokes to their neighbors, tease other children, etc., which gains them some attention and potential respect from their classmates. This compensates for their academic shortcomings which are known to *everyone* in the class. Make no mistake, children keep score. They always know how everyone else is doing, no matter how hard the teacher tries to disguise this, such as labeling reading groups "Bluebirds" and "Robins." Children will tell you in the blink of an eye that "I am in the Robins, that's the good reading group, but my friend Sarah is in the Cardinals, because she can't read."

One day I was walking with eight-year-old Mark from the classroom to the testing room. To make conversation I asked him, "I suppose you're a good reader. Do you like to read, Mark?"

Mark replied without pausing for breath, "I've read five more books than Joe already this semester, and he used to be the best reader in the class, but now I am."

Being the class clown or the class nuisance is a benign way of expressing anger, but the motive is anger nonetheless. Other children act out in much more destructive ways. We tested a child at our reading clinic who had severe reading problems. His mother was so distressed with him that they were scarcely on speaking terms. He had been in continuous trouble at school. The child was brought to two sessions, but before he came to the third, he stood up on a table in the middle of the school cafeteria and began screaming at the top of his voice. He was subsequently hospitalized. I can't finish his story, because we never saw him again.

Another child expressed her anger and anguish in a different way. Susie began to act bizarrely at school, paying no attention whatsoever to anything anyone told her to do. She interfered in other children's work. She bossed them around. She used her body in provoking and inappropriate ways, sticking her feet up on her classmate's desk, tipping over chairs. She was diagnosed "mentally retarded" by the school psychologist because she wouldn't respond during testing. Her mother came in despair, seeking our help.

Testing was impossible. Feet went up on the table and the test materials were scattered across the room. She never made eye contact at any time and sat backwards in the chair for much of the session. Her behavior was nearly "autistic." Eventually, all that could be done was to try to connect with her in some kind of conversation, and even this was difficult. Working with Susie continued to be a problem through the first few sessions, until she began to trust the teacher and began to try. Fortunately, she had a sense of humor and could be reached through humor. Susie, who was taught by my colleague, is now a perfectly normal and delightful child. She's popular with both adults and children, and is reading at grade level.

These examples are not untypical. Well over half of the children with behavioral problems and those labeled "attention deficit disorder," as well as the majority of juvenile delinquents, have serious reading difficulties. Susie is a reminder that children can literally be driven insane by what goes on in our schools. We often wonder what would have happened to Susie if her mother hadn't persisted and found us. By now she would be in a classroom for the "mentally retarded." She would be reading nothing and would have become a burden on her parents for the rest of her life. There are thousands of children like Susie across America, who are lost forever in special classrooms. When you see the consequences of this first-hand, it makes you aware of the cruel treatment that some schools can mete out to youngsters in need.

Fear

Fear is opposite to anger. It is the reaction of children or adults who desperately want to please and haven't the guile or gumption to impose their personality on others through acting out. Ultimately, these people can develop what is called "learned helplessness," a profoundly debilitating condition in which they come to believe that they need help in every phase of their life. This reaction poses a different kind of problem for a reading specialist in attempting to gain the trust of someone who is afraid that no one can ever make him self-sufficient.

Putting anything in print in front of someone like this causes instant panic, and the specialist needs to proceed slowly and cautiously, always being sure to begin each session at the place where the client experiences some comfort and sense of control. I am always particularly emphatic to parents about children who manifest these symptoms that they should not under any circumstances put any pressure on their child to read books to them until the remediation has progressed substantially. I also try to get parents to convey this message to the classroom teacher.

Fearful children and adults often have a finely developed ability to manipulate anyone who tries to teach them. Experience in classrooms has taught them that there is only one answer to any question, and their task is to find that right answer. They do this by a subterfuge that involves asking a question when they are given a question. They become adept at reading people's expressions, searching their face for clues that they are on target.

A case that epitomizes this type of emotional response is an adult in her late twenties whom I worked with. Eva had a severe speech defect that made her seem unintelligent, and her self-esteem was at zero. Her reading score was at the sixth-grade level, but even this was based on untimed tests which she took forever to complete. She had had years of speech therapy and years of remedial reading classes. Having been diagnosed "LD," she was currently struggling through junior college with a "tutor" (paid for by the taxpayers) who helped Eva with her written assignments. Eva gradually revealed that she had more or less manipulated this tutor into writing large portions of her essays. I spent considerable time convincing her that her life would be unmanageable if she had to conduct the rest of it with a tutor at her elbow!

As we began to work, she would take her eyes off the materials and stare into my face. If I asked her, "Which sound went away?" she would reply with a question, "The /b/?" and quickly scan my face for a clue to whether she was right. If I replied, "Are you sure?" she thought she had made a mistake and immediately substituted another question using another sound: "The /e/?" After a while my constant reminder: "You won't find the answer on my face" became a standing joke between us. It took her months to stop doing this.

Eva learned to read at the college level and improved her speech to the point where she sounded completely normal, causing her brother from out of state to burst into tears when he telephoned her to wish her Merry Christmas. She successfully interviewed for a job at a local bank and moved into her own apartment. She no longer needed her tutor and was writing her own essays and getting straight A's at the end of thirty-five sessions.

Depression/Withdrawal

Clinical descriptions of psychological distress can be ranked on an "energy" continuum. A person who is filled with anger/hostility has a much higher energy level than someone who is afraid (anxiety), which is, in turn, a higher level than sadness or depression. Some clinicians believe that prognosis in psychotherapy depends on the level of energy, and that people with extremely low levels of energy are much harder to treat. Depression is close to psychological "death." People who slip into a clinical depression can withdraw completely from human inter-action.

Children or adults who have reacted with depression to their read-ing problems are difficult to teach for just this reason. Some are so de-pressed and withdrawn that they are nearly mute, staring into their laps and mumbling inaudibly only when spoken to. It's exhausting to work with such clients because the specialist feels obliged to provide energy for the client as well as herself. This is like pouring water into a cup with a hole in it. Depressed people extract energy from everyone around them, but this does little to improve their condition. To deal with this type of client you must attempt to fix "the hole." This means explicit goal setting and exercises in self-awareness. The more the spe-cialist attempts to take responsibility for the client, the less responsibil-ity the client will take to remedy the situation. People whose depression is based *solely* upon their reading failure need a remedial program that involves more ongoing support, such as more frequent sessions and activities where the clients can estimate their progress: "Look how far you've come." This keeps them from slipping into ap-athy between sessions and keeps the goals in focus. If depression ap-pears to be due to other causes, this type of client should be referred to a suitable professional for psychological treatment.

Intellectualization

Intellectualizing a reading problem can be a tactic of the highly intel-ligent child or adult. We have already seen how Mike decided not to learn how to spell, because "spelling made no sense." Many very bright youngsters know they are clever because they are able to learn quickly and remember everything they hear or see. They usually get a lot of positive feedback from their parents about their abilities. When it tran-spires that they have some difficulty learning to read, they can invent some extraordinary kinds of rationalizations about this deficiency to protect their self-worth. These children can be challenging to work with because the teacher constantly has to outwit them.

Bobby was six and a half and had decided to stop reading altogether when he was brought to me for testing. His mother and father were both very concerned and both seemed motivated to get help for him. Bobby had an impenetrable set of logical arguments about why he didn't need to learn to read. He was quite a talented artist. He argued that as he was going to be an artist, artists didn't need to learn to read. After all, they never had anything to do with the printed word. I reasoned that if he was ever commissioned to produce a work of art, he would need to sign contracts and be able to read them, otherwise he could be cheated. He disagreed and said that he would only deal with honest people, and their contract would be a handshake. Furthermore, when he got famous (which was sure to happen), he would hire someone to deal with all the paperwork.

We had many similar discussions, which, of course, were a deliberate "time waster" that Bobby enjoyed promoting. In addition to his many intellectual arguments about not needing to learn to read, he had scores of premeditated behaviors to distract me from the task at hand. He would smuggle strange objects into the session and then begin to pull them out of his pockets at various intervals. His high intelligence extended to a masterful ability to manipulate adults, especially his mother. (If he came to a reading session, he got a treat.) I pointed this out to him on one occasion and he just grinned.

Obviously, I genuinely liked Bobby and we had great rapport. He also liked coming to sessions but not to learn to read. We would rarely work longer than about five or ten minutes before the fun and games began.

There was a more important aspect to this case. Bobby had a hidden agenda behind his manipulative games that he was too young to be aware of. When Bobby's parents were first interviewed, I asked whether there was anything in his life that was upsetting him, because his test scores revealed that there was basically nothing wrong with him. He had no deficits in any subskills related to reading. His mother hastily responded that everything was fine. His father, on the other hand, pointed out that Bobby had just lost a favorite grandparent and that his other favorite grandparent was in hospital at that moment. Bobby went to visit every evening. (This grandparent subsequently recovered.) Then the father confessed that he and his wife were in the process of separating for the third time. Yet the mother had stated "nothing was wrong."

Some time after we had been working together, Bobby returned from a month-long trip to visit his dad, the third separation now underway. Bobby's first remark came immediately after we began to work. He told me that the whole time he was with his dad, "he didn't make me read one word." Suddenly I saw a purpose in Bobby's behavior. He could hold his parents together by virtue of his continuous failure to learn to read. This upset was their common interest and it focused their attention on him. His dad could "punish Mom" by telling Bobby he didn't have to read when they were together, knowing

Bobby would convey this information, just as he did to me. Mom, who was trapped in the game, was practicing denial that anything in their family life could impact on Bobby. It's not surprising that I was having little success, because I became an unwitting pawn in this game. Although Bobby certainly had a minor reading problem that could easily have been remediated, he didn't need a reading specialist so much as an astute family therapist.

Intellectualization plus denial is common in the adult poor reader, as we saw with Mike in the last chapter. These are people who "can read," but very badly. They have poor decoding skills and have to reread the same passage over and over again. They also have serious spelling problems. However, they will fight everyone who tries to help them in order to protect their self-worth: "I don't really have a reading problem, I just don't like to read." "I don't really have a reading problem, I'm just a slow reader." They also worry that their fragile grasp of the writing system could be undermined by being taught a new method. They could be worse off than before. ("Better the devil you know.") There is some justification for this concern, as many poor readers have been in remedial reading programs already with no measurable outcome. It is hard to convince these people that there are programs that really work, something you need to be aware of if this description fits a family member. It is also something a reading specialist needs to be aware of when a surly client is dragged in protest to the clinic.

Incidentally, families often don't know how serious a reading problem is for an adult member of the household. Here is a trick you can use to find out. If you find something really interesting in a magazine or newspaper while you're in the same room, toss it to them and say: "Wow, have a look at this! This is amazing!" The first thing a poor reader will do is to put the magazine or paper down somewhere, on the coffee table or the floor. Then they will say something like: "I'll read it later," or "Why don't you tell me what it's about?" or "I'm just about to: (a) "watch TV," (b) "mow the lawn," (c) "go for a walk." This may be true, so repeat this experiment a few times. If these reactions occur each time, you know there is a problem.

This is a glimpse of the many kinds of additional issues that adults and children can bring to a reading clinic or reading specialist. I have given examples of relatively severe cases and not everyone will have such debilitating emotional reactions to reading problems. Children with minor deficiencies can be remediated fairly quickly and, because they see gains almost immediately, are easy to work with. Even in the more severe cases, the psychological distress will diminish as soon as the client begins to trust the teacher. However, when these symptoms do not disappear, or when a client devotes his entire energy to game playing, as in the example of Bobby, it is usually a sign that something else besides reading needs to be addressed. Because a reading specialist is not really in a position to recommend other forms of treatment, she is often in a difficult position with certain clients and must handle the situation with great tact.

THE REMEDIAL ENVIRONMENT

The School

In an ideal school no child would ever need "remediation." Some children might take longer to learn to read than others, but everyone would learn by the right method. Hopefully, one day, remedial reading specialists will become an extinct species and the schools will at last take on the job of doing what they are supposed to do, teaching all children to read. Until that time, there are millions of children who need help now and who cannot roll back the clock and start anew. Here is a brief outline of a model remedial program that should be implemented in every elementary school in America.

1. Each school would employ a reading specialist. This person should be trained in how to test and diagnose specific kinds of reading problems. She would have an understanding of child psychology and be aware of the types of emotional problems created by reading failure. She would know how to use methods like those discussed in this book.

2. The specialist would have her own quiet and self-contained space, big enough to work with children in small groups as well as individually.

3. The specialist would coordinate each child's curriculum with the classroom teacher. This would include separate stories, books, and worksheets, so that the child's time in the classroom was productive instead of being wasted.

4. The specialist would have regularly scheduled meetings with the parents and advise on homework and reading activities appropriate for each child.

5. The specialist would meet with the school psychologist or other professional to discuss children with special emotional problems.

The Private Clinic

A key issue for parents and for reading specialists in private practice is that parents have no knowledge about how to evaluate a reading specialist or a particular method. One of the main goals of this chapter is to provide information that will enable people to make an informed choice. Specific information on how to do this is provided in chapter 13. The layperson tends to equate specialists with "tutors," and doesn't understand why she should pay higher fees to specialists in private practice. A specialist is a professional and needs to pay rent, staff salaries, miscellaneous office expenses, and still make a living. A reading specialist using a good reading method will teach a child to read correctly in a short space of time, so that he can function to the maximum of his potential.

The atmosphere of the clinic is critically important. The work area should be quiet, peaceful, and uncluttered. Nothing should distract from the task at hand. Children should be made aware that what they do in this environment is a serious matter, and that the clinic is a special place where they will learn to read. For these reasons it is not a good idea for the specialist to teach children in their home (unless there is a self-contained room). This blurs the boundaries between the professional and the client and can create a situation where misbehavior is more likely to occur.

I once agreed to test a neighborhood child in my home. The clinic was about thirty minutes' drive away so it was inconvenient for both of us. I had about ten seconds to say, "Hello, Johnny," and then Johnny took off, running from room to room, up and down stairs, opening doors and cupboards, while Mom did and said nothing except to utter the unbelievable remark: "He doesn't usually act like this."

Whether a reading specialist is employed by the school system or operates a private practice or a clinic, the remainder of this chapter applies equally to these environments.

THE DIAGNOSTIC WORKUP

Mandatory Tests

Parents need to be informed about which kinds of tests are useful for diagnosing a reading problem and which are not. They also need to know that a reading specialist who does not use diagnostic testing is not doing her job properly.

No type of intervention should begin until the reading specialist has a profile of the client. Without this profile, she doesn't know where to attack the problem precisely. For example, a child or adult may have good phonemic awareness, understand the phonetic code perfectly in isolation, but be unable to apply this code when reading text. This would direct the specialist to focus more on blending and segmenting activities than on teaching phoneme awareness and sound/letter correspondences.

It isn't necessary to spend weeks or months waiting on the school system for special testing in order to determine whether a child needs remedial help. A simple reading test will reveal whether a child is reading below grade level. Other straightforward tests are all that are required to pinpoint specific weaknesses in perceptual or cognitive abilities that impact on reading. These five tests are the most useful in determining a diagnostic profile and apply equally to children and adults.

1. A standardized reading test that has the following properties: isolated word recognition and nonsense word decoding (word attack). Word recognition errors should be phonetically transcribed so the child's predominant reading strategy can be determined.

2. A test of phoneme awareness. The client is asked to listen to a word or nonsense word and be able to manipulate phonemes in the word.

3. A test of phoneme segmentation. The client hears a word and has to isolate (separate) each phoneme one at a time in sequence.

4. A test of blending. The client hears a series of isolated phonemes and is asked to blend them into a word.

5. Code knowledge. Letters or letter patterns from the spelling code are listed and the client has to decide how these would sound if they appeared in a word.

(Examples of these tests are provided at the end of this chapter. The standardized tests cannot be obtained by nonprofessionals.)

The purpose of the testing is to rule in or rule out certain processing problems that will impact on the speed at which the remediation will occur, as well as specific problem areas that the therapist needs to be aware of.

The reading test will show how the client performs relative to national norms, or to district norms if the test is also used in the school district. The nonsense word reading test measures pure decoding skill and reveals whether or not the client has any ability to decode phonetically. The client's reading strategy will be determined by the phonetic transcriptions of errors in the word recognition reading test.

Phoneme awareness test scores will reveal whether the client has a problem hearing and manipulating phonemes when they are embedded in words. Two tests are normed. These are the Lindamood Auditory Conceptualization test (Lindamood and Lindamood, 1971) and the Auditory Analysis Test (Rosner and Simon, 1971). Neither test is recommended for children younger than six, and they can be too difficult for some six-year-olds. Poor performance on either of these tests will direct the specialist to intensive training in phoneme awareness. A modified version of the AAT is at the end of this chapter.

Segmenting tasks, in which the client has to separate each sound in a word ("What are the sounds in the word 'frog'?"), illustrate the ability to analyze the sound sequences in words. Blending is the subskill that allows the client to put the sounds back together. It is common for poor readers to have one skill and not the other. Segmenting and blending tests are also at the end of this chapter.

Optional Tests

1. Writing sample. A person's writing sample is a powerful aid in determining the degree of confusion about the spelling code. For older children and adults it is useful to ask for a page of written work with spelling *uncorrected*. This is one way to identify the poor speller who might score well on the diagnostic tests. It is also beneficial later, when reading, spelling, and writing have improved, to illustrate the improvement to the client.

2. Reading fluency. It is useful to measure the speed it takes to read a standard passage, which can be compared at a later date after remediation. Although this gives the reading specialist little diagnostic information, it can be a big motivator to repeat this test during remediation.

3. Reading comprehension tests have little predictive value for diagnostic purposes. I have had clients take forty-five minutes to read twenty-five single sentence passages and score almost perfectly on these tests. However, for adult clients, a comprehension test can be informative. It provides a vivid impression of the effort it takes for a poor reader to extract any meaning from what they read. If the first ten to twenty items are timed, this provides a useful measure of improvement after remediation. Finally, it will expose the rare fluent decoder who

doesn't process the *meaning* (comprehend) of what he reads, indicating that comprehension itself may need special attention.

4. Spelling. A spelling test can be useful for children eight years and older. A "spelling recognition" test is essentially a reading test and should be avoided. Here the client chooses among possible spellings: clene clean cleen clien. A spelling dictation test should be given instead. The Wide Range Achievement spelling subtest is used most often in research and in many clinical settings (though it has some problems). A new spelling dictation test has been developed by Pro-Ed which provides separate scoring norms for phonetically regular and irregular words. Unfortunately, we do not have good spelling tests with sufficient range and good psychometric properties.

The Testing Climate

One day I was visiting a friend's clinic and observed a child being tested who was unable to focus on the task at hand for any length of time. He kept turning around to look at the door behind him and constantly squirmed uncomfortably in his seat. Fortunately, my friend was a sensitive person who bothered to ask him what was wrong. He was simply worried about when and whether his mother would return for him, and if she had been told what time he would be finished. Once reassured, he immediately settled down to focus on the test.

Someone else, sticking strictly to the test manual, might plunge ahead and write in her notes: "hyperactive behavior, possibly ADD?" I have seen people who should know better rush through testing, disregarding the emotional and physical state of the client. Children and adults arrive straight from school or work and may need to go to the bathroom or get a drink. These are routine courtesies that a specialist should extend. It sets the climate for testing in that the child or adult feels the tester's concern for her well-being.

The specialist should reassure clients that they will be given very few tests and none will be timed. Clients (and parents) often come to a testing session in a state of anxiety and even panic. They have often been tested over and over again with little outcome except humiliation. They need to know that the specialist is going to teach them how to read and not just send them back into the void. The purpose of the tests is not to upset them but to provide a set of guidelines for remediation.

Testers should *never* let a client continue if he has misunderstood the test instructions. The purpose of the tests is *not* to determine whether or not the client understands test instructions. The purpose of testing is to get a true measure of ability. Even when clients have been told that reading tests are untimed, they frequently rush ahead, scarcely looking at the words, to impress the tester with their speed. They should be told to slow down and be reminded that the test isn't timed. When transcribing errors, this is all the more important. A similar problem occurs in the nonsense word reading test. Clients start to invent real words for each example, reading 'bif' as 'bit.' They should be stopped and the instructions repeated. The purpose of the test is to force them to try to decode, so that the specialist has some idea whether or not they have any decoding skill.

Communicating Test Results

Many parents with a child who has been tested by the school system have experienced being handed a fistful of incomprehensible charts and tables and/or a jargon-laden narrative, which provides them with absolutely no information whatsoever. I have interviewed parents who have arrived with folders full of years of test score results, charts, and reports, most of which made no sense, even to me. The purpose of these reports seems to be to obscure what is actually wrong with the child.

A remedial reading specialist and the special ed staff at the school have a duty to the parents of a child or adult poor reader to communicate clearly and unambiguously the test score results and either a verbal or written explanation in plain English. They must be able to state the reason why the test was given. They must be able to state how *that particular test* defined a specific problem that impacts upon reading or spelling, and how that problem is manifest. They must be able to tell the client or parents how the intervention will be managed based upon the diagnostic test scores, how this will be measured, and finally, *how long this intervention will take* based upon the severity of the problem. A good reading clinic can give you a broad time estimate over the phone based on their experience, and a fairly accurate time estimate after testing. Never trust anyone who says they have no idea how long it will take (or how much it will cost). If someone tells you this at your child's school, seek outside help immediately.

In the following chapter we will look in detail at successful remedial programs, and the purposes and goals of each step of the process.

DO-IT-YOURSELF DIAGNOSTICS

The following tests are designed for parents and teachers to help evaluate a child. These tests will provide information on the child's reading skill, reading strategy, phonemic awareness, and knowledge of the advanced spelling code. These are not standardized tests, but they have been used in research and in the clinic. If a child is having trouble on any one of these tests, you need to seek further advice from a professional, or teach the child yourself based upon the information provided in chapters 8, 9, and 12.

Word Recognition and Strategies Test

Write the words listed below on white 3″ × 5″ cards, three words to a card, in large lower-case letters. Number the cards on the back from 1 to 15.

Hold up each card, or hand it to the child, and ask him to read each word carefully. There is no time limit.

This is also your scoring sheet. When the child makes an error, record *what he said* in the spaces provided (any spelling will do).

1.	no _____	16.	then _____	31.	plate _____
2.	an _____	17.	says _____	32.	warm _____
3.	be _____	18.	feet _____	33.	blow _____
4.	sat _____	19.	clock _____	34.	funny _____
5.	bed _____	20.	here _____	35.	river _____
6.	fox _____	21.	cold _____	36.	break _____
7.	book _____	22.	house _____	37.	shout _____
8.	to _____	23.	dear _____	38.	could _____
9.	bag _____	24.	log _____	39.	honey _____
10.	them _____	25.	said _____	40.	melon _____
11.	see _____	26.	dime _____	41.	watch _____
12.	good _____	27.	new _____	42.	exam _____
13.	dry _____	28.	uncle _____	43.	blue _____
14.	hot _____	29.	sheet _____	44.	answer _____
15.	gas _____	30.	anyone _____	45.	believe _____

SCORING WORD RECOGNITION TEST

Approximate grade placements are shown for reading all or most of the items correctly.

Items 1–6   Beginning first grade
Items 1–15   Middle first grade
Items 1–30   Beginning second grade
Items 1–45   Middle second grade

ASSESSING STRATEGIES

Pure Guessing. Child guesses a real word that has no connection to the word either in letter sound correspondence or in word length.

Examples: 'no' is read as 'fun' or 'look'

Modified Whole-Word Errors. Child decodes the first letter or letters correctly and guesses a real word with attention to word length and shape.

Examples: no   as 'not'
           sat   as 'say'
           them   as 'this'
           good   as 'great'
           clock   as 'clover'

Part-Word Errors. Child tries to break the word down into "sound bites." Typically reads nonsense words and reuses letters.

Examples: them   as 'the-hem'
           clock   as 'cloawok'
           sheet   as 'she-heat'
           anyone   as 'an-yunee'
           plate   as 'play-ate'

Orthographic Errors. Child reads phonetically, letter by letter from left to right, but decodes many letters incorrectly.

Examples: here   as 'her'
           house   as 'huss'
           dear   as 'dar'
           uncle   as 'unclee'
           plate   as 'plat'

Phonetic Errors. Child reads a phonetically probable rendition of the word, but misreads word.

Examples:	no	as 'naw'
	says	as 'saize'
	house	as 'hooss'
	anyone	as 'anyoan'
	blow	as 'blou'
	honey	as 'hoany'

The strategies are set out from the worst to the best. Code each error into the highest possible strategy. Example: 'her' may have been a guess but is also a phonetic decoding.

To estimate your child's predominant strategy or strategies, count each *type* of error and divide this number by the total number of errors. This will give you percentage of each type of strategy error.

Children with a year or two of reading instruction should be making mainly orthographic or phonetic errors. If this is not the case, you may want to get outside testing and remedial help or teach the child yourself.

Instructions for the Nonsense Word Test

This test can be used in two ways. If you use it *both* ways, be sure to give the reading test first and the word repetition last.

NONSENSE WORD REPETITION

Screening test for possible speech problem. Suitable ages: four to seven years. (Three-year-olds can do this test but a poor score doesn't mean anything.) If the child scores below average, you may want to get proper testing by a speech therapist.

Tell the child you are going to play a game by saying words in "Martian." His job is to repeat back the word exactly as you said it. Be sure to practice first so you can read each word fluently. It doesn't matter if you do not pronounce it correctly, but it *does* matter that the child repeats it exactly as you have spoken it. If he does, then score it correct.

The average scores for four to seven years are as follows:

4 years: 15–20
5 years: 20–30
6 years: 30–35
7 years: 36–40

NONSENSE WORD DECODING

To use this as a decoding test, print words on 3″ × 5″ cards, three words to a card, in large lower-case letters for your child to read.

There are no norms for this test. Anyone who knows the code can read every word because they are phonetically regular. However, this would be unusual, even for many adults. Younger children (ages six to eight) will not be able to read many of the multisyllable words. This test will give you information about whether or not your child has *any idea* about how to decode our writing system.

Nonsense Word Decoding

1.	dap	_____	21.	bloamite	_____
2.	fim	_____	22.	strŏŏkle	_____
3.	pob	_____	23.	varthip	_____
4.	tad	_____	24.	roilesh	_____
5.	bek	_____	25.	quomple	_____
6.	seef	_____	26.	lomramp	_____
7.	kug	_____	27.	chowmerg	_____
8.	doif	_____	28.	sharlfen	_____
9.	kibe	_____	29.	groithek	_____
10.	boosh	_____	30.	zichong	_____
11.	chuj	_____	31.	kagpeb	_____
12.	fowp	_____	32.	vifthung	_____
13.	thev	_____	33.	distroamber	_____
14.	woamp	_____	34.	sizchullen	_____
15.	feench	_____	35.	meminum	_____
16.	nempt	_____	36.	jozipesh	_____
17.	barng	_____	37.	zotrempering	_____
18.	gleth	_____	38.	chibbyreenom	_____
19.	straimp	_____	39.	quodistelpab	_____
20.	droiper	_____	40.	rinpohacherfelp	_____

Blending Test

Do not allow the subject to see the test. Tell the subject that you are going to say some sounds. He/she should tell you what word it sounds like. Sit near enough so the subject can hear you clearly and see your mouth. Explain that you can say the sounds only once and he/she should listen and watch carefully. Say each sound in the first word, with a one second interval between each sound... "p" "i" "g". Do not repeat the word. Write down the first response.

PART ONE		PART TWO	
p i g	_____	f r o g	_____
b u g	_____	g r a ss	_____
h a t	_____	s t i ck	_____
p i n	_____	p r i n t	_____
r a t	_____	c r u n ch	_____
b ir d	_____	p l a n t	_____
sh e ll	_____		
f i ve	_____		
b oa t	_____		

Interpretation Of Scores

14+ = good   - 14 = low moderate   - 11 = poor

Less than a perfect score on part one indicates that the subject has trouble blending or pushing together the sounds in three sound words.

Less than a perfect score on part two indicates that the subject has trouble pushing together sounds in four and five sound words.

Phoneme Segmentation Test

Do not allow the subject to see the test. Explain that you will say all the sounds in the word dog. If the subject offers a letter name say, "That's a letter. What's the *sound*?" If he/she persists at responding with letter names, mark those responses wrong.   Put a check for each correct answer in the corresponding space.   If he/she omits a sound mark it wrong, EX: "frog" = "f" "o' "g". You would mark these responses like this ✔ _X_ _✔_ _✔_. If he/she gives the wrong sound, mark it wrong, EX: "frog" = "f" "r" "a" "g". You would score these responses like this _✔_ _✔_ _X_ _✔_. If he/she blends two sounds together mark both sounds wrong, EX: "frog" = "fr" "o" "g".   You would mark these responses like this _X_ _X_ _✔_ _✔_. "f" "ro" "g" would be marked like this _✔_ _X_ _X_ _✔_.

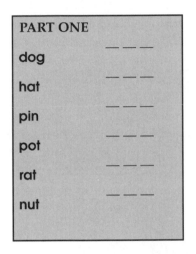

PART ONE		PART TWO	
dog	_ _ _	frog	_ _ _ _
hat	_ _ _	black	_ _ _ _
pin	_ _ _	nest	_ _ _ _
pot	_ _ _	trip	_ _ _ _
rat	_ _ _	milk	_ _ _ _
nut	_ _ _	drum	_ _ _ _

Interpretation Of Scores

40+ = good   - 40 = low moderate   - 36 = poor

____ offered a letter name more than 2 times EX: "dog" = "dee" "oe" "gee"
The subject may not understand that letters are symbols for sounds, and may be trying to recall the sound of the letter by thinking of the letter name, an unnecessary step requiring a translation.

____ omitted vowel sound or chunked it to a consonant sound 2 or more times
EX: "dog" = "d" "g" or "do" "g" or "d" "og"
The subject may be connecting a vowel sound to each consonant and may need training in the pronunciation of consonant sounds.

____ chunked consonants together or omitted one of them more than 2 times
EX: "frog" = "fr" "o" "g" or "f" "o" "g"
The subject may be having trouble isolating the separate sounds in words, causing him/her to leave sounds out   and add sounds that aren't there.

____ repeated the wrong sound 2 or more times EX: "frog" = "f" "r" "a" "g"
The subject may have a low auditory memory.

Auditory Processing Test

Do not allow the subject to see the test. Ask the subject to say the word pig. Now ask for pig without the sound "p". If he/she has trouble doing this, offer an example. Say, OK, if I wanted to say "dog" without the "d," it would be "og".

PART ONE

Say **pig** w/o the 'p' _____ (ig)
Say **pog** w/o the 'g' _____ (po)
Say **sip** w/o the 's' _____ (ip)

PART TWO

Say **stop** w/o the 's' _____ (top)
Say **nest** w/o the 't' _____ (nes)
Say **flag** w/o the 'f' _____ (lag)

PART THREE

Say **plum** w/o the 'l' _____ (pum)
Say **best** w/o the 's' _____ (bet)
Say **grill** w/o the 'r' _____ (gill)
Say **lost** w/o the 's' _____ (lot)

Interpretation Of Scores

+8 = good   +5-7 = low moderate   -5 = poor

____ was unable to score correctly on all of the first 3 test items
Subject is experiencing difficulty segmenting and isolating single sounds in simple words.

____ removed the adjacent consonant to the target sound in part two or three
   EX: flag with out the 'f' = "ag"
Subject is experiencing difficulty segmenting individual consonants.

____ unable to perform (no correct responses)
Subject is having difficulty understanding the nature of sounds in words.

Copyright Read America, Inc. 1-800-732-3868

Code Knowledge Test & Key

This page is the key for the code knowledge test on the next page. Use the next page as the cue sheet for the test. Do not let the subject see this page. After each sound is an example of a word or words containing that sound in case you are uncertain of the sound that the letter(s) represents. For example, the <ie> in the last column can represent the sound 'ie' as in the word die, or 'ee' as in the word chief. Begin by pointing to the first letter and asking: "If you saw this in a word, what sound would you say?" If subject says a letter name, you say: "That's a letter. I want to know what sound it stands for." If subject continues offering letter names, mark these answers incorrect. Only sounds are correct answers. Keep track of the number of correct and incorrect responses. The total correct times two is the percentage of code knowledge the subject has at this time.

___b	boy		fly	___eigh	**eigh**t
___c	cat				**h**eigh**t**
	city	___z	zipper	___ay	pl**ay**
___d	dog	___i	r**i**p	___ie	d**ie**
___f	fat	___e	n**e**t		ch**ie**f
___g	got	___a	m**a**t	___aw	s**aw**
	gentle	___o	m**o**p	___ee	s**ee**n
___h	hop	___u	n**u**t	___ey	k**ey**
___j	job	___sh	**sh**ip		th**ey**
___k	kid	___ch	**ch**ip	___ue	bl**ue**
___l	lap	___th	**th**is	___ew	f**ew**
___m	mop		**Th**ursday		n**ew**
___n	nod	___ck	du**ck**	___au	**Au**gust
___p	pat	___qu	**qu**ick 'kw'	___oo	w**oo**d
___r	rat	___ce	ni**ce**		m**oo**n
___s	sat	___ai	r**ai**n	___ui	s**ui**t
___t	top	___ou	**ou**t	___oy	b**oy**
___v	give		gr**ou**p	___oi	s**oi**l
___w	with		t**ou**ch		
___x	fox 'ks'	___ea	**ea**ch		
	exit 'gz'		st**ea**k		
			br**ea**d		
		___oa	b**oa**t		
		___ow	n**ow**		
			sn**ow**		
___y	yes	___igh	n**igh**t		
	happy				

Interpretation Of Scores

Raw score times two equals percentage of correct answers.
For older children and adults use the eight year-old values.

	good	low moderate	poor
6 years old	60-100%	50-60%	-50%
7 years old	70-100%	60-70%	-60%
8 years old	80-100%	70-80%	-70%

Code Knowledge Cue Card

b	x	oa
c	y	ow
d	z	igh
f	i	eigh
g	e	ay
h	a	ie
j	o	aw
k	u	ee
l	sh	ey
m	ch	ue
n	th	ew
p	ck	au
r	qu	oo
s	ce	ui
t	ai	oy
v	ou	oi
w	ea	

Chapter 12

REMEDIAL READING PROGRAMS

In chapter 8, I reviewed the training studies based on research on the "new paradigm." Many of these studies were short-term experimental programs or programs for younger children. In this chapter I will be describing remedial reading programs that work for everyone, and for all ages. There are only two of them, and they meet the following requirements for an effective reading method.

1. Published research supports large and consistent gains.
2. Uses phonemes as the platform or basis for teaching the alphabet code. Includes most or all of the spelling code.
3. Works for *everyone* at all ages.
4. Works quickly. It should take no longer than sixty hours *maximum* to teach anyone to read and spell.

I wish I could tell you about hundreds of good remedial programs—or even ten, or five—where you could be certain that your child or family member would learn to read, but I can't. This is not to say that there may not be other good remedial programs in the schools or the private sector. The problem is that most reading specialists do not do research. This means that one has to rely on the reading teacher's "belief" that her program works, and without published information, it's very difficult to find out about good programs. One of the goals of this chapter is to present these two successful programs in sufficient detail so that you can evaluate a reading program in your school or town.

Parents should be aware that traditional "phonics" programs don't get any better when transported to the clinic or to the special ed classroom. They have the same shortcomings they do in the regular classroom and don't miraculously improve simply because the child is working one-on-one with a specialist. Phonics programs do not teach phoneme awareness, nor do they teach the correct logic for the alphabet code. Some reading teachers in private practice have told me that they have had more success after providing phoneme awareness training *prior to* teaching phonics. This may be so, but this still does not eliminate the cumbersome and time-consuming instruction required by phonics logic in order to teach the entire spelling code.

That remediation is an unsolved problem in the school system has been documented by Steven Truch, formerly a consulting school psychologist in Alberta, Canada. He did a survey of the special ed "resource" teachers and asked what percentage of the children graduated back into the main classroom. The answers ranged from zero to an optimistic 20 percent. Most teachers estimated 0 to 10 percent. Robert Slavin and his colleagues report that special ed fails most of the time in U.S. inner-city schools where their research has been ongoing for over a decade.

I have already discussed the elements of a good reading program in chapters 9 and 10. The first key component is training in phoneme awareness. Phoneme awareness begins with the identification of all the phonemes in the language (not just some of them). Then the student must be trained in these skills: "auditory analysis," or the ability to manipulate phonemes in words (remove, insert, reverse sounds); the ability to segment words into isolated phonemes; and the ability to blend isolated phonemes back into words. *All three skills are equally important* and do not necessarily go together. That is, a child can have good segmenting and poor blending, or poor phoneme awareness. Variable performance on these three skills is not uncommon.

The programs described in this chapter differ in two fundamental ways from the classroom programs outlined in chapters 9 and 10, though the overall philosophy is the same. First, they require individual one-on-one training, which is critical for anyone with a reading problem. Each client must be monitored closely, and all errors dealt with immediately. The client has already lost valuable time (usually years) and cannot afford to waste any more.

Small-group instruction is considerably less effective. The reading therapist has to shift her focus of attention constantly from one pupil to another. Children tend to misbehave in small groups and distract one another from the task at hand. Children prompt each other with answers instead of waiting their turn. Children and adults alike are embarrassed about their reading difficulties and less likely to be forthcoming when asked to try something new in a group of strangers. Many adults have emotional problems or serious life problems that they cannot share in a group setting. This lesson learned from clinical practice is important for the special ed teacher working in the public schools. A special ed teacher cannot teach reading to a class or groups of children with serious reading problems successfully. Special ed funding could be sharply reduced if the teacher worked individually with each child to ensure he moved quickly back to the classroom. This is, of course, provided that she was using a method similar to those outlined in this chapter.

Speed of remediation is determined by the *total* amount of one-on-one time spent with each individual client. This rule applies to the individual versus small-group issue. You can multiply the amount of time it takes by the number of children in the group. It also applies to the *frequency* at which the training takes place. Four hours of work a day is nearly as effective as four hours a week, or four hours a month. Beyond this (four hours per year) the rule breaks down. The goal of remediation is to train missing subskills, eliminate incorrect strategies and replace them with correct ones, teach the complete code, and prevent what is gained during sessions from being lost over time, and the client slipping back into old habits.

The second difference between remedial programs and the classroom approach described earlier is that they are rapidly speeded up in information content. In part, this is because the child or adult has the entire focus of the teacher for the training period, but also because classroom instruction has the luxury of time. The classroom program outlined earlier is ultraconservative because it must be taught in small groups or to the whole class. It was designed so that no child can fall through the cracks. A remedial program has no luxury of time. Changes must be made fast. Clients have to see progress happening in real time, otherwise they become discouraged and apathetic. After all, many of them have been through this process before, with no measurable results.

The Lindamood-Bell Clinics

The Lindamood program was developed by Pat and Charles Lindamood in the 1960s. They combined Charles' expertise in linguistics and Pat's expertise in the speech-and hearing sciences to design a true "linguistic" reading program called "Auditory Discrimination in Depth" (ADD). Lessons are organized around the phonemes of the English language and begin with the discovery of how each of the forty-four phonemes is produced. Letters are introduced when this knowledge is secure. Instruction is always oriented *from* the phoneme *to* the letter, so the overall logic of our alphabetic writing system is consistent. The Lindamood program was the first true linguistic program of this century, at least for the English-speaking world. (The first linguistic program, designed by Nellie Dale in England in 1898, was discussed in chapter 5.) Today, Pat Lindamood operates several clinics, known as the Lindamood-Bell clinics, with her longtime colleague Nanci Bell and her daughter Phyllis Lindamood. Lindamood-Bell is headquartered in San Luis Obispo, California and has branches in many major cities across the nation. Each branch director has had special training and supervised teaching experience.

Other clinics are also using this method. These are the Morris Center in Gainesville, Florida, run by Ann Alexander, the Reading Foundation in Calgary, Alberta, run by Steven Truch, and the Langsford Center in Louisville, Kentucky run by Stephen McCrocklin. Both Alexander and Truch have published research to show the effectiveness of their programs, which was reviewed in chapter 8.

People who have trained to teach "Auditory Processing in Depth" at the Lindamood-Bell clinic are not certified in any way. Reading teachers who use this method in the clinic or in special ed classrooms (with or without training) must be distinguished from the Lindamood-Bell personnel. The ADD program, in and of itself, does not necessarily guarantee success. Even when a reading teacher has been trained in the method, she may lack the skill to teach effectively. The Lindamood program requires an in-depth knowledge of English phonemes and how they are physically produced. It also requires considerable sensitivity on the part of the teacher, because it relies extensively on a "questioning" technique of instruction. This isn't easy to train. The teacher must tune in to the client's thinking accurately and completely. This requires empathy and imagination. A didactic approach, where the teacher tells the client what to do, won't work with this program.

You can check on the effectiveness of a clinic or a special ed program using the ADD method by asking for evidence of results. In the hands of an expert it should take from about fifty to eighty hours and get gains ranging from one to four years or more depending on the age of the client. *Older clients tend to get higher gains.* Anyone who is using this program, but tells you she has no idea how long it will take, or whether there will be any gains, or how much it will cost, either isn't keeping records (which she should be) or isn't using the program properly.

The ADD program begins with linguistic and phonemic exercises. These involve practice in analyzing how phonemes are produced and the relationships between groups of similar sounds (linguistic categories) until these are made "super conscious." Clients use a mirror to watch mouth movements to enhance awareness of which parts of the mouth move to make which phonemes. Children and adults are taught in similar ways using the same materials and the same exercises. Lessons differ mainly in the speed at which clients proceed through the exercises. Those who "get it" easily go through the program much faster.

Due to the detailed training in speech production and auditory analysis, the program nearly doubles as a speech therapy program and is particularly powerful for those individuals with language delays or speech difficulties.

The program has these special features:

1. *Vocabulary.* The program teaches a new vocabulary to talk about phonemes. Phonemes are introduced in categories or families based on specific articulatory features. Voiced and unvoiced contrasts are taught as "brothers." Groups of similarly produced phonemes are taught as "cousins," such as the "nasals" /m/ /n/ /ng/. Phonemes are introduced with pictures of mouth postures, and the client learns special names for each of them based on articulatory features. "Lip popper" is the name for bilabial plosives /b/ and /p/, and "tip tapper" for dentals /d/ and /t/. Voiced and unvoiced consonant contrasts are called "noisy" and "quiet." The sound /d/ is a "noisy tip tapper." The sound /d/ is the "noisy brother" of /t/.

2. *Phoneme analysis and tracking.* There is extensive work in phoneme analysis using colored blocks to represent and manipulate sequences of phonemes in words and nonsense words. These are mainly carried out in tracking exercises as illustrated in chapter 9. Nonsense words form a major part of the training, based on the rationale that this is the most effective way to teach decoding skills. Using nonsense words avoids activating old habits or incorrect strategies that are prompted by the sight of real words.

The teacher begins a tracking exercise by asking the client to select a colored block for a sound, /i/, for instance. Then she says: "If that says 'i,' show me 'ip.'" The client chooses a different color (any color) for the sound /p/. Next she asks: "If that is 'ip,' can you show me 'pip'?" The student must now match the color of the last block in the sequence so far:

```
/i/              ■
/i/   /p/        ■  □
/p/   /i/   /p/  □  ■  □
```

The chain can proceed to a high level of complexity (CCVCC and CCCVCCC) depending on the client's skill.

3. *Basic Code.* Letters are introduced as a "Basic Code," much like the one described in chapter 9. Each of the forty-four sounds is assigned to one letter or digraph (w/wh—witch/which—are taught as 'two sounds'). Some spelling alternatives are taught at the same time. These are the spellings oi   oy, ou   ow, au   aw, and er   ur   ir. Single letters and digraphs are introduced together based on linguistic categories. For example, the sounds /j/ and /ch/ are voiced and unvoiced contrasts of the same articulatory pattern, so that the *letters* j and ch are introduced as a pair. The letters are first taught with pictures of mouth postures, then with a paper movable alphabet, and later, letter tiles are substituted. Phonemes are printed on the cards or tiles, so that some have single letters [c] some have digraphs [ch]. As the lessons progress, the student uses several types of manipulatives: pictures of mouth postures on cards, colored blocks, paper letters for initial training and "assembly" (see below), and letter tiles.

4. *Questioning technique.* The therapist guides the client to a correct solution by a sequence of questions *if at all possible.* Only when the client cannot answer is more information provided. The client is occasionally challenged even when his answer is correct, so that he can articulate his reasoning. The purpose is to help clients become independent and able to self-correct their errors with complete confidence.

An example of the teacher/client dialogue is extracted from the Manual and illustrated here. Note that to be able to engage in this dialogue, the client must first memorize the verbal "labels" for each sound:

T. If that says /ood/ show me /eed/. Which sound changed?

S. The round sound is gone. There's no round sound.

T. What kind of sound is the round sound, a consonant or vowel?

S. A vowel.

T. If it's gone, can our syllable be left without any vowel?

S. No

T. Why not?

S. Because it has to have one.

T. That's right. A syllable has to have a vowel. Let's check our mouth pictures. When I said /ood/, it was a round sound and a tip tapper. If the round sound is gone, that leaves us just a —?

S. Tip tapper.

T. I'll say the new pattern again. You see if that tip tapper is all alone, or if something else came where the round sound used to be: /eed/

S. A smile sound.

T. Good. When I change /ood/ to /eed/, the round sound goes away and a smile sound takes its place.————— If that says /eed/, show me /eep/.

S. The tip tapper goes away, and a lip popper takes its place.

[This sequence continues for two more pages.]

5. *Assembly.* There are several exercises which are repeated across sessions. Consonants are organized into categories using mouth pictures or paper letters, including: eight voiced/unvoiced consonant pairs ("brothers"), such as: /b/-/p/, /j/-/ch/, "nose sounds:" /m/ /n/ /ng/, "windy sounds:" /h/ /w/ /wh/, etc. Vowel letters are assembled on a printed vowel chart, which contains slots set out in a "vowel circle" and other slots for additional vowels. This provides training in sequencing vowels according to similar mouth postures and in bringing attention to the shifting positions of the tongue, lips, and jaw.

Most of the higher-level work is carried out with the movable alphabet tiles. This work includes most (not all) consonant clusters, basic prefixes and suffixes, and practice at the multisyllable level using words up to five syllables long. At the multisyllable level, the client learns to segment by syllable and represent each syllable with a large, colored felt square. Next, the client must analyze the phoneme sequences in each syllable and represent this in letter tiles or cards on top of each felt square. The syllable level is not covered in depth in the published program, but is during teacher training. Steven Truch writes in a recent research report that he has expanded this level at his clinic.

A multisyllable sequence set up in manipulatives would look like this for the word **softer:**

Some spelling rules are taught, such as the e-control principle, the rule that governs the pronunciation of the letter <u>c</u> (<u>c</u> sounds /s/ when it precedes the letters <u>e</u>, <u>i</u>, <u>y</u>), and the rule for dropping the final <u>e</u> in e-controlled spellings when adding a suffix, like <u>ing</u> and <u>es</u>. Spelling alternatives (the advanced code level) are dealt with minimally. Altogether about sixteen spelling alternatives are taught for both consonants and vowels.

The entire set of materials is contained in a small box, and the client works with these same materials throughout all sessions. The teacher's manual contains many examples of nonsense word chains for "tracking" and word lists for spelling real words and nonsense words. Clients do some spelling dictation.

6. *Visualizing-verbalizing.* The program has expanded to add another training module for reading comprehension. This was designed by Nanci Bell and is used for clients who have difficulty comprehending what they read. The client is trained to be able to visualize objects, landscapes, persons, etc. in order to establish a mental picture while he reads. The program appears successful from early reports, though there is no published research on this program.

Most Lindamood-Bell™ clinics have moved nearly exclusively to an "intensive" time schedule. Clients are taught for two to four hours each day, five days a week, for four to eight weeks. Reading "technicians" rotate between clients every hour to avoid boredom and fatigue for both teacher and client. Intensives are particularly useful for families who have to travel great distances to reach a clinic. Information about Lindamood-Bell clinics and other clinics using this method recommended by Lindamood-Bell are provided in the Appendix to this chapter.

Read America

Read America is a reading clinic and research center. It also publishes curriculum materials. Read America was founded by Geoffrey and Carmen McGuinness in Orlando, Florida. Read America developed a clinical reading program to take advantage of all the research reported in this book. The program is called "Phono-Graphix." The Phono-Graphix structure and curriculum is the brainchild of Carmen McGuinness. Research on Phono-Graphix was presented in chapter 8.

The central philosophy and guiding principles of Phono-Graphix stemmed from the research described in chapters 6 and 7, including our own research at the University of South Florida. Other contributing factors to this program are C. McGuinness' extensive experience teaching children and running a school and our joint efforts running a reading clinic where ideas could be tried out in an applied setting.

Phono-Graphix incorporates these principles:

1. A true linguistic program in which the phoneme is the basic unit for teaching the writing system.
2. Comprehensive training in phoneme awareness, phoneme segmenting, and blending.
3. An analysis of the English alphabet code (spelling alternatives/ code overlaps). This is the organizing principle for an extensive curriculum.
4. Knowledge of the cognitive and intellectual development of the child and the applied testing of this knowledge. Management of the complexity of the code through carefully sequenced lessons, one type of logic at a time.
5. Automaticity. Eliminate letter names, all exercises or language that conflict with the logic of the code, or that add an unnecessary memory load. Keep strictly to the motto: "Teach nothing that must be discarded later on." Create a "reflex" response to the print code by instilling the appropriate strategy through repetition.
6. Involve the parent or adult mentor directly in homework so she has a positive role and can maintain gains between sessions and after sessions have ended.

Phono-Graphix was developed to teach every important skill necessary to read, write, and spell, and to teach them as rapidly as possible. Local clients participate in a one-on-one twelve-hour program. The maximum time to date is twenty-four hours (one adult client). The sessions are held weekly and a family member supports the client in one to two hours of homework each week using specially designed curriculum materials. If the client is coming from a distance, he or she is taught in "intensives," and these are set up according to the needs of the clients and their families. Two-hour sessions, plus one hour of homework per day, is optimum. This program takes six days.

From second grade on, gains on standardized reading tests have been found to be equivalent whether or not the client is taught over twelve weeks or in intensives over six days. First graders get slightly lower gains in intensives than in weekly sessions. Gains are similar to those for the Lindamood program, ranging from one to four years depending on the age of the client. However, they occur *seven times faster,* based on test score gains per clinical hour (standard score units).

Phono-Graphix differs from other remedial programs in a number of ways. Each of these new approaches contributes to the incredible speed of remediation.

The program and curriculum materials are set up in three levels. These levels would roughly approximate what a child would learn if he was taught to read properly in the first place. However, not every level is necessarily taught to the poor reader. On the basis of diagnostic testing, each client begins at a level, or at a place within a level, most suited to his ability and knowledge. The diagnostic tests were presented in the previous chapter.

These are the three main levels:

*Level 1. Basic code: 1-to-1 mapping only: one sound–one letter (*no digraphs). Skills training covers phoneme analysis, segmenting, blending, reading, and spelling. These skills are mastered in simple three-sound words and words containing consonant clusters.

Level 2. Advanced code level: The first part of this level includes consonant digraphs. Next come vowel digraphs followed by phonemes with multiple spellings: 1-to-many mapping. Code overlap (many-to-1 mapping) is integrated with teaching spelling alternatives. The advanced code level is the most extensive in the program and continues to teach segmenting, blending, reading coded text, analysis of text through "sound targetting" worksheets and stories, and in spelling and writing.

Level 3. Multisyllable level: Multisyllable words through five syllables are taught. Clients are trained to build words by syllable and to decode by syllable, reducing long words to manageable "chunks." They do this by analyzing phoneme sequences within syllables and reassembling syllable "chunks" into a word. The final step at this level introduces common Latin suffixes taught as multiphoneme "phonograms:" cian, tion, cious, etc.

Curriculum

A curriculum of hands-on materials was designed for each of the levels. There are picture cue cards with "sound-picture" cards to construct the word in the picture. There are phoneme analysis cards for phoneme awareness training and over 1,000 word cards. All materials are organized *by phoneme* except for code overlap exercises and Latin suffixes. There are also worksheets, games, specially written stories with controlled vocabularies, as well as stories in coded text to help train the eye to notice which letters work together to stand for one phoneme. A story series in coded text was written for the following age groups: Kindergarten—Reading Fundamentals. First and second grade—"Snuffy Puppy" series. Second to fourth grade—"The Clubhouse" series. Third to ninth grade—"Things in Nature" series. Adult—"Bob's Life."

Teaches the Entire Code

The curriculum is organized in sequence according to the child's age or skill *and* according to the mapping logics involved. The client learns all possible spelling alternatives and all possible code overlaps in over 1,000 words, from the single-syllable level through the multisyllable level. Consistent spelling patterns are taught as "tendencies" or "expectancies," never "rules": (the sound /ae/ tends to be spelled ay at the ends of words and sometimes ey). These "tendencies" are taught by *exposure,* by sequencing the materials so that the client discovers these patterns during controlled exercises.

The Adult Mentor

The homework materials consist of a packet of over 250 worksheets, stories, and games designed to reinforce what was taught at the clinical sessions. Each client's packet contains materials from the place where the client begins in the program through the remainder of the curriculum. The materials are constructed to promote the correct strategy. This packet becomes the property of the adult mentor or client. One hundred percent of parents replying to an anonymous survey at follow-up reported they were still using the home materials.

Speed of Remediation

Through appropriate diagnostic testing, it is possible to begin clients in the curriculum sequence most appropriate for their level of skill. No time is wasted teaching what the client already knows or can do. For example, if a client has very poor phoneme awareness, he will begin at Level 1, "auditory processing" training. If a client has good phoneme awareness, he skips this level altogether. However, segmenting and blending are practiced at all levels, as can be seen in the examples below.

In remedial settings, where most clients are older, progress can be speeded up by interleaving the levels of logic. Vowels with digraphs can be introduced together with lessons on spelling alternatives, and followed immediately by sessions on code overlaps where necessary.

The explanations given to the client are highly important. An example of a lesson is given below. There are five goals to this lesson:

1. To make the client understand the "sound picture" nature of written language, so that he can begin to organize the written code.

2. To teach the client to recognize the specific sound pictures of the written language.

3. To make it clear that sometimes one letter, and sometimes two or more letters, can represent a single "sound." The client learns that digraphs and phonograms are a *unit* and not separate letters that work together because of a "rule."

4. To show that there is more than one way to represent most sounds.

5. To train the client to segment sounds in words at the same time as he "maps" the word (saying each sound as he writes). This establishes a clear understanding that both reading and spelling proceed from left to right, and that the code is reversible: Reading involves decoding from symbol to sound, and writing involves encoding from sound to symbol.

As a first step, the client needs to understand the concept of a "sound picture," which underpins the logic of everything that follows. This is shown in the following lesson:

One of the things that all good readers need to understand is that written words are like a code. Each sound that we say is shown through a code symbol. So, let's take an example of the word "cat." If we want to show this word, we can do it like this. [Teacher draws a cat on a white board.] This is a picture of a cat. Or, we can do it in code. The code we use is a sound code. We have to find out which sounds are in the word "cat." What is the first sound in "cat"? [The client says /k/.] This is the picture of the sound /k/. [The teacher writes c̲ on the board.] [The lesson proceeds through each sound until c̲ a̲ t̲ is spelled out.]

So written words are really nothing more than just pictures of sounds. Right now you know most of the sound pictures really well, but you don't know them all. We're going to work on the hard ones. The hard ones are mostly long ones too, like this. [Teacher writes o̲a̲ on a white board.] Lots of people think that these are two sound pictures [Teacher says /o/ and points to o̲, and says /a/ and points to a̲], but they aren't. They are just a code for the sound /oe/.

[Teacher draws a picture of a balloon on a string.] It's just like, this can be a balloon, but if you add this [draws petals on it], it can be a flower. This [writes o̲] is a picture of /o/, and this [adds an a̲ to make o̲ a̲] is a picture of /oe/.

As part of the lesson, clients are trained to say *each* sound separately as they write the "picture" for that sound, a process called "mapping." Clients must isolate each phoneme in sequence: /b/ /l/ /e/ /n/ /d/ (**not** /bl/ /e/ /n/ /d/ or /b/ /l/ /e/ /nd/). Clients should not "map" silently because they may not be thinking of sounds or may be thinking of letter names. They also cannot write in cursive. Each "sound picture" must have a beginning and an end and not be run together.

The lesson proceeds by teaching the client the various spelling alternatives for the sound /oe/. The client sees word cards or a list of words in coded text, in which the digraphs are bolded, and a worksheet that looks like Figure 12–1.

When the client reads the first o̲-e̲ spelling in the word list, the teacher says: "This sound picture is really odd. It's separated. See here, this should look like this:"

The teacher writes this on a white board: **n   o e   t**

FIGURE 12–1

n o t e	th r ow	c r ow	g r ow
sh ow	b o l d	t o t e	g r oa n
t o n e	kn ow	h o p e	b oa t
h o s t	h o l d	fl oa t	n o
g oa t	c o n e	l oa f	c oa t
m o s t	s o	t oa s t	m o l d
r oa s t	g l ow	h o m e	

oe	oa
ow	o

FIGURE 12-2

oa	oe
boat	note
toast	cone
goat	tone
roast	tote
float	hope
groan	home
coat	
loaf	

ow	o
show	hold
glow	bold
grow	most
know	host
throw	so
crow	no
	mold

"Instead, somebody decided that this part of it [indicates the e̲] should be at the end of the word, even though the sound happens here." [points to the o̲].

The client writes the word (correctly) using "mapping," while the teacher says each sound *for him* to model so that there is no additional sound when he writes the e̲. The client should not be told that the e̲ is "silent." Instead, it works with the o̲ to represent the sound /oe/. When the client is finished, the worksheet looks something like Figure 12-2.

When the client has progressed with learning a few vowel digraphs and has practiced sorting words with the same vowel sound into their correct spelling categories, he is introduced to "code overlaps." The teacher points out that some of these spelling patterns ("sound pictures") have been seen before, and that they stood for *different* sounds. Figure 12-3 is an example of a code overlap exercise:

FIGURE 12–3

sh ow	c l **ow** n
c **ow**	c r **ow**
h **ow**	b r **ow** n
g r **ow**	**kn** ow
th r ow	g l **ow**
t **ow**	t **ow** n
n **ow**	d **ow** n
f l **ow**	
f r **ow** n	

the sound 'oe'	the sound 'ow'
know	brown
show	town
grow	clown
glow	frown
throw	down
flow	now
tow	cow
crow	how

Special Techniques for Handling Errors

The client is kept actively engaged at all times, mentally and physically, and the teacher keeps the questions and explanations to the minimum. However, much of the success of the program is due to how the clients' errors are handled, so they understand clearly and quickly what they did wrong and how to correct it. When the client makes an error, he is informed immediately of what he did.

In Figure 12–4, the child is being asked to do a tracking exercise as described in chapter 9. She was told to change the word 'cot' into the word 'pot.' She has chosen the wrong letter, the letter m.

The teacher says, "That says 'mot.' We want 'pot.'" The teacher says

FIGURE 12–4

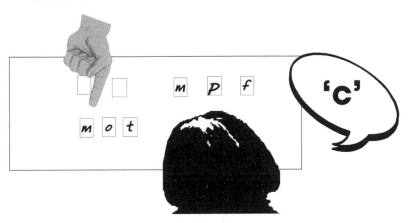

the whole word without segmenting the sounds and points to each "sound picture" in turn as she does so. If, after a few tries, the client does not make the correct change, then the teacher segments each sound.

"We need to make 'cot' say 'pot:' /p/—/o/—/t/." The teacher points to each "sound picture" as she says this. Clients will be successful at this step.

Here is another example:

The client reads a word, segmenting each sound accurately. When asked to blend the sounds together to make the word, she blends them incorrectly:

"/m/ /a/ /p/——— cap."

The teacher says, "You said all the right sounds, but when you blended them you read 'cap.'" [The teacher points to each sound in turn as she says the word.] "If this was 'cap,' then this [points to m] would be the sound /k/. But it isn't. It's /m/. Try again please."

The combination of the carefully sequenced logical structure, unambiguous language, and the extensive controlled exercises produces progress that is so rapid, it is almost immediately noticeable to the client. This, along with the variety and novelty of the materials, maintains the client's interest. Through clear and helpful explanations, the client learns exactly what he did, and why, and what to do next. In a short space of time, he is able to self-correct his own errors and become an independent reader and speller.

Information about the clinics and where they are located is provided below.

APPENDIX: READING CLINICS

Read America

Directors: Geoffrey McGuinness
             Carmen McGuinness
370 Whooping Loop, Suite 1142
Altamonte Springs, FL 32701
Tel   407-332-9144
      1-800-READ-TO-U
Call for list of approved Phono-Graphix trainers.

Lindamood-Bell

Headquarters: 416 Higuera St., San Luis Obispo, CA 93401
Tel   805-541-3836
      1-800-233-1819
Lindamood-Bell clinics are located in these cities:

California	*National*
Berkeley	Boston
Newport Beach	Dallas
Palo Alto	Miami
Sacramento	New York
San Diego	Washington, DC
San Luis Obispo	
Santa Barbara	

Other clinics using the Lindamood-Bell programs:

The Langsford Center	*The Reading Foundation*
Director: Stephen McCrocklin	Director: Steven Truch
The Belknap Building	200 Rivercrest Dr. SE #250
1810 Sils Ave.	Calgary, Alberta TC2 2X5
Louisville, KY 40205	Tel 405-279-8639
Tel 502-473-7000	

Chapter 13

WHAT'S A PARENT TO DO?

Parents have many questions that range across a broad spectrum of issues, from how to teach subskills to preschoolers to how to find remedial help for a child in trouble. Family members and friends of adults with reading problems also have questions. In this chapter, I will do my best to answer the many questions people have asked me over the years.

Parents all want to know when a child should begin reading and when to intervene if they suspect there is a problem. The simple answer is that it is never too late to teach anyone to read, and that there is no special time to begin teaching a child to read. Children in Scandinavian countries learn to read two years later than children in most other European countries. This works fine because parents are under strict orders to do nothing in the home prior to the time the child begins school, and they willingly comply. It also works because most schools are doing their job. Finland, Sweden, and Norway have the highest literacy rates in the world.

But Scandinavian children, like children in Germany, Spain, and Italy, learn a much more straightforward alphabetic writing system. Because our alphabet is so complex and causes so many problems when it is taught incorrectly (which is most of the time), parents in English-speaking countries are justifiably concerned about whether their child will learn to read.

So the issue is really more subtle than when to begin to teach reading or when to begin to worry. The issue is rather that because inappropriate teaching methods are the norm, the child can easily develop incorrect decoding strategies. The more these strategies are practiced, the worse things become. A parent can intervene either preventively before this happens or after the fact. Parents need to be aware that *if* a child is in trouble, they must seek help immediately. The longer the child practices reading and spelling using the wrong strategy, the further he will fall behind his classmates. All the evidence shows conclusively that poor readers *do not catch up* simply because they get older. Don't believe any teacher who tells you this.

THE PRESCHOOLER

Let's begin at the beginning, with the preschooler. What can parents do to help rather than hinder their child's progress in learning to read?

The answer can be divided into three categories: what is helpful, what is harmless, and what is harmful.

Helpful Activities

Talk to Your Child. Talk even if you're just expressing your thoughts out loud about what you're doing or thinking. An amazing study was carried out by Betty Hart and Todd Risley. They studied forty-two families from three social groups and recorded how mothers spoke to their infant children during the first two and one-half years of life. They recorded everything that was said to each child for one hour per month. The average number of words addressed to the child ranged from 1,500 to 2,500 per hour in homes classified as "professional," 1,000 to 1,500 in the middle-class homes, and 500 to 800 in homes of welfare mothers. By the age of three, it was estimated that children in professional families had heard nearly 35 million words; middle-class children, just over 20 million words; and children of welfare mothers, around 10 million words. These differences were found even though welfare mothers spent more time overall in the same room with the child.

The speech addressed to the child also varied in terms of the richness of vocabulary and style of speaking. Mothers in the "professional" group used a more complex sentence structure, a richer vocabulary, and a highly affirmative feedback style: "that's right," "that's good," along with a more positive tone of voice. Welfare mothers by contrast, often used a negative tone, and lots of explicit disapproval: "stop that," "don't spill it," "don't do it that way." Welfare mothers, however, did not differ in any other measures such as affection, concern for their child, the cleanliness of the environment, and appropriate reactions to a child in need. Nor was race a factor in any of the data.

The various measures of the mother's speech, taken together, were highly correlated to the child's linguistic skills later on, to their vocabulary development, to vocabulary use, and to standardized measures of IQ, vocabulary, and a test of language use. These relationships were much more powerful when based solely on parenting speech style than when correlated to socioeconomic status. The correlations between the mother's speech output and style to the child's later verbal and intellectual ability were high at age three and also at age nine (correlations ranged from .74 to .82).

We saw earlier that vocabulary and IQ are not strong predictors of reading success, because the major problem of the poor reader is weak or absent phonemic awareness and a lack of knowledge of the English alphabet code. However, when children do learn to read spontaneously, or are in situations where phoneme awareness *is* taught and the appropriate method *is* used, then vocabulary becomes much more important. Reading accuracy and fluency are enhanced if the word you are decoding already exists in memory. This is obvious in the difficulty people have in decoding strange words like those in "Bad Fruit" in chapter 2. Also, as discussed in chapter 10, decoding accuracy and fluency are the major predictors of reading comprehension.

Read to Your Child. Reading to your child has lots of spin-offs for teaching prereading and early reading skills. It familiarizes children with the format of books. There are pages that turn in a fixed order. It familiarizes children with the print code, if the parent points this out. For example, the parent can trace along the text with a finger as she reads, training the child that our print code goes in rows from left to right and from top to bottom down the page. She can begin to train early awareness of how our alphabetic writing system works, by showing the child how to decode a word:

"Oh, let's see. Let's sound this word out." The mother points to each letter or letter pair (digraph) and says each sound separately: /f/ /r/ /o/ /g/ and then blends it into the word 'frog,' moving a finger swiftly under the letters in the word as she blends the sounds together. Be sure the child sits beside you and can see what you're doing. The child learns that *letters* are ordered from left to right in a word, that letters stand for *sounds,* that words are made up of these sounds, that sounds in words can be broken apart and put together.

In addition, the child learns all the other important aspects of language and literature, such as new vocabulary, that stories have a beginning, middle, and end, that stories can be "made up," and so forth. Parents can enhance comprehension and awareness by asking questions like: "Why did the baby dinosaur have to wear a coat?"

Prewriting Skills. Get materials from the bookstore or supermarket so that the child can begin to practice tracing and connecting dots, in order to develop manual control over a pencil, pen, or crayon. Let the child write with "imaginary" writing: "Why don't you write a letter to Grandma, and draw her a picture?"

Harmless Activities

The research evidence shows clearly that rhyming activities do not impact on learning to read as scientists once thought. The rhyme component of a word contains more than one sound. It consists of the final vowel sound plus any consonants that follow it. Multisound units, such as the rhyme, are not the basis for our alphabet code, so teaching rhymes specifically is a waste of time. Pointing them out in structured lessons, where rhyming patterns and "word families" are taught as a basic decoding strategy, is actually detrimental: "the letters ay-tee sound /at/ in 'the cat sat on the mat.'" Instead, the child should learn that the *sound* /a/ is spelled a anywhere in a word, and the *sound* /t/ is spelled t anywhere in a word.

This doesn't mean that children shouldn't learn nursery rhymes, poems, or songs, and use word play. It's something young children enjoy very much. Remember the finding that pig latin correlates with reading skill? If you want to teach a word-play game that actually might be beneficial, this is a better choice, because it involves picking off a single phoneme from the front of a syllable, putting it at the end, and adding /ay/: oo-day oo-yay ikelay eadray-ingay?

Harmful Activities

One of the most harmful things you can do is to force children to do "reading activities" they don't want to do. Children are highly active learners, and they decide what they want to learn at any moment in time. And so they should, unless their particular activity is harmful to someone or something. (My son, age two, used to tip over furniture from various angles, to see "if it would break," as he explained it to me, an experiment on the force of gravity on falling objects. After a while, I could intercept him in this activity by listening for grunting noises.)

You should know the other harmful activities by now. The first is teaching letter names, forcing your child to memorize and recite the alphabet, having him read ABC books and memorize the names of capital and lower-case letters. You can teach the alphabet a much better way, should the child show any interest. Begin with only lower-case letters and *say the sound the letter stands for as you write it or point to it,* not its letter name: /d/ /o/ /g/. If your child's preschool teacher is teaching letter names, you'll just have to live with it, or tell her to stop.

Teaching letter names is more benign than teaching whole words by sight, which sets up completely the wrong logic. If your child recognizes a word, points, and says: "That says 'dog,'" find out how she did it.

Don't shriek, "Oh! She's reading!!"

Ask her to show you what cues she was using. If she can't do this, then you show her. Say something like, "That's right. How did you know that? Can you tell me what you *see* that makes you know it says 'dog?'"

If she can't do this, other than to say, "It starts with a dee," or "I just know it does," then prove to her it does.

"Let's prove that it says 'dog,' shall we? The first letter is for the sound /d/, the next letter for the sound /o/ (say /ah/ not /oh/), and the last letter for the sound /g/. Let's put it together: /d/ /o/ /g/ 'dog.' Aren't you a clever girl to figure this out!"

As a general principle for preschool children, they are better off learning *nothing* about reading than learning something that is detrimental to the reading process. If they don't want to have anything to do with activities related to learning to read, then so be it. Doing nothing is not going to hurt them.

THE KINDERGARTNER

What should my child be learning in kindergarten?

Oh dear! Here is where the problems begin. Your child should be doing everything described in the first sections of chapters 8 and 9. But odds are that your child will be doing none of these things, and instead, she will be learning letter names and sight words.

The first thing you have to do is find out from the teacher what she intends to teach the children. Then you have a choice: You can ask the teacher to leave your child out of the lessons, which is not easy for her to do. You can take your child to another school, but chances are, nothing will be different there. A Montessori school is the safest place to go. You can decide to home-school, which isn't always a good idea, because your child will be socially isolated. You can teach your child at home *and* send her to school, and hope that you have more influence over your child's thinking than the teacher does, because what you will be doing is directly opposite to what she is doing. The final option is to take your child to a good reading clinic, but there are few who take children this young.

I can't help you make this decision, but I can give you some idea of what to teach at home.

If you find out that the teacher is actively teaching the wrong things, then you have to create a pact with your child *if and only if* your child finds this a problem. If your child says something like: "Mrs. Bowers doesn't do it this way," you reply: "Never mind what Mrs. Bowers is doing, we are going to learn to read the proper way."

If this issue doesn't come up, then just ignore it. More subtly, you can also ignore your child's developing skill in reciting the alphabet and pointing to letters and saying their names. Don't give any praise or re-inforcement for these behaviors. Give her the *sound* the letters stand for instead: "Yes, that letter says /b/." If your child is learning "sight words," then go through the routine I showed you earlier, *especially* with words that are phonetically regular. If they are not, and they are truly "sight words" (see chapter 10), like the words: 'the' (thuh), 'one' (wun), 'of' (uv), then say nothing.

If you are serious about teaching your child at home, you will need to work with the exercises in chapter 9 and/or get one of the programs or sets of materials described in the Appendix to that chapter. "Reading Reflex" is the only complete parent program that teaches all elements of reading correctly. Also, purchase a good audiotape of English phonemes.

The materials should train the child in left-to-right sequencing, symbolizing (that symbols can stand for something else), and how to segment sounds and blend sounds into words. Any type of more complex auditory analysis is too difficult at this age. Begin by teaching around eight to ten sounds, one at a time. Teach one sound and show the child the letter that stands for that sound. When you have taught a few sounds, you can begin combining them into little words, like the ones listed at the end of chapter 9. You can also create little phrases and stories from the word lists in chapter 9.

Go slowly and don't force the issue, because kindergartners are extremely variable in their aptitude for these tasks. Some children will just take off and start reading, others will struggle and want to quit. Be patient.

THE FIRST GRADER

When should I know if my child is learning to read or not?

A six-year-old should be able to read simple stories by the second semester of first grade. Around the middle of first grade, he should be able to read most simple words, especially three-sound words like those listed at the end of chapter 9. He should be able to write his letters correctly, even though the handwriting leaves something to be desired. He should be able to spell his name and also common, phonetically regular three-sound words.

If none of this is happening, then start to become concerned. Ask your child to read simple text to you. Listen to what he is doing, and reread chapter 2 to see if he is using a bad strategy. Be suspicious if he is spelling like Donny in chapter 1. If your child can't read a word by the middle of first grade, you need to take action. Get him to a good reading clinic, or bite the bullet and try to teach him at home. The longer the reading problem continues, the further behind your child will become. There are simple tests provided at the end of chapter 11 to check on his strategy, phoneme awareness, and decoding skills, and later in this chapter, I will show you how to find a good reading clinic.

AFTER FIRST GRADE

Is my child LD?

Well, the problem with this question is that you're never going to know until the child is about one to two years below grade level, at which point he gets tested, diagnosed LD, and put in a special classroom, or visited in the main classroom by the special ed teacher. And of course, as you are already aware, *there is no such thing as LD anyway* (see chapter 6). If you wait for a diagnosis, the earliest most children can become "LD" is around age eight, because this is the first time that a child of average intelligence can be far enough below age norms in reading. This means that he will have lost at least two years of school, and will go on losing ground in most special ed classrooms.

The dilemma for many parents is in the gray area between the end of first grade, when parents recognize there is a problem, and waiting for the child to qualify for special services. Start by giving the screening test battery at the end of chapter 11. If your child has problems on any of these tests, my advice would be to get him tested at a good reading clinic or by a school psychologist in private practice. Chances are you will not be able to get testing at the school unless the child is "severe" and acknowledged by all to be "severe." But you can try.

School psychologists in private practice are trained to give tests and write reports summarizing the test results. By and large, they are not trained as diagnosticians. Most school psychologists do not remediate the poor reader. If they did, they would be much more likely to use tests that had greater diagnostic value. They can tell you *that* your child has a reading problem, but not *what* to do about it.

School psychologists in private practice also tend to be expensive, and this can be a function of testing "overkill." It is often difficult to get a school psychologist to give only a reading test, which is what you need initially. You can make a few phone calls and see if anyone is willing to do this. Ask for two specific tests: the Woodcock Reading Mastery subtests "Word Identification" and "Word Attack." These are the best tests to show whether your child is reading below grade level. Don't confuse these tests with the Woodcock-Johnson Psycho-Educational Battery, which has less valid reading subtests. This is a time-consuming (expensive) test battery and isn't what you want. If the school psychologist also administers one of the two phoneme awareness tests, the LAC test or Rosner and Simon's AAT, then ask for this also.

In spite of these shortcomings, a good school psychologist can screen for other problems, such as cognitive deficiencies like poor memory, weak vocabulary, auditory and visual perceptual difficulties, problems with fine-motor coordination, speech dysfunction, and so forth. If you suspect any of these problems, then it will be a good idea to have a complete test battery. A school psychologist is one of the few professionals who is qualified and licensed to give an intelligence test.

Another option is to phone a local reading clinic. Call a few reading clinics in the Yellow Pages to find someone who will give a reading test. Some reading clinics, especially those based on the small-group "tutorial model," don't do any testing at all. Tell them that you want your child tested for grade-level placement on "word recognition" and "word attack" *only,* using either the Woodcock Reading Mastery Test or the Wide-Range Achievement Test. Be sure to ask how much it will cost before you make an appointment. Testing should take about twenty to thirty minutes maximum.

If your child is not at grade level on one or the other of these tests, then you will need to schedule more testing and proceed through the inquiry process described on pages 339–340, or attempt home intervention. If your child is only marginally behind, you might want to teach him yourself. Follow the methods set out in chapters 9 and 10. The parent program "Reading Reflex" is also good for children who are below grade level. Be sure to obtain a good audiotape of English phonemes. (Do not purchase "Hooked on Phonics." Over half the parents who come into the Read America clinic have purchased this program. It doesn't work.)

If your child is reading a year or more below grade level or has serious problems in any one of these areas: phoneme awareness, segmenting, blending, code knowledge, then you may need to get outside help. It will be much faster, more effective, and will cause far less friction between you and your child.

If, after testing, you find out that your child scores normally or above grade level in reading, but is still having problems in school, then you will need to address other issues. Is there a family problem the child is not coping with? Are there other problems that would impact on school work, like difficulty with handwriting or a personality conflict with a particular teacher? Schedule a conference with the classroom teacher and ask her to pinpoint specifically the weaknesses your child has. Don't accept vague statements like: "He just isn't paying attention. I think he's 'ADD' ['dyslexic,' 'developmentally delayed,' 'emotionally disturbed']" *or* "He isn't motivated to learn," *or* "He never finishes his work." There could be twenty reasons why he isn't paying attention, isn't motivated, or doesn't finish his work. One reason could be boredom. You want specific information:

> His handwriting is illegible and it takes him forever to write anything. *[Get him training in fine-motor control from a tutor who specializes in penmanship: or teach him yourself. Purchase wide-lined paper at the supermarket or stationer.]*
> He reads just fine, but he can't spell. *[Get him tested at a read-*

*ing clinic and get remedial help. If he can't spell, he doesn't un-
derstand the code.]*

I sometimes wonder if she can hear properly, because when I
ask the children to do something, she behaves as if she hasn't
heard a word. *[Get her a hearing test.]*

He finishes his work correctly in about five minutes and just
stares out the window, and recently he's stopped doing work altogether. *[Ask for testing for gifted placement, or get him moved
up a grade, or change schools.]*

Earlier I reviewed the evidence to show that speech difficulties impact on reading. Speech problems need to be remediated, especially if
they persist to the age of six. Take your child to a speech therapist. If
you can't see any significant progress, change therapists.

Some children have visual problems. If your child gets tired while
reading and keeps rubbing his eyes, then he may need glasses. If he
reads in funny postures, looking sideways at the print, and complains
that he "can't see," he may need to be tested by an optometrist who
specializes in diagnosing and treating problems with binocular fusion
and tracking. These children may be able to read isolated words on a
reading test, but not be able to do sustained reading activities because
the print is constantly going in and out of focus.

IF YOUR CHILD HAS BEEN DIAGNOSED LD

The immediate and urgent question you must ask is whether or not
your child has made any progress. If your child has been diagnosed
"LD" and is receiving special services, then she should show noticeable
improvement within six months. She should be back in the classroom,
reading at grade level, in one year *at the latest*. If this isn't happening,
get help fast somewhere else. Although some special ed programs are
excellent, most are not, and far too many special ed classrooms are
merely baby-sitting operations for children with multiple handicap-
ping conditions.

If your child has been diagnosed LD, and you are going to a "staffing
conference," or want to schedule one, then it is your right, under federal guidelines, to know the answers to the following questions:

1. How far is my child reading below grade level?
2. Which diagnostic tests did you give?

3. What skills do these diagnostic tests measure?
4. How do these skills impact on learning to read and spell?
5. What methods are you using to remediate my child's reading problem?
6. Which diagnostic tests did you rely on to set up an individual education plan (IEP) for my child?
7. What is the scientific evidence that your reading method works? Could you provide me with published reports on this research?
8. How long will it take you to teach my child to read?

If you're unhappy with any or all of the answers to these questions, take your child to an outside reading clinic immediately, or read the earlier chapters carefully and try to teach your child yourself. If the school psychologist and the special ed teacher do not know why they give certain diagnostic tests, or how these tests would predict progress in a specific reading method, they don't know what they are doing and cannot teach your child to read. If they cannot cite research evidence in support of the program they are using, they don't know why they are using it.

Before moving on to the issue of how to find a good reading clinic, I want to say a few words about the adult with reading problems.

THE ADULT POOR READER

The adult poor reader can be someone who has made do with an extremely ineffective strategy or someone who gave up long ago and can't read a word. Most adult poor readers will not be reading this book. The motivation to get help has to come from the outside, from a family member or friend who insists that help really exists and that the poor reader can be taught to read.

Here, I am not describing someone who somehow missed out on reading instruction or an immigrant who speaks another language. These people will probably do well in a community-based adult reading program. I am talking about people who didn't miss out, and who will *not* be fine in an adult reading program. Someone needs to reach out to these people, IF you can find them, because often they develop ingenious means for disguising their disability. Others are in denial that they have a reading problem, as we saw earlier. In the Adult Literacy Survey reported in chapter 1, 75 percent of the adults classified as "functionally illiterate" told testers that their reading skills were "good!" Adults with reading problems are often reluctant to get help and need to be reassured that help will actually make a difference. Let them know they are not alone. There are forty-two million functionally illiterate adults in America, many of them highly intelligent. Read them the book *The Teacher Who Couldn't Read* by John Corcoran, so they can see they're not unique and that remediation really does work.

If you are a relative or friend of someone with a reading problem, the next section applies to you as well as to parents of children with reading problems.

FINDING A GOOD REMEDIAL CLINIC

Reread chapter 12 so you will have a clear idea of what a good remedial reading program looks like. If programs similar to these are offered in your school as part of special ed instruction, *say a prayer of thanks!* I know firsthand that there are excellent special ed programs and instructors, but they tend to be the exception. If your special ed program does not match up, or if you have a child in special ed who is making no progress, you will have to go outside the school system for help. Don't waste any time.

Sources of Information

The best source is someone else who has had successful reading therapy for himself or for a child. But this information can be hard to come by. Adults are humiliated by their reading problem and won't talk about it. Parents can be embarrassed about their child's reading problem and often reluctant to mention it because they blame themselves. If a parent does recommend someone, you need to ask for specific information about *how* her child was helped. She should be able to tell you the actual gains the child achieved, how long it took, any changes in status (no longer LD), and improvement in grades, behavior, and attitude toward reading. On rare occasions, a parent will recommend someone who actually never helped her child. Instead, she got a diagnosis: "dyslexia," plus the information that it could take years for her child to learn to read and still never be "cured." This may have made her feel better, because parents feel guilty when their child can't read, but it did nothing to help her child. Getting this kind of "diagnosis" gets some parents off the hook.

The classroom teacher or special ed teacher at the school can be helpful in recommending someone, but again you will need to be cautious. Most teachers care enormously about children, and their attitude is one of selfless concern. If they have had experience with a good reading clinic, they will gladly share it with parents. Some teachers are threatened if an outsider can teach a child to read when they have failed, and will be less forthcoming, or even negative, about getting outside help. We have found this to be the case as well with some teachers in special ed, particularly if they are having little success. A successful reading clinic threatens their job and prestige. It also brings the wrath of the parent down on their head if the child has spent a year or more in their classroom.

Evaluating a Reading Clinic

Gather whatever information you can and then begin to interview reading specialists by telephone. They are listed in the Yellow Pages under various headings, such as "reading," "schools," and "tutoring."

Write out the questions listed below onto a notepad with space for answers. Don't expect a receptionist to be able to answer them. Ask to speak to the director or assistant director. Begin by telling the person something about your child, spouse, relative, or friend, his/her age, whether or not he/she has been tested, and your specific concerns about reading, spelling, and writing. Then ask the following questions in this order:

1. Could you tell me a little bit about your program? What method do you use? [If they give you the name of a program: "We use Reading Mastery," and expect you to know what they mean, ask for more information.]
2. Do you see people in individual or small-group sessions?
3. How long does each session last?
4. How many sessions per week do you recommend?
5. How long does the training take overall? [The answer may be in hours or in weeks or months.]
6. What kinds of gains should I expect to see? Will my child be reading at grade level by the end of training?
7. Do you do any diagnostic testing? What kinds of tests do you give?
8. How long does this testing take?
9. What does it cost?

10. What does the training cost?

11. Do you give out names and phone numbers of satisfied customers?

12. How soon could you schedule my child (friend, brother, etc.) if I decide to do this program?

If you are calling about an adult:

13. What is your success rate with adults?

Then say thank you very much and hang up. Here's what you are looking for.

Every good clinic should be able to give you a clear idea of the method they use. Let the person keep talking. If you don't understand, say so. If they can't explain it to you in plain English, they won't be able to teach it. NEVER enroll your child in a clinic where they teach "sight words" or tell you that they tailor the reading program to the child's "learning style." There is only one right way to teach reading effectively.

Avoid programs that use small-group instruction, especially if your child (spouse/relative) has serious problems. Use the answers to questions 3 to 5 to compute how long it is going to take. Sixty hours should be the maximum for children. Multiply this by the answer to number 10 if they give you an hourly rate. This will give you the total cost. Most good remedial programs charge around $45 to $55 per hour. Some programs give a discount for a package of remediation for a fixed time period. Often this makes it well worth paying in advance, especially if you are impressed by the clinic and its staff.

Be suspicious if they have no idea about gains. Clients have told us about a reading "tutor" who charges $5,000 "no matter how long it takes." This is $50 an hour for 100 hours! Be equally suspicious if they give you exact information about gains for your child. Reading therapy can be unpredictable. Gains can only be approximate. A responsible clinic will give you approximate figures for the majority of their clients. They will also tell you that they will be able to predict more accurately after diagnostic testing.

If the answer to question 7 is that they do not do diagnostic testing, this is a strong negative. If they give too many tests, this is another strong negative. You don't need testing "overkill" to diagnose a reading problem. Be aware that some clinics *earn the major part of their income* from testing rather than from remediation. The answer to questions 7 and 8 will give you an idea if the clinic is going overboard on testing.

Testing should take from one to two hours. The cost of testing should be in the range of zero (some clinics give free testing) to around $200. The higher the cost, the more information you will receive about additional skills like vocabulary or reading comprehension, and the more likely you are to get a full written report. With free testing you will get diagnostic test scores and a verbal explanation.

A good reading clinic has no hesitation in giving out phone numbers of satisfied customers. They will also be able to provide you with personal statements that former clients and parents have made about their impressions of the program, and mail you a brochure describing the program.

For adults, it is more difficult to predict the time in remediation. Some adults are motivated and make rapid progress. But for those who have lost the better part of their life without experience with the printed word, bringing them up to an "adult" reading level takes time. Also, some adults are likely to bring emotional baggage to the clinic which can slow down the remedial process. Some are depressed, or believe they are stupid, or take up time relating life experiences. Although adults usually make striking gains in a good program (four years or more is not uncommon), those who begin as nonreaders may still be reading only at the fourth- or fifth-grade level at the end of sessions. What they need next is *practice* and support, plus help with more advanced academic skills like writing letters/memos and reading material with technical language. Reading clinics will supply this help, but it can be equally effective from a family member.

Finally, question 12 on the list gives you information on whether there is space available now for your child, relative, or friend.

If all the answers are reasonable, you will be very lucky, and the next step is to schedule testing and meet the person who will be seeing your child *if possible*. Often the person who does the diagnostic testing is not the person who will be working with your child. Ask to meet this person even if it's just for a minute. If there are multiple reading instructors, such as with the Lindamood-Bell format, this would not be practical.

More likely, the answers to the questions will be variable, some pluses some minuses, and you will have to weigh them carefully. If it is a great program, with great results, you may have to pay for expensive testing. If everything looks good, and testing fees are reasonable, you may have to be satisfied with small-group instruction. If there are too many negatives, you might want to consider traveling to one of the clinics listed in chapter 12. Work out the costs carefully, because a program that takes one to two years to remediate a poor reader can cost more than two cheap airfares, a motel room, and one to four weeks of training. At least you will be sure ahead of time that your child, spouse, or relative will learn to read, and you won't waste any more of your child's valuable time in the classroom.

IS ANYONE IN THE SCHOOLS LISTENING?

Now that we have the answers to teaching all children to read, you might think that classroom teachers, special ed teachers, principals, curriculum specialists, and so forth will rush to adopt these excellent programs. This is not going to happen. Let me tell you a story.

Once upon a time there was a company called XYZ Corporation. It was entirely funded by taxpayer dollars and had no competitors. For over 100 years, it produced products with serious flaws. The product fail rate in some factories was as high as 60 to 75 percent. Laws mandated that everyone had to have this product, so you couldn't refuse to buy it or shop elsewhere. Not only was there a high fail rate, but the manufacturing process itself was toxic. It destroyed millions of people's lives. They were unable to get or hold a job, to participate in higher education, to get off welfare, or to escape the inner city, and many were sucked into a life of crime. These additional problems cost tax payers billions of dollars more for welfare programs, courts, attorney fees, and new prisons.

XYZ Corporation told legislators that they wanted to fix things. To do this they needed more tax dollars for product-recall schemes ("We care"). They hired thousands of product-recall specialists, including a fleet of administrators. The fail rate of products "fixed" by the Recall Division of XYZ Corporation was 90 percent. Additional product-recall programs were initiated at more expense to taxpayers, and took over space belonging to institutions like community colleges, universities, public libraries, and local community centers.

XYZ Corporation is still in business. No one can shut down this company. No one can replace it with anything better or do anything to fix it. XYZ Corporation owns you. Its local board of trustees demands your tax dollars; if you don't pay up, you will lose your home on the courthouse steps. Its state and federal boards of trustees demand your tax dollars; otherwise you will be fined and thrown in jail.

For 100 years, XYZ Corporation had two standard answers for critics: (1) There is nothing wrong with our product. (2) We have a chronic shortage of cash. With the failure of the Product Recall Division, XYZ Corporation shifted the focus of attention to the raw material, claiming it is flawed. They have no control over the raw material, and everyone knows you can't make a silk purse out of a sow's ear. What's more, the "sows' ears" are to blame for being flawed. They have bad parents. They have bad genes. They have brain disorders with Greek names. They have "emotional," "developmental," "behavioral," "conduct," etc. disorders and need to be put on medication.

Meanwhile, ABC Corporation down the road can take the same raw material and turn out a product with no flaws. They can do this much faster at far less cost, *and* their manufacturing process is completely nontoxic. So why not purchase products from ABC Corporation? Well, you can if you're rich. But most people aren't rich. Their spare cash goes to pay XYZ Corporation.

When you look at public education this way, you can scarcely believe this story. Imagine owning a company like this one:

Customer required by law to purchase your product

No competition

Unending source of free capital

No product guarantee

Not accountable to its customers

Cannot be sued for product failure

When critics demand accountability, resorts to fraudulent misrepresentation of data

Responds to external tests of accountability with lies

Twice as many administrators as workers

Two-thirds of revenues allocated to administration

Worker training has little or no relevance to on-the-job skills

Fifty percent worker attrition rate every five years

The workers' union is part of corporate management, and is the only union in the United States that "owns" its own cabinet department

Now add these other ingredients and stir:

University departments of elementary education contribute directly to the toxicity problem by ignoring the scientific research, or by failing to recognize what is scientific research and what isn't, and by failing to incorporate new discoveries into teacher training programs. While there are good, and even great, departments of education, like those at Columbia, Harvard, and Stanford, their voices are drowned out in a cacophony of edu-babble.

The education publishing industry is controlled by university departments of education and by district and state administrators. Publishing houses flourish only to the extent that they stay friendly with the right people in the right places. When parents are overly vocal about their dissatisfaction with the public schools, education publishers are at the ready with scores of new product lines, costing tens of thousands of dollars per school or even per classroom.

The collapse of whole language provides a golden opportunity for a real revolution. We have solved the problem of literacy. Research reports are there, available for all to see. Sadly, there will be no revolution in education publishing or in the classroom. In the summer of 1996, the floodgates opened and an avalanche of new reading programs, complete with readers, worksheets, and spellers, descended on classroom teachers all across the country. Do the new curricula look anything like the reading programs discussed in this book? Of course not. Education publishers have rummaged in their archives and dredged up the same old stuff. New curricula come in three flavors: "super-phonics" and two types of eclectic reading programs, "eclectic chaotic" and "eclectic sequential."

"Super-phonics" is the same old 26 letters–26 names–26 sounds formula, plus a few hundred spelling rules that don't work. It has all the problems discussed in chapters 2, 4, 5, 8, and 10. "Eclectic chaotic" derives from the belief that a little bit of everything is better than just one thing. We saw the consequences of this in chapter 8 when "Success for All" departed from its basic floor plan. "Eclectic sequential" is an attempt to sequence every known reading method (except the right one) in some kind of order. This order mirrors what children do when they are forced to teach themselves to read. Maladaptive strategies become the platform for the program. "Eclectic sequential" begins with whole words ("sight words"), then graduates to syllables, and then to syllable fragments ("word families"). Sprinkle in whole language activities for a year or two, and when children are thoroughly confused, teach them the "sounds of letters" followed up with spelling rules and lists of spelling words they can't read. This sequence takes four to five years.

Parents are optimistic about the return of phonics, but there's nothing to be optimistic about. Even the best phonics programs have a fail rate of around 30 percent. This is far short of zero, which is where we should be and *where we could be*. Remember, too, that the success of phonics depends on having teachers with appropriate training who have been practicing in the classroom for several years. There aren't many of these teachers left. Professors of elementary education have been on the whole language bandwagon for about fifteen years. They are not going to be able to change their spots that easily, much less train teachers in phonics.

Even if by some miracle a scientifically proven reading curriculum was adopted by the schools, teachers would need extensive retraining. This would entail workshops and ultimately a complete overhaul of elementary education departments in nearly every university. This isn't going to happen in the foreseeable future. The trend has been, and continues to be, to avoid anything explicit or rigorous in teacher training. This is why education is continually losing ground, a process known as "dumbing down." It's difficult to break out of this mind-set. Half-baked ideas and misrepresentation of other people's work are standard fare for trainee teachers.

"Invented spelling" is a prime example. Supposedly based on Montessori's "discovery learning," it's devoid of everything that Montessori stood for, including her valuable observations and insights about how children learn. Gone is the important work on subskills that makes discovery learning possible. Gone is Montessori's fundamental point that children must practice only with materials that promote *error-free performance*. In his book on Montessori, John Chattin-McNichols points out that there is a profound difference between error-*free* repetition and error-*filled* repetition: "Error is information only if it is correctable—otherwise it *becomes* the information."

Montessori was in the classroom every day. She developed her methods from years of observing how children learn. All good teachers know what works and what doesn't. Teachers see firsthand that what they were taught at university has little practical value, and that much of it doesn't even make sense. It is unlikely this is going to change in a hurry. In our research and our teacher workshops, we have heard teachers complain that they were taught next to nothing about how to teach reading. They learned a lot of "theory" which had little applied relevance, and were given nothing practical to do to teach reading effectively. Louisa Moats reports on survey material which reveals the impoverished (and often absent) training teachers receive in the alphabet principle, knowledge of the sounds of the English language, and the spelling code.

When we do research in the schools, teachers frequently ask: "Could you test this child? I have no idea whether she has a reading problem or not." A teacher who attended one of our workshops came up to us afterward with this story. Dissatisfied with reading instruction during her undergraduate training, she subsequently completed a master's degree in "Reading Instruction." When she finished this program she still didn't know how to teach reading. She told us she had learned more in our four-hour workshop than in *six years* of teacher training at university.

If you believe that the phonics backlash will truly make a difference, don't hold your breath. Nor is it likely that anyone outside the system will have an impact on the public schools. The glue that holds the system together is money and power. There are state and local boards of education with fleets of administrators and curriculum specialists. The National Education Association (NEA) is one of the most powerful unions in America. It has two million members and collects dues of approximately $750,000,000 each year. The NEA controls accreditation requirements for teacher training, which means that no one without a credential can get employment in the public schools, no matter how much teaching experience she or he has had in the private sector.

NEA blocks initiatives that would make schools accountable or open up the system to excellence, despite the fact that its charter lists "excellence" as a primary goal. It opposes school choice, a Republican initiative, *and* charter schools, a Democratic initiative. The NEA claims to represent the wishes and viewpoints of its members to state and federal legislators, but never polls its members about anything. It talks legislators into believing that it can deliver votes, when it cannot: Most teachers voted for Reagan in both presidential elections.

I can report on a personal experience of the difficulty of trying to change the system. I joined a cooperative venture to start a charter school in Florida. Charter schools are supposed to introduce fresh ideas and wrest the armlock on education from the bureaucrats. Instead, the education lobby put such pressure on Florida's legislators that no one would dare open a charter school *unless they were already a public school.* Charter schools must conform to the same requirements as the public schools: credentialed teachers; random allocation of pupils; handicap access ramps; special teachers for the blind, deaf, and mentally retarded; not-for-profit status, and so forth, *but* charter grants are limited by district and only the school board is allowed to decide who gets a charter. No startup capital (furniture, equipment, playgrounds, remodeling) is provided, *and* if the school board doesn't like what you're doing at the end of three years, they have full authority to revoke your charter (and take over your school (including furniture, equipment, etc.). The school board sits in judgment on the charter schools, but no one sits in judgment on the public schools. There is no provision in the legislation for how to recover your up-front costs or meet your contractual and ethical obligations to your staff, to say nothing of your lost time and effort. This is a concrete example of why we are unable to reform our schools. Only the fabulously rich would dare venture forth with these kinds of odds.

So, what's a parent to do? First and foremost, protect your own self-interest. Teach your children to read or find someone else who can. Monitor what your children are learning in the classroom. Insist on excellence, but be cooperative and not adversarial. Remember, teachers are as much victims of the system as you are. They aren't responsible for their inadequate training, and they are well aware of its shortcomings. They're doing 120 percent of their best.

Another alternative is to become an activist, though most people don't relish this role. It requires commitment, passion, and a lot of time and savvy. If you decide to take it on, be aware of what you're up against. Speaking at PTA meetings or writing vitriolic letters to the newspaper won't cut it. Unless you have good organizational and leadership skills, your best alternative is to bombard your elected officials with information about what you, other parents, and teachers really think. California turned its back on whole language for three major reasons: overwhelming proof of skyrocketing illiteracy rates, lots of media attention, *and* parents' outrage.

Remember, the legislators aren't the bad guys. Many truly want to do something about our education system, but are frustrated in knowing how to break the stranglehold of the public school education "industry." They are aware of how far we lag behind countries in Europe and the Far East in literacy, mathematics, and science. Legislators are up against education lobbyists and special interest groups like the NEA. Legislators need to know that the NEA does not represent the opinions of its members and that it *cannot deliver votes of those members.* Campaign finance reform couldn't hurt.

As we approach the twenty-first century, we have solved the mystery of literacy. We have pinned down *exactly* what skills and knowledge a child needs to be able to read and spell. We have proved this in careful research. We have shown that *everyone* can learn to read unless he or she is mentally retarded. We have shown that it isn't even *hard* for children to learn to read. This is exciting news, but there has to be a major groundswell, a grass roots movement, before anything can change.

Until then, parents and teachers are left holding the bag, while they and other taxpayers foot the bill for a system that hasn't worked for 100 years. I have done my best to give you a better idea of the scope and seriousness of the bag you are holding. I have also tried to give you something practical to do to rescue our children. I hope I have succeeded.

NOTES AND REFERENCES

CHAPTER 1. READING REPORT CARD

Notes

1. An international survey: W.B. Warwick, 1994, *The IEA Study of Reading Literacy: Achievement and Instruction in Thirty-Two School Systems,* London: Pergamon Press, reports American fourth graders as scoring just behind top-ranked Finland (narrative prose) and behind only Finland and Sweden (expository prose) in a survey of thirty-two countries. This study lacks the rigorous controls of the NAEP study (unsupervised testing by the classroom teacher, multiple choice answers only, sampling problems, etc.). In the U.S. sample, 7 percent of the children were excluded as "untestable" and there was an 82.5 percent compliance rate for the remainder. Thus, only 75 percent of the U.S. sample was represented in these data. Most countries had 99 to 100 percent compliance rates. The author states that compliance rates of less than 80 percent are regarded as "suspicious." This study is frequently cited as proof that there is nothing wrong with American education.

   Secretary of Education Robert Riley (C-Span, June 17, 1996) stated that the discrepancy in the IEA and NAEP reports was due entirely to the higher difficulty level of the NAEP tests. According to this interpretation, American children are reading just fine compared to the rest of the world, but Americans have higher standards for literacy. This conclusion is not supported by the results from an international adult literacy survey conducted by Statistics Canada. This study used similar methodology to the U.S. Adult Literacy Survey, and also measured U.S. and Swedish literacy rates. For the youngest group tested (sixteen to twenty-five years), Statistics Canada reported that six times more Americans scored at Level 1 (functionally illiterate) than top-ranked Sweden (23.5 percent versus 3.8 percent), and there were twice as many Americans scoring at Level 1 as Canadians (23.5 percent versus 10.7 percent). Forty percent of Swedes scored at the proficient and advanced levels (Levels 4 and 5), versus 13 percent in the U.S. The literacy rates for Americans in the Statistics Canada study were nearly identical to the rates from the U.S. Adult Literacy Survey across all age groups, indicating solid methodology. Unless we assume that American children read superbly in fourth grade (IEA study) but suddenly become illiterate in high school (U.S. and Canadian data), the only possible conclusion is that the IEA study is methodologically flawed and grossly inflates U.S. fourth-grade literacy levels.

2. Educational Testing Service personnel reported to me that the IEP exclusion rates are beyond their control under federal law. The IEP team consists of parents and special ed teachers who have full authority to declare a child "untestable." Preliminary research on this issue has shown that a proportion of children declared "untestable" are, in fact, testable. The ETS team has available a number of options (unlimited time, oral reporting of answers, Braille versions of the test items) to accommodate IEP students. This is a problem they recognize and are attempting to solve.

References

Adult Literacy in America (1993). Office of Educational Research and Improvement, U.S. Department of Education.

Cannell, J.J. (1988). Nationally normed elementary achievement testing in America's public schools: How all 50 states are above the national average. *Educational Measurement Issues and Practice, 7.*

Linn, R.L. (1991). Test Misuse: Why is it so prevalent? Office of Technology Assessment. U.S. Congress.

Literacy Economy and Society: Results of the First International Literacy Survey (1995). Organization for Economic Cooperation and Development, Statistics Canada.

NAEP 1992. Reading Report Card for the Nation and States (1993). Office of Educational Research and Improvement. U.S. Department of Education.

NAEP 1994. Reading Report Card for the Nation and States (1996). Office of Educational Research and Improvement. U.S. Department of Education.

Projections of Education Statistics to 2003. (1993). U.S. Department of Education.

Slavin, R.E. (1989). Students at risk of school failure: The problem and its dimensions. In: R.E. Slavin, N.L. Karweit, & N.A. Madden (Eds.). *Effective Programs for Students at Risk.* Boston: Allyn and Bacon.

Sykes, C.J. (1995). *Dumbing Down Our Kids.* New York: St. Martins Press.

CHAPTER 2. READERS READING: HOW DO WE DO IT?

References

Bryant, P.E., MacClean, M., Bradley, L.L., & Crossland, J. (1990). Rhyme, alliteration, phoneme detection and learning to read. *Developmental Psychology, 26,* 429–38.

Flesch, R. (1955/1985). *Why Johnny Can't Read.* New York: Harper and Row.

Goodman, K. (1967). Reading: A psycholinguistic guessing game. *Journal of the Reading Specialist.* May, 126–35.

McGuinness, D. (submitted). Strategies as a predictor of reading skill: A follow-on study.

Rayner, K. & Pollatsek, A. (1989). *The Psychology of Reading.* Englewood Cliffs, NJ: Prentice-Hall. Chapter 4. The work of the eyes.

Dr. Seuss. (1991). *How the Grinch Stole Christmas.* From: *Six by Seuss.* New York: Random House.

CHAPTER 3. TRANSCRIBING TALK

Notes

1. Childe, G. (1941). *Man Makes Himself.* London: Watts. p. 187.
2. "Schooldays" translated by S.N. Kramer (1963). *The Sumerians.* Chicago: Chicago University Press, pp. 237–40.

3. Chomsky, C. Approaching reading through invented spelling. Paper presented at a conference on Theory and Practice of Beginning Reading Instruction. University of Pittsburgh, 1976. EDRS document (ED 155 630). p. 3.
4. Quotes cited in Groff as they appear in order:
   a. Weaver, C. (1988). *Reading Process and Practice.* Exeter, NH: Heinemann, p. 178.
   b. Smith, F. (1985). *Reading.* New York: Cambridge University Press. p. 146.
   c. Smith, F. (1973). *Psychology and Reading.* New York: Holt, Rinehart and Winston. p. 79.
   d. Smith, F. (1985). *Ibid.* p. 53.
   e. Weaver, C. (1980). *Psycholinguistics and Reading.* Cambridge, MA: Winthrop. p. 86.
   f. Weaver, C. (1980). *Ibid.* p. 86.
   g. Goodman, K. (1986). *What's Whole in Whole Language?* Exeter NH: Heinemann. p. 37.
   h. Smith, F. (1986). *Understanding Reading.* Hillsdale, NJ: Lawrence Erlbaum Associates, p. 188.

References

Whole Language: pages 32–34

Goodman, K. (1976). Behind the eye: What happens in reading. In: H. Singer & R. Ruddell (Eds.). *Theoretical Models and Processes in Reading.* 2nd Edition. New York: I.R.A.
Goodman, K. (1993). *Phonics Phacts.* Portsmouth, NH: Heinemann.

Early Writing Systems: pages 35–51

Bridge, E.A.W. (1977) *The Book of the Dead.* The hieroglyphic transcript of the papyrus of ANI. Secaucus, N.J.: University Books Inc.
Coulmas, F. (1993). *The Writing Systems of the World.* Oxford: Blackwell.
Crystal, D. (1987). *The Cambridge Encyclopedia of Language.* Cambridge: Cambridge University Press.
Gordon, C.H. (1965). *The Ancient Near East.* New York: W.W. Norton and Co., Inc.
Kramer, S.N. (1963). *The Sumerians.* Chicago: Chicago University Press.
——— . (1981). *History Begins at Sumer.* Philadelphia: University of Pennsylvania Press.
Lichtheim, M. (1975). *Ancient Egyptian Literature. Vol I. The Old and Middle Kingdoms.* Berkeley: University of California Press.
Lloyd, S. (1978). *The Archaeology of Mesopotamia.* London: Thames Hudson.
Lui, I.M., Chiang, C.J., & Wang, S.C. (1975). *Frequency Count of 40,000 Chinese Words.* Taiwan: Luck Books (in Chinese).
McArthur, T. (Ed.) (1992). *The Oxford Companion to the English Language.* Oxford: Oxford University Press.
Oates, J. (1979). *Babylon.* London: Thames and Hudson.
Rayner, K. & Pollatsek, A. (1989). *The Psychology of Reading.* Englewood Cliffs, N.J.: Prentice-Hall.
Robinson, A. (1995). *The Story of Writing.* London: Thames and Hudson.
Schele, L. & Freidel, D. (1990). *The Forest of Kings: An Untold Story of the Ancient Maya.* New York: William Morrow and Co.
Taylor, I. & Olson, D.R. (Eds.). (1995). *Scripts and Literacy.* Dordrecht, Netherlands: Kluwer Academie Publishers. See chapters by Che Kan Leong, 163–83; Shin-Ying Lee, D.H. Uttal, & Chuansheng Chen, 247–63.

Whole Language Issues: pages 51–55

Groff, P. (1991). Teachers' opinions of the whole language approach to reading instruction. *Annals of Dyslexia, 41,* 83–95.

Stevenson, H.W., Stigler, J.W., Lucker, W. & Shin-ying, L. (1982). Reading disabilities: The case of Chinese, Japanese and English. *Child Development, 53,* 1164–83.

CHAPTER 4. ALPHABETS: SPLITTING SOUNDS

References

Chall, J. (1967/1983/1996). *Learning to Read: The Great Debate.* New York: McGraw-Hill.

Coulmas, F. (1993). *The Writing Systems of the World.* Oxford: Blackwell.

Crystal, D. (1987). *The Cambridge Encyclopedia of Language.* Cambridge: Cambridge University Press.

Denes, P.B. and Pinson, E.N. (1993). *The Speech Chain.* New York: W.H. Freeman and Co.

Flesch, R. (1955/1985). *Why Johnny Can't Read.* New York: Harper and Row.

Healey, J.F. (1990). *The Early Alphabet.* London: British Museum.

Gelb, I. (1963). *A Study of Writing.* Chicago: Chicago University Press.

Kramer, S. (1963). *The Sumerians.* Chicago: Chicago University Press.

Robinson, A. (1995). *The Story of Writing.* London: Thames and Hudson.

Schele, L. and Freidel, D. (1990). *The Forest of Kings: An Untold Story of the Ancient Maya.* New York: William Morrow.

Stevenson, H.W., Stigler, J.W., Lucker, W., and Sing-Ying, L. (1982). Reading disabilities: The case of Chinese, Japanese and English. *Child Development, 53,* 1164–83.

Taylor, I. & Olson, D.R. (Eds.). (1995). *Scripts and Literacy.* Dordrecht, Netherlands: Kluwer Academie Publishers. See chapter by Takeshi Hatta & Takehito Hirase, 230–46.

CHAPTER 5. THE ENGLISH ALPHABET CODE

Notes

1. The opening lines of the *The Vision of Piers Plowman.* William Langland. C text Preface written A.D. 1385–1386. Bodleian MS 814. Oxford, Bodleian Library. The translation is mine.
2. E. Raleigh. Letter to Sir Robert Cecil. HMS Cecil 5, p. 396. Hatfield House.
3. Preface to Johnson, S. (1755/1773). *Dictionary of the English Language.* 4th Edition. London: Strahan. p. 21.
4. Preface to Webster, N. (1828). *A Dictionary of the English Language.* English Edition. Covent Garden: Black, Young and Young. pp iv–v.
5. All quotes are from Webster, N. (1870). *Improved Spelling Book.* Manchester: Abel Heywood. pp 8–11.
6. Webster, N. (1783). *A Grammatical Institute of the English Language. Part 1.* Facsimile (1968). Menston, England: The Scholar Press Ltd., p. 29.
7. The probability structure of American Spelling as set out in these tables was based on over 3,000 common English words. This probability structure is *not* based on the work of Hanna, P. R., Hanna, J.S., and Hodges, R.E. (1966). *Phoneme-Grapheme Correspondences as Cues to Spelling Improvement.* OE-32008. Washington, DC: U.S. Department of Health, Education, and Welfare. This is a 1,716-page document which estimates the probability structure of spelling patterns in over 17,000 words by position of each phoneme in the syllable.

This was a valuable and important undertaking and it is a minor tragedy that there are so many errors in this work. For example, the authors state that there are fifty-two phonemes in English, and their classification duplicates many vowel and consonant sounds. 'Silent' /h/ is classified as a 'phoneme' (heir).

They misunderstand the consonant spellings which use e̲ as a diacritic: ce, se, ze, ve, ge, dge, le, the, and classify them instead as vowel spellings. Examples are: choose = oo̲-e̲; juice = ui̲-e̲; license = e̲-e̲, dodge = o̲-e̲. There are hundreds of phonological errors in the word lists themselves (too many to count), possibly the fault of data entry personnel. For example, words containing the vowel phoneme /o͞o/ (soon) are classified with words that contain the phoneme /ue/ (cue) (i.e., cue is not 'coo,' nor cute 'coot'). These problems make it impossible to rely on Hanna et al.'s probability estimates of English spelling patterns.

A further problem is that the frequency estimates are based on the entire corpus of 17,000 words. However, spelling patterns and hence their probabilities differ for common English words (including those of French origin) and for Latin words, and should be analyzed separately. This is especially important for designers of early reading and spelling curricula.

Richard Venezky [Venezky, R.L. (1970). *The Structure of English Orthography.* The Hague: Mouton] worked out all possible spelling patterns (letters) for a corpus of 20,000 words. These were set out from letter(s) *to* sounds (code overlaps only). This effort is of academic interest, but this is not how the alphabet code was written, nor how it works. No attempt to assess the probability structure of these overlaps was provided. Spelling patterns are illustrated with only a few examples, and rare spellings are given equal prominence to common spellings. Again, this type of analysis is of little use to people who design reading or spelling curricula.

References

Old English Writing: pages 79–84

Aelfred. *Preface to Pope Gregory's Pastoral Care.* A.D. 890–895. MS Hatton 20. Oxford: Bodleian Library.

Aelfric. *A Grammar.* A.D. 987–988. St. John's College MS 154. Oxford: St. John's College Library.

Asser. *Life of King Alfred.* A.D. 893–894. Translated by L.C. Jane (1966). New York: Cooper Square Publishing, Inc.

Bede. *Ecclesiastical History of the English People.* A.D. 731. Translated by L. Sherley Price. Revised by R.E. Latham (1990). London: Penguin Books.

Ellis, P.B. (1995). *Celt and Saxon.* London: Constable.

Grant, M. (1981). *Dawn of the Middle Ages.* London: Weidenfeld and Nicholson.

Jones, C. (1989). *A History of English Phonology.* London: Longman.

Marckwardt, A.H. and Rosier, J.L. (1972). *Old English.* New York: W.W. Norton.

Moody, T.W. and Martin, F.X. (Eds.) (1978). *The Course of Irish History.* Cork: The Mercier Press.

Smyth, A.P. (1995). *King Alfred the Great.* Oxford: Oxford University Press.

Sprockel, C. (1965). *The Language of the Parker Chronicle.* Vol. 1. Phonology and Accidence. The Hague: Martinus Nijhoff.

Wood, M. (1981). *In Search of the Dark Ages.* London: British Broadcasting Corporation.

Middle English: pages 84–87

Anderson, G.K. (1962). *The Literature of the Anglo-Saxon.* New York: Russell and Russell.
Burrow, J.A. and Turville, T. (1992). *A Book of Middle English.* Oxford: Blackwell.
Clanchy, M.T. (1994). *From Memory to Written Record.* England 1066–1307. Oxford: Black-well.
Gottfried, R.S. (1983). *The Black Death.* New York: Free Press.
Jordon, R. (1974). *Handbook of Middle English Grammar: Phonology.* The Hague: Mouton.
Platt, C. (1994). *Medieval England.* London: Routledge.
Scragg, D.G. (1974). *A History of English Spelling.* Manchester: Manchester University Press.

Samuel Johnson: pages 87–91

Heminge, J. and Condell, H. (1623). *Mr. William Shakespeare's Comedies, Histories and Tragedies.* The Norton Facsimile: *The First Folio of Shakespeare* (1968). New York: W.W. Norton.
Johnson, S. (1755/1773). *A Dictionary of the English Language.* 4th Edition revised. London: Strahan.
Wain, J. (1994). *Samuel Johnson.* London: PaperMac.

Noah Webster/Nellie Dale: pages 91–97

Dale, N. (1898). *On the Teaching of English Reading.* London: J.M. Dent and Co.
———. (1902). *Further Notes of the Teaching of English Reading.* London: G. Philip and Son.
Rollins, R.M., ed. (1989). *The Autobiographies of Noah Webster.* Columbia: University of South Carolina Press.
Webster, N. (1783). *A Grammatical Institute of the English Language. Part I.* Facsimile (1968). Menston, England: The Scholar Press Ltd.
———. (1828). *Dictionary of the English Language.* (English edition). Covent Garden: Black, Young and Young.
———. (1856). *The Illustrated Webster Spelling Book.* London: Ward and Lock.
———. (1858). *British and American Spelling and Reading Book.* London: Dean and Son.
———. (1870). *Improved Elementary Spelling Book.* Manchester: Abel Heywood.

The Logic of the Code: pages 100–101

Adams, M.J. (1994). *Beginning to Read.* Cambridge, MA: M.I.T. Press.
Pribram, K.H. (1971). *Languages of the Brain.* New York: Prentice-Hall.
Stanbach, M.L. (1992). Syllable and rime patterns for teaching reading: Analysis of frequency-based vocabulary of 17,602 words. *Annals of Dyslexia, 42,* 196–221.

CHAPTER 6. SCIENCE TO THE RESCUE

Notes

1. Goodman, K. (1993). *Phonics Phacts.* New York: Heinemann. pp. 57–58.
2. Rutter, M. & Yule, W. (1975). The concept of specific reading retardation. *Journal of Child Psychology and Psychiatry, 16,* 181–97. p. 194.
3. Fletcher, J. M., Shaywitz, S.E., Shankweiler, D.P., Katz, L., Liberman, I. Y., Stuebing, K.K., Francis, D.J., Fowler, A.E., and Shaywitz, B.A. (1994). Cognitive profiles of

reading disability: Comparisons of discrepancy and low achievement definitions. *Journal of Educational Psychology, 86,* 6–23. p. 20.

4. Stanovich, K.E. & Siegel, L.S. (1994) Phenotypic performance profile of children with reading disabilities: A regression-based test of the phonological-core variable-difference model. *Journal of Educational Psychology, 86,* 24–53. p. 48.

5. Pennington, B. (1991). *Diagnosing Learning Disorders.* New York: The Guilford Press. pp. 53, 54.

6. Pennington, B. (1991). *Diagnosing Learning Disorders.* New York: The Guilford Press. p. 55.

7. Rosner and Simon were not the first to publish this type of test. A phoneme deletion test was published by Bruce in England [Bruce, D.J. (1964). The analysis of word sounds by young children. *British Journal of Educational Psychology, 34,* 158–70.] However, children younger than seven years could not perform this test. Further, Bruce never correlated performance on his test to reading and reported that it *did not* correlate to oral spelling. It is unknown whether Rosner and Simon were aware of Bruce's work. They do not cite it in their paper.

8. Aasved, H. (1989). Eye examinations. In: H-J. Gjessing & B. Karlsen (Eds.). *A Longitudinal Study of Dyslexia.* New York: Springer-Verlag. pp. 192–209. Quote on p. 209.

References

What Science Is and Isn't: pages 114–15

Goodman, K. (1993). Phonics Phacts. Portsmouth, NH: Heinemann.

Is Dyslexia a Special Reading Disorder? pages 117–23

Fletcher, J.M., Francis, D.J., Rourke, B.P., Shaywitz, S.E., & Shaywitz, B.A. (1992). The validity of discrepancy based definitions of reading disabilities. *Journal of Learning Disabilities, 25,* 555–61.

Fletcher, J.M., Shaywitz, S.E., Shankweiler, D.P., Katz, L., Liberman, I.Y., Stuebing, K.K., Francis, D.J., Fowler, A.E., & Shaywitz, B.A. (1994). Cognitive profiles of reading disability: Comparisons of discrepancy and low achievement definitions. *Journal of Educational Psychology, 86,* 6–23.

Galaburda, A.M. (1989). Ordinary and extraordinary brain development: Anatomical variation in developmental dyslexia. *Annals of Dyslexia, 39,* 67–93.

Hynd, G.W., Semrud-Clikeman, M., Lorys, A.R., Novey, E.S., & Eliopulas, D. (1990). Brain morphology in developmental dyslexia and attention deficit disorder/hyperactivity. *Archives of Neurology, 47,* 919–26.

Larsen, J.P., Hoien, T., Lundberg, I., & Odegaard, H. (1990). MRI evaluation of the size and symmetry of the planum temporal in adolescents with developmental dyslexia. *Brain and Language, 39,* 289–301.

Leonard, C.M., Lombardino, L.J., Mercado, L.R., Browd, S.R., Breier, J.I., & Agee, O.F. (1996). Cerebral asymmetry and cognitive development. *Psychological Science, 7,* 89–95.

Leonard, C.M., Voeller, K.K., Lombardino, L.J., Morris, M.K., Alexander, A.W., Andersen, H.G., Garofalakis, M.A., Hynd, G.W., Honeyman, J.C., Mao, J., Agee, O.F., & Staab, E.V. (1993). Anomalous cerebral structure in dyslexia revealed with magnetic resonance imaging. *Archives of Neurology, 50,* 461–69.

Pennington, B.F. (1991). *Diagnosing Learning Disorders.* New York: The Guilford Press.

Pennington, B.F., Gilger, J., Olson, R.K., & DeFries, J.C. (1992). The external validity of age-versus IQ-discrepancy definitions of reading disability: Lessons from a twin study. *Journal of Learning Disabilities, 25,* 562–73.

Richardson, S.O. (1989). Specific developmental dyslexia: Retrospective and prospective views. *Annals of Dyslexia, 39,* 3–23.

Rutter, M. & Yule, W. (1975). The concept of specific reading retardation. *Journal of Child Psychology and Psychiatry, 16,* 181–97.

Share, D.L., McGee, R., McKenzie, W.S., & Silva, P.A. (1987). Further evidence relating to the distinction between specific reading retardation and general reading backwardness. *British Journal of Developmental Psychology, 5,* 35–44.

Shaywitz, S.E., Escobar, M.D., Shaywitz, B.A., Fletcher, J.M., & Makuch, R. (1992). Evidence that dyslexia may represent the lower tail of a normal distribution of reading ability. *New England Journal of Medicine, 326,* 145–50.

Stanovich, K.E. & Siegel, L.S. (1994). Phenotypic performance profile of children with reading disabilities: A regression-based test of the phonological-core variable-difference model. *Journal of Educational Psychology, 86,* 24–53.

A Gene for Bad Reading? pages 124–25

Olson, R., Forsberg, H., Wise, B., & Rack, J. (1994). Measurement of word recognition, orthographic, and phonological skills. In: G.R. Lyon (Ed.). *Frames of Reference for the Assessment of Learning Disabilities.* Baltimore: Paul Brookes. pp. 243–77.

Olson, R.K., Wise, B., Conners, F., Rack, J., & Fulker, D. (1989). Specific deficits in component reading and language skills: Genetic and environmental influences. *Journal of Learning Disabilities, 22,* 339–48.

Pennington, B.F. (1991). *Diagnosing Learning Disorders.* New York: The Guilford Press.

———. (1996). The development of dyslexia: Genotype and phenotype analysis. Invited address at the 47th annual conference of The Orton Dyslexia Society. Boston, Nov. 6–9.

Phonological Awareness and Reading: pages 125–37

Adams, M.J. (1990). *Beginning to Read.* Cambridge, MA: M.I.T. Press.

Ben-Dror, I., Frost, R., & Bentin, S. (1995). Orthographic representation and phonemic segmentation in skilled readers: A cross-language comparison. *Psychological Science, 6,* 176–81.

Brady, S.A. & Shankweiler, D. P. (Eds.) (1991). *Phonological Process in Literacy: A Tribute to Isabelle Y. Liberman.* Mahwah, NJ: Lawrence Erlbaum Associates.

Calfee, R.C., Lindamood, P.C., & Lindamood, C.H. (1973). Acoustic-phonetic skills and reading—kindergarten through 12th grade. *Journal of Educational Psychology, 64,* 293–98.

Denckla, M.B. (1972). Color-naming deficits in dyslexic boys. *Cortex, 8,* 164–76.

Denckla, M.B. & Rudel, R.G. (1976). Rapid automatized naming (R.A.N.): Dyslexia differentiated from other disorders. *Neuropsychologia, 14,* 471–79.

Liberman, A.M., Cooper, F., Shankweiler, D., & Studdert-Kennedy, M. (1967). Perception of the speech code. *Psychological Review, 74,* 431–61.

Liberman, I.Y. (1973). Segmentation of the spoken word and reading acquisition. *Bulletin of the Orton Dyslexia Society, 23,* 65–77.

Liberman, I.Y., Shankweiler, D., Fischer, F.W., & Carter, B. (1974). Reading and the awareness of linguistic segments. *Journal of Experimental Child Psychology, 18,* 201–12.

Lindamood, C.H. & Lindamood, P.C. (1971). *Lindamood Auditory Conceptualization Test.* Austin, TX: Pro-ed.

Lundberg, I., Olofsson, A., & Wall, S. (1980). Reading and spelling skills in the first school years predicted from phoneme awareness skills in kindergarten. *Scandinavian Journal of Psychology, 21,* 159–73.

Mann, V.A. & Liberman, I.Y. (1984). Phonological awareness and verbal short-term memory. *Journal of Learning Disabilities, 17,* 592–98.

McGuinness, D. (1985). *When Children Don't Learn.* New York: Basic Books.

McGuinness, D., McGuinness, C., & Donohue, J. (1995). Phonological training and the alphabet principle: Evidence for reciprocal causality. *Reading Research Quarterly, 30,* 830–52.

Morais, J., Cary, L., Alegria, J., & Bertelson, P. (1979). Does awareness of speech as a sequence of phones arise spontaneously? *Cognition, 7,* 323–31.

Morais, J., Bertelson, P., Cary, L., & Alegria, J. (1986). Literacy training and speech segmentation. *Cognition, 24,* 45–64.

Read, C., Yun-Fei, Z., Hong-Yin, N., & Bao-Qing, D. (1986). The ability to manipulate speech sounds depends on knowing alphabetic writing. *Cognition, 24,* 31–44.

Rosner, J. & Simon, D.P. (1971). The auditory analysis test: An initial report. *Journal of Learning Disabilities, 4,* 384–92.

Shankweiler, D.P., Liberman, I.Y., Mark, L.S., Fowler, C.A., & Fischer, F.W. (1979). The speech code and learning to read. *Journal of Experimental Psychology: Human Learning and Memory, 5,* 531–45.

Share, D. L., Jorm, A.F., Maclean, R., & Matthews, R. (1984). Sources of individual differences in reading acquisition. *Journal of Educational Psychology, 76,* 1309–24.

Vandervelden, M.C. & Siegel, L.S. (1995). Phonological recoding and phoneme awareness in early literacy: A developmental approach. *Reading Research Quarterly, 30,* 854–75.

Wagner, R. K. & Torgesen, J. K. (1987). The nature of phonological processing and its causal role in the acquisition of reading skills. *Psychological Bulletin, 101,* 192–212.

Wagner, R.K., Torgesen, J.K., & Rashotte, C.A. (1994). The development of reading-related phonological processing abilities: New evidence of bi-directional causality from a latent variable longitudinal study. *Developmental Psychology, 30,* 73–87.

Wolf, M. (1991). The word retrieval deficit hypothesis and developmental dyslexia. *Journal of Learning and Individual Differences, 3,* 205–23.

Yopp, H.K. (1988). The validity and reliability of phonemic awareness tests. *Reading Research Quarterly, 23,* 159–78.

Speech and Language and Reading: pages 137–42.

Bishop, D.V.M. & Adams, C. (1990). A prospective study of the relationship between specific language disorders and reading retardation. *Journal of Child Psychology and Psychiatry, 31,* 1027–50.

Hull, F.M., Mielke, P.W., Timmons, R.J., & Willeford, J.A. (1971). The national speech and hearing survey: Preliminary results. *ASHA, 3,* 501–9.

McGuinness, D. (1995). *When Children Don't Learn.* New York: Basic Books.

Merzenich, M.M., Jenkins, W.M., Miller, S.L., Schreiner, C., & Tallal, P. (1996). Temporal processing deficits of language-learning impaired children ameliorated by training. *Science, 271,* 77–81.

Moats, L.C. (1994). Honing the concept of listening and speaking. In: G. R. Lyon (Ed.). *Frames of Reference for the Assessment of Learning Disabilities.* Baltimore: Paul Brookes. pp. 229–41.

Post, Y. (1996). Vowel length and voice onset time in consonants as indicators of reading difficulty. Paper presented at the 47th annual conference of The Orton Dyslexia Society. Boston. Nov. 6–9.

Shankweiler, D., Crain, S., Katz, L., Fowler, A.E., Liberman, A.M., Brady, S.A., Thornton, R., Lundquist, E., Dreyer, L., Fletcher, J.M., Stuebing, K.K., Shaywitz, S.E., & Shaywitz, B.A. (1995). Cognitive profiles of reading-disabled children: Comparison of language skills in phonology, morphology, and syntax. *Psychological Science, 6,* 149–56.

Snyder, L.S. & Downey, D.M. (1995). Serial rapid naming skills in children with reading disabilities. *Annals of Dyslexia, 45,* 31–49.

Tallal, P. (1980). Auditory temporal perception, phonics, and reading disabilities in children. *Brain and Language, 9,* 182–98.

————. (1988). Developmental language disorders. In: J.F. Kavanagh & T.J. Truss (Eds.). *Learning Disabilities. Proceedings of the National Conference.* Parkton, MD: York Press. pp. 181–272.

Tallal, P., Miller, S.I., Bedi, G., Byma, G., Wang, X., Nagarajan, S., Schreiner, C., Jenkins, W.M., & Merzenich, M.M. (1996). Fast-element enhanced speech improves language comprehension in language-learning impaired children. *Science, 271,* 81–84.

Tallal, P. & Piercy, M. (1974) . Developmental aphasia: Rate of auditory processing and selective impairment of consonant perception. *Neuropsychologia, 12,* 83–93.

Tallal, P. & Stark, R.E. (1981). Speech acoustic-cue discrimination abilities of normally developing and language-impaired children. *Journal of the Acoustic Society of America, 69* 568–74.

Tallal, P., Stark, R.E., & Mellits, D. (1985). The relationship between auditory temporal analysis and receptive language development: Evidence from studies of developmental language disorder. *Neuropsychologia, 23,* 527–34.

Tunmer, W.E., Nesdale, A.R., & Wright, A.D. (1987). Syntactic awareness and reading acquisition. *British Journal of Developmental Psychology, 5* 25–34.

Werker, J.F. & Tees, R.C. (1987). Speech perception in severely disabled and average reading children. *Canadian Journal of Psychology, 41,* 48–61.

Intelligence and Reading: pages 143–45

Bradley, L. & Bryant, P.E. (1985). *Rhyme and Reason in Reading and Spelling.* Ann Arbor: University of Michigan Press.

Bryant, P.E., Maclean, M., Bradley, L.L., & Crossland, J. (1990). Rhyme, alliteration, phoneme detection and learning to read. *Developmental Psychology, 26* 429–38.

Gjessing, H.-J. & Karlsen, B. (1989). *A Longitudinal Study of Dyslexia.* New York: Springer-Verlag.

McGuinness, D., McGuinness, C., & Donohue, J. (1995). Phonological training and the alphabet principle: Evidence for reciprocal causality. *Reading Research Quarterly, 30,* 830–53.

Stanovich, K.E., Cunningham, A.E., & Feeman, D.J. (1984). Intelligence, cognitive skills, and early reading progress. *Reading Research Quarterly, 19,* 278–303.

Wagner, R.K., Torgesen, J.K., & Rashotte, C.A. (1994). The development of reading-related phonological processing abilities: New evidence for bi-directional causality from a latent variable longitudinal study. *Developmental Psychology, 30,* 73–87.

Vision and Reading: pages 145–47

Aasved, H. (1989) Eye examinations. In: H.-J. Gjessing & B. Karlsen (Eds.). *A Longitudinal Study of Dyslexia.* New York: Springer-Verlag. pp. 192–209.

Calfee, R.C., Fisk, L.W., & Piontowski, D. (1975). On-off tests of cognitive skill in reading acquisition. In: M.P. Douglas (Ed.). *Claremont Reading Conference, 39th Yearbook.* Claremont, CA: Claremont Graduate School.

Gjessing, H.-J. (1989). Function analysis of literacy behavior. In: H.-J. Gjessing & B. Karlsen (Eds.). *A Longitudinal Study of Dyslexia.* New York: Springer-Verlag. pp. 106–59.

Rayner, K. (1985). Do faulty eye movements cause dyslexia? *Developmental Neuropsychology, 1,* 3–15.

Rayner, K. & Pollatsek, A. (1989). *The Psychology of Reading.* Englewood Cliffs, NJ: Prentice-Hall.

Stein, J.F. & Fowler, M.S. (1993). Unstable binocular control in dyslexic children. *Journal of Research in Reading, 16,* 30–45.

CHAPTER 7. THE CHILD'S MIND AND READING

Notes

1. Aelfric's Grammar, A.D. 987–988. Quote is from the Introduction starting at the first line in Saxon English. St. John's College MS 154. Oxford: St. John's College Library.
2. Piaget, J. (1964/1993). Development and learning. In: M. Gauvain & M. Cole (Eds.). *Readings on the Development of Children.* New York: Scientific American Books/W.H. Freeman. pp. 25–33. Quote on p. 32.

References

Making Sense of the World: pages 151–56

Flavell, J.H. (1963). *The Developmental Psychology of Jean Piaget.* Princeton, NJ: Van Nostrand.

Landau, B. & Gleitman, L.R. (1985). *Language and Experience: Evidence from the Blind Child.* Cambridge, MA: Harvard University Press.

McGuinness, D., Pribram, K.H., & Pirnazar, M. (1990). Upstaging the stage model. In: C.N. Alexander & E.J. Langer (Eds.). *Higher Stages of Human Development.* New York: Oxford University Press. pp. 97–113.

Montessori, M. (1972). *The Discovery of the Child.* New York: Ballantine Books.

Piaget, J. (1954). *The Construction of Reality in the Child.* New York: Basic Books.

———. (1964/1993). Development and learning. In: M. Gauvain & M. Cole (Eds.). *Reading on the Development of Children.* New York: Scientific American Books/W.H. Freeman. pp. 25–33.

———. (1971). The theory of stages in cognitive development. In: D.R. Green, M.P. Ford, & G.B. Flamer (Eds.). *Measurement and Piaget.* New York: McGraw-Hill

Logics for the Advanced Code Level: pages 156–61

Ceci, S.J. & Roazzi, A. (1994). The effects of context on cognition. In R.J. Sternberg & R.K. Wagner (Eds.). *Interactionist Perspectives on Human Intelligence.* New York: Cambridge University Press.

Piaget, J. (1977). *The Development of Thought: Equilibration of Cognitive Structures.* New York: Viking Press.

Pinker, S. (1994). *The Language Instinct.* New York: William Morrow and Company.

Richards, F.A. & Commons, M.L. (1990). Postformal cognitive-developmental theory and research: A review of its current status. In: C.N. Alexander & E. Langer (Eds.). *Higher Stages of Human Development.* New York: Oxford University Press.

Rosch, E. (1978). Principles of categorization. In: E. Rosch & B. Lloyd (Eds.). *Cognition and Categorization.* Hillsdale, NJ: Lawrence Erlbaum Associates.

Development of Language and Learning to Read: pages 161–64

Gleitman, L.R. (1981). Maturational determinants of language growth. *Cognition, 10,* 103–14.

Gleitman, L.R. & Newport, E.L. (1995). The invention of language by children: Environmental and biological influences on the acquisition of language. In: L.R. Gleitman & M. Liberman (Eds.). *Language.* Vol. 1. Cambridge, MA: M.I.T. Press.

Liberman, A.M., Cooper, F.S., Shankweiler, D.P., & Studdert-Kennedy, M. (1967). Perception of the speech code. *Psychological Review, 74,* 431–61.

McGuinness, D. (1985). *When Children Don't Learn.* New York: Basic Books.

Tees, R.C. & Werker, J.F. (1984). Perceptual flexibility: Maintenance or recovery of the ability to discriminate non-native speech sounds. *Canadian Journal of Psychology, 38,* 579–90.

Werker, J.F. (1995). Exploring developmental changes in cross-language speech perception. In: Gleitman, L.R. & Liberman, M. *Language.* Vol. 1. Cambridge, MA: MIT Press. pp. 87–106.

Werker, J.F. & Tees, R.C. (1984). Cross-language speech perception: Evidence for perceptual reorganization during the first year of life. *Infant Behavior and Development, 7,* 49–63.

————. (1992). The organization and reorganization of human speech perception. *Annual Review of Neuroscience, 15,* 377–402.

Control of Attention: pages 164–68

Deci, E.L. & Ryan, R.M. (1992). *The Initiation and Regulation of Intrinsically Motivated Learning and Achievement.* New York: Cambridge University Press.

Haier, R.J., Siegel, B.V., MacLachlan, A., & Sonderling, E. (1992). Regional glucose metabolic changes after learning a complex visuospatial motor task: A positron emission tomographic study. *Brain Research, 570,* 134–43.

Haier, R.J., Siegel, B.V., Neuchterlein, K.H., & Hazlett, E. (1988). Cortical glucose metabolism rate correlates of abstract reasoning and attention, studied with positron emission tomography. *Intelligence, 12,* 199–217.

Haier, R.J., Siegel, B., Tang, C., & Abel, L. (1992). Intelligence and changes in regional cerebral glucose metabolic rate following learning. Special Issue: Biology and intelligence. *Intelligence, 16,* 415–26.

Katz, L. (1987) . Early education: What should young children be doing? In: S.L. Kagan & E.F. Zigler (Eds.). *Early Schooling: The National Debate.* New Haven: Yale University Press.

McGuinness, D. (1985). *When Children Don't Learn.* New York: Basic Books. Chapters 9 and 10.

————. (1989). Attention deficit disorder, The Emperor's Clothes, Animal Pharm and other fiction. In: S. Fisher & R. Greenberg (Eds.). *A Critical Appraisal of Biological Treatments for Psychological Distress.* Hillsdale, N.J.: Lawrence Erlbaum Associates.

———. (1990). Behavioral tempo in preschool boys and girls. *Journal of Learning and Individual Differences, 2,* 315–26.

McGuinness, D. & Pribram, K.H. (1980). The neuropsychology of attention: Emotional and motivational controls. In: M.C. Wittrock (Ed.). *The Brain and Educational Psychology.* New York: Academic Press.

Pribram, K.H. & McGuinness, D. (1975). Arousal, activation and effort in the control of attention. *Psychological Review, 82,* 116–49.

———. (1992). Attention and para-attentional processing. *Annals of the New York Academy of Sciences, 433,* 65–92.

Raichle, M.E., Fiez, J.A., Videen, T.O., & McLeod, A-M.K. (1994). Practice-related changes in human brain functional anatomy during nonmotor learning. *Cerebral Cortex, 4,* 8–26.

Williamson, P. (1989). *Good Kids: Bad Behavior.* New York: Simon and Schuster.

CHAPTER 8. THE PROOF OF THE PUDDING: READING PROGRAMS THAT WORK

References

Training Studies at Preschool and Kindergarten: pages 173–78

Ball, E. W. & Blachman, B.A. (1988). Phoneme segmentation training: Effect on reading readiness. *Annals of Dyslexia, 38,* 208–25.

———. (1991). Does phoneme awareness training in kindergarten make a difference in early word recognition and developmental spelling? *Reading Research Quarterly, 26,* 49–66.

Blachman, B.A., Ball, E.W., Black, R.S., & Tangel, D.M. (1994). Kindergarten teachers develop phoneme awareness in low-income, inner-city classrooms. *Reading and Writing, 6,* 1–18.

Byrne, B. & Fielding-Barnsley, R. (1989). Phonemic awareness and letter knowledge in the child's acquisition of the alphabetic principle. *Journal of Educational Psychology, 81,* 313–21.

———. (1993). Evaluation of a program to teach phonemic awareness to young children: A 1-year follow-up. *Journal of Educational Psychology, 85,* 104–11.

Elkonin, D.B. (1963). The psychology of mastering the elements of reading. In: B. Simon & J. Simon (Eds.). *Educational Psychology in the U.S.S.R.* London: Routledge and Kegan Paul.

Foorman, B.R., Francis, D.J., Beeler, T., Winikates, D., & Fletcher, J. M. (in press). Early interventions for children with reading problems: Study designs and preliminary findings. *Learning Disabilities: A Multi-Disciplinary Journal.*

Lundberg, I., Frost, J., & Petersen, O.-P. (1988). Effects of an extensive program for stimulating phonological awareness in preschool children. *Reading Research Quarterly, 23,* 263–84.

McGuinness, C., McGuinness, G.D., & McGuinness, D. (submitted). "Reading Fundamentals." Success of a new reading approach for the preschool classroom.

Tangel, D.M. & Blachman, B.A. (1992). Effect of phoneme awareness instruction on kindergarten children's invented spelling. *Journal of Reading Behavior, 24,* 233–61.

———. (1995). Effect of phoneme awareness instruction on the invented spelling of first-grade children: A one-year follow-up. *Journal of Reading Behavior, 27,* 153–84.

Preventive Programs for At-Risk Children: pages 178–88

Bartlett, E.J. (1979). Curriculum, concepts of literacy, and social class. In: L.B. Resnick & P.A. Weaver (Eds.). *Theory and Practice of Early Reading.* Vol. 2. Hillsdale, NJ: Lawrence Erlbaum Associates.

Blachman, B.A. (1987). An alternative classroom reading program for learning disabled and other low-achieving children. Proceedings of The Orton Dyslexia Society symposium on "Dyslexia and Evolving Educational Patterns." Airlie, VA, June 19–21.

————. (1994). Early literacy acquisition. The role of phonological awareness. In: G.P. Wallach & K.G. Butler (Eds.). *Language Learning Disabilities in School-Age Children.* New York: Merrill.

Blachman, B. A. (Ed.). (1997). *Foundations of Reading Acquisition and Dyslexia: Implications for Early Intervention.* Mahwah, NJ: Lawrence Erlbaum Associates.

Bradley, L. (1987). Categorizing sound, early intervention and learning to read: A follow-up study. Paper presented at the British Psychological Society London Conference. December.

Bradley, L. & Bryant, P. (1985). *Rhyme and Reason in Reading and Spelling.* Ann Arbor: University of Michigan Press.

————. (1991). Phonological skills before and after learning to read. In: S.A. Brady & D.P. Shankweiler (Eds.). *Phonological Processes in Literacy.* Hillsdale, NJ: Lawrence Erlbaum Associates.

Engelmann, S., Becker, W.C., Hanner, S., & Johnson, G. (1978). *Corrective Reading: Decoding B.* Chicago: Science Research Associates.

Engelmann, S. & Bruner, E.C. (1983). *Reading Mastery I and II: DISTAR Reading.* Chicago: Science Research Associates.

Kuder, S.J. (1990). Effectiveness of the DISTAR reading program for children with learning disabilities. *Journal of Learning Disabilities, 23,* 69–71.

Slavin, R.E., Karweit, N.L., & Madden, N.A. (1989). *Effective Programs for Students at Risk.* Boston: Allyn and Bacon.

Slavin, R.E., Madden, N.A., Dolan, L.J., & Wasik, B.A. (1996). *Every Child, Every School. Success for All.* Thousand Oaks, CA: Corwin Press.

Wallach, M.A. & Wallach, L. (1976). *Teaching All Children to Read.* Chicago: Chicago University Press.

Wilson, B.A. (1988). *Wilson Reading System Program Overview.* Millbury, MA: Wilson Language Training.

School-Based Studies Using Normal Children: pages 188–90

Howard, M. (1982). Utilizing oral-motor feedback in auditory conceptualization. *Journal of Educational Neuropsychology, 2,* 24–35.

————. (1986). Effects of pre-reading training in auditory conceptualization on subsequent reading achievement. Doctoral dissertation. Brigham Young University.

Lindamood, P.C., Bell, N., & Lindamood, P. (1992). Issues in phonological awareness assessment. *Annals of Dyslexia, 42,* 242–59.

McGuinness, D. (1985). *When Children Don't Learn.* New York: Basic Books. Chapter 11 reports on the Santa Maria study.

McGuinness, D., McGuinness, C., & Donohue, J. (1995). Phonological training and the alphabet principle: Evidence for reciprocal causality. *Reading Research Quarterly, 30,* 830–52.

Remedial Programs: pages 191–205

Alexander, A., Andersen, H., Heilman, P., Voeller, K.K., & Torgesen, J. (1991). Phonological awareness training and remediation of analytic decoding deficits in a group of severe dyslexics. *Annals of Dyslexia, 41,* 193–206.

Center, Y., Wheldall, K., Freeman, L., Outhred, L., & McNaught (1995). An experimental evaluation of Reading Recovery. *Reading Research Quarterly, 30,* 240–63.

Clark, D.B. (1988); Clark, D.B. & Uhry, J.K. (1995). *Dyslexia: Theory and Practice of Remedial Instruction.* Parkton, MD: York Press.

Fletcher, J.M. & Satz, P. (1980). Lag-deficit characterization of the disabled reader: Some alternative interpretations. Paper presented at the 80th annual meeting of the International Neuropsychological Society, San Francisco. February.

Juel, C. (1988). Learning to read and write: A longitudinal study of 54 children from first through fourth grades. *Journal of Educational Psychology, 80,* 437–47.

Juel, C., Griffith, P., & Gough, P. (1986). Acquisition of literacy: A longitudinal study of children in first and second grade. *Journal of Educational Psychology, 78,* 243–55.

McGuinness, C., McGuinness, D. & McGuinness, G.D.J. (1996). Phono-Graphix™: A new method for remediating reading difficulties. *Annals of Dyslexia, 46,* 73–96.

Pinnell, G.S., Lyons, C.A., De Ford, D.E., Bryk, A., & Seltzer, M. (1994). Comparing instructional models for the literacy education of high-risk first graders. *Reading Research Quarterly, 29,* 8–39.

Shanahan, T. & Barr, R. (1995). Reading Recovery: An independent evaluation of the effects of an early instructional intervention for at- risk learners. *Reading Research Quarterly, 30,* 958–96.

Shaywitz, B.A., Holford, T.R., Hoahan, J.M., Fletcher, J.M., Stuebing, K.K., Francis, D.J., & Shaywitz, S.E. (1995). A Matthew effect for IQ but not for reading: Results from a longitudinal study. *Reading Research Quarterly, 30,* 894–907.

Truch, S. (1994). Stimulating basic reading processes using Auditory Discrimination in Depth. *Annals of Dyslexia, 44,* 60–80.

Williams, J.P. (1979). The ABDs of reading: A program for the learning disabled. In: L.B. Resnick & P.A. Weaver (Eds.). *Theory and Practice of Early Reading.* Vol. 3. Hillsdale, NJ: Lawrence Erlbaum Associates. pp. 179–95.

———. (1980). Teaching decoding with an emphasis on phoneme analysis and phoneme blending. *Journal of Educational Psychology, 72,* 1–15.

CHAPTER 10. MASTERING THE ADVANCED CODE IN READING, WRITING, AND SPELLING

References

Byrne, B., Freebody, P., & Gates, A. (1992). Longitudinal data on relations between word-reading strategy, comprehension, and reading time. *Reading Research Quarterly, 27,* 141–51.

Foorman, B.R., Francis, D.J., Shaywitz, S.E., Shaywitz, B.A., & Fletcher, J.M. (1997). The case for early reading intervention. In: B. Blachman (Ed.). *Cognitive and Linguistic Foundations of Reading Acquisition: Implications for Intervention.* Mahwah, NJ: Lawrence Erlbaum Associates.

Juel, C., Griffith, P.L., & Gough, P.B. (1986). Acquisition of literacy: A longitudinal study of children in first and second grade. *Journal of Educational Psychology, 78,* 243–55.

CHAPTER 11. HELPING THOSE WHO DIDN'T MAKE IT

References

Lindamood, C.H. & Lindamood, P.C. (1971). *Lindamood Auditory Conceptualization Test.* Austin, TX: Pro-ed.

Rosner, J. & Simon, D.P. (1971). The auditory analysis test: An initial report. *Journal of Learning Disabilities, 4,* 384–92.

CHAPTER 12. REMEDIAL READING PROGRAMS

References

Bell, N. (1986). *Visualizing and Verbalizing for Language Comprehension and Thinking.* Paso Robles, CA: Academy of Reading Publication.

Dale, N. (1898). *On the Teaching of English Reading.* London: J.M. Dent and Co.

Lindamood, C.H. & Lindamood, P.C. (1975). *Auditory Discrimination in Depth.* Austin, TX: Pro-ed.

McGuinness, C., McGuinness, D., & McGuinness, G.D.J. (1996). Phono-Graphix™: A new method for remediating reading difficulties. *Annals of Dyslexia, 46,* 73–96.

Slavin, R.E., Karweit, N.L., & Madden, N.A. (1989). *Effective Programs for Students at Risk.* Boston: Allyn and Bacon.

Truch, S. (1991). *The Missing Parts of Whole Language.* Calgary: Foothills Educational Materials.

CHAPTER 13. WHAT'S A PARENT TO DO?

References

Chattin-McNichols, J. (1992). *The Montessori Controversy.* Albany, NY: Delmar.

Corcoran, J. & Carlson, C.C. (1994). *The Teacher Who Couldn't Read.* Colorado Springs: Focus on the Family.

Hart, B. & Risley, T.R. (1995). *Meaningful Differences.* Baltimore: Paul Brookes.

Moats, L.C. (1994). The missing foundation in teacher education: Knowledge of the structure of spoken and written language. *Annals of Dyslexia, 44,* 81–102.

Sykes, C.J. (1995). *Dumbing Down Our Kids.* New York: St. Martin's Press.

GLOSSARY

alphabet   A writing system based on the phoneme.

case grammar   Word forms for nouns, pronouns, and adjectives, marking gender, object/agent of action, etc.

categorical perception   The inability of a native speaker to hear acoustic transitions between two consonant sounds, and the tendency to hear only one *or* the other.

character   In Chinese writing, a symbol standing for a word or syllable.

classes   In categorizing, where objects sharing similar features are grouped together.

classifier   In Chinese writing, a symbol acting as a determiner.

class inclusion   One class nested within another class (red balls versus balls). Hierarchical category relations.

co-articulation   In speech, phonemes coming later in a word modify the production of phonemes coming earlier in the word, creating a complex acoustical envelope.

code overlap   All possible phonemes that a letter or letter pattern can represent.

consonant   A phoneme that involves movement and/or contact between one or more of the speech articulators

   voiced consonant   Engages the vocal folds.

   unvoiced consonant   Does not engage the vocal folds.

consonantal alphabet   A writing system based on the consonant in which vowels are inferred from context.

consonant cluster   Two or three consonants in sequence in a word: 'str' in street.

criterion-based testing   A test designed to measure expected or anticipated aptitude for a particular age.

decoding   Translating from symbols into words or into speech sounds.

determiner   A symbol standing for a category (e.g., plant).

diacritic   A special mark or extra letter written above, below, or beside a letter to indicate pronunciation.

digraph   Two letters standing for one phoneme: <u>ch</u> in 'church.'

diphone system   A writing system based on a consonant-vowel (CV) phonological unit.

diphthong   A vowel sound that combines two vowels in rapid succession: /e/ + /ee/ = /ae/, in 'late.'

e-control principle   The letter <u>e</u> used as a diacritic to signal a new vowel sound, for vowel letters: a, e, i, o, u only. Extends backwards across one consonant, but not two: 'hate' vs. 'hat.'

encoding   Translating words or sounds in speech into symbols.

etymology   The study of the origin of words.

hieroglyphic   A writing system used on religious or public monuments for sacred or political purposes.

homophones   Words that sound exactly alike but with a different meaning.

invented spelling   A spelling method in which the child creates own spelling system based on knowledge of letter names and/or sounds.

logograph   An abstract symbol standing for a word.

mapping   A process by which units of one type are assigned to units of another type.

orthography   Predictable or probable spelling patterns within a system of spelling.

phoneme   The smallest unit of sound in a word that people can hear.

phoneme awareness   The ability to hear and remember the order of phonemes in words.

phonics   A generic term for any reading method that teaches the sounds for letters of an alphabet.

phonogram   Three or more letters standing for one phoneme: 'ough' in plough.

phonological processing   A generic term for the ability to hear and remember various units of sound within a word: syllable, rhyme, syllable fragment, phoneme.

phonology   The study of sounds in speech.

pictograph   A pictorial symbol standing for a word.

prefix   A syllable added to the beginning of a word to change meaning: 'un' in unfit.

propositional logic   The ability to think of a feature in two or more classes at the same time.

relations   In categorizing, where objects share some features but not others.

rime   Vowel + consonant endings to words. Identical rimes "rhyme": 'at' in cat.

schema   A mental structure that integrates dimensions or features of perceptual experience.

sight word   A word memorized by "sight" rather than sounded out phonetically.

silent letter   A letter in a word that isn't sounded: 'de<u>b</u>t.'

spelling alternatives   All possible spellings of one phoneme.

standard deviation   The square root of the sum of the squared difference of each score to the mean for all scores in a population.

standardized test   A test given to a large population in which scores are "standardized" using standard deviations to fit a bell-shaped curve.

statistical significance   A probability estimate in which the outcome of a measurement is less than 5 percent (5 in 100) of occurring purely by chance.

suffix   A final syllable added to a word to change meaning: live, living.

syllabary   A writing system based on the syllable.

syllable   A unit within a word containing only one vowel plus any consonants.

whole language   An approach to learning to read in which a child relies on natural language ability to discover how the writing system works.

word family   Same as **rime**.

AUTHOR INDEX

SUBJECT INDEX

ABDs of Reading, 197–99
Accounting tablet, 35, 36
Adult Literacy Survey, 9–10, 337–38
Adult poor readers, 337–38, 340
Advanced Spelling Code, 249–79
  code overlaps in, 266–67
  logic for, 156–61
  multisyllable words in, 273–74
  Phono-Graphix and, 318
  sight words and, 267–73
Aidan, Bishop, 80–81
Akkadian writing system, 58
Alfred, King, 81, 86, 101
Alfric, Bishop, 81, 82, 152
Allographs, 200, 250, 254–61
  address for, 247
  final consonants and, 260–61
  initial consonant clusters and,
    258–60
  initial consonants and, 255–56
  major goals of, 254–55
  sight words and, 267–68
  vowel spelling alternatives and,
    261–66
Allographs Book I, 254, 273
  address for, 279
Allographs Book II, 254, 273
  address for, 279
Alphabet code, 6, 16, 22, 24, 30,
    76–107, 181, 210: see also Ad-
    vanced Spelling Code; Basic
    Code; Spelling code
  in kindergarten and preschool, 174
  logic of, 97–99
  phonics and, 73–75
  Phono-Graphix and, 204
  in reading programs, 172, 212
  in remedial reading programs,
    191–92
  reversibility of: see Reversibility
  structure of, 101–7
Alphabets, 56–75
  consonantal, 59–60, 66, 67, 72, 78
  Etruscan, 80
  Greek: see Greek alphabet/language

as "natural" representation, 51
Phoenician, 57–58, 59–60, 66, 67,
  68
preschoolers and, 331
Roman, 80
split sounds in, 66–72
as transparent writing systems, 71
Alphaboxes, 248
Alternative spellings: see Spelling alter-
  natives
American Speller, The, 91–95
Analogies, 21
Aspirated consonants, 218, 237t.
Attention, control of, 164–68
Attention deficit disorder (ADD), 164,
  166, 167, 169, 247–48, 287
Attention span, 165–66
Auditory analysis/discrimination,
  127–29, 155, 201, 310
Auditory Analysis Test (AAT), 127–28,
  131, 132, 133, 144, 295, 334
Auditory Discrimination in Depth
  (ADD), 199–200, 204
  address of, 247, 248
  description of, 311–16
  evaluation of, 188–90
  special features of, 313–16
Australia, 133, 193
Automaticity, 154–55, 317

Basic Code, 97, 101–5, 211, 217–35
  Auditory Discrimination in Depth
    and, 314
  consonant clusters in, 227–29
  consonant digraphs in, 229–30
  e-controlled vowel spellings in,
    232–33
  getting started in, 221–25
  Phono-Graphix and, 201, 318
  redundant consonant letters in,
    230–31
  segmenting, blending, and tracking
    in, 225–27
  vowel digraphs in, 231–32
  vowel plus r in, 233–34